HAYMARKET MOTIVE POWER DEPOT, EDINBURGH

Haymarket's own J36, No. 65243 *Maude*, **heads the Queensferry Goods past the shed en route to Haymarket Yard in early BR days.** *Bill Lynn collection*

A panoramic view of the 'new' Haymarket diesel shed in the 1960s, taken from the 'Caley Brig'. The main line signals are still semaphore signals, but the steam shed has long gone. Gone too are the coaling plant and the turntable, and a completely new shed stands on the site. The late 1950s rebuild of the steam shed (Nos 6, 7 and 8 roads), however, stands out clearly on the right side of the newer shed, and the big water tower still stands immediately to the right of the signal gantry. The new administration block is located in the centre of the picture, and the east yard, no longer filled with wagons of locomotive coal, plays host to the steam breakdown crane and support vehicles (ex St. Margaret's) as well as some DMU sets. In the foreground are two Class 26s, Nos D5309 and 26017, and a Class 25, No. 25078. *Courtesy Gavin Morrison*

HAYMARKET
MOTIVE POWER DEPOT,
EDINBURGH

A HISTORY OF
THE DEPOT, ITS WORK
AND LOCOMOTIVES
1842–2010

HARRY KNOX, FIRO, MCIT, CMILT

Lightmoor Press

For my own 'Top Link'

Alexander Fraser, Thomas Ross, Elliot Peter, Hope Catherine, Max Fraser,
Ross, Eilidh, Archie Alexander, Sam Keith and Joe Grant

Haymarket Atlantic No. 9510 *The Lord Provost*, **assisted by ex-GNR Class 'D1' No. 3065, lifts a heavy 14-coach Aberdeen to Edinburgh Sunday service out of Inverkeithing Tunnel and onto the 1 in 70 climb up to the Forth Bridge in the 1920s.** *Bill Lynn collection*

© Harry Knox and Lightmoor Press 2011.

Designed by Nigel Nicholson.

British Library Cataloguing-in-Publication Data. A catalogue
record for this book is available from the British Library.
ISBN 9781 899889 58 7

LIGHTMOOR PRESS
Unit 144B, Lydney Trading Estate, Harbour Road, Lydney, Gloucestershire GL15 5EJ
www.lightmoor.co.uk
Lightmoor Press is an imprint of Black Dwarf Lightmoor Publications Ltd.

Printed & bound by TJ International, Padstow, Cornwall.

CONTENTS

FOREWORD 7

INTRODUCTION 9

1   THE EARLY DAYS: THE EDINBURGH & GLASGOW RAILWAY COMPANY 11

2   THE ORIGINAL SHED 17

3   THE NEW SHED 21

4   DIESEL DAYS: THE RECONSTRUCTION OF THE SHED 35

5   THE TRACTION MAINTENANCE DEPOT 43

6   FOOTPLATE LIFE 49

7   ALLOCATED TRAIN WORKING OVER THE YEARS 57

8   SHED WORK 69

9   EDINBURGH & GLASGOW RAILWAY LOCOMOTIVES 79

10   NBR 0-6-0 FREIGHT LOCOMOTIVES 85

11   NBR 2-4-0 AND 4-4-0 LOCOMOTIVES: THE HURST, WHEATLEY, DRUMMOND AND HOLMES ERA ... 89

12   NBR 4-4-0 LOCOMOTIVES: THE REID ERA 91

13   THE NBR AND NER 4-4-2 ATLANTICS 97

14   THE GNR 4-4-0 LOCOMOTIVES 101

15   THE L&NER 4-4-0 LOCOMOTIVES 103

16   L&NER PACIFICS: THE GRESLEY A1S AND A3S 107

17   L&NER PACIFICS: THE GRESLEY A4S 113

18   L&NER LOCOMOTIVES: THE GRESLEY P2S 119

19   L&NER LOCOMOTIVES: THE GRESLEY V2S AND V4S 127

20   L&NER LOCOMOTIVES: THE THOMPSON 4-6-2 PACIFICS 129

21   L&NER LOCOMOTIVES: THE THOMPSON B1S 131

22   L&NER LOCOMOTIVES: THE PEPPERCORN 4-6-2 PACIFICS 133

23   OTHER STEAM LOCOMOTIVES 139

24   HAYMARKET AND THE NON-STOPS 147

25   THE DMU DAYS 153

26   THE DIESEL ELECTRIC LOCOMOTIVES 161

27   THE ENGLISH ELECTRIC NAPIER DELTICS 171

28   LOCOMOTIVE MAINTENANCE 177

29   TRAINING AND COMPETENCY OF DRIVERS AND FIREMEN 181

30   HAYMARKET ON FILM 187

31   ACCIDENTS AND INCIDENTS 189

32   FINALE 205

BIBLIOGRAPHY 207

FOREWORD

Dr W. Rhind Brown

Is it not strange that a famous locomotive depot which formed half the East Coast Main Line (as far as traction was concerned) has had to wait so long to have a detailed and comprehensive account of it made public? After all, it began life as far back as 1842, being a two-road stone engine house, without a turntable and only able to boast of a handful of primitive locomotives, when the Edinburgh & Glasgow Railway was opened.

It still remains today, in a vastly different place and form, as a modern diesel multiple unit maintenance depot, having seen the halcyon days of steam – the pre- and post-war non-stop and other prestigious expresses between Edinburgh and London King's Cross. It was also to go further, providing locomotives for the Glasgow, Carlisle (Waverley route), Perth, Dundee and Aberdeen roads. Haymarket has long outlived its opposite number, King's Cross 'Top Shed', in the south.

Yes, there have been many books published about Gresley, his inspired locomotives and their work, and also of the men who worked them. One such earlier work was a semi-autobiographical book by a driver at Haymarket and another, by our present author, about the last days of steam at Haymarket shed, amongst many others; but none, until now, has provided us with such an overreaching history of 64B.

In Harry Knox we have a railwayman to his finger-tips, and an enthusiast who is ever-aspiring. He began work on the lowest rung of the ladder and relished every moment, telling us of the toil, tears, sweat and humour that went into turning out groomed locomotives, tuned to the highest degree and shining like new pins, under working conditions which could neither be employed, nor would be tolerated, today. He shares with us his encyclopædic knowledge of the men, the trade unions and the management, as well as sharing the mysteries of the link structures, and in doing so, errors which have over the years been set in stone by the gospels of others have, with sound evidence, now been corrected.

On a personal note, I remember and have travelled behind ex-NBR Atlantics, especially No. 9903 *Cock o' the North*, on the Perth road, and also behind these same locomotives, with pilots, on the Aberdeen line, and followed the developments since that time. I am also grateful to our author's account of the P2s. His is a balanced view, not relying on personal likes or dislikes, both of which crept into past writings, and which were then copied with a little speculation being added each time.

There was nothing 'hush-hush' about the new *Mikado*. Speculation about its name was rife and reached the *Railway Magazine* by April 1934. C.J. Allan waxed lyrical about No. 2001 *Cock o' the North*, carrying the name of its illustrious forebear, on the trial run with 649 tons behind the tender on the 19th June 1934. '*Such tractive effort seems almost too much to lavish on the east coast of Scotland*' he opined, but by January 1936 their success in both the work and road for which they were designed was to have been well documented. As a teenager, I enjoyed several (illicit) footplate trips on Nos 2002, 2003 and 2006 north of Dundee on ordinary service trains, and met welcoming, kind, understanding drivers and firemen; great railwaymen they were but, alas, memories have become confused over the intervening years.

It is an honour to be asked by Harry to write a foreword to his excellent book and in expressing my gratitude, may I wish him every success with his work … '*a fire built up behind the door and down the sides, a good head of steam and the green flag for the "off"*.'

W.R.B.
Glasgow 2009

FACING PAGE: The chime whistle fitted to P2 No. 2001 *Cock o' the North* stirs the echoes as she passes Dalmeny Junction on her way up to the Forth Bridge at the head of a heavy Edinburgh–Aberdeen express. The driver has shut off steam and the engine will drift up the hill losing speed to enter the bridge at the required limit. There is a clear road ahead with all distants 'off'. The line coming in from the right is the Winchburgh Junction (E&GR main line)–Dalmeny Junction chord line. Behind the signal box is the bing (waste tip) of the Dalmeny Oil Company, used for the residue of the oil shale burned in retorts to produce crude oil. Interestingly, this bing is still *in situ* today, and has been hollowed out to provide a bund inside which the massive storage tanks for North Sea Oil are contained, hidden from view. *Bill Brown collection*

A light and shade study, and most atmospheric, taken inside 64B in 1963, showing Gateshead shed's A4 No. 60020 *Guillemot* sharing a shed road with a new English Electric Type 4 diesel electric locomotive. The deteriorating condition of the shed roof can be clearly seen, making work within the shed somewhat of a trial for staff during inclement weather. *Courtesy Dugald Cameron*

INTRODUCTION

Having completed a book of personal reminiscences concerning my own days, both on and off the footplate, at Haymarket Motive Power Depot (MPD) in Edinburgh *circa* 1957, I realised that I had become, during the course of writing, very conscious of the fact that I was merely reflecting a small slice (in terms of time) of the overall history of Haymarket MPD and that there has not been, to my knowledge, any serious attempt to document the detailed history of this famous and long-lived engine shed.

This line of thought has now prompted me to follow on from my first book with what, I hope, might be considered a definitive history of Haymarket Shed (coded by BR as 64B). A shed which, in reality, must be one of the earliest and long-lasting 'engine houses' anywhere in the UK. However, in saying that, a disclaimer: this work does not seek to list *all* locomotives or *every* locomotive class which may have had an association with the shed, but is, rather, an attempt to highlight the more significant classes shedded there at one time or another.

Haymarket, in the golden days of steam traction and on into the main line diesel days, served the northern end of the East Coast Main Line (ECML). I believe that there is thus some justification for such a book, similar to that excellent earlier book by Peter Townend about King's Cross Top Shed, which served the southern end. Unlike Top Shed, Haymarket shed did not follow steam out, but survived dieselisation and has gone on, although in much-changed guise, to survive the almost total demise of the locomotive as the means of passenger traction on the railways of the UK, and now embraces the modern, self-contained diesel multiple units. There is little doubt, however, that the 'glory days' at 64B occurred during that momentous period between 1928 and the late 1950s, when steam reigned supreme, and hence no apologies are made for dwelling at some length on these times within this work. During this time, Haymarket was probably the only ECML depot to challenge King's Cross Top Shed as the top Gresley shed, since the Haymarket Gresleys (and all other engines allocated there, it must be said) were generally kept cleaner and better maintained, and were more skilfully driven than at most other sheds.

Over the decades of steam working, Haymarket had a spectacular array of notable engines allocated – through the NBR days, into L&NER days and on into BR days. Even as steam was being phased out, Haymarket was given an allocation of the new English Electric Type 5 Napier Deltic diesel electric locomotives, the famous 'Deltics', which followed on in the proud footsteps of the NBR Atlantics and the L&NER Pacifics (Gresleys, Thompsons and Peppercorns), and began returning performances on the ECML far and away beyond the capability of any of their steam predecessors.

Now in the twenty-first century and the brave new world of the privatised railway, Haymarket still exists as the First ScotRail Diesel Multiple Unit Maintenance Depot which thus has an important place in this book. Indeed, it is likely that Haymarket, already much extended, will go on to see some other significant changes with the current on-going electrification project for the soon to be re-opened Edinburgh to Airdrie via Bathgate rail link, and the fact that electrification of the Edinburgh & Glasgow main line will now follow.

I have relied heavily on works by other Scottish railway historians which, whilst not necessarily primary sources, have nevertheless proved to be invaluable and reliable sources for much information. I did think that life in this respect would be somewhat easier when researching the NBR days at the shed, because of the writings of one Norman McKillop, under his pen name 'Toram Beg' (and for those who have long pondered this pen name, it means quite simply, in Gaelic, 'Little Norman'). He was a noted Haymarket railwayman through and through, a senior driver and a quite prolific writer. Here, regrettably, I encountered some real problems, and what I did discover was that his version of events did not necessarily accord with the versions obtained from either other locomotive men at the depot, or other recorded and reliable sources. McKillop held very strong and often biased opinions which surfaced frequently in his documented works and magazine articles.

I met him only once, in my early days at Haymarket, during which time he was Editor of the then Scottish Region Staff Magazine and I was but a humble clerk. However, as an indication as to the nature of the man, I have, on good authority from no less than the person involved, been told of an incident which occurred at the same General Office at Haymarket. McKillop, the Editor, appeared at the enquiry window one day and asked to see the Shed Master. The office boy, who knew not the great man, asked, very politely, who he was and what his business was. He was soon put right and on being admitted to the office, McKillop slapped the office boy across the head 'for his insolence'. Try that with a 'junior' now!

So the reliable source that I thought I might have for, say, the P2s and D1s, and the work they did, was worth little. McKillop did not like either class and so both were deemed, in his eyes, to be useless and not fit for purpose. This he said in various articles and also more than once in *Enginemen Elite*, but I have found no other source of such severe criticism from any other engineman regarding these particular engines. Indeed, other responsible railway commentators of the times have written of some splendid work carried out by some of these engines. So who is right? Sadly, there were so many other contradictions between what McKillop penned and what other railway commentators and records say, that I have chosen carefully and have tried to steer a middle course through many of the more contentious items which are, in truth, now merely history in any case.

In passing comment on McKillop's writings, however, I wish to make it absolutely clear that he was, at all times, a first-class engineman who could, with his beloved *Spearmint*, rise to the occasion as demanded, and did so many, many times. His professionalism as a driver can never be in doubt, but, with his other interest in writing (he was the Founder, Editor and a chief contributor to the short-lived *Locomotive Express* between 1946 and 1954), he was wont sometimes to court controversy.

A Class 109 DMU two-car set leaves Haymarket station bound for Dundee and is just passing Duff Street Junction (right foreground). On the immediate left is the black, ramshackle garage owned by well-known Edinburgh coal merchants Bruce Lindsay Ltd, which was a long-time landmark on the approach to Haymarket station from west and north directions. Immediately behind the DMU is the original E&GR 'train shed', the terminus for the original Edinburgh & Glasgow Railway, until the railway was extended through to Waverley via the new Haymarket tunnels. This train shed is clearly identified by the white, triangular end boards and stands alongside the 'new' Haymarket station. *Courtesy John Furneval*

I am also fortunate enough to have spent some of my early railway career on the footplate at Haymarket during the latter days of steam and whilst there I was able to discuss with, and question, men who had actually experienced life with such engines as the P2s, the 'Ponies' and the ex-NBR classes – and what a valuable primary source of factual material that turned out to be, 'straight from the horse's mouth'.

To prepare a book such as this, a historical work, much of the research for the period of time outside my own knowledge and experience has had to be gleaned from many historical sources such as the comprehensive former railway company minutes, papers, etc. held by the National Archives of Scotland in West Register House, Edinburgh. Sound and valuable sources of information they indeed proved to be. My thanks go to the duty archivists and archives staff for the help and courtesy afforded. Likewise, the North British Railway Study Group membership provided a valuable source of information.

The National Library of Scotland Map Room has also been most helpful in sourcing and providing OS maps showing both the original and new Haymarket locomotive depots over the years. The OS maps reproduced herein are included by the kind permission of the Trustees of the National Library of Scotland and my grateful thanks go to them and to the staff of the Map Room.

To Kerry Black, Syndications Executive, Scotsman Publications Ltd, Edinburgh, Barry Hoper, Transport Treasury, and Mary White of the Search Engine, NRM, York, for kind assistance in sourcing the photographs requested, and to Gavin Morrison, Stuart Sellar, David Anderson, John Furnevel, Dugald Cameron and Ian Musgrave for access to their respective photographic collections, my sincere thanks. A particular thank you must go to R.W. (Bill) Lynn for allowing me full and free access to his absolute treasure trove of early photographs and other information on all things NBR, and likewise to David Dunn for his support and assistance with photographs also.

To Peter Lund, who provided much information about his late, and highly-respected, father, Geoffrey Lund, a well-known face at Haymarket in the 1940s and '50s, and who also kindly permitted me to use photographs supplied from his personal collection, my sincere thanks.

To my friends in the Silver Link Club for photographs and articles, and in particular to both Robin Nelson for assistance on signalling

matters and Jim Summers for general train working information, a special thanks. I am, however, especially deeply indebted to Dr Bill Rhind Brown, also a member of our small, select band of brothers, not only for photographs so generously provided but also for his kind words in the foreword he has prepared for this book – I consider it both a privilege and a pleasure to have had him do so. He has been the font of much valuable information regarding the Gresley P2s. Bill not only photographed them at work in Scotland, but also could recall footplate trips on these locomotives north of Dundee, and I am pleased to be able to reflect some of his fine photographs herein.

I wish also to particularly thank Mary Grant, former Managing Director, First ScotRail, for allowing me free and open access to the present Haymarket Maintenance Depot; and to Steve McCredie, Depot Manager, Ray Murison, Production Technical Manager, and Alan Poyner, for their long-suffering patience in dealing most adequately with all my queries and wishes on my visits there. Without them all, an important part of this history would not have been possible. Also a special thanks to Ray for photographs provided, and to Stephen Murphy, Safety Manager, First ScotRail, for supplying the 'before and after' drawings of the present Haymarket depot.

My sincere thanks to Centaur Media for permission to quote from a paper included in *The Engineer* of 1939 and also to Ian Allan Publishing Ltd for permission to quote from *Enginemen Elite* by the late Norman McKillop.

Throughout this book I have quoted all times using the 24-hour clock for the sake of consistency since this became BR standard practice in the 1970s. The views and opinions expressed herein are, of course, mine, and mine alone, and for which I accept full responsibility.

Last, but in no way least, a special thank you to my wife, Heather, for her patience and forbearance, as this history, and all things Haymarket, became the focal point of life in the Knox household for such a long time. To her, this book is, in part, dedicated – but it must also be dedicated in the greater part to all the many men and women (past and present) who were, and are, part of the great Haymarket story. I am indeed privileged, and proud, to have been one of their number, and that story.

Harry Knox,
Linlithgow 2010

1 THE EARLY DAYS:
THE EDINBURGH & GLASGOW RAILWAY COMPANY

The Edinburgh & Glasgow Railway Company (hereafter referred to as the E&GR, a term originally, and still affectionately, used by Scottish railwaymen for this line of route) was incorporated by an Act of Parliament (*The Edinburgh & Glasgow Railway Act*, 1838), and was the first railway company to construct and open a real main line in Scotland. This main line connected the two principal Scottish cities, Edinburgh, capital city of Scotland, and Glasgow, by this time rapidly becoming what was to be known as 'the second city of the British Empire'. Interestingly, well over half the invested income for this project came from England, with Lancashire money being especially prominent.

The route finally chosen was not the preferred option, but rather the second-choice, both options having been prepared by the railway engineering firm Grainger & Miller of Edinburgh, ably assisted by the great George Stephenson himself. In surveying possible routes, these engineers had initially sought to place the consideration of gradients and the convenience of north-bound connections before what might be the shortest distance. The preferred route as proposed by Grainger & Miller and endorsed by Stephenson was, in its final form, to run via Bathgate and Slamannan to connect with the Garnkirk & Glasgow Railway near Coatbridge. However, their Bill containing this route failed at the Commons Committee stage in May 1832, most probably on account of opposition by local canal interests.

The alternative route proposed, which had previously been considered by Stephenson alongside the preferred route, was one which closely followed the route of the new Union Canal from Edinburgh to Falkirk – a contour canal, level throughout and following the 240-foot contour line – and thereafter was to follow the route of the Forth & Clyde Canal. But this had not found particular favour with him, and in his Report to the Board of Directors, dated 6th June 1831, he wrote:

> … *whilst the line of the Forth and Clyde canal is, in itself, of favourable gradient, owing to the extreme rough and hilly surface of the intervening country, the entrance into to it, both from Edinburgh and Glasgow, could be effected only with an immense sacrifice of directness to the extent probably of ten miles, and by the ruinous expenditure of money in the formation of the line.*

Nevertheless, it was over this second-choice route that, in 1835, the same firm of Grainger & Miller was appointed to engineer the line, with a younger partner of the firm, James Miller, being given the heavy responsibility for the overall management of the project – but subject to the 'superior' advice being sought from time to time from some prominent railway engineers of the day, including Joseph Locke and Charles Vignolles. The advantages of this 'second choice' in terms of ease of gradient were proportionately much greater than the 'preferred route', and the £550,000 estimate was deemed to be acceptable by the promoters. The authorising Act of Parliament was finally enacted on the 4th July 1838 and whilst the first contract

was let in the autumn of 1938, the onset of winter meant that little progress could be achieved before the spring of 1839. The overall work was split into twenty-one contracts, with two contracts being devoted to viaduct construction.

When finally constructed, the majority of the line was, to all intents and purposes, level throughout – with only one short, rising quarter-mile-long gradient of any consequence, the 1 in 600 on the Down line between the 22¾ and 22½ mileposts at Polmont, not meeting the objective of having no gradient any more severe than 1 in 800. It was also largely straight. In this context it has been described as 'Stephensonian' in concept, in that it followed the great man's ideals of bridging valleys and penetrating hills, rather than placing strain on his progeny locomotives with too many gradients. Only in the final two miles or so at the western end did the line of route turn sharply south and drop down on a falling gradient of 1 in 45 in order to pass under, by means of a 1,000-yard-long tunnel, the 'Cut of Junction' Canal (joining the Forth & Clyde Canal and the Monklands Canal) near Port Dundas, and enter the new Glasgow Queen Street terminus.

As a consequence of this careful attention to such detail, the route was, and still is, marked by many notable (and now listed) civil engineering works resulting from the aspirations to maintain minimal gradients throughout. These structures include such immense works as the 7-arch and 36-arch viaducts over the Almond valley beyond Bathgate Junction (now Newbridge Junction) – the latter viaduct now being probably one of the finest examples of a railway viaduct anywhere in the UK – Winchburgh Tunnel and the 4-mile-long Winchburgh cutting, the 23-arch Avon Viaduct west of Linlithgow, Falkirk Tunnel, Castlecary Viaduct, and the deep rock cutting at Croy. Both the Almond and Avon viaducts are today Grade 'A' listed structures. These immense works led to the new line being considered as nothing less than one of the finest engineered lines of the great Railway Age. The line over the 46 miles[1] between the two cities was opened for traffic on the 18th February 1842.

When first constructed, malleable iron rail weighing 65 lbs per yard was laid down on whinstone blocks measuring roughly 2 feet × 2 feet × 13 inches, with the occasional transverse wooden sleeper being provided. Even in 1838 this was old-fashioned railway technology, but the consulting engineers, Rastrick, Locke and Vignolles, as well as James Millar himself, were much influenced by the abundance of this material available immediately adjacent to the line of route. One William Chambers, a knowledgeable and noted

---

1 Forty-six miles (45 miles 1716 yards to be precise) was the actual distance between Glasgow Queen Street and the original Haymarket terminus, but thereafter the line was extended to an overall distance of 47 miles 242 yards, through to the Edinburgh Waverley terminus, when the first Haymarket Tunnel was opened in 1846. Indeed, up until the demise of British Rail, it was possible to see many of the original E&GR cast-iron mile posts, showing the aggregated mileage as 46 miles, on the lineside between Glasgow Queen Street and Greenhill Junction and, even today, one original example has pride of place in Queen Street station.

correspondent of the day, wrote to *The Scotsman* newspaper in September of 1839, pointing out the serious problems encountered by the Kingstown & Dublin Railway when employing similar track technology and the fact that complete renewal of their line of route had been required within only five years. He wrote:

Sir, I observe that at a meeting of the Shareholders of the Edinburgh & Glasgow Railway, it has been resolved to use stone blocks as sleepers for the rails. Perhaps the company have decided correctly in coming to this determination, but from the following fact I fear the contrary is the case. The railway from Dublin to Kingstown was first laid with stone blocks (granite) but it has been found necessary to lift the whole of these and supersede them with wooden beams, which are now placed longitudinally beneath the rails. When I passed along the line lately, I saw the displaced blocks of stone scattered about, and of no value whatsoever. I was informed that the stone blocks were found unavailing from their unyielding property, which caused immense damage to the vehicles, and the noise made by the train was altogether unbearable; in short, that it was found absolutely necessary to dismiss the stone blocks and adopt wood in their place, although at greater expense. At present, the train goes in a smooth delightful manner, with very little noise. It is quite possible that the Edinburgh & Glasgow Railway Company may possess some facts leading to the conviction that stone is best for the purpose, but such a fact as that which I relate is surely worthy of their investigation before ultimately committing themselves in this very important manner.
I am, Sir, yours.
William Chambers.
19, Waterloo Place, Edinburgh.
11th September, 1839

Chambers was a member of a noted family from the border town of Peebles. In later years he was to become the Chairman of the Peebles Railway (*Peebles Railway Act* of 8th July 1853), and he and his brother established the highly-respected Edinburgh publishing house of W&R Chambers. He was also later to become a much-revered Lord Provost of the city. It will also be noted in passing that he resided almost next door to what was to become the headquarters of the North British Railway Company (the NBR) (No. 23 Waterloo Place).

This was a warning which was valid in the extreme. However, despite such dire warnings from persons with first-hand knowledge of this technology, the Board of Directors remained intransigent. The upshot, as Chambers quite accurately predicted, was a railway line which was hard and unyielding, causing unending damage to locomotives and rolling stock, and on which the track fittings and fastenings became loose and almost impossible to maintain. Inevitably, within only seven years, the whole route had to be relaid with wooden sleepers at considerable expense. As a matter of interest, some of these original whinstone 'sleepers' can still be seen today, lining the northern edge of the Union Canal basin immediately above Linlithgow station.

At the eastern end of the line, the original Edinburgh terminus of the E&GR which opened in 1842 was on the outskirts of the city at Haymarket. This station comprised a handsome sandstone building at street level housing the ticketing and other commercial facilities and the Station Master's house, which led down to a train shed located immediately on the north side of the present Haymarket station. This train shed was to be a continuing, although largely redundant, feature at Haymarket station, sitting on the north side of No. 1 platform with the bay siding extant underneath, after the lines were extended through the Haymarket tunnels to Edinburgh

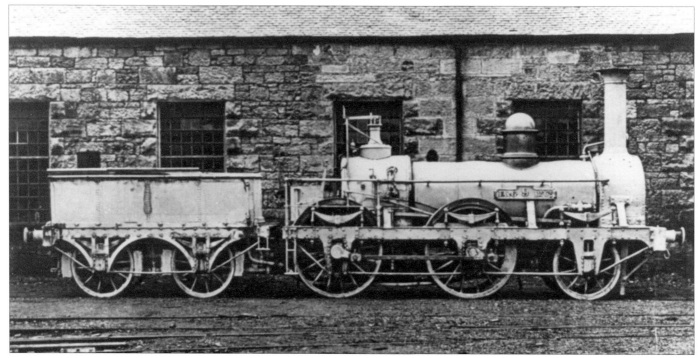

Original 2-4-0 'Luggage' engine No. 9, as supplied for the opening of the Edinburgh & Glasgow Railway in 1842. It was built by R&W Hawthorn, Leeds in 1841 and allocated to Haymarket shed where this photograph was taken. This was one of three such engines ordered by James Millar, along with a further nine 2-2-2 passenger engines from the same builder. The engine had a role in the Winchburgh collision of 1862, when acting as pilot engine in place of a smaller Bury locomotive; the pointsman, in the failing light, mistook the first train engine, No. 57, for No. 9, and let a train enter the already occupied single-line section and a head-on collision ensued in which fifteen people were killed. *J.F. McEwan collection/Courtesy of Strathkelvin Libraries*

Waverley. It was, in fact, only finally removed in 1982/83 as part of the station refurbishment which was completed in 1984. Happily the train shed was moved and re-erected to form an integral part of the Bo'ness terminus for the Scottish Railway Preservation Society's Bo'ness & Birkhill Railway where it can be seen still in use to this day. As a matter of interest, recent modernisation work (in 2007) has brought the former bay siding (now relaid) back into use as the new bay Platform 0 (sic) at Haymarket station.

In the minutes of the meeting of the E&GR Plans & Works Committee on the 23rd October 1840, it is recorded thus:

Mr. Miller's letter of 19th Inst. having been read and fully considered, the Meeting were inclined to recommend that, as experience had not yet sufficiently shewn whether Engines on Bury's or Stephenson's Plan were to be preferred, an equal number of Engines of each kind should be ordered, say nine of each, but they would wish the matter to be considered by the General Board next week in presence of their Engineers. It was agreed with reference to Mr. Miller's letter to recommend that the following carriages be ordered.

The minute then went on to list the recommended numbers and type of carriages and other rolling stock. Another issue which was exercising the minds of the Board even as late as 1841 was, quite unbelievably, an ongoing debate as to what the gauge of the railway should be; whilst it appeared to have been agreed that the standard gauge of 4 feet 8½ inches would apply, in the minutes of the board meeting of the 5th December 1840 it is revealed that the board members were still split on this matter and a further amendment was proposed at that time calling for a gauge of 5 feet 6 inches to be adopted. The Chairman, Mr Leadbetter, most sensibly begged to

move a further amendment to the effect that the resolution of the board meeting, dated 14th May 1840 and agreed by the shareholders at a meeting on the 25th August 1840, confirming the adoption of the standard gauge, should be adhered to. An agreement at last, 4 feet 8½ inches it was to be!

In the line's inaugural year, Willox's *Guide to the Edinburgh and Glasgow Railway*, published in that year, listed the daily train service as being four trains in each direction. Three were 'all stations', namely the 07.00, 15.00 and 17.00 from both Edinburgh and Glasgow, serving the original ten stations on the line, with one express service at 11.00 in each direction and calling at Linlithgow, Falkirk and Castlecary only. Journey times were 2½ hours by stopping services and 2¼ hours by the fast trains. There was also a 06.00 luggage train each morning in each direction. By 1844 there were six passenger services in each direction and carrying five classes of passenger, namely first, second, third, fourth (stand up) and parliamentary. By 1862 it was recorded that eight trains were running in each direction, with the best giving a journey time of 80 minutes.

From the outset, the E&GR courted adverse criticism by running Sunday trains. Sunday services began on the 13th March 1842, and consisted of one morning service and one evening service in each direction. This brought a hail of fire and brimstone down upon the Directors from both the Edinburgh and Glasgow Presbyteries, with passengers also being informed that, by travelling on a Sunday, they had purchased tickets, not for the rail journey, but to Hell. The furore did not pass, and eventually what has been described as 'an unholy alliance' between the Sabbatarians and the mercenary English shareholders in search of greater dividends, toppled the existing E&GR Board, and Sunday services were discontinued from 1st November 1846. Sunday services were not to be resumed until

E&GR 2-2-2 passenger locomotive No. 57 at Haymarket shed. Built by Beyer Peacock and delivered to Harmarket in 1856, this engine was originally numbered 87, being renumbered as No. 57 in 1862 and further renumbered as No. 218 when taken over by the NBR in 1865. Rebuilt by Drummond between 1880 and 1882, it was renumbered yet again in 1895 as No. 808, and again in 1901, becoming No. 1008. In 1880 it was given the name *Winchburgh* and was finally withdrawn in 1907. An attractive and well-proportioned design and splendid performers always, this class of locomotive gave long and distinguished service on the E&GR main line.

The engine is seen here in original condition, standing alongside the old Haymarket shed. It was this engine which was acting as the ballast-train engine during single-line working between, strangely enough, Winchburgh and Linlithgow in 1862, when, owing to a pointsman's error, a serious collision occurred with many fatalities. No. 57 was not involved in the actual collision. *J.F. McEwan collection/Courtesy Strathkelvin Libraries*

the amalgamation of the E&GR and NBR in 1865, and Sunday trains continued their quiet progress, in peace, thereafter.

Although promoted as a passenger-carrying railway, from the 10th October 1842 the E&GR became a carrier of freight traffic. Initially this was domestic coal traffic from the Redding coalfield near Polmont, through which the line ran, and consigned to Hay Market (*sic*) Goods Yard on behalf of one James McNaughton, an Edinburgh coal merchant. McNaughton had been quick to recognise the benefits offered by rail for the carriage in bulk of, as he himself described it, '*fresh coal of superior quality*'.

In keeping with the practice then prevailing, the Engineer-in-Chief of a new railway was not only responsibility for the construction works, but thereafter continued in office as a sort of Traffic/Operations Manager. And so it was on the E&GR. The Engineer of the line, James Miller, had vested in his position responsibility for not only construction works, but also procurement of locomotives and rolling stock. Prior to the opening of the line, Miller was instructed to order, as a consequence of his recommendation recorded herein, a total of twenty locomotives, ten from the English builder, Bury, and ten from R&W Hawthorn. These were described in the later board minutes as being seven passenger engines and three 'luggage' engines from each company. Seven engines from each manufacturer were supplied in time for the opening of the line, the remainder coming later.

The first Locomotive Engineer of the E&GR, or rather Superintendent of Locomotives, as he was grandly titled, was William Paton, based at Cowlairs, with Robert Thornton appointed as Locomotive Superintendent at Edinburgh Haymarket. Thornton was appointed at the grand salary of £100 per annum, but neither, despite their grand titles, were to have any say in the procurement and allocation of the first locomotives, this being left to Miller. As stated, James Miller obviously continued to enjoy a considerable degree of autonomy in general running matters after the opening of the line and, in March 1842, William Paton was censured by the Board for non-compliance with a Miller 'Instruction' regarding the working of the Cowlairs incline.

The E&GR engines, not too good to start with, were greatly overworked and under-maintained in these earliest days; problems quickly arose with boiler and tube leakages, with many of these problems being linked to the poor standard of permanent way provided. These same problems were to manifest themselves in a dramatic and tragic event at or near Ratho (discussed at Chapter 31). Nevertheless, some of these engines were to go on to give good service, being rebuilt and surviving to the end of Wheatley's reign at Cowlairs in 1874.

Paton also had a works built for the repair and erection of locomotives and carriages at Cowlairs, close by the top of the Queen Street incline; this was also to include the main 'engine house' for some twenty-six locomotives until replaced by the new Eastfield Motive Power Depot in 1904 (built by the NBR).

In Edinburgh, the original E&GR Haymarket locomotive shed was a much smaller affair, and it is upon this shed, its small beginnings, eventual relocation and replacement, and the ongoing changes over the intervening years to the present time, that we must now focus.

The NBR line from Berwick-upon-Tweed to Edinburgh was completed and opened for traffic in 1846, and at 07.00 on the morning of Monday, June 22nd the first NBR passenger train pulled out of Berwick-upon-Tweed for Edinburgh. Six weeks later,

the E&GR completed the extension of its double line of railway into the North Bridge station (the forerunner of Waverley station) via a tunnel running from Haymarket station through to Princes Street Gardens and a further shorter tunnel below the Mound, thus bringing Glasgow into the eastern line of Anglo-Scottish communication. On the 1st August 1865 the NBR absorbed the E&GR.

1890 should have been a year of triumph for the NBR with the opening of the Forth Railway Bridge. When the bridge opened, owing to a quite inexplicable lack of foresight, absolutely no account had been taken by the NBR management as to the inevitable increase and altered flows of rail-borne traffic likely to result, and thus the NBR system around Edinburgh quickly became overwhelmed by the sheer volume of traffic which was now passing by rail. The NBR, forever parsimonious, had not seen fit to provide loops and/or refuge sidings along the main lines of route and thus, with burgeoning levels of freight, the main lines quickly became clogged with trains. Chaos reigned, with freight trains often not moving a wheel over a full shift (and at that time twelve- to eighteen-hour days were the norm for train crews). It is on record that one Glasgow to Carlisle freight train took 24 hours to travel the 47¼ miles to Edinburgh and it was not an uncommon sight to see trains standing detained at every signal on the approach to Edinburgh from Saughton Junction.

Even passenger trains were not spared running problems over this stretch, and it has been recorded that express passenger trains sometimes took well over an hour to cover the three miles between Saughton Junction and Waverley. The result was what came to be known as the infamous 'Waverley Block', where the inability of the NBR to handle trains to any shred of a published timetable made effective train operation well nigh impossible. This, in turn, had a detrimental knock-on effect by severely delaying services which then had to be handed over to run via the lines of other companies. This was nothing less than a national scandal and it was clear that drastic and urgent action was required. To make matters much worse, if indeed this were possible, on Sunday, 17th August 1890 the roof of Winchburgh Tunnel collapsed, effectively blocking the E&GR main line. Although single line working was quickly restored, the tunnel was to remain partially closed for some nine months. Some through trains to Glasgow were diverted via Bathgate and others were run round the Winchburgh Junction/Dalmeny Junction/Saughton Junction triangle; however the reversing of the Glasgow trains at Dalmeny, in the face of traffic coming off the Forth Bridge, only compounded the already near impossible chaos.

In an effort to help ease the situation, although the solution was neither quick nor cheap, the lines in and out of Edinburgh Waverley were eventually quadrupled from Waverley to Saughton Junction, requiring the boring of duplicate tunnels at Haymarket and the Mound (and Calton Hill at the eastern end of the station). A general reconstruction and widening of the station was undertaken in parallel, this work being carried out between 1892 and 1900. The horrors of that summer of 1890 were never to be repeated, lessons having been learned the hard way.

The E&GR main line, however, contained some significant inherent problems for the operators despite its all-but-level line of route, not least of which was the 1 in 42 gradient, partly in tunnel, for the first 1¼ miles out of Glasgow Queen Street station. If ever railway operators had a millstone hung round their necks, the E&GR certainly did from the word go, with this most difficult of inclines. The incline was worked by rope haulage operated from a winding house at Cowlairs, the rope being attached to the front

E&GR No. 101, a 2-4-0 passenger engine, was designed by William Steel Brown – whose term of office with the E&GR was to be of short duration – and built at Cowlairs works in 1862. This was the first of eight such engines, the last four of the class were completed by W.S. Johnston, Brown's successor. The coupled wheels were 6 feet in diameter and they proved to be a useful class of engine. It was renumbered No. 351 by the NBR. The class was rebuilt by Holmes in 1882. Renumbered yet again in 1909 as No. 1007, this locomotive was eventually withdrawn in 1915. Contrary to E&GR/NBR practice, this class had the driving position on the right-hand side, a feature disliked intensely by Haymarket drivers. As No. 351, this was the train engine involved in the dreadful collision which occurred at Manuel, on the E&GR main line, in 1874. *J.F. McEwan collection/Courtesy Strathkelvin Libraries*

coupling of the locomotive of an Up (Edinburgh) train – the train being hauled from Queen Street station up the hill to Cowlairs. Down trains had to stop and detach the locomotive at Cowlairs and the train was taken down by special brake trucks, again on the rope. Light engines going to work trains descended the incline at a very reduced speed and under the control of the driver.

From the outset it had been generally unthinkable that this incline could be worked by adhesion, but in January 1844 there emerged from Cowlairs works a new, special engine that Paton had designed and had built for this purpose – a six-coupled tank engine, *Hercules*, weighing 26½ tons and with a superior braking system. This locomotive proved it could haul a twelve-coach train of some 57 tons up the incline at a steady speed of 15 mph. So successful did this engine prove to be that a second engine, *Samson* – similar, but with larger cylinders – was soon introduced and the rope working was abandoned, temporarily, as things turned out. In fact, the two locomotives were proving to be too good, and regularly caused damage to the inadequate track, whilst the severe, hammering blast of their exhaust damaged the tunnel lining. Rope working was reinstated on the 4th March 1847 (but with an untwisted wire rope eventually replacing the hemp rope), and was to continue for a further sixty-two years. This method of operation was as cumbersome as it was slow, but persisted until 31st October 1908 (although empty coaching stock had not been required to use rope assistance after 11th February of that year). Thereafter,

rear-end banking became the norm, and was perpetuated until the demise of steam.

Once clear of the incline, the smooth curves and easy gradients invited high-speed running, but the line of route had the misfortune to cross extensive measures of coal, fireclay and oil shale, all of which were being mined, thus posing subsidence problems owing to the associated network of underground workings. The company had but two choices, either to accept long-term temporary speed restrictions resulting from mining subsidence, or to pay compensation for (that is, purchase) the mineral rights, thus leaving the mineral reserves undisturbed below the tracks. The company chose the latter option in several instances, buying fireclay reserves to safeguard the Castlecary viaduct, the oil shale measures under the seven-arch viaduct between Winchburgh Junction and Bathgate Junction and coal seams in the Cowlairs area in order to safeguard a bridge and a signal box. Overall, the minutes of the NBR Finance Committee record, in the early years, considerable sums of money being paid out to purchase seams of oil shale in West Lothian, either under or adjacent to the railway. Nevertheless, despite all the early precautions taken, problems with old mine workings were later, in BR days, to plague the line; the Falkirk Tunnel had to be closed for almost a full year in 1980 because of instability caused by old coal workings, whilst, not so very far away, at Roughcastle, BR had to undertake an exercise to inject massive quantities of liquid concrete into old mine workings, again to stabilise the solum of the trackbed.

The OS map dated 1852 shows the original Haymarket engine house of the E&GR adjacent to the one-time terminus station. By this date, one double-line tunnel has been driven through to what will become Edinburgh Waverley, and so Haymarket is now a through station. The orientation of the shed in relation to the magnificent Donaldson's Hospital is clearly shown; the shed itself is a stone-built two-road through shed. There is no turntable shown at this time, but engines were turned at the Edinburgh terminus. As a matter of interest, at the bottom left of the map is the early Dalry Road Shed belonging to the Caledonian railway.   *Courtesy of the Trustees of the National Library of Scotland*

2 THE ORIGINAL SHED

A small 'engine house' was constructed close by the Haymarket terminus at the eastern end of the E&GR main line of 1842 (OS Grid Ref. NT238731). The shed was actually situated just west of Haymarket station, on the north side of the line (then merely one double line of railway) and an early Ordnance Survey map (1852) shows that this was a small, two-road through shed, but with no turntable being provided at that time – even though in 1841 Miller had been charged with ordering twenty 14-foot and thirty 12-foot turntables. It is assumed that these turntables were wagon turntables, but no evidence has been unearthed to say exactly when the locomotive turntable at Haymarket was provided. A locomotive turntable was, however, installed in the E&GR-part of the former Waverley station after the line had been extended through from Haymarket terminus. The shed accommodation, ready for occupation by the opening of the line in 1842, was substantial, being constructed of stone with a longitudinal pitched and partially glazed roof, and with thirteen glazed windows along the length of the south wall, as can be seen in photographs of the time. This original shed stood very close to the site of the much later wooden shed constructed by the well-known Edinburgh coal merchants, Bruce Lindsay, which in itself was a notable lineside landmark at Haymarket, surviving well into diesel days. The actual site of the original Haymarket shed is now more or less underneath the Institution of Chartered Accountants headquarters, built a few years ago within what was the former Haymarket goods yard.

On the 18th January 1842 it was thus reported in *The Scotsman*:

On the 17th, a party of Directors paid a visit of inspection to the works of the line, this probably being the last before the opening, examining the line from end to end … After inspecting the station-house containing booking and other offices, they proceeded to *examine the capacious sheds for passengers, goods, engines and carriages, repair shops etc. The ample space which the Company has secured at this terminus will offer abundant accommodation for a very extended traffic.*

An 1876 Ordnance Survey map shows this original Haymarket shed, now much extended and in NBR ownership, with the two-road through shed still extant and lying parallel to the main line, but with a new, larger shed to the north side (quite probably a maintenance/fitting shed), with two dead-end roads on the west side and a single dead-end road on the east side. A smaller through single-road shed lay immediately to the east of this, in the yard area with a 40-foot (?) turntable situated on the eastern end of this shed road. When the turntable was actually installed is unclear, although it is known that it was *in situ* by 1874 (see the Bo'ness Junction, Manuel accident, 27th January 1874, Chapter 31).

Interestingly, more recent construction work undertaken in the area of what was Haymarket goods yard partially exposed the circular edging of this old turntable. The shed was immediately in line with, and to the south of, Donaldson's Hospital in Haymarket Terrace, the latter being an extremely handsome building designed by the noted Edinburgh architect, London-born William Henry Playfair (1789–1854), which was opened in 1850 as a school for deaf children. It dominated the area then, as it still does today, and it is reputed that so impressed was Queen Victoria by the architectural grandeur, she offered to give up Holyrood House (her official Scottish residence) in exchange. It is the appearance of the towers of this magnificent building in the background of many locomotive photographs of the time which helps to accurately mark the location of the original shed.

This Haymarket shed pre-dated the NBR works and shed at St.

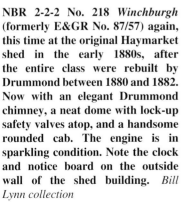

NBR 2-2-2 No. 218 *Winchburgh* (formerly E&GR No. 87/57) again, this time at the original Haymarket shed in the early 1880s, after the entire class were rebuilt by Drummond between 1880 and 1882. Now with an elegant Drummond chimney, a neat dome with lock-up safety valves atop, and a handsome rounded cab. The engine is in sparkling condition. Note the clock and notice board on the outside wall of the shed building. *Bill Lynn collection*

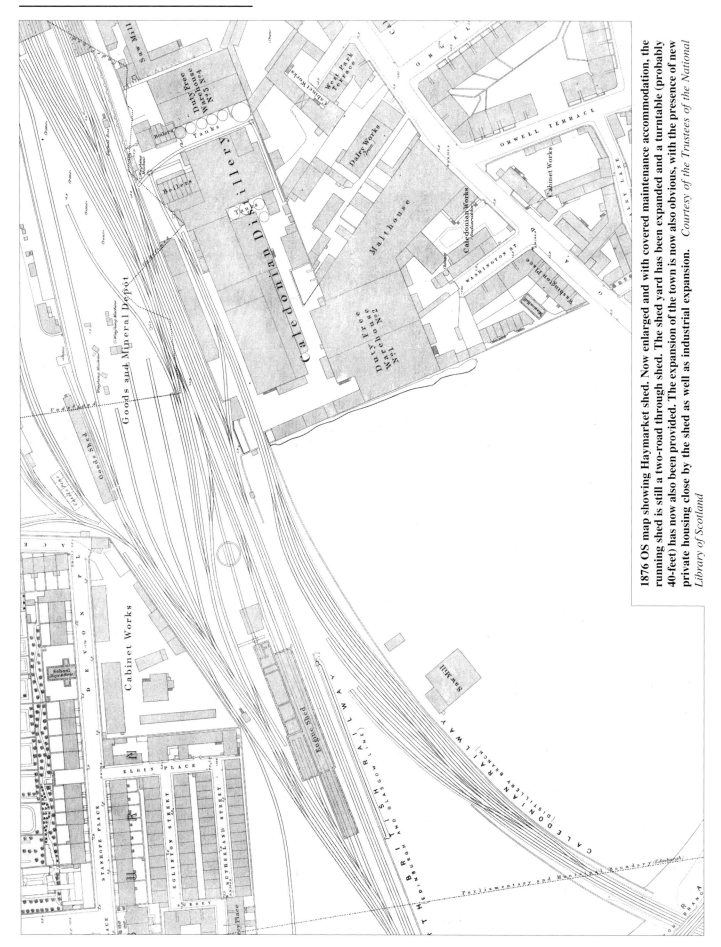

1876 OS map showing Haymarket shed. Now enlarged and with covered maintenance accommodation, the running shed is still a two-road through shed. The shed yard has been expanded and a turntable (probably 40-feet) has now also been provided. The expansion of the town is now also obvious, with the presence of new private housing close by the shed as well as industrial expansion. *Courtesy of the Trustees of the National Library of Scotland*

NBR 2-2-2 No. 211 (formerly E&GR No. l *Haymarket*), originally built by Beyer Peacock in 1856, standing at Haymarket old shed after rebuilding by Drummond in 1882. In the middle background are the towers of Playfair's magnificent Donaldson's Hospital, with Herdman's Flour Mills above the tender. *Bill Lynn collection*

Margaret's in Edinburgh by some three years. Robert Thornton, who had trained with R&W Hawthorn at Newcastle, was the first Locomotive Superintendent at Haymarket, and under his stewardship the first allocation of twelve E&GR engines performed well and with some reliability, although leaking fireboxes were an ongoing problem. The E&GR was, however, short of engines overall, partly due to recurring failures (due in no small part to the hard and unyielding track), and between October 1845 and September 1846 it is recorded that they hired, on an 'as required' basis, locomotives from the NBR, whose line to Berwick was not completed by the time their first new engines were delivered. This 'hiring' was based on turns run, and the cost to the E&GR was not inconsiderable. The NBR charged the E&GR for each trip of 46 miles, that is, each single trip between Edinburgh and Glasgow, and for the period from 9th October 1845 until 30th September 1846 the E&GR paid a total of £754 for the use of five NBR locomotives, Nos 1, 2, 3, 4 and 7.

It is known that by 1844 the E&GR owned and ran a total of twenty-six locomotives, of which ten had iron fireboxes and sixteen had copper fireboxes. This information is contained in the report into the accident which occurred at or near Ratho on the 19th May 1844 (see Chapter 31). As a consequence of this rear-end collision, a Glasgow cattle and spirits dealer who had hired a special train to take him from Glasgow to Edinburgh was killed. In the evidence given at the trial, which took place in Edinburgh on the 3rd and 4th November 1845, Hawthorn-trained Robert Thornton, then described as Locomotive Superintendent in Edinburgh (Haymarket shed), stated that he had twelve engines allocated to Haymarket shed out of a company total of twenty-six. Of the engine involved – *Napier*, of the E&GR and one of the original Bury four-wheelers of 1841 – he confirmed that it had been examined on arrival in Edinburgh on two occasions in the seven days prior to the accident and the first examination revealed that the engine was '*in a good state*' but at the later examination '*it was leaking badly*'. He further confirmed that all engines upon arrival at Edinburgh were examined

before going back into traffic. The truth of the matter was that *Napier* was, on the day in question, in a very poor state of repair with leaking tubes and boiler and should never have been allowed into traffic. Some of the original Bury and Hawthorn locomotives, although rebuilt, lasted well into the final years of Wheatley's reign, being scrapped around 1874.

On James Miller's recommendation to the Directors of the NBR, Thornton was 'head-hunted', to use modern parlance, by the NBR, and was subsequently appointed Locomotive Superintendent in January 1846. Thornton was responsible for building and equipping the workshops which were to become known as St. Margaret's – so named after its close proximity to St. Margaret's Well, one of the many famous wells lying below the shadow of Arthur's Seat. The NBR also augmented the footplate staff numbers at St. Margaret's by enticing engine drivers away from the E&GR shed at Haymarket with the offer of an additional 6*d*. (2½ pence) per day in wages. However, niggardly to the last, once the men had signed up, the NBR management withdrew the extra 6*d*. per day, and there was nothing the men could do about it. Indeed, in 1850, a driver and firemen who quit without notice were jailed for three months.

When the NBR absorbed the E&GR it was obvious that this first Haymarket shed was to continue serving the E&GR main line and branches, and was to be very much subservient to the main Cowlairs shed, whilst St. Margaret's continued to serve the Berwick and Hawick main lines and branches. However, the workshops at St. Margaret's were eventually to be closed and the work previously undertaken there absorbed by the former E&GR Cowlairs works.

One interesting aside was the fact that Edinburgh's own Co-operative Society, St. Cuthbert's Co-operative Society, was originally founded by a group of twelve men in 1859, some of whom were employees of the E&GR at what is recorded as 'Haymarket Workshops', and it has been possible to find a very old photograph showing one of these men, John (Jock) Lawrie, posing in front of an early locomotive at the original Haymarket shed, where he was the blacksmith (see page 21).

The OS map of 1914, showing the new Haymarket shed. The extent of the reclaimed ground on which the new shed was built, causing it to sit on a higher elevation compared with the surrounding area, is clearly delineated. The shed is an eight-road through shed and the coaling stage (manual) is apparent, situated at the south-west corner. The 50-foot turntable is also shown, as is the original brick-built sand kiln, located between the two fans of shed roads at the eastern side of the depot. The surrounding area is still largely rural and the polo ground will later be swallowed up by the construction of the rugby football stadium for the SRU. At the foot of the map can be seen the chord lines which form the Gorgie triangle when they converge at Gorgie East Junction on the Edinburgh and South Side Suburban Railway. This is where the larger locomotives were turned until a new, longer turntable was provided at the shed. *Courtesy of the Trustees of the National Library of Scotland*

3 THE NEW SHED

The situation – or as perhaps better described, shambles – as highlighted in Chapter 1, which lasted up until the widening work was completed, had led to a significant increase in the level of industrial unrest amongst the grossly over-worked staff including signalmen, drivers, fireman and guards; NBR staff joined the national agitation for shorter working hours and longer rest period between shifts. The main locomotive sheds involved were those which handled most of the freight traffic; so, although Haymarket men had the same long hours of duty, because in the main they worked passenger trains they were not quite so badly affected as, for instance, were the St. Margaret's crews. Inevitably, the agitation led to a widespread six-week-long strike, not only on the NBR, but elsewhere in Scotland; it included men from both the Caledonian Railway and the Glasgow & South Western Railway, and lasted from December 1890 until January 1891.

At around this same time, when work was underway quadrupling the running lines and doubling the Mound and Haymarket tunnels after the opening of the Forth Bridge, it became increasingly obvious that the original Haymarket shed was wholly unsuitable for the sheer number of engines now allocated, and the opportunity was grasped to have a new, custom-built larger shed constructed on an open site, some 678 metres to the west of the original shed.

In the minutes of the NBR Works Committee dated 29th September 1891 it is recorded, '*Offers for the erection of a new engine shed to the west of Haymarket were submitted and referred to the Secretary to arrange a contract*', and in the minutes dated 15th October 1891 appeared the following: '*Committee approved of there having been placed with Messrs. James Young & Sons, Edinburgh, the contract for the erection of the new engine shed to be created in the west of Haymarket, at the price of £14,500, the work to be completed by 1st June, 1892.*' An ambitious timescale indeed!

Construction of the new engine shed commenced in 1892. Work was soon stopped as the foundations were found to be unstable, most likely because the area of ground had been an infill site. The minutes of the NBR Works Committee dated 30th March 1893 stated:

Secretary reported as to the condition of the new engine shed in course of construction at Haymarket and stated that it would be necessary to carry out additional work in connection therewith and at an additional cost of about £7,300. It was remitted to the General Manager and Secretary to examine and report.

It would appear that the foundation piers had shown some signs

NBR 2-4-0 No. 418 stands at Haymarket old shed with regular driver John Walker on the footplate. Designed by Wheatley and built at Cowlairs in 1873, this engine was fitted with simple vacuum brake equipment to enable it to work East Coast Joint coaching stock. Named *Bonnybridge* during the Drummond era, this locomotive was to be further rebuilt by Reid in 1914. In the right centre of the worthies standing in front of the locomotive is blacksmith Jock Lawrie who was a founder-member of Edinburgh's own St. Cuthbert's Co-operative Society. *Bill Lynn collection*

of subsidence, but the contractor failed to alert the Company Engineer of this; drains supported by brackets from the piers, and the stonework on top of the piers, were then installed until the piers actually shifted. In the minutes of the meeting of NBR Directors (held in London) dated 22nd June 1893, the situation was noted and the blame placed on the resident NBR engineering representative, one Inspector Bruce, with the Directors ordering that '*he be dispensed with*'. Harsh treatment indeed!

Owing to the continuing instability of the site it was to be late 1893 before work commenced once more; but finally, in 1894, a new and substantial shed was opened. However, stability problems aside, in the minutes of the meeting of the Works Committee dated 26th October 1893 it was recorded that:

The Committee approved a contract having been placed with Messrs. Wm. Beattie & Sons, Edinburgh, for the erection of a coaling stage at the new locomotive shed to the west of Haymarket at a price of £694.10/-, the work to be completed by January, 1894 under penalty of £2 per day.

In the November minutes it was recorded that the cost of the new Haymarket shed was £14,500 and that the Company had withheld £1,524.11/1d, paying out only £13,719. This obviously was their way of obtaining some compensation for the overrun in construction. Thereafter, there is no mention made of the new shed or its problems, and even the opening went unrecorded. This perhaps says a lot about the relatively minor role Haymarket shed played in the early days of the NBR.

The engine shed was of typical NBR design, brick built, and consisted of a double-ended, straight, eight-road through shed with transverse-pitched roofs and raised smoke vents. The shed was 100 yards in total length, with ten transverse pitches in the roof. The roof was originally covered in slate – but in the latter years, with wear and tear, and the result no doubt of many engines 'blowing off' in the shed, the roof was deteriorating and a tarred felt covering was used as a replacement in part, and certainly at the eastern end of the shed. However, by the mid-1950s, the roof was anything but waterproof and the smoke vents were just open holes. On the south side of the shed each side wall section supporting the roof pitch, ten in all, had two arched and glazed windows, plus a round, wooden-slatted ventilation louvre set high into the peak.

As originally built, the north-side wall of the shed was similarly fitted with arched windows and louvres, but the addition of a new sand kiln in the mid-1930s, and the 1947 new workshop along the north side, covered up the windows, and the louvres were eventually bricked up.

The shed measured some 40 yards in width and, as built, each of the eight roads was fitted with closing wooden doors at either end – although, through wear and tear, these soon disappeared. The Ordnance Survey map of 1893/94 in the National Library of Scotland, although now in poor condition and of small scale, shows sidings and a shed, named 'engine shed', in the general location of what was to become the new shed, but in no great detail; so it is obvious that work was well underway at this time, although the 'old' shed is also still extant on this map. The new shed is indicated on the Ordnance Survey map of 1914, with the area of infill clearly shown.

This new shed (OS Grid Ref. NT229728) lay more or less on an east/west axis, parallel to and on the north side of, the North Main and South Main lines. It was in what later became the Edinburgh

NBR 2-2-2 No. 1003, formerly E&GR No. 213 *Polmont*, as rebuilt by Holmes in 1897. The engine stands outside the new shed at Haymarket in the very early 1900s, being prepared for the next turn of duty by its driver. Immediately behind the tender is the original sand kiln at this shed. Built originally by Beyer Peacock in 1856 for the E&GR, this was the first engine of eight designed by Charles Beyer which were to continue to give sterling service until withdrawn in 1909. *Bill Lynn collection*

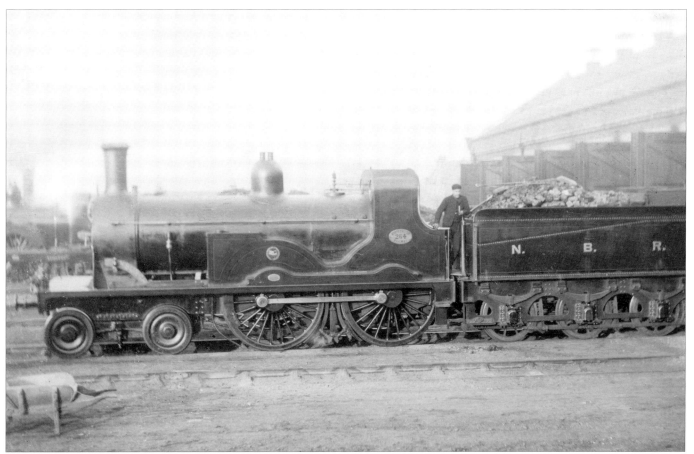

NBR 4-4-0 No. 264, designed and built by Wheatley at Cowlairs in 1871 and in the same class as the ill-fated No. 224 which went down with the first Tay Bridge in 1879, stands at Haymarket new shed after 1896. The engine is typical Wheatley with all the austere look of his engines. The tender is also standard Wheatley, with its close-set wheels. This engine worked over the E&GR from Haymarket until withdrawn in 1917. *Bill Lynn collection*

West Parliamentary Constituency (Murrayfield/Cramond Ward) and, as the surrounding area was built up, was eventually to be bounded to the eastern side by Russell Road, which passed under the running lines, and to the north and west by Roseburn Street which again passed under the running lines. To the south, across the main lines, lay a triangular area of open ground which was later to become the Russell Road Cleansing Depot of Edinburgh City Corporation. This in turn was bounded on the south side by the Caledonian Railway's Edinburgh Princes Street (Dalry Middle Junction) to Haymarket West Junction link line which, in 1876, gave the 'Caley' access to, and running powers over, the E&GR main line to Larbert Junction and the Scottish Central main line.

To the eastern side of the shed yard was the Caledonian Railway's Edinburgh Princes Street to Leith North branch line, which diverged from the Haymarket West link line (described above) at Dalry Middle Junction, crossing over the NBR main lines at right angles on a north to south axis. This overbridge was thereafter, until it was finally removed in the late 1960s, always referred to by Haymarket crews as 'the Caley Brig'. Access and egress to and from the shed to the North and South Main lines was controlled from Haymarket Central Junction signal box which lay on the south side of the main lines immediately west of the aforesaid bridge.

Over the years the location of the new Haymarket shed was to become bounded, in part, by Edinburgh's brewing/distilling industry and other equally odoriferous establishments, as can be seen on the Ordnance Survey maps. In later years (and well

into the 1960s), Jeffrey's Caledonian Brewery in Russell Road, Bernard's Brewery at Gorgie and the McEwan's Fountainbridge Brewery complex vied with both the North British and Caledonian Distilleries, Cox's Gorgie Mills Glue Works, the NB Rubber Works, Duncan Flockhart (formerly T.H. Smith) Industrial Chemists, Weston's Biscuit Factory and the confectionery works of J. Ross & Co., in emitting a variety of all-pervading smells. These smells, whilst individually not unpleasant, were, when mixed together in the cold air and particularly at night, a stomach-churning mélange which often made shed life at 64B unpleasant, and left indelible memories with all who ever worked there.

The layout of this new shed was to establish a protocol for the ordered movement of locomotives from the time they came on shed, right up to the point where they were presented at the shed outlet signal ready for traffic, and the daily operation of the shed is described in detail at Chapter 8.

A 50-foot turntable was provided at the south-east corner of the east shed yard, and the large wooden hand-coaling stage referred to above was provided at the south-west side (adjacent to the main lines) of the west yard, the latter area being commonly known amongst Haymarket loco-men as the 'top-end' of the shed. Engines coming 'on shed', after turning (if required) on the turntable, ran up alongside the southern wall of the shed to the manual coaling stage and, after coaling, ran on to ash pits at the top end. After fires/ashpans and smokeboxes had been cleaned, the engines were then placed in the allocated shed road, this movement taking place

NBR 4-4-0 No. 423, built by Wheatley in 1873 and rebuilt by Holmes in 1890 – when it received the typical Holmes characteristics, except for the solid bogie wheels – stands on the original short 50-foot turntable at Haymarket around the turn of the century. Mainly working over the Waverley route, the engine is seen here with Driver Andrew Manzie, a well-known Haymarket character, who was to finish his days on the Haymarket yard pilot. *Bill Lynn collection*

via the long headshunt which crossed Roseburn Street and lay parallel to the main lines. This headshunt extended towards the area of ground which now accommodates the Scottish Rugby Union's Murrayfield Stadium. After the mechanical coaling plant had been constructed in the early 1930s, the track layout at the top end was altered to provide for two dedicated ash pit roads.

In the shed proper, each of the eight roads had a continuous brick-lined pit facility (non-illuminated), but with roads 7 and 8 at some later date being partitioned off and used as maintenance and fitting roads. No. 7 road was also to be interrupted and buffer-ended approximately one engine length inside the eastern end of the shed, with the western portion contained within the partitioned area and closed off by a sliding door. Roads 1 to 6 were then the running shed roads, with each road equipped with a wooden boarded crossing facility running across all the pits approximately one third of the way up the shed from the eastern end. Adjacent to the boardwalk on No. 6 road, and mounted on the north wall which divided the fitting area from the running shed, was the 'engine arrangements board'. This large board contained details of all booked Haymarket turns and also all turns worked by foreign engines booked to come on-shed before returning homewards – the engine number and the road where each was stabled was chalked-in alongside the relevant turn. This is where preparation crews found the number of each of the engines they were required to prepare on their respective diagrams, and also from whence the chargeman cleaner directed his particular operation. The arrangements board was kept updated by the shift assistant running foreman (third man).

At the south side of the east shed yard, adjacent to and at the east end of the turntable, lay the shed office block for the Shed Master and clerical support staff. This was, when built, a long single-storey brick building, with a longitudinally pitched and slated roof. At the eastern end there was a small store room, originally a kit store, but post-war it only held supplies of paraffin and rape oil for filling lamps, and was the repository for the headboards for the named express passenger trains. It was here that the turntable crew took refuge. Of the two adjacent offices, the easterly one accommodated two clerks and served as the paying-out office on Thursday afternoons and Fridays. The next along was the General Office with five incumbents, and the Shed Master's office was the most westerly office, but was only accessible through the General Office.

Immediately to the south-west corner of the Shed Master's office lay the turntable. On the north side, at the north-west end of the east shed yard, shear legs were provided for the lifting of locomotives. Here the stores block lay adjacent to the pathway leading up from Roseburn Street.

East of this facility lay another long single-storey brick-built building. At the west end were the enginemen's locker room and the booking-on lobby with notice cases and locomotive diagrams. The Running Foreman's Office was in the centre front of the building with a clear view across the east yard to the turntable, and the booking-on staff and the roster clerk sat in the room directly behind. At the eastern end of the block lay the drivers and firemen's bothy (mess room). These offices and messing facilities survived

A fine view of Haymarket top end immediately post-grouping, with a wide selection of NBR engines to hand. The shed roof, some twenty-odd years old by now, is still intact and in excellent condition. The locomotives are, from left to right, Atlantic No. 9875 *Midlothian*, an unidentified Class 'J' (D29) 4-4-0, Class 'B' (J35) 0-6-0 No. 848 and Class 'N' 4-4-0 No. 896. All these engines were allocated to Haymarket. There is some work being carried out above the shed doors to Nos 3, 4 and 5 roads, at which, you can be sure, the present day Health & Safety Executive would look in horror. *Bill Lynn collection*

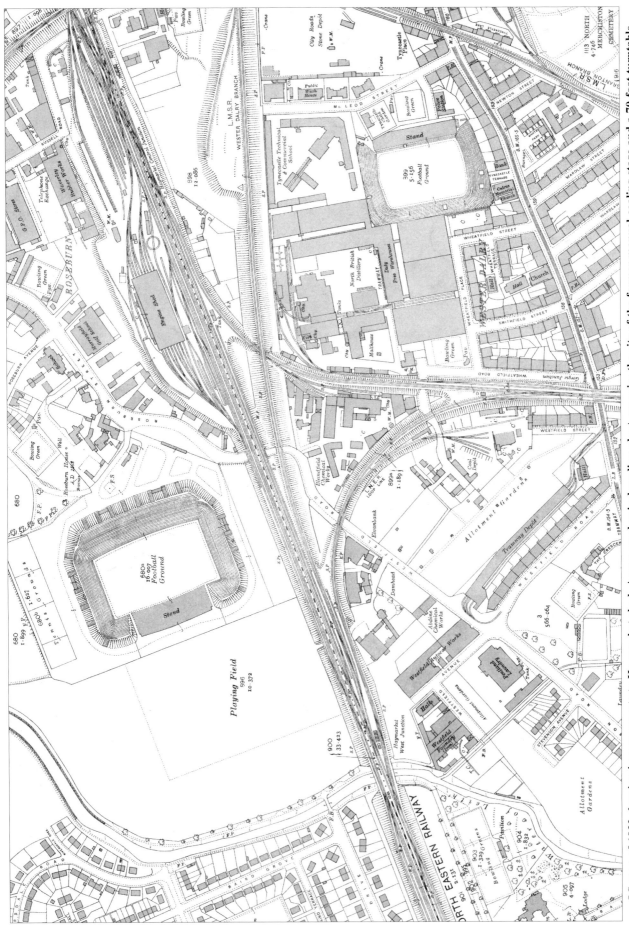

OS map of 1932 showing improvements to Haymarket shed. A new mechanical coaling plant occupies the site of the former manual coaling stage and a 70-foot turntable has now been installed. The sand kiln is still extant, but will be gone by the mid-1930s, replaced by a new kiln on the north-east corner of the running shed. Haymarket shed basically survived in this form until the demise of steam, with the only alterations being the addition of a new two-road fitting shop constructed on the north side of the shed in 1947. Haymarket, however, is now well and truly in Edinburgh, with new housing and industrial development continuing apace. *Courtesy of the Trustees of the National Library of Scotland*

until post-dieselisation. The cleaners were initially housed in an old coach body to the west of this office block.

When opened, the shed had a brick-built sand kiln located between Nos 4 and 5 roads in the east-end yard and, whilst the date of removal is not known, it certainly was extant in the early 1930s and after the turntable and coaling plant alterations, but was gone by 1938. The east shed track layout was remodelled in 1947 in consequence of the construction of the new fitting shop. As part of the track alterations, the shed roads were extended forward at the east end to provide greater engine standage, with new connections laid for the lines to the new machine shop and the siding which ran around the north side of it. A new sand kiln was built before the original was removed, butted onto the north wall of the shed and immediately outside the new machine shop, along with a staff toilet block. This new sand facility had a furnace which heated and dried the sand, and a constant supply of dry sand for locomotives was obtained via small chutes located in a small recessed space on the north wall inside the shed.

The E&GR had purchased the Union Canal outright in 1849, and with it came the canal-feeder water supply in the shape of Cobbinshaw Loch, located in the Midlothian/Lanarkshire county march and deep in the heart of Caledonian Railway territory.

When the new (1894) shed was built, a piped water supply for locomotive watering purposes was run from the Union Canal in the vicinity of Slateford, via the South Suburban line to an elevated water tank sitting atop a brick base and located in the V formed by the Haymarket Central/Gorgie Junction chord of the Suburban line and the Down South Main line. This water tank was replaced in the early 1950s by the new large elevated water tank alongside the south wall of the shed, which was to become a feature of Haymarket over many years. This new water tank continued to be fed from the same source. At first, water cranes were located at the top end, with one single water crane on the south side of No. 1 road at the east end, plus a further water crane at the converging point of Nos 4 and 5 roads, where engines could take on water just before going off-shed. With later changes, water cranes were provided between each set of shed roads immediately outside the east end of the shed, and the water crane at the shed exit was removed.

The engines which came to the new shed were still, in many cases, the rebuilds of the original E&GR locomotives, plus the engines introduced in the Hurst years of the NBR. However, the passenger engines built by Wheatley and Drummond soon replaced these earlier engines and they, in turn, were superseded firstly by

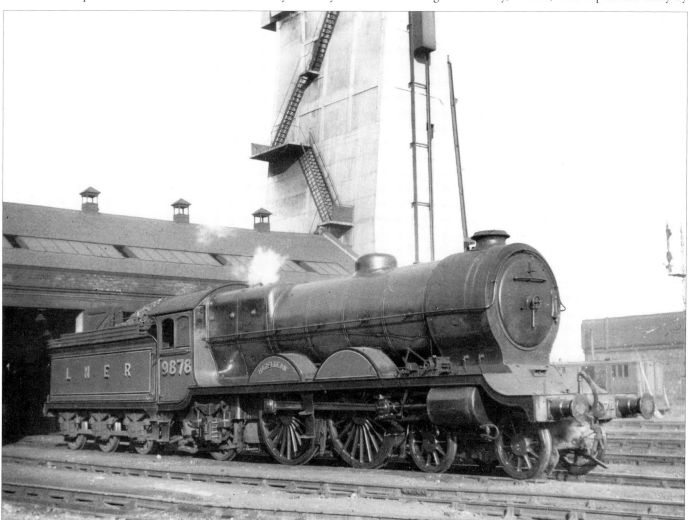

Ex-NBR Atlantic No. 9878 *Hazeldean* stands at the top end of Haymarket. This was Tom Henderson's engine and was one of three fitted with water scoops for working through to Newcastle. The date is just after 1930: the coaling plant is still new and in clean condition, and No. 9878 has by this date been supplanted in the Top link by Gresley A1 No. 2563 *William Whitelaw*. In the right background is a rather decrepit NBR coach body, serving as the messing room for firedroppers – a less than salubrious facility! *Bill Lynn collection*

Ex-NBR Atlantic No. 9902 *Highland Chief* at Gorgie whilst turning on the triangle, the 50-foot turntable at Haymarket being too short for these engines. This engine had just worked in from Dundee on the heavy Aberdeen/London 'fish' train, an important service almost always entrusted to the Atlantics.   *Bill Lynn collection*

the new Holmes passenger engines and then, of course, by the new locomotives of the Reid era at Cowlairs.

The NER, in exercising the running rights between Newcastle and Edinburgh which they had negotiated, required the NBR to find and allocate shed space for up to ten engines as part of the agreement. Initially, the NBR management suggested that the NER be allocated space which was available at Leith Walk Goods, but the NER rejected this out of hand and insisted that space be found for their purposes in St. Margaret's shed. By 1904, however, the NER were finding that the St. Margaret's premises were becoming far too cramped for their locomotives, and so that year they relocated their locomotives to the new and more spacious shed at Haymarket

where they were allocated the use of Nos 7 and 8 roads on the north side of the shed.

Up until the 1930s, when the shed was further modernised, a huge coal stack lay at the top end (the west end) to the area north-west of the shed roads. The NBR, and subsequently the L&NER, like most railway companies of the time, bought considerable amounts of coal both to hedge against future price increases and as insurance against the unrest which swept the mining industry from time to time, and created huge stacks of locomotive coal 'for a rainy day' as it were. In 1920 this was done under an Instruction issued by the wartime Government Coal Commissioner. The First World War had seen the NBR's supply of coal dwindle, with stocks reducing in

A strangely quiet time at Haymarket shed in September 1938. This view across the front of the shed shows quite clearly the General Offices on the left with the coaling plant behind. The original brick sand kiln stood in the area between Nos 4 and 5 roads (centre) but had been removed by this time. An NER Atlantic stands in No. 8 road, one of the two shed roads allocated to the NER. The carriage body on the right is the cleaners' bothy (mess room), with the stores block behind.   *P. Fox/Transport Treasury*

ABOVE: NBR Atlantic No. 9510 *Lord Provost* heads a Perth express past Haymarket in the mid-1930s. The new coaling plant rises above the train, a landmark on the Edinburgh skyline until it was finally demolished. In the left background are the elegant towers of Donaldson's Hospital, whilst to the right, behind the water tank and chimneys, is the bulk of Edinburgh Castle.   *Bill Lynn collection*

BELOW: It is the end of May 1947, and the new machine/fitting shed is under construction at the north side of the shed. This facility, when completed, housed a new electric wheel-drop pit and provided a more amenable location for heavy repairs.   *Bill Lynn collection*

Haymarket, even in the later days of BR ownership, maintained close contact with ex-NBR locomotives – both with those still allocated and with the frequent visitors from Fife. Here, D29 No. 62412 *Dirk Hatteraick*, one of the original saturated 'Scotts', stands in the shed loop waiting to work home to Dunfermline shed later in the day. The date is pre-1950, since No. 62412 was taken out of traffic and condemned in September 1950.   *Courtesy David Dunn*

consequence, and much of the coal then being supplied was of poor quality. In 1920 every railway company was ordered to lay down at each depot the equivalent of six month's supply of locomotive coal, and for the NBR this meant 98,000 tons in total. With only 42,000 tons in hand, this was to prove an uphill struggle and was only achieved in part by appropriating many of the coal trains passing through the system (with Government authority). Coal was the life-

blood of steam traction, and any problem which might interrupt the constant supply of coal for locomotives could be costly in the extreme. Coal was only taken from these stacks as a last resort. This practice of stockpiling coal was phased out at Haymarket as supplies stabilized, ending after the mechanised coaling plant was provided at the south-west corner of the running shed, practically on the site of the hand coaling stage.

The front of Haymarket shed in the 1950s, with the line from the turntable up the south side of the shed to the coaling plant clearly shown. An engine is having its tender replenished as another wagon of coal is tipped into the hopper to keep supplies topped up. Otherwise, it appears to be a (rare) quiet time at the shed.   *Bill Lynn collection*

Haymarket west (top) end in 1952. To the right are the ashpits with a 'Director' standing thereon, and to the left of the shed roof is the black bulk of the new 1947 machine shop. Haymarket was always covered in a pall of smoke. *Bill Lynn collection*

Another busy day at Haymarket, in September 1957, as engines are prepared for the next turn of duty. Five Pacifics are in the picture with A1 No. 60162 *Saint Johnstoun* wearing the headboard for the 'Heart of Midlothian', the 13.30pm Edinburgh to London King's Cross express, forever known to Haymarket men as 'The Diners'.

The 1930s modernisation provided not only for a new, electrically-operated, pre-cast-concrete coaling plant to the design of Henry Lees & Co., who provided many similar coaling plants for the L&NER, but also provision of a bigger, Ransomes & Rapier 70-foot manual turntable which was commissioned in 1931, and which was, in the immediate post-war years, to be fitted with a vacuum operated tractor. The coaling plant, with a twin hopper capacity of around 400 to 500 tons, cost some £15,000 to erect, and the new turntable saw a further expenditure of £1,481. The 'cenotaph' concrete coaling plant was to be a familiar landmark on the western Edinburgh skyline for many years to come. The changes are clearly indicated on the Ordnance Survey map of 1932.

Surrounded by rich coalfields, Haymarket received the bulk of its locomotive coal from local collieries and in 1920 there were more than sixty collieries in the supply chain. In the 1950s, the main pits

supplying coal to the shed from the rich seams of good quality steam coal then being worked in the Lothians and Fife coalfields were:

West Lothian pits
- Riddochhill   Lady Morton Jewel coal
- Whitrigg   Lady Morton Jewel coal, Wilsontown splint

Midlothian pits
Newbattle collieries
- Lady Victoria ⎫
- Lingerwood   ⎬ Jewel seam
- Easthouses   ⎭
- Burghlee   Jewel seam
- Ramsay   Jewel seam
- Woolmet   Jewel seam

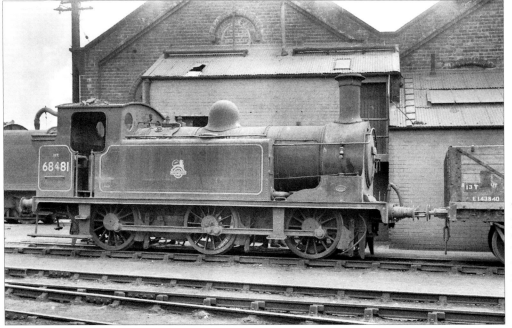

The former No. 1 Waverley west pilot, Class J83 No. 68481, stands outside the new sand kiln which was built onto the north wall of the shed around 1947. The engine is coupled to a five-plank wooden wagon which may contain sand awaiting off-loading to the kiln hopper. *Courtesy David Dunn*

The roof support pillars inside Haymarket shed made it extremely difficult to get good photographs, but this is a nice example of the light and shade within the depot, with shafts of sunlight illuminating Haymarket A4 No. 60024 *Kingfisher* in the final days of steam in 1963. An ex-NBR survivor, a Class J36, lurks in the background and is most probably No. 65243 *Maude*. *Courtesy Dugald Cameron*

Fife collieries
- Bowhill   Lochgelly splint
- Kinglassie   Lochgelly splint
- Lindsay   Dunfermline splint.

The coal supplied post-war was generally good quality steam coal and was used on all engines across the board, there being no differentiation made between engines scheduled for goods work or passenger work. Small amounts of hard Yorkshire coal also made an appearance, but in the main, locally-produced coal was used. However, for all non-stop workings the selected coal was the high quality Grade 'A' Jewel coal from the Newbattle collieries, one of the two hoppers in the coaling plant being reserved for the storage of this coal in the summer months.

The 1930 modernisation was partly driven by the original manual coaling and turntable facilities becoming life expired; but also, insofar as the turntable was concerned, the fact that the larger NBR and NER Atlantic class locomotives, at 53 feet 2 inches for the former, could not be accommodated on the 50-foot turntable. By this time the first Gresley Pacifics had also been allocated, with the likelihood of many more arriving sooner rather than later. This led to all these big engines having to be run round the 'Gorgie triangle' – formed by the chord lines from Haymarket Central Junction and Haymarket West Junction, running to Gorgie Junction on the Edinburgh South Side Suburban Railway (the 'Sub') – each

time a turn was required, a movement which was usually carried out on an 'as required' basis before the engines came on-shed after train working duties. It was, however, a practice which was time consuming, occupied valuable line capacity and carried the potential to inject delay into timetabled services on the running lines.

Further improvements were effected at Haymarket in the late 1940s, just prior to nationalisation, including the provision of a new machine/fitting shed consisting of two new double-ended through roads (9 and 10). Lying on the north side of the existing shed in a new, custom-built workshop, this shed was constructed with half-height brick walls, a corrugated iron upper half and pitched roof, and was painted black from the outset. A new Ransomes & Rapier electrically-operated wheel-drop pit was provided on No. 10 road, which did away with the need for shear legs, plus, in the workshop proper, there were modern machining facilities and equipment for blacksmiths, fitters, turners, machinists and the solitary joiner. Alongside the north wall of the 'new' shed lay accommodation consisting of the ambulance and first aid room, the mutual improvement meeting room, and the joiner's shop. The office of the Mechanical Foreman was also located in the south-east corner of the new building, but at an elevated level and accessed via a stone stairway. This workshop remains today as roads 9 and 10 of the former BR, and latterly ScotRail DMU, maintenance depot. The original stores building was also greatly extended in 1947 to cater for the many additional spares then requiring to be held.

An office/bothy for the examining fitters and 'running' fitters, consisting of a low, square brick (utility) building with a flat concrete roof was built adjacent to the south-east corner of the shed at No. 1 road. This building formed the basic design for other improved messing facilities around the depot. A similar utility building was provided for the cleaners between the stores and the Running Foreman's Office, replacing an old coach body which had served previously. The author had considerable experience of this 'new' facility; it had never been particularly comfortable to begin with, and over the years it had suffered in the hands of the many 'inmates' – in his time there was little glass left in the windows. This new bothy contained a single cast-iron stove, a single stone wash-hand basin with cold running water only, some coat pegs, a few trestle tables and wooden benches. The Ritz it was not!

Another new bothy, similar in design to that provided for the fitters and cleaners, was built at the top-end yard, to the west side of the coaling plant and coal storage roads, for use by the conciliation staff (labourers) – but again providing little in the way of creature comforts. This building replaced an even more decrepit coach body which had served as mess room up to that time.

Nothing much else was done to the existing buildings thereafter, although a glass verandah was erected on the north side along the front of the two general offices, to provide shelter for men queuing for wages, etc. In the post-war years, a canteen was built behind the Running Foreman's Office, which was accessed through the booking-on lobby. This facility opened at 07.00 and remained open until around 18.00 Mondays to Fridays and 14.00 on Saturdays; it provided warm and weatherproof accommodation offering a greater degree of comfort than did the official bothies, thus it was well used by all grades of shed staff. In the 1950s, all the buildings, including the south-facing wall of the actual shed, were painted in a terracotta-coloured distemper, which was quite unique. Overall, however, life at Haymarket changed very little until the demise of steam.

With the onset of hostilities in 1939/40, brick and concrete air-raid shelters were provided at both the top-end (west yard) and the east-end of the shed, the latter gaining some notoriety at a later date as a repository for purloined pianos.

The management/supervisory and grading structure during the 1950s was:

- Shed Master   (Special Class B)
- Mechanical Foreman   (days) (Special Class A)
- Mechanical Foreman   (nights)   (Class 1)
- Running Foreman ×3   (3 shifts)   (Class 1)
- Asst. Running Foreman ×3   (3 shifts)   (Class 2)
- 3rd Man ×3   (3 shifts)   (Drivers)
- Chargehand Fitters (Workshop) ×2
- Chargehand Fitters (Running) ×3   (3 shifts)
- Chargehand Cleaners ×3   (3 shifts)
- Chargehand Conciliation grades   (days only)
- Head storekeeper
- Chief Clerk   (Class 1)
- Roster Clerk   (Class 2)
- Staff Clerk   (Class 2)
- Mechanical Foreman's Clerk   (Class 4)
- Clerks (general) ×3   (days)   (Class 4)
- Office Boy   (Junior Clerk)
- Typist   (Shorthand Typist).

Management relief (such as annual leave, absence or sickness) was covered by 'stepping up', as was the relief for the running foreman. Clerical relief was either provided internally, by overtime, or by assistance from the pool of relief clerks under the control of the District Motive Power Superintendent (DMPS), Edinburgh.

Maintenance was overseen by the mechanical foreman and his chargehand fitters; more is said regarding locomotive maintenance in Chapter 28.

Classic view of the front of Haymarket shed in the early 1960s, with every road occupied by a Gresley pacific. From left to right, A4s No. 60004 *William Whitelaw* and No. 60016 *Silver King* (the latter a visitor from Gateshead), Carlisle Canal's A3 No. 60095 *Flamingo*, then Haymarket's A4 No. 60024 *Kingfisher* and A3 No. 60097 *Humorist*. This was a typical view of Haymarket and was not posed in any way. *C. Lawson Kerr/Bill Brown collection*

4 DIESEL DAYS:
THE RECONSTRUCTION OF THE SHED

New main line diesel electric locomotives, in the shape of BRCW 1160 bhp D/E units, started to be allocated to Haymarket in 1959. Initially housed temporarily at the former Leith Central station, this by now being the home of the Edinburgh-area DMU fleet, after entering revenue-earning service they inevitably had to share shed space with their steam counterparts at Haymarket. This was an undesirable situation, since diesels demanded a significantly cleaner environment for servicing and maintenance. Work started in the summer of 1959 on the conversion of the existing Nos 6, 7 and 8 roads, the last two having been turned over solely to the purposes of steam locomotive maintenance at an earlier time. The work consisted of demolition of the roof and shed walls at the east and west ends of the shed and the reconstruction of that part of the running shed to provide a new, clean and entirely separate workshop dedicated to diesel electric traction. The 'new' diesel maintenance facilities were segregated from the main steam shed, now consisting of Nos 1 to 5 roads only, by a partition wall running the full length of the shed. This new facility provided continuous pits running the length of the shed on the three roads, with wheeled 'tables' which permitted access to diesel locomotive body-sides and hatches. The flooring was finished in an easy-clean, anti-slip material. However, the diesel locomotives still had to be stabled cheek by jowl with steam in the 'old' shed whilst in revenue-earning service, something

which did absolutely nothing for the external appearance of the diesels.

At the top end, on the north-west side, four new storage tanks for diesel fuel oil were constructed at street level, with a new discharging siding for rail tankers running alongside but at depot level. Temporary refuelling facilities were provided at the west end of the shed loop adjacent to the main lines until the demolition of the coaling plant, when custom-built refuelling facilities were then built on the site at the west end of the shed.

This redevelopment was very much an interim 'make-do-and-mend' – the new diesel maintenance facility remained unaltered for several years and within the modern ScotRail maintenance facility, the existing Nos 6, 7 and 8 shed roads are still in the original converted area of the former steam shed, although now much improved with new, elevated roads with illuminated pit facilities to ease maintenance, but otherwise as described above. The new Nos 9 and 10 roads are, in fact, merely a continuation of what was the former 'new' steam machine shop, provided after the advent of the Gresleys, and this shed and the roads are still in use today, mainly for lifting (with jacks) purposes. The exterior changes of this half-and-half conversion are clearly shown on the 1960-revision Ordnance Survey map.

The diesels brought the need for a new grade of technician,

Probably taken in late 1963 or in 1964; diesels hold sway, but work has yet to start on the remodelling of the remainder of the old steam shed roads 1 to 5. English Electric and Sulzer Type 4s dominate the picture whilst, just below the coal chute of the coaling plant, right, can be seen the bulk of Edinburgh Castle some 1½ miles to the east. *Courtesy Ian Musgrave*

Another later view of Haymarket top end, probably in early 1965. The rebuilding of the remains of the former steam shed has started, with the roof having been completely removed. The support columns and walls remain and the diesel locomotives stand quite unconcerned in the middle of the destruction and mayhem. The earlier-modernised diesel facility in Nos 6, 7 and 8 roads can clearly be seen on the left of the photograph. *Courtesy Ian Musgrave*

Electrician. The electricians, in turn, brought their own problems, mainly involving lines of demarcation and 'who should be doing what'. This led to a period of much disharmony, but a semblance of order was restored when the post of Electrical Foreman, graded Special Class, was created. The first incumbent, Ian MacIntosh, did much to restore order to the new situation and was, through sheer

personality, able to work closely with his mechanical counterparts, which was to the benefit of all – a benefit which was to see Haymarket return impressive availability figures for the new diesel fleet, as will be discussed later.

Steam was finally transferred away from Haymarket in September 1963 and further rebuilding was commenced in March 1965 on

Former Nos 6, 7 and 8 roads of the steam shed were part demolished and rebuilt as a diesel maintenance facility in 1959. Here, in February 1964, the conversion is long completed and a new, light and airy space has been created, separated from the remainder of the steam shed by a partition wall. This area is provided with low-maintenance, easily cleaned, non-slip floors and exudes a degree of cleanliness quite foreign to most steam sheds. Note the wheeled 'tables' provided to give access to bodyside doors on the locomotives. In No. 6 road, four EE Type 4 locomotives are waiting or undergoing attention, whilst an unidentified Deltic Type 5 lurks at the bottom of No. 7 road. A Class 17 (Clayton) and some Class 26s complete the line-up. *Courtesy Ian Musgrave*

Class 27 diesel electric locomotive No. 27204 stands on the breakdown train tool van in the east yard at Haymarket on 3rd June 1978. Haymarket fell heir to the former St. Margaret's steam breakdown crane, No. ADM1254/50, upon closure of that shed in 1967. Class 27s were, apart from the modified units for the E&GR push-pull services, not generally allocated to Haymarket. *Courtesy Gavin Morrison*

the site of the original steam shed roads 1 to 5, but with the new maintenance facility still using the same configuration of the shed roads and within the 'footprint' of the old steam shed. No. 1 road in the new facility was the underframe wash road, the adjacent No. 2 road was the 'bogie lift' road, Nos 3, 4 and 5 roads were the servicing roads, and roads 6, 7 and 8 were used for examination and maintenance. Nos 9 and 10 roads in the machine shop were used for heavier repairs. Later, with the disappearance of diesel locomotives, modifications were made to accommodate DMUs, with No. 2 road latterly being used for modification/heavy works.

The turntable was removed and the pit filled in, and the coaling plant, for so long a feature of the west-Edinburgh skyline, was demolished. The stores block was extended and modernised. A new two-storey administration block, with an integrated booking-on point, train crew and engineering staff mess-rooms, as well as a diesel training school on the upper level, was constructed almost immediately opposite the old General Office facilities on the north side of the east shed yard and adjacent to the access road from Russell Road. At this time, Haymarket was still both a train crew depot as well as a maintenance depot, with shift locomotive supervisors looking after drivers and secondmen. The retention of train crews at Haymarket continued well into the 1980s, although with the advent of the HSTs, diesel multiple units and the E&GR push-pull trains, and as the use of locomotives diminished, drivers were more and more, after booking-on, being required to travel to Waverley or some other location to take charge of trains, rather than taking locomotives 'off shed'.

In the mid-1970s, the resignalling of some 220 route miles

under the Edinburgh and East of Scotland Resignalling and Track Rationalisation Scheme – ranging from the regional boundary at Marshall Meadows and fringing with Motherwell SC (at Auchengray & Benhar Junction), Polmont, Longannet and Cupar signal boxes – with control being centralised in the new Edinburgh Signalling Centre, was well underway. The closure of Leith Central as a diesel multiple unit depot followed. Waverley station was then used to stable and clean DMUs on the nightshift, while all maintenance was carried out at Haymarket, with considerable transferring of sets to and from the station being required throughout the night hours. Increasing use of multiple units displaced more and more diesel electric locomotives, until finally Haymarket became a multiple unit running and maintenance depot only. The HST sets were stabled, serviced and maintained at Craigentinny Carriage Depot, which had been modernised as a proper coaching stock maintenance depot.

In April 1967, St. Margaret's Motive Power Depot was closed completely, and Haymarket fell heir to that most jealously-guarded facility, the 36-ton steam breakdown crane, No. 1062/36. Ordered by the NBR in 1914 from Cowans Sheldon & Co. at a cost of £3,290, it was delivered new to St. Margaret's, bearing at that time the NBR number 770517. Renumbered 972567 by the L&NER and renumbered yet again by BR, it lasted only a short time at Haymarket before being transferred on to Dundee, from where it was taken into preservation by the SRPS at Bo'ness where it can still be seen today. Haymarket then received a Cowans Sheldon 50-ton steam crane, No. ADM1254/50, which was joined in 1988 by a new Cowans Sheldon 50-ton diesel crane. For a time, both

ABOVE: Two Class 40s, Nos 40066 and 40160, await their next turn of duty on 2nd September 1979. The rebuilt steam shed is in the background. To the immediate left is the former steam stores building (black corrugated iron) with its new brick extension just visible in the picture. *Courtesy Gavin Morrison*

Two Class 55s, Nos 55008 *The Green Howards* of Gateshead depot and 55022 *Royal Scots Grey* of Haymarket depot, share space with an unidentified Class 47 outside Haymarket on 18th April 1981. This photograph clearly shows the part of the original steam shed which was converted in 1959, immediately behind the engines, with the more modern and completely rebuilt portion of the shed on the left. In the right background, immediately behind the white car, is the original steam-era stores building. *Courtesy Gavin Morrison*

50-ton cranes sat side by side at the depot while all members of the breakdown gang were trained in the workings of the new diesel crane. Finally, in 1989, the 50-ton steam crane was sent south for preservation, to the Great Western Railway Centre at Didcot.

Eventually, in May 1984, all Edinburgh-based passenger train crews were relocated to the new custom-built operations centre in Waverley station, built on the site of the old Nos 4, 5 and 6 platforms at the east end of the station. All the Edinburgh train crews (guards, drivers and drivers assistants) for passenger workings were centralised here, with Haymarket reverting to being a purely maintenance and exterior cleaning depot. Millerhill, however, continued then, as it docs today under the freight operator, English, Welsh & Scottish Railways (EWS, rebranded DB Schenker from 1st January 2009), to be the base for drivers working freight trains.

Craigentinny, having been largely reconstructed by BR and converted from being purely a carriage cleaning/maintenance yard and shed, was provided with new covered accommodation and facilities, including refuelling facilities, for the maintenance of the new HST sets – and continues to service the HST and ECML 225 electric train-sets. In addition, since privatisation, Craigentinny has provided facilities for the Voyager train-sets of Virgin and, more recently, Arriva CrossCountry.

At Haymarket depot, as part of the modernisation works, a new automatic exterior cleaning plant was provided between the North

Main lines and the depot buildings, and it remains in use today. The removal of the last visible external evidence of the old Haymarket steam shed came with the removal in 2002 of the large, high water tank on the south side of the shed, adjacent to the main lines, to allow for the extension of a headshunt. It has to be mentioned that, in the true, unfathomable traditions of the former BR, this tank had just been repainted at great expense immediately prior to its demise.

Up until the late 1980s, all movement of train-sets within the depot was carried out by certified drivers in the line of promotion, and therein lay a problem. This task was traditionally carried out by drivers who were employed on 'light work' duties, and so it had been back into the mists of antiquity. In the '80s, with all footplatemen now being concentrated at Waverley, depot shunting/ unit movement was incorporated into the train running links – and suddenly, instead of 'old hands' who knew the depot inside out, new, younger, drivers were being required to make all movements within the shed limits, working with the depot shunters; or so it should have been. Very quickly, the incidence of collisions, side-swipes and derailments started to increase, not only within Haymarket, but also at maintenance facilities elsewhere in the region. The outcome of a regional risk assessment exercise, with which the author was associated, recommended that the eminently sensible solution would be to make maintenance staff responsible for everything occurring within the parameters of the depot, including the movement of sets. The drivers' trade union, ASLE&F, naturally had a moan, based on the grounds that the driving task should be carried out by drivers in the line of promotion only, but, with privatisation looming, the day was won, common sense prevailed, and the collision/incident rate diminished considerably.

With the advent of new diesel multiple unit trains, the diesel electric locomotives and coaching stock on Scottish Region (by this time branded Regional Railways) internal passenger services were rapidly displaced. At the same time, the HST fleet and the newer InterCity 225 electric trains gained the monopoly of the InterCity ECML services between Aberdeen, Inverness and

ABOVE: **The new Cowans Sheldon 50-ton diesel crane, as delivered new to Haymarket in the 1980s, displacing the 50-ton steam crane, stands in the east shed yard.** *Courtesy Ray Murison*

RIGHT: **The 50-ton diesel crane shows off, lifting Class 08 shunting locomotive No. 08764, possibly during breakdown gang familiarisation with the new equipment at Haymarket.**
Courtesy Ray Murison

The new order! Class 47 No. 47268, Class 55 No. 55018 *Ballymoss* **and Class 40 No. 40142 stand in the old Nos 6, 7 and 8 'steam' roads on Saturday, 3rd June 1978.**   *Courtesy Gavin Morrison*

London. The diesel electric locomotives were soon confined to working the overnight sleeping car services, the few diesel electric locomotives so involved being out-stabled at Edinburgh Waverley and Craigentinny. By the mid-1980s, Haymarket was turned over solely to DMU maintenance and, as such, upon rail privatisation in March 1994 it passed into the hands of the new private train operating company (TOC) National Express (NX), who were awarded the first franchise for train operation in Scotland. NX continued to operate train services in Scotland under the former BR name, ScotRail, the branding brainchild of that most charismatic BR general manager, C.E.W. (Chris) Green, who was, in fact, to become that TOC's first managing director.

The front of the diesel shed in final form, standing in the footprint of the former steam shed, looking west. On the extreme left is the DMU washing plant. In the background, behind and between the wash road and the shed, can be seen the overbridge which carried the former ex-LM&S line from Princes Street to Haymarket West Junction, now the Western Approach Road, over the Edinburgh South Side Suburban Railway (the Sub). At this point the Sub climbs away to the left towards Gorgie Junction. All roads in the new shed complex can clearly be identified – with Nos 6, 7 and 8 being very evident because of the transverse roof which, of course, was the old steam shed as modified for diesels in 1959. From left to right, No. 1 road is the bogie underfame wash road, No. 2 road, previously bogie lift road, is now used for modification works, Nos 3, 4 and 5 roads are servicing roads, and Nos 6, 7, 8, 9 and 10 roads are the maintenance and heavy maintenance roads.   *Courtesy Ray Murison*

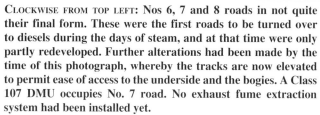

CLOCKWISE FROM TOP LEFT: Nos 6, 7 and 8 roads in not quite their final form. These were the first roads to be turned over to diesels during the days of steam, and at that time were only partly redeveloped. Further alterations had been made by the time of this photograph, whereby the tracks are now elevated to permit ease of access to the underside and the bogies. A Class 107 DMU occupies No. 7 road. No exhaust fume extraction system had been installed yet.

Class 150 and 170 stand on jacks in Nos 9 and 10 roads.

Nos 9 and 10 maintenance roads and the former 'new' machine shop of the steam era – with a Class 150, No. 150285, receiving attention and Class 170 No. 170423 elevated on jacks.

A pair of Class 170 'Turbostars' stand in Nos 7 and 8 roads at Haymarket.

A general view inside Nos 6, 7 and 8 maintenance shed showing the final arrangement of the former steam shed, with state-of-the-art exhaust fume extraction system and maintenance facilities. Turbostar No. 170431 stands in No. 8 road whilst an unidentified Class 158 stands in No. 6 road.   *All courtesy Ray Murison*

ABOVE: A panoramic view of Haymarket diesel maintenance depot in BR days, with a Class 47/7 heading an Up E&GR push-pull train past the shed. By this date the line had been completely resignalled and the semaphore signals were but a memory. In the shed foreground, from left to right, can be seen several Class 47s, at least one Deltic, and various Class 26s and DMUs. In the middle background is the new two-storey administration block. The various stages of the shed modernisation can be clearly seen, with completely new sheds for roads 1 to 5 (from the main line), and with the converted steam shed, roads 6 to 8, also quite identifiable. The concrete base in the foreground in front of the locomotive is the site of Haymarket Central Junction signal box, removed under the resignalling scheme. *Courtesy John Furneval*

Class 158s receive attention in Nos 6 and 7 roads. *Courtesy Ray Murison*

A Class 170 undergoes heavy repairs as it stands on the jacks in No. 10 road. *Courtesy Ray Murison*

5 THE TRACTION MAINTENANCE DEPOT

In 1994, with the privatisation of the railways, Haymarket Diesel Multiple Unit Maintenance Depot was handed over to the new owners, National Express, who took over the BR ScotRail services and the Class 150, Class 156 and Class 158 'Sprinter' units that were based at Haymarket. The depot, as modernised for diesel traction by BR, remained basically unaltered throughout the period of their control. In 1999 the new three-car Class 170 'Turbostars' started to come on stream, deposing the Class 150s and 156s, and relegating the Class 158s to lesser passenger duties. The new sets took over the running of the Edinburgh/Glasgow/Aberdeen services and, as further train-sets arrived, they were also to be seen on Edinburgh/Glasgow/Stirling/Perth services. After National Express had failed to win a second term of the franchise in 2005, the new owners, First ScotRail (First Group), took possession and revolutionised both the depot and train services in Scotland.

The diesel shed, as rebuilt by BR, had been further modified to deal with the two-car DMUs which formed the allocated fleet at the time. With the introduction of the Turbostars, which are three-car units, further modifications had to be made to the servicing and examination roads to accommodate the longer units; even today a single Turbostar unit is too long for No. 1 road – the underframe wash road – and any Class 170 set receiving attention there has to be moved about as required.

With the increase in the Turbostar fleet under First ScotRail stewardship, in 2006 work commenced on providing an additional covered maintenance area to supplement the existing maintenance facility which had been built in BR days. This new area was required to provide increased covered maintenance facilities for the existing fleet of Class 158s and the expanding fleet of Class 170 'Turbostar' DMUs. These multiple units were now forming almost all of the internal ScotRail services – with, of course, the exception of the electrified lines where EMUs reigned supreme, and the overnight ScotRail Caledonian sleeping car trains which are hauled on a 'hook and pull' contract operation by both diesel electric Class 66 and electric Class 90 locomotives, owned and provided by the freight operator DB Schenker. The EMUs running the Edinburgh to North Berwick services are maintained at Shields Depot in Glasgow, with the Caledonian sleeping cars being serviced at Craigentinny and Polmadie (Glasgow).

The new facility at Haymarket consists of a large covered shed, located directly to the east of the current depot, in the area formerly occupied with the east yard storage sidings. Lying parallel to and above Russell Road, it consists of three roads, 'A' (Alpha) and 'B' (Bravo) for light maintenance, and 'C' (Charlie) for heavy maintenance, providing the most modern facilities, all under cover, plus new external storage sidings. Haymarket depot employs a staff

The construction of the new maintenance shed at Haymarket, on the site of the former east yard sidings, started in 2006. Providing valuable additional space for the maintenance of the 158 and 170 fleets under cover, planning and construction were undertaken by First ScotRail. Examples of both these DMUs can be seen stabled to the right of the new building. *Courtesy John Furneval*

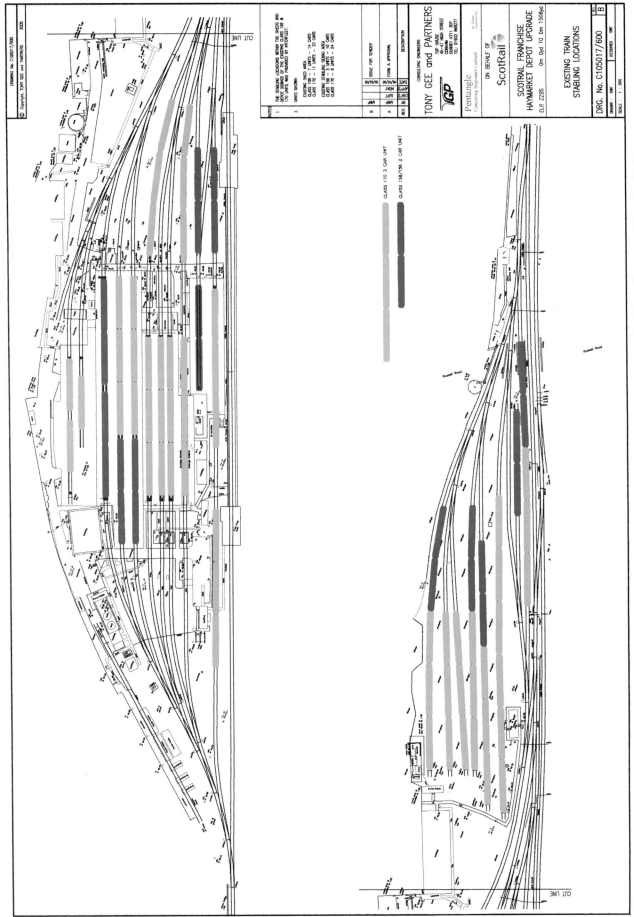

Plan showing the pre-2007 track and facilities, showing the depot more or less as it was first rebuilt for diesels by BR.   *Courtesy of First ScotRail*

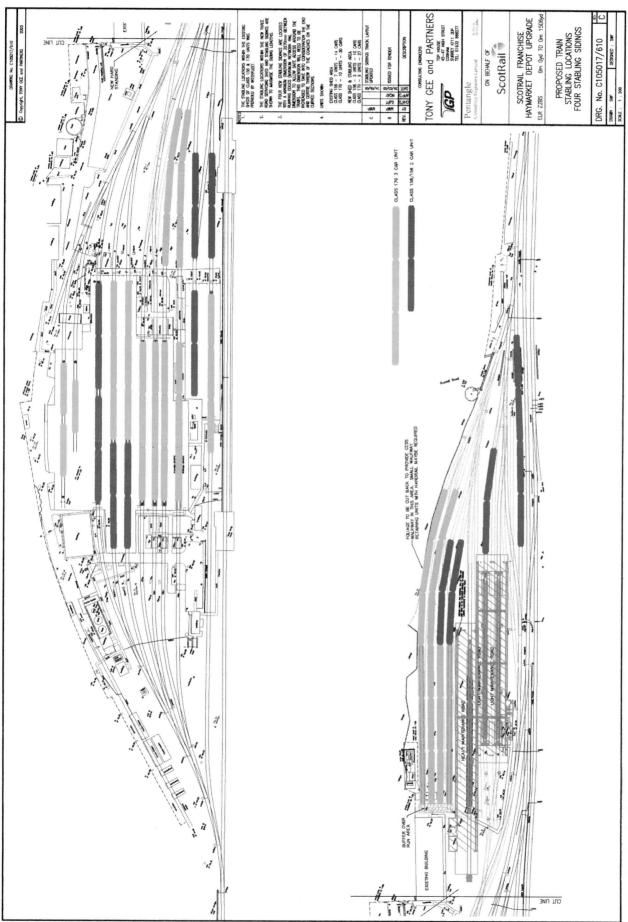

Plan showing the 2007 extension of the maintenance facilities, with one heavy maintenance road and two light maintenance roads, and the four new stabling roads. *Courtesy of First ScotRail*

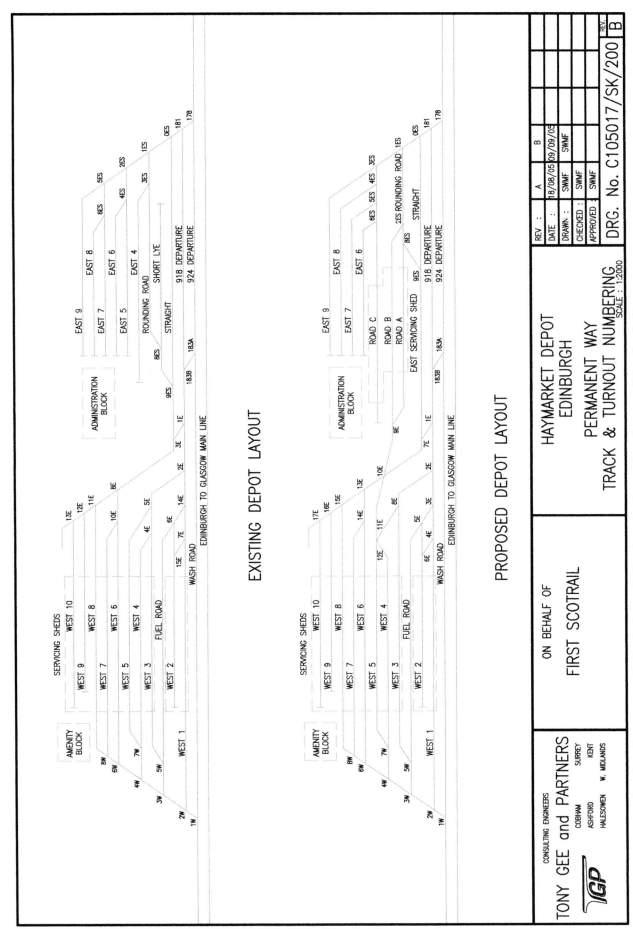

Schematic diagram of track and turnout numbering before and after the extension work. *Courtesy of First ScotRail*

The superstructure of the new maintenance shed looking due west towards the existing Haymarket facility. In the right background can be seen the steelwork which is the covered stands of the Scottish Rugby Union's Murrayfield Stadium. *Courtesy John Furneval*

of 140 persons and undertakes all examinations, running repairs and heavy maintenance of their own allocated fleet, and the heavy repairs in regard to the Eastfield and Inverness DMU allocation. The original DMU maintenance shed and the expanded facility are clearly shown on the enclosed plans.

In the latter part of 2008, First ScotRail intended to improve the train service on the Fife Circle after EWS gave up the allocated train paths over the Forth Bridge route for their Longannet coal traffic (in late November this began to pass over the newly-reopened

Stirling to Alloa route). First ScotRail had sought additional Class 170 Turbostars for this in order to alleviate peak overcrowding problems, however a delivery date of two years was the best that could be obtained. Instead, two full sets of older Mk II coaching stock owned by First ScotRail were brought back into service and the freight operator DB Schenker, using Class 66 diesel electric locomotives, was contracted to provide the motive power for an additional two loco-hauled trains per day on this route. By June 2009 this had been extended to four loco-hauled trains per day.

Another view of the near-completed shed in 2007, again with attendant Class 158 and 170 DMUs. The complex was officially opened in 2007. *Courtesy John Furneval*

The sheer size of the new maintenance facility at Haymarket can be appreciated as it nears completion. The new complex is surrounded by Class 158 and 170 units. The approach road leading up to the shed is that laid down by the NBR in 1896. Sadly, this last link with the original shed and the NBR Company will soon be lost, since the new Edinburgh Tram scheme will pass over Russell Road (immediate foreground) by way of a new bridge and then take the line of the original approach road to pass behind the shed proper.   *Courtesy John Furneval*

6 FOOTPLATE LIFE

FOOTPLATE STAFFING STRUCTURE

Right from the outset, the emerging railway industry offered an attractive form of employment, better paid than farming and more interesting than factory work. It also offered job security, with the added bonus of the opportunity for advancement. The downside was that, once in, the men were owned, body and soul, and were locked into an industry where the company will was enforced by a rigid hierarchy and iron discipline. Many early railway managers had been serving military officers, and the principles of military discipline ran through the railway industry – mainly, it has to be said, to the benefit of the industry. Instant dismissal for any infraction of the laid-down rules and regulations was the order of the day, and the men had no right of redress against unscrupulous employers. As mentioned in Chapter 2, a driver and a firemen who tried to leave the NBR in 1850 without notice were actually jailed for three months.

The E&GR *Rule Book*, such as it was, clearly reflected the military style of strict footplate discipline pertaining at the time, in that it required that:

> *During the whole of the journey the Engineman shall keep a sharp lookout forward so as to instantly observe any obstruction which may be on the road, or signal made for his convenience. He shall on no account sit down, or allow the Firemen to sit down on either the engine or tender. The Engineman shall not allow any person whatever to light tobacco at the Engine fire or lamps.*

Firemen were required, when not firing, to stand on the footplate keeping a sharp lookout backwards, ready to act on any signal from the guard, and were even instructed on such things as maximum pressure of steam in the boiler. This same *Rule Book* also required all employees to turn out for Sunday duty, whilst also expressing a hope that such hours would allow these same employees to attend church!

In the early days of railways, footplate staff (drivers) were often recruited from men who had had some experience of boilers and steam engines, such as colliery boilermen and winding-engine men and, thereafter, these recruits were very much on their own, learning the art of railway operation through often bitter experience. Insofar as the E&GR was concerned, it is more than likely that William Paton obtained at least some of the drivers he required from the earlier local railway concerns such as the Glasgow & Garnkirk or the Monklands & Kirkintilloch, men who had some degree of training and experience in steam traction. Firemen were mere labourers, but the fact that they worked with, and thus learned from, the drivers made it a logical move to promote firemen to driving when vacancies arose.

From these early days, the footplate manning structure became based on boys starting as engine cleaners, being 'passed' to act as firemen and being appointed as firemen as vacancies arose, thereafter going through a similar long (or not so long in some cases) learning curve to become drivers. Particularly for cleaners, the 'passing out' for firing duties in earlier times was a most casual affair and did not generally include any examination in Rules, the ability to read being deemed sufficient. This structure, although existing as a basic model for promotion, was not cast in tablets of stone and, certainly up until the First World War, within the NBR the locomotive superintendent or indeed foreman at each shed had a big say in the matter. A cleaner, in being passed out for firing duties, had, essentially, to look strong.

From contemporary reports and works such as McKillop's book *Enginemen Elite*, a clear picture emerges of what it was like to gain, and retain, employment in the footplate grades on the NBR, and at Haymarket in particular. A lot depended on the size and strength of the applicant. A big strong lad could, in fact, find himself on firing duties very quickly, if not almost immediately. Others who, like McKillop, were on the slight side, had many obstacles placed in their way and had to prove themselves in a very hard school. So, a foreman's opinion, or a driver's recommendation, could, and frequently did, shape futures, and promotion on the long ladder to driver was in no way automatic.

Up until the end of the First World War, this freedom in promotion was common, with cleaners appointed firemen and firemen to drivers in a somewhat haphazard manner and largely based on the personal preferences and opinions of other drivers and, of course, the aforesaid foremen. After 1919 and the establishment of the first national agreements, footplate promotion became much more structured. Thereafter, boys starting as engine cleaners were formally 'passed out' for firing duties by theoretical and practical examination and, in strict seniority, were then appointed as firemen as vacancies arose. Indeed, in BR days there was a 'Firing Instructor' – who was a locomotive inspector with specific duties regarding the training and passing out of cleaners as competent to act as firemen – attached to each District Motive Power office. Firemen were in turn 'passed out' by examination in both their theoretical and practical competence for driving duties and then, by seniority, were promoted to drivers when vacancies arose.

In the early days there was very little moving away from a home shed for promotion (other than moves caused by redundancy) but, with the coming of the grouping and the formation of the L&NER, vacancies in the footplate grades were to become advertised throughout the Scottish Area and cleaners and firemen could opt to move to other sheds for promotion. Later, post-nationalisation, a regional vacancy list, published at regular intervals and covering all vacancies at all former railway company sheds, was open to applications from all footplate staff within the Scottish Region; as before, however, selection was on a strict seniority basis. Many Haymarket cleaners and firemen decided to just stay put, waiting for vacancies to arise at their home depot – but promotion could take many years, particularly at Haymarket because of the mileage work, and up to the closing days of steam the shed was never to be short of footplate staff. As an example, when the author first went to Haymarket in the early part of 1957, the most senior passed fireman at the shed had a seniority date of 1935 and, twenty-two years later, still was not an appointed driver. Indeed, the Shed Master at Haymarket, with a complement of 100 plus cleaners, was able to allow passed cleaners to voluntarily go 'on loan' to motive power depots in the London area and other large conurbations south of the border where recruitment was virtually at a standstill in the late 1950s.

The medical requirements for footplate staff were also tightened up over the years, with high standards in fitness and eyesight being paramount, and with medical checks on a regular basis (see Chapter 29). There was one relaxation which came later, that which concerned the wearing of glasses. On steam traction, if a driver or other member of the footplate grade required glasses for anything other than reading, this automatically led to removal from main line duties for obvious reasons. With modern traction, and with the driving task now being undertaken in enclosed cabs, the risk to eyes through glasses being broken is much reduced, and so, provided the minimum standards can be attained, the wearing of spectacles no longer impacts on the driving task.

By the early 1960s, when steam was quickly disappearing everywhere, this abundance of footplate staff at Haymarket was presenting its own problems as the need for firemen decreased significantly. Younger firemen and passed cleaners were then being offered financial inducements to leave railway service in order to streamline the manning levels consistent with train working demands. Diesels did not actually need firemen as such, but double-manning on diesel locomotives was to remain a requirement for a long time to come, not only because of trade union pressures, but also because, in the days of the iniquitous steam-heating boilers that were fitted to the earlier classes of diesel locomotives for train heating purposes, the boilers did require attention en route. Single manning had been achieved very quickly with the advent of the DMUs, but right up into the 1980s young men were still being recruited as driver's assistants and secondmen, as firemen were now known, and still accompanied drivers on main line working. During this period, the promotional ladder was driver's assistant, secondman, senior secondman (passed fireman) and driver. Training in diesel traction became much more structured since there was a need for each driver, secondman and traction assistant to have an in-depth knowledge of every type of locomotive/multiple unit they were likely to handle, and the faulting and failure procedures associated with each, with, it has to be said, the latter knowledge being an absolute must, given the failure rate of the diesel fleet. The Scottish Region of BR maintained a driver's training school in Edinburgh, at Haymarket Depot, right up until privatisation.

Gradually, more and more single-manning was being introduced under the fairly strict parameters as set down by Her Majesty's Railway Inspectorate (HMRI), the rail industry 'watch dog', until single-manning eventually, and sensibly, became the norm. The one exception, which remained until 1994 and the new privatised railway, were those services booked to run at speeds exceeding 110 mph; these were, in the main, the HSTs, where two drivers in the line of promotion were required on every train booked to run at such speeds, up to 125 mph. Come the brave new world of privatisation, the new train operating companies – no longer shackled by national agreements, and with the ability to set new contracts of employment, including wages – soon got rid of this last archaic requirement and, through financial 'carrots', even

reintroduced lodging turns, albeit in much more salubrious accommodation – namely the Newcastle crews working through from Newcastle to Aberdeen and Inverness under the GNER term of office on the ECML – a practice perpetuated by the new operators of the franchise, East Coast Holdings. In fact, on one diagram a Newcastle driver worked north to Aberdeen in late afternoon and then travelled by taxi to Inverness to work the following morning's 'Highland Chieftain' HST service south to King's Cross as far as Newcastle; this was due to the incoming Newcastle man on the evening north-bound service to Inverness being unable to have the required twelve-hours rest period. Changed days!

PAY AND CONDITIONS OF SERVICE

Footplate life was Spartan and very hard in the early days. Shifts were long, at least twelve hours in duration, days off were few and the foreman's word was law. There is a record of an inspector reminding a passenger guard, who had protested about being asked to work another turn after completing eighteen hours on duty, that there were twenty-fours in every day and every hour belonged to the company. However, in comparison with other jobs, the pay was not bad and the job did carry some status in society. The E&GR paid their drivers quite an unusually high daily rate of 7/6d. (37½p) – which in 1862 led to a wages dispute between drivers and the company, with the drivers lobbying for a reduction in wages of 6d. per day, since the higher rate made them liable for income tax. In comparison tables with the earnings in other comparable industries that were produced in the early 1920s, engine drivers sat at the top of the earnings list.

Other 'perks' included, for some, company housing provided at reasonable rents, and all enjoyed reduced travel. Each NBR employee was entitled to one free pass per year (later to be increased to three), although in reality men had little or no spare time in which to take up this privilege, holidays with pay being unheard of. Each company could, and did, dictate to staff exactly where they had to reside, and this somewhat draconian authority was carried over into the 1950 *Rule Book* and was applied well into the late 1950s. The author of this volume, as a passed cleaner at Haymarket in 1957, was obliged at his shed master's direction to take 'digs' in Edinburgh, even although his home was a mere fifteen miles from the depot. Even in the early days of the nationalised railway, staff on shift work had little say in this matter.

Around 1912 Haymarket had at least one 'Drummond' 0-6-0, and most likely two out-stationed at Ratho for the Ratho pilots and the Broxburn Goods workings. Haymarket crews were merely instructed 'to book on at Ratho' for these turns (thus avoiding travelling time), but no provision was made to allow them to travel out and back by train or, indeed, by any other means of transportation – in fact using the passenger train service was strictly forbidden unless the men actually purchased tickets. The company simply did not care how the men got there and made no provision for travel, but get there on time they must. Trawling through the NBR Board of Directors' minutes reveals that the question of staff travelling whilst on duty, and how this should be regulated, was discussed at length. Lodging was another sore point – where men were required by virtue of their diagrammed work to lodge away, by and large they had to arrange their own accommodation. McKillop records an amusing account of just how he and his driver travelled out to Ratho when on the pilot turns, and at a later point describes how when on a lodging turn to Fife he slept overnight in the empty coaches of his train at Anstruther. Hard days indeed; but, as a relief station master in the mid-1960s this author found himself in much the same position, sleeping on first-aid stretchers or the like at stations where an early shift or late visitations to remote signal boxes precluded the use of public transport and before he acquired his own 'wheels'. Some things took a long time to change!

By the mid-1850s drivers and firemen nominally worked a twelve-hour day over a 144-hour fortnight, but within these 144 hours, shifts of fifteen or sixteen hours were the norm, there being no definition of what a 'normal' day's labour entailed.

The NBR as a railway company had been, and was even then, parsimonious in the extreme when it came to proper staffing levels and the provision of adequate resources and infrastructure – in consequence trains suffered long delays and men worked exceedingly long hours. By 1871, working days of fifteen hours and more were common, and around that time Wheatley, recognising the risks posed by excessive working hours, appealed to the NBR Board to limit the working day for his drivers and firemen to twelve hours duration. This was approved but was in fact impossible to adhere to because of the inadequate railway infrastructure then existing. In 1872 drivers submitted a memorial to the NBR Board requesting payment for overtime incurred and for Sunday duty worked, but, more importantly, requesting that a normal working day be defined. The NBR Board evaded this latter issue, although (minimal) payment for overtime/Sunday working was conceded. The demands of traffic overrode all other considerations!

At the time the NBR employed a 'trip' or 'contract' arrangement for goods and mineral trains, whereby each train was allocated a set journey time, say eleven hours, and this is what the driver's and fireman's daily wage would be calculated upon, even though in practice the actual journey may have taken sixteen to eighteen hours, or even more, to accomplish; even more incredibly, men coming back on shed after such long hours could be forced to go back out with another train.

Long hours and inadequate rest took their toll. On the Scottish railways, in the single year of 1890, eighty-four railway employees were killed whilst on duty and a further 229 received serious injuries. The shambles following the opening of the Forth Bridge had exacerbated the problem of long hours, particularly amongst the goods and mineral train crews. Haymarket had a lesser exposure, being in the main a passenger depot, but nevertheless the drivers there also had some very long shifts for similar reasons. It is on record that during this period a freight train from Dundee to Portobello took eleven hours to travel from Inverkeithing to Portobello, a journey normally of only one hour's duration. This was becoming par for the course. One NBR driver is recorded as incurring 100 hours and 30 minutes on duty in a mere six days, and over 49 days averaged 16½ hours per day; whilst the working hours of another freight driver were revealed in a wholly independent investigation over five consecutive days to be a quite incredible 21½, 21½, 19, 19 and 24 hours.

Split shifts were also to be a continuing feature of the NBR locomotive-man's lot. This was an arrangement which was

Class D34 No. 62467 *Glenfinnan* **is slipping out to the shed exit signal on the way home to Thornton. On the right are the General Offices, where the glass verandah provided for staff comfort can be clearly seen.** *Courtesy David Dunn*

Ex-NBR 'Scott' Class D30 No. 62441 *Black Duncan* **of Dunfermline shed is being turned to face home after bringing in a Fife local service to Edinburgh Waverley. Running back to shed light engine has been done with the Class B train headlamp code unaltered, a sin in the eyes of the powers-that-be. A Class J83 is alongside the kit store platform, waiting to follow onto the turntable. The General Office can also be clearly seen. The weather is obviously fine and warm, and has tempted six stalwarts (probably spare crews) out of the bothy (behind them) and into the sunshine where they can take their ease and sit and watch others at work. The small wooden hut to the right of the bothy is the Chargehand Labourer's Office, whilst above the tender of the 'Scott' is the bulk of Jeffrey's Brewery in Russell Road, now long gone and replaced by up-market flats.** *Courtesy W.S. Sellar*

perpetuated right up to the grouping. Men worked part of a shift, were then booked off duty, often through the middle of the day, and resumed work mid-to-late afternoon to complete the diagram – but being paid only for the hours worked. Haymarket suffered less than other depots in this respect, but the crews who worked the Rosyth Dockyards, for instance, did so on a split-shift arrangement. Obviously this state of affairs could not continue.

Even in those difficult days, the railway companies, the NBR included, were proud to regard their employees as free and independent men – unlike, for instance, the miners – yet these same 'independent' men were to be denied the right to form a trade union to speak out on their behalf. This was to be reflected in no small way in the problems during the years ahead.

The shambolic situation which arose after the Forth Bridge opened – with the resultant severe dislocation of traffic, particularly the goods and mineral traffic – was to be the straw which broke the camel's back insofar as the already grossly over-worked NBR drivers and firemen (and guards and signalmen) were concerned. The general UK-wide unrest and agitation for shorter working hours amongst railway workers spilled over into a six-week general strike, commencing on Sunday, 21st December 1890. The striking men were portrayed as the villains of the piece from the outset, with the NBR Board (and CR and GSWR Boards) insisting the strike was merely about an increase in wages. Many of the leading newspapers, under, it is presumed, pressure from these boards and/or central Government, also followed this line in their very-much biased reporting of the situation, and some went so far as to suggest a conspiracy theory – although there was much sympathy for the cause in other quarters.

The strikers won very little as a result of the strike which lasted a full six weeks, and some of the striking men were never to be re-employed. The Caledonian Railway had been extremely harsh in their dealings with the striking men, even resorting to eviction from railway-owned housing in the Motherwell area. Such were the political implications of the strike, however, that a parliamentary committee was established (the Select Committee on Railway Servants Hours of Duty) with the remit '*to inquire whether, and, if so, in what way, the hours worked by railway servants should be restricted by law.*' The committee started deliberations on the 10th March 1891 and, with the dreadful state of affairs existing, was soon thrust into the public limelight. The NBR was soon to be revealed, and reviled, as the worst offender amongst all railway companies.

With the committee proceedings underway, it became patently obvious to the NBR Board that changes were inevitable, and in February 1891 they submitted an order to Matthew Holmes at Cowlairs for an additional thirty new locomotives. The committee reported to Parliament in 1892 to the effect that '*overwork on the railways of the United Kingdom is widespread and, in general, systematic, and not accidental or exceptional*', a damning report by any standards, but the outcome at that time was to be equivocal.

Working hours for footplate staff, although not reduced, were thereafter to be calculated on a 72-hour week (still a 12-hour day) but with overtime to be paid for any excess hours worked. Train running turns were reduced to a 10-hour day, but with a further 1½ hours added for preparation and disposal duties. The iniquitous trip/contract arrangement was abandoned, and by 1910 the 10-hour day had been introduced across the board – although, interestingly, whilst ten hours had become the norm, at the same time, a day's work on the Waverley pilot was set at eight hours because '*the work was exacting.*'

By 1890 the daily rates of pay for footplatemen were 5/6d. (27½ pence) to 7/6d. (37½ pence) for passenger drivers, 5/6d. to 6/6d. (32½ pence) for goods drivers, and 4/6d. (22½ pence) to 5/6d. for pilot drivers. Passenger firemen were paid between 3/2d. (16 pence) and 4/- (20 pence) per day, goods firemen between 3/6d. (17½ pence) and 4/- per day, and pilot firemen 3/2d. per day. These rates of pay did not materially alter up to the First World War.

In 1912 a new link was created at Haymarket known as the 5/6 link. Quite simply, for a daily wage of 5/6d. drivers accepted that they would drive anything, anywhere, and undertake any other duties, as required. Much of the work in the 5/6 link consisted of covering for regular main line drivers, relieving, disposal, and working of special trains as necessary. In short, it was the precursor to what was to become the Senior Spare and Junior Spare links. It is interesting to consider that in those days there was no basic rate of pay for a driver or fireman, but men were paid on the basis of work being undertaken. We have looked at the 5/6 link, but drivers on the Edinburgh/Glasgow main line were being paid a daily rate of 6/6d., some 1/- (5 pence) more than their lesser colleagues. As may be expected, the Atlantics carried the greatest financial rewards of all, with drivers being paid 7/6d. and firemen 4/4d. (22 pence) per 10-hour day. This latter rate applied to only nineteen sets of men across the NBR system. This small differential payment of 6d. (2½ pence), at a time when the weekly wage for drivers had been established at around 7/- (35p) per day, and firemen at 4/- per day, caused much animosity amongst the lower orders.

There was no formalised link working at Haymarket in pre-grouping days, with allocated diagrams around which the drivers and firemen rotated. In those days, a driver, with his own locomotive – and all main-line drivers did have their own engines – could opt to work the same turn of duty for long periods of time, and did so for years in some cases. Some drivers took an almost paternal pride in their engine to the point where the engine's welfare was put before schedule – in consequence they were stuck in the same rut for many years, with all promotion bypassing them completely. Some small links were formed, such as the Aberdeen Atlantic link, but with no progression round the link – that is, the same five drivers, each with his own engine, worked the same train in the link, week in, week out. The overall situation that existed was much less structured, and remained so until post-grouping days.

Haymarket, like most locomotive depots, was to suffer severe staff shortages during the First World War. Many young firemen, (McKillop included) had 'joined up' and gone into the British Army before the railways were eventually declared a reserved occupation. Indeed, whilst the government of the day had agreed that railwaymen would not be recruited, army recruiting personnel were choosing to ignore this directive, which led W.F. Jackson, the then (firebrand) General Manager of the NBR, to threaten one particular army Commander-in-Chief that, if he did not get back the NBR men who had enlisted without permission, he would reduce the train service, thereby denying the government the service they would require in any emergency which might arise. Jackson got most of his men back and, considering his situation, McKillop was perhaps unique in that he was not recalled back to footplate duties – and even more fortunate to escape his army service without injury. Of the 4,836 members of NBR staff who enlisted in the armed forces, 775 did not return. At Haymarket, as elsewhere, by 1916 the manning situation was really desperate, with drivers being required to return to firing duties and firing to other drivers as senior as themselves.

It was not only a problem with staffing. Like most railway companies, the NBR was quite devitalised by the end of the war and was in dire straits for locomotives, some 20 per cent of the fleet being out of use as 'non-effective'. The situation was extremely difficult for everyone and led to a bitterness which was to last well into the post-First World War days, and the grouping.

Throughout the years of the First World War, all the railway companies were controlled by a single body, the Railway Executive Committee, on behalf of the government, and it was with this committee that the two big rail unions, NUR and ASLE&F, now much stronger and far better organised, negotiated at national level on behalf of all railway staff. Following the general election in December 1918, the government, under Lloyd George, summoned a national industrial conference which duly recommended that a maximum working week of 48 hours and minimum pay rates be established across the board. Thus, through 1919, Whitley councils and trade boards were being formed in most industries. The railway industry was one such industry, and trade unions became a recognised force when final negotiations – pushed through by Jack Bromley, the then General Secretary of ASLE&F – set the date for the establishment of a national 8-hour day (48-hour week) for railwaymen, and this became a national standard on the 1st February 1919. The first national agreements were the outcome of some protracted negotiations between February and August 1919. These first agreements set in tablets of stone the 48-hour week, overtime, night and Sunday payments, a 12-hour minimum rest period (with conditions) and one week's annual leave with pay for all staff with twelve years' service or more.

These agreements had a far-reaching effect on locomotive depots right across the country. Because of the shorter working day, and with an annual leave commitment now to cover, increased staffing levels, and in particular more drivers, were required. Young firemen were immediately elevated to drivers' positions and cleaners to firemen after just a few years service. McKillop at Haymarket was one who became a registered driver whilst still short of his thirtieth birthday, in 1919, and was never again rostered to work as a fireman.

Minimum wages also increased for drivers and firemen, with standard rates of pay being set across the rail industry. There were the war increases which raised the rate of pay for a driver to 15/- (75 pence) per day, 7/- to 9/6d. (35 pence to 47½ pence) for firemen and 4/- (20 pence) per day for cleaners.

Further improvements in conditions of service were won in subsequent years, with the eventual setting of the 44-hour working week for all locomotive men. Since all weekday rostered work was spread over six days, with only Sunday work counting as an extra shift, it can be seen that the 6-day week (8-hour day) consisted of 48 working hours. However, the 44-hour week also saw the introduction of 'rest days', whereby each member of the footplate staff had one paid rest day every fortnight. This resulted in alternating working weeks of 48 hours and 40 hours – and to comply with the 44-hour week, four hours remained unpaid in the week consisting of 48 hours of work, but were then added to the 40-hour 'rest day' week, thus giving an 88-hour fortnight. However, despite the 8-hour day being the official norm, within the various engine diagrams pertaining, daily hours in excess of the laid-down eight hours were often required, this being rostered overtime, as can be seen from the sample 1955/56 Winter Engine Working Sheets for the Haymarket Class 8 engines (page 61).

Nevertheless, despite the advent of national agreements, the lot of footplate staff was not necessarily to improve. The L&NER adopted quite a cavalier attitude towards their staff during the difficult time of the depression of the 1930s. The position of engine cleaners and young firemen became deplorable as redundancies struck. Junior members of staff, and here we are talking of men with five to ten years footplate service, were the first to become redundant; to secure ongoing service and a job, many of these young men were forced to relocate, not just once, but sometimes on several occasions. This led to many of these young men leading an almost nomadic existence, transferring from depot to depot to maintain employment. This, regrettably, was no trek of unencumbered young men, since many were married and had to leave wives and families, and they themselves then had to seek out and pay for lodgings wherever this nomadic life took them. The company contributed little to these men during this period. The late Charlie Meacher, in his book *LNER Footplate Memories*, gave a stirring account of one young man (himself) caught up in these unhappy times at Haymarket, having to transfer to work as a cleaner at Carlisle Canal shed, and on the coaling bench at Carlisle London Road.

In happier days, post-depression, the interests of the various grades of staff at smaller establishments were represented by a station committee, formed by trade union representatives and managers, where such items such as rostering were discussed. At the larger stations and depots, with staff numbers of fifty and above, staff were represented by a local departmental committee (LDC), the staff side of which was elected by a voting system and was again formed by trade union (staff) and management representatives. At Haymarket there was an elected LDC who represented the interests of both the footplate staff and shed conciliation staff (labourers, fire-droppers, timekeepers etc.), and amongst other things this committee considered diagram and work allocation, annual and lieu leave, rostering and the like, but specific to the depot.

Under the national agreements the management side was obliged to advise and discuss with the staff side any matters which would impact on the working of the depot, but depending on the particular issue the discussions either took the form of 'negotiation' or 'consultation'. There were clear, laid-down instructions about what constituted a topic for the negotiation or consultation processes.

So what was the difference between the two procedures? Under negotiation, the matter(s) to be considered – normally a subject or subjects placed on the agenda by management – had to be properly presented and briefed, then discussed 'round the table'; following which, even if there was no agreement from the staff side, the management had the right, after the negotiation process had been complied with, to then implement the proposals anyway. There simply was no 'failure to agree' provision under the negotiation procedure. Items covered by negotiation were such things as resignalling, track rationalisation schemes, electrification and changes in working practices (such as train radio).

Items referred for consultation, however, had to be agreed by both sides, disagreement by one or other side being possible. Failure to agree a consultation matter at local (LDC) level led to the issue being raised to the next level in the consultation process, which was the regional sectional councils, again formed by trade union and management representatives, but dealing with regional issues and any matters referred upwards by LDCs. McKillop was for many years a staff-side representative on the Haymarket LDC. Consultation included link structures, rediagramming issues, claims for reclassification in grade, and so on.

Rest day rostering was managed in different ways at different depots, and on the LM&S the rest day was generally incorporated in the link diagrams with each link carrying its own rest-day relief arrangements. Thus, in a twelve-week link there would be eleven train-working turns with five of these turns having a rest day on an 'every second week' basis. The men on the twelfth weekly turn provided the rest day relief for these five rest days and then had a rest day themselves on the sixth day.

At Haymarket the rest days were allocated to each individual member of staff, each of whom was allocated a 'rest day group'. Thus, on a progressive basis, the rotation mean that, for instance, Group A had a rest day on the Monday one week, Tuesday in the next rest day week and so on, in order that each man was ensured a 'long weekend' every fourteen weeks. Each of the groups rotated in this way and there were twelve rest-day groups, thus ensuring that roughly the same number of men were on rest day each day over a working fortnight so as to ease coverage requirements.

The allocation of work involving the Newcastle link reflected the situation existing at Haymarket since the NER/NBR days, both prior to and immediately following the grouping, with the East Coast work, involving 256 miles running, being wholly concentrated in this small five-man senior link. When payment for mileage was negotiated and established under the national agreements of 1919, the trade unions won conditions which set the normal day's work for train running as 140 miles, after which, for every additional 15 miles run, one hour's payment was made over and above the agreed eight-hour day. It was clearly evident with the disproportionate number of Newcastle, and thus high-mileage, turns in No. 1 link, that there needed to be a restructuring of all allocated work in order to ensure an equalisation of earnings (sharing) for all the senior drivers and firemen at Haymarket.

Additional mileage work arising at a later date then required a further recasting of diagrams around the links at Haymarket, and this reallocation of work and diagrams spread out the Newcastle mileage turns more equitably. It also ensured that drivers in the top four passenger links worked over a variety of different roads regularly, thereby maintaining their route knowledge.

By the early 1950s the Haymarket Top link were enjoying four Newcastle turns spread over the twelve diagrammed turns of duty. Initially the summer non-stop working (two diagrams) was addressed by inserting two extra turns into No. 1 link for the summer timetable only, thus making it a fourteen-man link (summer only); but by the mid-1950s the Top link was to be left as a fourteen-man, fourteen-diagram link throughout the year, with all of the seven A4s now allocated on a regular-manning basis to two drivers per engine in that link. The additional summer non-stop diagrams thereafter required a regular biannual rearrangement of the work allocation in the other three senior passenger links at Haymarket (all consisting of twelve turns of duty), and these link rearrangements were prepared each May (ready for the summer

A visiting V2, No. 60865 from Heaton shed, stands in a positively Arctic top-end in February 1963, during the extremely severe winter of 1962/63. The shed area was by this time very quiet, with steam numbers now significantly depleted. The V2 is waiting to have the fire dropped and, whilst this was generally an unpleasant and warm task, on this day it would be a welcome one for the staff involved. *Courtesy Ian Musgrave*

timetable at the beginning of June) and August (for the winter timetable effective from September).

No. 2 link had three Newcastle turns, No. 3 link also had three Newcastle turns, No. 4 link had the three Carlisle (202 miles) turns and No. 5 link – which was the goods link – had a single Carlisle freight working every twelve weeks. This resulted in the sharing, in a fair and equitable way, of the considerable mileage earnings potential amongst the senior train crews at Haymarket. It was these very same mileage turns (plus the additional mileage turns inherent in the many special and additional summer trains) which thereafter caused promotion through the links at Haymarket to be particularly slow.

In terms of mileage, 256 miles (Edinburgh–Newcastle shed-to-shed return) was the longest single working turn for Haymarket men; but at other depots across BR there were daily mileage turns which far exceeded this (for instance, Crewe North men worked through to Perth, a total of just over 300 miles per night). However, mileage work at Haymarket was neither conducted on a 'contract' basis, nor did it involve 'double-home' working; so it was normal, for example on night turns on the Edinburgh/Newcastle route, for drivers and firemen to work either six or seven consecutive days/nights of 256 miles, covering up to an aggregated 1,792 miles in their normal working week. When this aggregated mileage is then compared with the other high-mileage turns (aggregated) system-wide, it can be seen that Haymarket men were right up there amongst the top group of enginemen in the UK working exceptionally long-distance and high-mileage turns on a regular basis. All men in the

link worked these turns, and promotion through these links was the normal procedure based on seniority, unlike the former LM&S, where much of the long-distance work was based on a 'volunteer' system.

As a matter of interest, drivers and firemen of Newcastle (Gateshead) shed worked the ECML night trains through to King's Cross and lodged on a double-home volunteer basis. The link was, sad to say, forever known locally on Tyneside as 'the blackleg link'. Similarly, King's Cross Top Shed created a volunteer link which worked to Newcastle on a double-home basis. Haymarket men came close to having one regular lodging turn created (apart from the summer non-stop working) when trials were carried out working a Haymarket engine and crew through to Leeds, via Carlisle and Ais Gill, on the 10.05 Edinburgh to London St. Pancras 'Waverley' diagram, but nothing more came of it.

These conditions of service remained by and large the same through the diesel years and on into the latter days of BR, but with some altered conditions appropriate to the new forms of traction being handled and the new operating procedures evolving. The introduction of 'in cab' radios and single-manning were the big events for the negotiating tables, plus issues such as level crossing automation and resignalling projects which would impact on footplate staff. All national agreements were to be largely swept away when the brave new privatised railway and train operating companies came into being in 1994. New contracts were almost imposed, and national conditions and national rates of pay ceased to exist. Market forces now dictated salaries. Changed days indeed!

Not the best of photographs, but one which records an important milestone. NBR 4-4-0 Class 'M' No. 293, one of the class built by Holmes between 1890 and 1895 with 6-foot 6-inch driving wheels and 18-inch cylinders. This was a famous Haymarket steed – with Driver Joe McGregor and Fireman John Berry it ran the Edinburgh to Dundee section during the 1895 Railway Races to the North on the last three nights of racing. On the last night, the 60.1 miles to Dundee were reeled off in one minute under the even hour. Here Driver McGregor and Fireman Berry pose with their engine soon after the event, alongside the very new brickwork of Dundee Tay Bridge shed. *Bill Lynn collection*

7 ALLOCATED TRAIN WORKING OVER THE YEARS

Over the many years that both the original and new (current) shed at Haymarket have been in existence there have been many changes. Ownership of the original shed passed from the E&GR Company on the 1st August 1865 when that company amalgamated with the NBR Company, and approximately one hundred E&GR locomotives were also transferred. This amalgamation meant that the NBR also inherited the large locomotive works at Cowlairs; thereafter the works at St. Margaret's, which had been the hub of NBR motive power building activities up to that time, was to be phased out. From this amalgamation in Edinburgh, Haymarket shed was initially to continue in a fairly minor role in the greater scheme of things; it continued to service the bulk of the Edinburgh/ Glasgow trains over both the E&GR main line and other routes such as the secondary Bathgate/Airdrie/Glasgow route, and, following the opening of the Forth Bridge in 1890, Haymarket was also allocated a small share of Edinburgh/Aberdeen/Perth main line workings (until 1908) – whilst St. Margaret's continued to operate the Berwick (later Tweedmouth) services, Perth services and, of course, the Waverley route to Carlisle.

Pre-Grouping Years

With the opening of the Forth Railway Bridge, and the final link with the railways in Fife and to the north established, the NBR was swamped with traffic emanating from the north. As a result, the section of line from Saughton Junction to Haymarket over the one set of double E&GR lines was to become a severe bottleneck – as was discussed in Chapter 1. The severe delays being incurred on a regular basis meant that NBR engines were 'off shed', and thus unavailable for other work, for very long periods, and so additional engines were introduced into the system, putting a severe strain on the old E&GR shed at Haymarket. The result was the new, expanded and modern replacement which was opened in 1894.

Haymarket (new) shed was actively involved in the 'Railway Races' to Aberdeen between the West Coast companies and the East Coast companies in 1895, and provided both locomotives and crews to work the penultimate stage of the race from Edinburgh through to Dundee on the 130-mile 'race' northwards to Aberdeen. The locomotives used were the Holmes Class 'M' (later to be L&NER D31) 4-4-0s with 6-foot 6-inch driving wheels and a boiler pressure of 150 p.s.i. With both sides sparring during the period of the 1895 summer timetable, things reached a climax in August of that year. On the morning of the 15th August, the NER handed the northbound express over to the NBR at Waverley 10 minutes early. Locomotive No. 293 of Haymarket took over, but the station authorities, perversely, held the train to time. When No. 293 finally got away, it ran to Dundee (59.2 miles) in a mere 64 minutes and 15 seconds.

During the 'Races', running which can only be described as 'reckless' took place, culminating on the third night of the racing, the 21st August, when Driver Joe McGregor, Fireman John Berry

and No. 293 averaged 60.25 mph between Waverley and Dundee, arriving there in one minute under the even hour. Driver McGregor and his mate had been involved in all three of the 'racing nights' north from Edinburgh as far as Dundee over the duration. On that last night, Driver Charlie Spalding and Fireman Peter Anton, with No. 262, all from Dundee Tay Bridge shed, then went on to average 56.25 mph for the last leg over the 70 miles to Aberdeen. The overall time from London King's Cross to Aberdeen over the ECML had been run in a record time of only 520 minutes for the 523.5 miles. The joint East Coast companies called off the 'racing' on the 22nd August, reverting to the proper timetable, but the joint West Coast companies had one more go at regaining the record, and jointly ran the 539.8 miles between London and Aberdeen in 512 minutes at an average speed of 63.3 mph, a record which stands today.

In 1869 the NER had advised the NBR that the company proposed to exercise the running rights they had previously won between Berwick and Edinburgh, and intimated that they intended to work ECML passenger trains right through from Newcastle to Edinburgh; they thus sought accommodation and facilities for up to ten locomotives to be out-based in Edinburgh. Part of Leith Walk goods depot, as initially proposed by the NBR as suitable accommodation, was rejected out of hand and the NER insisted that space be found at the St. Margaret's depot.

Through running of NER-worked trains commenced on the 1st June that year. The presence of the NER 'over the border' was to be a point of great dissension within the NBR over the coming years, and there were some acrimonious exchanges when the NBR discovered that the NER drivers were requesting pilot assistance by NBR locomotives north of Berwick, causing no less a person than Wilson Worsdell, CME of the NER, to admit that his engines were not up to the task of timing the ECML expresses.

Matters came to a head in 1894, when the NBR decided to take over the running of East Coast expresses between Berwick-upon-Tweed and Edinburgh, over their own metals and using their own engines and men, and so gave its old ally notice to quit. In giving the NER notice to cease running north of the border, the NBR somewhat shot itself in the foot, since the prestige express trains were tightly timed over the whole 125 miles of the route between Newcastle and Edinburgh and, as we have seen, even the NER had been stretched to the limit and beyond. Locomotives now had to be changed at Berwick-upon-Tweed *within* that running time and without disturbing the sensitive timings. This required some very hard running by the NBR north of Berwick, using the Holmes 633 class, and occasionally 592 class, locomotives, helped by some of the older Drummonds. Two locomotives headed every train and some extremely high speeds were obtained in the downhill running from Grantshouse to, and over, the Lothian plain. The NBR takeover was conditional upon the subsequent performance, to be monitored by the Railway Commission, since there had been inferences from NER sources to the effect that the punctual and efficient working was beyond the capabilities of the former company.

The takeover commenced on the 14th January 1897, but, barely one year into the altered workings, early in the morning of the 3rd January 1898, the gods nodded. Owing to an error of judgment on the part of the signalman at Dunbar, a shunting move across the main lines was permitted after the 23.30 passenger from King's Cross (the 06.12 from Berwick) had been accepted. The passenger train, consisting of a mix of ten coaches and vans hauled by Holmes No. 642 and Drummond No. 492, passed both the Dunbar Down Distant signal (the lamp of which was unlit) at caution and Down Home signal showing danger at high speed and ran headlong into the goods train. Damage was absolute, but fortunately for the NBR – albeit unfortunate for the victim – only one passenger was killed, although it has to be said that the NBR came very close to dispatching the Superintendent of the Glasgow & South Western Railway. Later in that same year the Railway Commission gave its long-awaited ruling on this dispute and came down on the side of the NER. In 1900, the NBR admitted defeat and the 'status quo', with the NER engines working through, was reinstated.

As discussed earlier, by 1904 St. Margaret's was becoming too cramped and so the NER had their passenger locomotives reallocated to the new Haymarket shed, where better and more modern facilities existed. Here they were allocated Nos 7 and 8 roads at the eastern end of the shed. It must not be thought that the NER had undisputed rights to the facilities at Haymarket. The reality was that the NER were required to rent the accommodation for their out-based locomotives from the NBR at a cost of £25 per locomotive per calendar year, and they chose to reserve space for up to ten engines on a daily basis. However, with the considerable increase in traffic levels, and with the advent of the NBR Atlantics, it was decided by higher NBR authority in 1908 to also transfer four NBR Atlantics, plus their regular crews, cleaners and booked Aberdeen passenger workings, from St. Margaret's to the more spacious layout at Haymarket. These Aberdeen turns were the 07.40, the 09.30 and the 10.42 express trains from Edinburgh – which the Haymarket men worked through to Aberdeen, returning with afternoon trains. Haymarket's star was now in the ascendancy and was to continue so, culminating in the final rearrangements of the Pacific diagrams during the mid-Second World War years.

The old inter-company bitterness flared up again in 1922, in the dying days of the old companies – the use of NER engines and crews on all East Coast expresses north of Berwick still being a bitter pill for the NBR men to swallow. With their NBR Atlantics, the NBR drivers felt that they could compete on equal terms with the NER and thus should be able to claim a share of this main line working. The result, after the running of two, albeit very belated, trials (referred to in more detail in Chapter 12), proved that the NBR Atlantics could, and thus should, share in the running of the express trains over the ECML to Newcastle. This set the scene for the creation of a new joint NBR/NER Top link at Haymarket – this Newcastle link consisted of three NER crews with NER Atlantics and two NBR crews with NBR Atlantics, all with their own engines, rotating round four Newcastle and a single Glasgow turn.

The NER Newcastle link apart, prior to the grouping and for some time thereafter, the role of Haymarket shed was to be the provider of locomotives and men to work main line services over the north and west of the NBR system out of Edinburgh. These being, in order of importance:

- The main line to Aberdeen (but with the advent of the eight-hour day came engine changing at Dundee)
- Edinburgh/Perth (shared with Perth and St. Margaret's)
- Edinburgh/Glasgow via Falkirk High (shared with Eastfield shed)
- Edinburgh/Glasgow (Hyndland) via Bathgate (shared with Bathgate shed)
- Dunfermline/Stirling/Alloa via the Forth Bridge (shared with Dunfermline and Stirling sheds)
- Semi-fasts to Dundee direct and via the East Neuk of Fife (shared with Thornton and Dundee Tay Bridge sheds)
- Local passenger services to Kirkliston/South Queensferry.

The principal Aberdeen workings had been entrusted to Haymarket and the NBR Atlantics after 1908. Even in the mid-1920s, when the then-new Gresley A1s had been allocated to dedicated crews in the Haymarket Top (Newcastle) link, an Aberdeen link (No. 2 link) consisting of three Atlantics and six crews was established to work six Edinburgh to Dundee and return diagrams. Eventually these workings were taken over by the 'Directors', the A3s, then in turn were to be worked by the P2s, and eventually the A4s and the Peppercorn A1s which were to be allocated to No. 1 link and No. 2 link. The never-popular (with Haymarket crews) 04.15 turn, which was to be later retired to have an earlier 03.57 departure from Edinburgh, was known to all and sundry at Haymarket as the 'Early Aberdeen', with the ungodly 02.00 book-on time This was the train which came to grief at Burntisland in 1914, in the hands of an Aberdeen crew.

Without any shadow of a doubt, the most important and spectacular express passenger train to run on NBR metals was the 07.35 Edinburgh to Aberdeen. This train had run in the same path, although with a slightly altered departure time on occasions, and in the hands of Haymarket men, since 1908; in the latter days of the NBR it even conveyed through coaches from both King's Cross and St. Pancras every weekday, plus a through coach from Penzance to Aberdeen on a Sunday. This heavy train, loaded to fourteen coaches and often more on a regular basis, saw the train engine, a Haymarket Atlantic, being piloted by a saturated 'Scott' (D29), or, later, a 'Pony' (D1), as the norm. The advent of the A3s (once cleared for the route), the P2s and the A4s saw the end of piloting. This train continued to run all through the L&NER and BR days.

The other night express from London, the famed '8.00pm' (20.00) was, of course, the train which was involved in the 'Railway Races' of 1895 and was a train which Haymarket latterly worked on a nightly (or more accurately, an early morning) basis between Edinburgh and Dundee. Whilst at that time not enjoying the fame of the 07.35 Aberdeen, it was nevertheless an important train in its own right and one which was to become 'The Aberdonian' in L&NER days, conveying sleeping-car accommodation only. Over the NBR years this was another train entrusted to the NBR Atlantics, and was for some time until the demise of the twelve-hour day worked as a return leg of the out-and-home journey by Aberdeen (Ferryhill) Atlantic crews.

The 'Fife Coast Express', as reintroduced in 1921, was a complicated working indeed – involving two daily express passenger trains (summer only), both named, connecting Edinburgh and Glasgow with the holiday villages in the East Neuk (east coast corner) of Fife. This was the post-First World War reintroduction of a train which had run from Glasgow Queen Street to Dundee via the Fife coast between 1911 and 1913. In 1921, one train, the 'Fife Coast Express', left Glasgow Queen Street at 16.10 and ran non-stop to Dalmeny via Winchburgh Junction. At Dalmeny, passengers for Thornton and Cameron Bridge transferred to a following train, the other 'Fife Coast Express', which left Edinburgh Waverley at 16.52. The Glasgow (first) train then ran forward to Dundee via the Fife coast, followed by the Edinburgh train, both trains having alternating stopping patterns. The Edinburgh train then terminated at Crail (not Anstruther as stated by McKillop) (see Chapter 11), and after an overnight stop involving lodging, left at 07.25 the following morning for a 09.11 arrival back at Waverley.

Otherwise, Haymarket continued in its lesser role after the grouping. Freight working was minimal and, all in all, including the three NER Atlantics, Haymarket had a relatively small allocation of locomotives, totalling no more than thirty-seven in the days immediately following the grouping. This allocation included, according to R.D. Stephen, five NBR Atlantics, six superheated Scotts, three non-superheated Scotts, seven D31s, one D27, two D28s, three D25s, three C15s, three J83s and one J35. The allocated engines were, as a rule, utilised on the following workings:

- Atlantics worked the Edinburgh/Aberdeen express passengers (and the Edinburgh/Newcastle expresses after 1922)
- Superheated 'Scotts' had the monopoly of express passenger workings on the E&GR main line
- Saturated 'Scotts' worked the stopping passenger trains on the Edinburgh/Perth/Dundee and Glasgow routes as did the residual Class D31, D27 and D28 locomotives
- The '7 footers', Nos 595, 596 and 597, were used as pilot engines on the heavy Aberdeen road
- The C15s worked local and suburban passenger services
- The Class 'C' tanks (J83 and J88) provided shunting power both on and off shed, two of the former covering No. 1 and No. 2 Waverley west station pilot duties.

However, we do know from Norman McKillop that, pre-grouping, Haymarket did also have out-based engines – with the engines for the Broxburn Goods and Ratho pilot workings being stabled at Bathgate Junction (Ratho), and the engine for the Edinburgh/Dalmeny passenger service, a 4-4-0 tank engine, No. 98, designed and built by Drummond at Cowlairs in 1881, stabled at Dalmeny. After the grouping, and certainly by the 1930s, Bathgate shed took over provision of power and manning of the Bathgate Junction pilots, two per day, leaving Haymarket with the Broxburn trips, the South Queensferry trips and the Suburban and Prestonpans trip workings which it retained until the final days of steam.

POST-GROUPING YEARS

With the fall of the 'invisible barrier' at Berwick for NBR men just prior to the grouping, not only did the regular NBR drivers who went into the Newcastle link then have to learn the road from Berwick through to Newcastle Central station and over the Tyne to Gateshead shed (and also out to Blaydon shed), but the Haymarket 'spare' drivers were also required to have this route knowledge. Consequently, a new link at Haymarket was established, the 'Senior Spare' link, for this very purpose, the 'Junior Spare' link (the former 5/6 link) still being relegated to covering ex-NBR territory services. This position did not last for long; whilst both Spare links survived at Haymarket until dieselisation in the shape of Nos 6 and 7 links, the drivers in both links became, by necessity, fully conversant with every route and every type of train worked by Haymarket shed. Initially the bulk of the running to Newcastle remained with the

ex-NER men, since they were completely familiar with the road and also the methods of working south of the border, but as these NER men retired, so they were replaced by Haymarket men, born and bred, and the Newcastle link became a true Scottish working.

The creation of this Senior Spare link at Haymarket in 1923 to provide coverage for the combined Newcastle link, with all drivers in the link required to learn and sign for the Newcastle 'road', was merely the beginning; the Senior Spare link thereafter went on to greater things following the arrival of the Gresley A1s, A3s, A4s and P2s. Several of the drivers learned and signed for the road right through to Doncaster, so that the Pacifics could be worked there for shopping (for example, for general repair), and the engines, ex-works, could be returned directly into traffic to Haymarket. The same spare men worked some of the P2s north as they entered traffic in the 1930s. This practice was discontinued at the onset of the Second World War, and never reinstated. McKillop infers that he alone was responsible for this latter working, a claim which must be viewed with some suspicion. Strangely, although all drivers in No. 1 link (the top link) had thereafter to learn and sign for the road right through to York – a requirement dictated by their sharing in the various non-stop and Streamliner workings – Haymarket spare drivers were not required to learn this route, which led to some convoluted rostering when regular No. 1 link men fell unavailable.

The 1920s and '30s were momentous years for Britain's railways; Haymarket progressively took more and more pride of place in the express-running exploits of the L&NER during this period of time. With the advent of the Gresley Pacifics, Haymarket quickly became recognised as a 'big engine' shed. The footplate staff and fitting staff had quickly taken to the Gresleys, and the latter soon became extremely capable and proficient in dealing with the vagaries of the conjugated valve gear.

Up to the early days of the Second World War, Gresley Pacifics had also been allocated to a few other sheds on the ex-NBR system (St. Margaret's, Eastfield and Dundee Tay Bridge), but this had resulted in very poor utilisation and abnormally high coal consumption figures (average coal consumption of the Scottish A1 Pacifics was recorded as 72 lbs per mile in 1927). These were exactly the same problems as encountered by the P2s in the years to come. Come the war, Haymarket was to be recognised, insofar as was possible in those troubled times, for the excellence in the maintenance and running of the Gresleys by the shed's fitting and footplate staff. The depot, with more than adequate space, enjoyed modern maintenance and servicing facilities; it was undoubtedly these factors, plus the excellence of the staff and the very real potential for increasing the daily mileages, which led the L&NER Scottish Area motive power officers to take the decision to concentrate the working of all Gresley Pacifics in the Scottish Area upon Haymarket. This initiative, by necessity, led to a complete recast of engine diagrams involving the Pacifics, and the consequential reallocation of the cream of all the passenger work, north, south, east and west out of Edinburgh, to Haymarket shed.

St. Margaret's lost a good number of their passenger turns at this time, in particular the Perth and Carlisle turns, but to compensate gained most of the local freight working in and around Edinburgh, plus the bulk of the main line fast freight workings. It was also decided that it would be common sense if the Carlisle Canal Pacifics, by then working over the Waverley route, were to work into Haymarket rather than St. Margaret's; conversely, from that time, Haymarket men commenced to work on a regular basis over the Waverley route with their own Haymarket Pacifics. Haymarket became a truly pro-Gresley depot right across the board – 'The Glamour Boys' had arrived! This nickname, based on service slang for RAF personnel, was not, however, to be accorded to Haymarket footplate staff until around 1946.

It is known that, immediately pre-grouping, both the NBR and NER drivers who comprised the Newcastle link were allocated their own engines on the 'one engine–one man' basis, and this continued even after the A1 Pacifics arrived. It is also known that the NBR crews in the senior links at both St. Margaret's and Haymarket were also allocated their own engines, in particular the Atlantics and the 'Scotts', on a similar 'one engine–one man' basis. This merely followed what was common practice across almost all the old railway companies, and is a clear indication of just how these companies (the L&NER included in the early days) were prepared to accept poor annual mileage figures and very restricted utilisation and availability from the locomotives – although, on the plus side, the engines were consequently maintained and cleaned to perfection.

Some interesting steps were taken at Haymarket in the mid-1920s with the NBR Atlantics and dedicated crews. Here they established a double-shifted method of working, whereby each engine worked round a link of fixed train workings, but with two dedicated crews on a daily early and late turn.

Thus a new No. 2 link was established at Haymarket, but at the time it was solely intended to improve efficiency of crew utilisation and engine mileage, and break down the 'one engine–one man–one job' practices which were still largely the norm. Three Class 'C11' Atlantics, Nos 9874, 9875 and 9877, each now with two dedicated crews, were placed in a link, working six Aberdeen trains on a double-shifted early and late basis, with each engine and crew rotating round the link as follows:

9874	04.15 Edinburgh–Dundee	07.59 Dundee–Edinburgh
	14.15 Edinburgh–Dundee	17.30 Dundee–Edinburgh
9875	07.35 Edinburgh–Dundee	11.39 Dundee–Edinburgh
	16.25 Edinburgh–Dundee	19.33 Dundee–Edinburgh
9877	09.30 Edinburgh–Dundee	14.38 Dundee–Edinburgh
	18.31 Edinburgh–Dundee	21.20 Dundee–Edinburgh.

This was to become the basis for a structured approach to regular manning and train working at Haymarket in the future, the spin-off benefits being the increased availability and mileage run by Haymarket engines. Link working was to be established thereafter, with the most important trains allocated to the top and second links, and other workings going to the lower links. Each link had twelve allocated turns around which the crews (and engines in Nos 1 and 2 links) rotated. The links were manned on a strict seniority basis with a variety of destinations allocated to each to ensure retention of route knowledge. The Gresley A1s which were still at that time allocated on a one engine–one man basis at Haymarket in the Newcastle (Top) link were also to be so diagrammed later. The Aberdeen turns listed above were to continue to run in the hands of Haymarket crews, albeit spread over the top three links, throughout BR days until the 1960s.

The LM&S was the first railway company to abandon dedicated locomotives/drivers and move to common-user right across the board in order to increase locomotive utilisation and thus achieve economic mileages. In the 1930s the LM&S management recast all locomotive diagrams in order to increase average daily locomotive mileage from around 85 miles to 120 miles or more. This meant that locomotives, now common-user, were often lost to their home depots for up to five days or more at a time, but the loss of regular maintenance was considered worthwhile when measured against the reduction of unproductive time. Thereafter, much illogicality was gradually swept away, such as the practice of 'one engine–one man', but this was often to the detriment of working at the depot. Come the Second World War, the personal element had been abandoned and, except where, like Haymarket, double shifting had been adopted, locomotive maintenance suffered in consequence.

Because of this new structured link working at Haymarket, through engine workings to Aberdeen were quick to cease after the advent of the eight-hour day, at least until the late 1950s. In terms of locomotive availability, such working was somewhat pointless and impossible to accommodate within an eight-hour shift. In any case, the trade unions cavilled at any suggestion of an engineman's daily diagram which exceeded eight hours – though such diagrams were not unusual and at Haymarket, up to the final years of steam, there were some diagrammed daily train workings involving just over ten hours on duty with rostered overtime. Instead of through working, an equivalent daily mileage or more, with much improved engine utilisation, could be obtained by one engine making two return trips to Dundee. The through running, and limited utilisation, had in fact proved to be a poisoned chalice for the P2s as we shall see.

In 1946, almost immediately after the end of hostilities, arrangements were put in hand at Haymarket to reinstate the structured, regular manning of the passenger locomotives of the 1920s. No. 1 link had, more or less, continued to man the A4s throughout the hostilities and regular manning was thus quickly regularised in that link. Regular manning was then extended to resurrect No. 2 link with two drivers being allocated to each engine on an 'early shift/late shift' basis as before. The A4s went back to the Top link and A3s were allocated to No. 2 link – each link, including

A specially-posed photograph, but a worthwhile addition nevertheless. The date is 1954/55 and four Top link drivers pose with their regular engines in front of Haymarket shed. From the left, Driver Tony McLeod and Driver Bill McLeod stand in front of A4 No. 60024 *Kingfisher*, Driver Jimmy Swan stands in front of A4 No. 60004 *William Whitelaw*, and Driver Jimmy Paterson stands with his engine, A4 No. 60009 *Union of South Africa*. Each locomotive carries the headboard of a train regularly worked by Haymarket Top link, although 'The Flying Scotsman' was a back working from Newcastle only. The two McLeod's, Swan and Paterson all retired around the same time and this may be marking that occasion. A splendid photograph, with three impeccably turned out Haymarket A4s. Note the burnished buffers, couplings, lamp brackets and cylinder covers. However the 'shark's jaw' door on No. 60009 does not appear to be fitting terribly well. *Courtesy Mr Peter Lund*

To: _____   From: Chief Operating Supt's Office,
                              GLASGOW.

                              February, 1956.

PASSENGER ENGINE WORKINGS.
WINTER 1955/56.
HAYMARKET PASSENGER ENGINES.

Turn No. 1.   Class 8 P. (A.1)

		Book on	Book off	H.	M.
	Engine prepared				
	Haymarket E.S.	9.38am. LE.			
9.44	Edinburgh	10.10	9.23	5/50	8.27
12.42	Newcastle	3.10			
5.30	Edinburgh	5.34 LE.			
5.40	Haymarket E.S.				
	Engine prepared				
	Haymarket E.S.	9.50pm. LE. SX.	9/35	6. 5	8.30
9.55	Haymarket G.L.	10.10 EC. SX.			
10.23	Edinburgh				
	Haymarket E.S.	9.55 LE. SO.	9/40	5.45	8. 5
10. 1	Edinburgh				
	do.				
(c) 1.10	Newcastle	10.40			
	do.				
5.43	Edinburgh	2.58 MX.			
5.55	Haymarket E.S.	5.50 LE. MX.			
	Newcastle				
5.21	Edinburgh	2.58 SUN.			
5.35	Haymarket E.S.	5.30 LE. SUN.			
	(d) 1.15am. SUN.				

Turn No. 2.   Class 8 P. (A.4)
(Amended 5.3.56)

11.26	Haymarket E.S.	11.20am. LE.			
	Edinburgh	12. 0	10.20	6/20	8. 0
2.11	Newcastle	3.37			
5.55	Edinburgh	6. 4 LE.			
6.10	Haymarket E.S.				
	Engine prepared				
	Haymarket E.S.	9.41pm. LE. SX.	9/26	7.35	10. 9
9.46	Edinburgh	10.15 SO.	9/26	7. 26	10. 0
1.12(b)	Carlisle	1.25am. LE.			
1.30	Canal E.S.	3.43 LE.			
3.48	Carlisle	4. 8 Pcls.			
7.18(c)	Edinburgh	7.20(d) LE.			
7.25(d)	Haymarket E.S.				

          (b) 1.16am. Sundays.
          (c) 6.56am. Sundays.
          (d) 10 minutes earlier Sundays.

LEFT: The first page of the winter 1955/56 Class 8 engine diagrams. The Turn No. 2 late shift shows the booked crew diagram of 10 hours and 9 minutes SX on a mileage (Carlisle) turn – an illustration of how the eight-hour day had to be exceeded on certain turns, much to the dislike of the trade union ASLE&F. The link workings were arranged from these sheets of engine diagrams, this occurring twice each year. *Author's collection*

BELOW LEFT: On 15th August 1952, the last year of the non-stop running as the 'Capitals Limited', Haymarket A4 No. 60004 *William Whitelaw* swings the Up working round the curves at Chaloners Whin Junction, south of York. By this point the crew will be the King's Cross men who will have taken over from the Haymarket crew at or near York. *E. Blakey/ Transport Treasury*

BELOW RIGHT: Haymarket A4 No. 60011 *Empire of India* hurries the Down 'Elizabethan' over the flatlands of Lincolnshire. The date is not recorded, neither is the exact location. The A4 is turned out in true Haymarket fashion and the two coaches behind the locomotive are the Aberdeen portion of the train which will go forward on the 16.15 Aberdeen departure from Waverley. *Transport Treasury*

The picture which says everything about Haymarket in the 1950s. Never short of cleaning staff, all Haymarket engines were cleaned on a regular basis, but special attention was (naturally) paid to both No. 1 and No. 2 link locomotives. Here, A1 No. 60162 *Saint Johnstoun*, a No. 2 link engine allocated to Driver W. (Willie) Bain at that time, sets the benchmark for cleanliness and was probably, under his ownership, the cleanest engine anywhere on BR. The date is the 29th August 1953, and No. 60162 pulls out of Edinburgh Waverley at the head of the 12.00 noon southbound Pullman service 'The Queen of Scots' for London King's Cross. The clock on the tower of the North British Hotel (above the engine) shows just a few minutes fast to assist would-be rail travellers. The tradition is maintained to this day! *John Robertson/Transport Treasury*

How the mighty have fallen. One-time star of the non-stop workings, and for a long time the chosen steed of one 'Toram Beg', A3 No. 60100 *Spearmint*, now fitted with a double chimney and German 'trough'-style smoke deflectors, reverses off the ash pits at the top end of the shed, en route to stabling – despite the fact that the smoke box door is unsecured. The date is early 1961. *Courtesy David Dunn*

the lower train-working links with common-user locomotives, had twelve turns of duty arranged on the early/late basis, although No. 1 link (the Top link) was to become a 14-turn link in the 1950s. The benefits of regular manning meant that more intensive mileage could be guaranteed, but with engines returning to their home shed on a daily basis. Thus best practice preventative maintenance could be perpetuated, with the locomotives being kept in first class mechanical order and clean appearance by both their regular crews and the shed staff. The benefits were also very quickly apparent in the high mileages being achieved by the allocated locomotives between main works general repairs. On the down side, regular manning of engines did still impact somewhat upon availability and utilisation. Common-user engines on the other hand were often lost for days or even weeks within the rail network, suffering the inherent detrimental effects of slip-shod and minimum levels of maintenance, and the general lack of interest afforded to 'foreign' locomotives as a consequence.

Followers of Norman McKillop may very well have gained the impression that the Pacifics were once again allocated on the basis of 'one engine–one driver', since he wrote at great length over the years about his partnership with 'his' A3 No. 60100 *Spearmint*. This was definitely not the case at Haymarket, since this arrangement would merely have perpetuated the abysmal mileage and availability figures of pre-war days. The best achievable daily mileages, in order of routes worked over (based on shed-to-shed mileages), would have been as follows:

Newcastle	256 miles
Dundee	120 miles
Perth	100 miles
Glasgow	104 miles

This was patently unacceptable, given the rundown state of locomotives and infrastructure post-war, and thus, from the outset, each Gresley was allocated to two drivers, although at no time did McKillop ever either identify or acknowledge his opposite number on No. 60100.

However, McKillop does relate, in his book *Enginemen Elite*, and

in some considerable detail, his reacquaintance with No. 60100 and the steps taken by him and his fireman to reinvigorate this famous A3. *Spearmint* had been one of the outstanding Haymarket 'stars' in the pre-war non-stop running (see Chapter 24), and his description of the subsequent years of neglect and what it had meant to this one engine, portrays, in considerable detail, the problems and home-truths of the 'common-user' engine policy.

This manning arrangement almost doubled the daily mileage figures being achieved, and in 1946 the L&NER 'Use of Engine Power' annual return indicated that the Scottish Area-based Gresleys (A3s and A4s) were achieving the highest average annual mileage, well above that of either the North Eastern or Southern areas. This was a great tribute to both the concept of regular manning (since, on certain diagrams, Haymarket A3s and A4s, and later the A1s, were accumulating some 3,600 miles per week) and the high standards of maintenance existing at Haymarket – although, it must be said, the 'soft' Scottish water did also play a part. At Haymarket, periods between boiler wash-out could be as long as fourteen days or more, unlike south of the border where boiler wash-outs were, by necessity, around weekly at best. This did assist in improving the availability figures considerably.

Without any shadow of a doubt, and as previously stated, Haymarket shed had become very much a 'pro-Gresley' shed; later, one Top link driver was overheard to say that '*Mr Thompson's new ideas (and locomotives) do not go down terribly well at all.*' The engines allocated to both Nos 1 and 2 links were Gresleys through and through, and it was not until the advent of the Peppercorn A1s that the situation changed, certainly insofar as No. 2 link was concerned.

POST-NATIONALISATION

The Haymarket allocation of locomotives at nationalisation included seven A4s, fourteen A3s, two A2/1s, three A2/2s, one A2, fourteen V2s, eight B1s, eight D49s, ten D11/2s, four D30s, two J36s, three V1/V3s, five J83s, two N15s and two J88s, a total of eighty-five locomotives. This allocation was to remain almost static throughout the 1950s, dropping to eighty around 1957.

Following the restoration of regular manning in 1946, the allocated workings for No. 1 link (the Newcastle link) had been as follows:

Early	06.50	Newcastle	Late	17.00	Glasgow
Early	10.15	Newcastle	Late	22.40	Newcastle
Early	07.30	Dundee	Late	19.50	Newcastle
Early	10.00	Dundee	Late	16.00	Glasgow
Early	10.40	Newcastle	Late	14.00	Newcastle
Early	08.10	Glasgow	Late	16.10	Dundee

With, yet again, a serious imbalance in the allocation of mileage turns (six Newcastle turns every twelve weeks) the diagrams were re-cast to take into account the increasing number of additional relief and special trains now diagrammed to and from Edinburgh over the ECML – such as the overnight 21.15 Glasgow Queen Street to Colchester, put on to accommodate the large number of national servicemen then travelling, plus the additional night sleeping car services to support the regular 'Night Scotsman' and 'Aberdonian' overnight services. The passenger links at Haymarket were to continue to be structured as discussed above, until the demise of steam.

New ECML day services, in addition to the long-standing services such as 'The Queen of Scots' Pullman, followed after the Second World War. A new mid-morning, summer-only, non-stop service was introduced in 1949, to run in front of the 10.00 departure, 'The Flying Scotsman'. Whilst it was to continue to run as the 10.00 thereafter with a Newcastle stop only, 'The Flying Scotsman' ceased to be the summer non-stop working after the 1948 summer season.

In the Festival of Britain year of 1951, from the 7th May the former mid-day service between Edinburgh and King's Cross became the 'Heart of Midlothian', departing both London King's Cross and Edinburgh at 14.00. The new train was equipped with the new BR Standard coaches and restaurant cars and was, particularly in summer, of very heavy formation – so much so that diagrammed relief trains had to be run on a regular basis during the summer months to cater for the high demand. Haymarket was allocated the Edinburgh/Newcastle section of the journey. Just like its predecessor, the former 13.50 Edinburgh to London, this train was known to all and sundry as 'The Diners'. Haymarket also manned most of the reliefs run in connection with this new service.

In the summer diagrams, No. 1 link (the Top link) always shared in the working of the non-stop service. Initially this was following the pre-war practice with the 10.00 'The Flying Scotsman', but the non-stop running was taken up in May 1949 by a new and re-timed train, departing Edinburgh at 09.45 and London King's Cross at 09.30, 'The Capitals Limited', which itself was soon to be renamed 'The Elizabethan' in the Coronation year of 1953 (see Chapter 23). The non-stop was the only 'lodging turn' worked by Haymarket crews, lodging turns having been largely discontinued by the L&NER at the onset of the Second World War because of perceived problems with food rationing, diminishing suitable accommodation, and the undesirability of staff having to be absent from home depots in wartime conditions.

Haymarket had had several lodging turns in earlier days, such as York and Newcastle on the 'Coronation' workings, the Edinburgh/Hyndland working via Bathgate, where on arrival the men worked

The date is 17th September 1956, the time is just a few minutes after 16.00, and an immaculate A4, No. 60031 *Golden Plover,* **driven by her regular driver, Tommy Smith of Haymarket's Top link, wheels the very first run of the new high-speed Edinburgh Waverley to London King's Cross express passenger service 'The Talisman' through the reverse curves at Portobello station and past a large admiring audience. The signal box on the right-hand side is South Leith Junction which plays no part in controlling the main ECML at this point. The train was timetabled to arrive in Newcastle at 18.06 and thereafter run non-stop to London, arriving at 22.40.** *Courtesy Scotsman Publications*

round the north Clyde suburban network and lodged at Hyndland. Aberdeen, and even Crail, in Fife, were other locations where Haymarket drivers and firemen had at some time or other been required to lodge overnight – although, perversely, at Crail they were in clear view of their home town across the wide expanse of the Forth estuary.

From 17th September 1956 a new mid-afternoon (Saturdays Excepted) express passenger train service was provided between Edinburgh and London King's Cross and return, the 16.00 'The Talisman'. For the first year, the Edinburgh/Newcastle leg of this working and the return working with the northbound service was allocated to the Top link at Haymarket. In the following year, from 17th June 1957, a morning equivalent was established between Edinburgh and London King's Cross, also named 'The Talisman', departing Edinburgh at 07.30, and Haymarket No. 3 link fell heir to this working. Two coaching sets of 'limited load' formation were employed, consisting of, in the Up direction, BSK, FK, CK, RFO, RK, SO, SK, SK and BSK of BR Mk I coaches, all fitted with roller bearings, with each train-set weighing 307 tons tare and each set completing the full return journey of 786 miles between Edinburgh and London daily. From the 16th September of that year, the morning train was extended to run from and to Perth, and was renamed 'The Fair Maid', departing Perth at 06.40, with an 08.30 departure from Edinburgh, and Perth men working the Perth to Edinburgh leg. However, the Perth extension made it impossible for the same coach sets to take up the afternoon return workings, and thus by the end of 1958 the Perth leg of the journey was abandoned and the train reverted to become, once more, the morning 'Talisman', but with the 08.30 departure from Edinburgh being retained. By 1958, No. 3 link at Haymarket had both early and late 'Talisman' services in their link, and both A3s and A4s were regularly to be seen on this working – but with A3s gradually taking the lion's share after being fitted with the 'Kylchap' draughting arrangements.

Right up to the demise of steam, Haymarket continued to engine and crew many additional summer trains, such as the 'Starlight Specials', working these through from Glasgow St. Enoch's to Newcastle if and when required. Haymarket shed was also called upon to work, at very short notice, many of the portions carried on the ECML services where, owing to late running, these portions had lost their forward connection from Edinburgh. Portions were regularly conveyed on ECML trains for Perth, Aberdeen and Glasgow, and on the occasions where these had to be worked forward as trains in their own right, a motley collection of motive power and young (and often inexperienced) crews were turned out. Latterly the 'Directors' and 'Shires' were utilised, thus giving them a chance to 'stretch their legs' away from the usual empty coach workings in and around the city, and also giving the young bloods amongst the passed firemen and passed cleaners the opportunity to 'strut their stuff'.

In the year 1957, the booked number of turns every twenty-four hours for which Haymarket had to provide engines and crews on a diagrammed basis were as shown in Tables 7.1 and 7.2 below. These were the regular diagrammed services; but Haymarket was also required to cover special train workings as contained in the weekly Special Traffic Notices, which in the winter would be an average of one or two turns daily, but in the summer could be up to a dozen additional relief or special workings every day with even more on each Saturday throughout the major holiday periods. There would also be the late-running portions off the ECML expresses, which

had to be specially worked to destination on an 'as required' basis. Over and above all these train working, special and relief train diagrams, Haymarket also had to provide crews (and engines as required) for the following supporting diagrams on a permanent and ongoing basis:

Waverley west

No. 1 and 2 station pilots	3 shifts	2 engines	6 crews
Haymarket yard pilot	3 shifts	1 engine	3 crews
Gorgie pilot No. 1	3 shifts	1 engine	3 crews
Shed pilot	3 shifts	1 engine	3 crews
Coal pilot	2 shifts	1 engine	2 crews
Turntable	3 shifts		3 crews
Disposal	6 shifts		6 crews
Preparation	24 diagrams		24 crews

Such were the pressures in summer that, despite the large Spare links at Haymarket, at the weekend, and Saturdays in particular, enginemen frequently had to be drafted in from adjacent sheds such as Bathgate and Polmont, and even on occasions from Hawick, to assist in disposal and preparation duties, thus freeing up Haymarket men for train working.

The introduction of overnight car/sleeper trains in 1958 saw more work for Haymarket. There was a Fridays Excepted 'Car Sleeper Limited' between Perth and London King's Cross departing Perth at 20.00 (weekdays) and 19.40 (Sundays), and King's Cross 20.05 northbound. The train consisted of sleeping cars plus GUVs for the conveyance of cars. At this time there was also a 'Highland Car Sleeper' which ran Saturdays Only between Inverness and York, departing Inverness at 21.45 southbound, and York at 21.55 northbound. These became very popular services with holidaymakers from the south being spared the long drive before setting out for, and returning from, a highland holiday. Haymarket men were allocated the Newcastle/Edinburgh and Edinburgh/Perth legs of the journey, and this saw the formation of a new link which, because of the Newcastle mileage, was required to be slipped in between the existing Nos 3 and 4 links, becoming link 4A.

Haymarket also gained additional work in 1960 with the advent of the 'Anglo-Scottish Car Carrier' service, a train consisting of coaches and GUVs. The train ran between London (Holloway) and Edinburgh, departing at 19.50, while the southbound train departed Edinburgh at 23.40.

POST-DIESELISATION

Diesel locomotives started replacing steam on a progressive basis from around 1960. Most of the services of the late 1950s mentioned above continued to run; in later days the night sleeping cars services ran via the WCML to London Euston, and they have continued into the new private railway of the twenty-first century under the privatised ScotRail TOC as the 'Caledonian Sleepers'.

At Haymarket, drivers and passed firemen extended their expertise into this new field of rail traction, as did the maintenance staff, and continued to set up quite exceptional runs with the new Deltics, and later with the HSTs. At the same time, maintenance at Haymarket was proving to be of the highest quality, with superior availability figures regularly being returned, particularly in regard to the English Electric Type 4s which were not always the most reliable performers and, of course, the famous Deltics.

As the railway network contracted under the infamous and

TABLE 7.1   WINTER TIMETABLE (FEBRUARY 1957)

00.28 Meadows Yard–Glasgow Sighthill	00.30 Niddrie West–Heaton
00.30 Craigentinny–Edinburgh ECS	00.40 Edinburgh–Carlisle (Stobs)
01.28 Edinburgh–Heaton	01.45 Niddrie West–Craiginches
01.45 Relieve Waverley pilot and ECS working	02.15 Niddrie West–Heaton
02.25 Portobello–Hawick	02.45 Edinburgh–Glasgow (newspapers)
03.30 Edinburgh–Dundee	04.20 Niddrie–Heaton
04.26 Edinburgh–Glasgow (West Highland sleepers)	05.05 Edinburgh–Thornton
05.25 Edinburgh–Carlisle	05.47 Edinburgh–Glasgow (parcels)
05.55 Edinburgh steam heat & turn mail vans via Gorgie	05.58 Edinburgh–Dundee
06.07 Edinburgh–Craigentinny ECS & 07.30 Glasgow	06.08 Edinburgh–Stirling
06.25 Edinburgh–Glasgow	06.28 Edinburgh–Perth
06.35 Edinburgh–Ratho Broxburn pilot	06.36 Edinburgh pre-heat & 07.30 Dundee
06.38 Edinburgh–Carlisle	06.40 Edinburgh–Dundee
06.40 Niddrie–Heaton	06.50 Edinburgh–Newcastle
06.58 Haymarket–South Queensferry (goods)	07.05 Haymarket–Corstorphine Sub (goods)
07.05 Craigentinny to Edinburgh & 08.12 Glasgow	07.34 Corstorphine–Edinburgh
07.40 ECS Edinburgh–Craigentinny & 10.40 Dundee	07.40 Edinburgh–Perth
07.53 Craigentinny–Edinburgh & 09.10 Dundee	08.02 Corstorphine–Edinburgh
08.05 Edinburgh–Thornton	08.34 Corstorphine–Edinburgh & 10.05 Carlisle
08.45 Gorgie pilot No. 2	09.05 Edinburgh–Glasgow
10.00 Edinburgh–Dundee	10.00 Edinburgh–Glasgow
10.10 Edinburgh–Newcastle	10.12 Edinburgh–Perth
10.27 Edinburgh–Newcastle	11.34 Craigentinny–Edinburgh & 12.15 Glasgow
12.07 Niddrie–Heaton	12.00 ECS ex Craigentinny & 13.20 Thornton
12.00 Edinburgh–Newcastle	12.00 Edinburgh–Glasgow
12.05 Edinburgh–Carlisle	12.38 ECS Leith Central–Edinburgh & 13.00 Glasgow
12.46 ECS Craigentinny–Edinburgh & 13.30 Thornton	13.00 ECS Craigentinny–Edinburgh & 13.50 Glasgow
13.04 Edinburgh–Corstorphine	13.18 Edinburgh–Galashiels via Peebles
13.30 Edinburgh–Ratho–Broxburn pilot	13.50 Edinburgh–South Queensferry pilot
13.58 Haymarket Yard–Niddrie West	14.00 Edinburgh–Perth
14.00 Edinburgh–Newcastle	14.15 Edinburgh–Dundee
14.18 Edinburgh–Newcastle (meat)	14.27 ECS Craigentinny & 15.00 Glasgow
14.33 Edinburgh–Carlisle	14.40 Edinburgh– Dundee
14.51 Corstorphine–Edinburgh & 17.17 Galashiels	15.43 Edinburgh–Larbert
15.50 ECS Edinburgh–Craigentinny & 18.00 Glasgow	16.00 Edinburgh–Perth
16.00 Edinburgh–Newcastle	16.00 Edinburgh–Glasgow
16.15 Edinburgh–Dundee	16.40 Edinburgh–Glasgow
16.38 ECS Craigentinny–Edinburgh & 17.20 Dundee	
16.43 Edinburgh–Corstorphine & 18.10 Thornton	17.00 Edinburgh–Corstorphine
17.15 Edinburgh–Corstorphine & 18.35 North Berwick	17.15 Edinburgh–Glasgow
17.52 Edinburgh–Carlisle	18.15 ECS Craigentinny–Edinburgh & pre-heat Postal
18.35 Niddrie–Heaton	18.45 Edinburgh–Dundee
19.13 Edinburgh–Newcastle (parcels)	19.55 Edinburgh–Carlisle ECS (Class 'C')
20.00 Edinburgh–Glasgow	20.00 Edinburgh–Newcastle (mail)
20.05 Leith Walk–Heaton	20.30 Steam Heat ECS & 22.45 North Berwick
22.10 ECS Haymarket & 22.40 Newcastle	22.15 Edinburgh–Newcastle
22.20 Edinburgh–Newcastle	23.20 Edinburgh–Newcastle
23.25 Haymarket–Heaton	23.30 Edinburgh–Newcastle

TABLE 7.2 SUMMER TIMETABLE (1957)

00.05 Edinburgh–Newcastle (parcels)	00.15 ECS Craigentinny–Edinburgh
00.25 Niddrie–Tweedmouth	00.40 Haymarket Yard–Carlisle
02.13 Niddrie–Heaton	02.15 Haymarket–Heaton
02.25 Portobello–Hawick	02.28 Edinburgh–Perth
02.56 Edinburgh–Dundee	03.13 Edinburgh–Dundee
03.39 Edinburgh–Dundee	03.45 Edinburgh–Glasgow
04.05 Edinburgh–Perth	04.55 Edinburgh Glasgow
05.05 Edinburgh–Thornton	05.25 Haymarket Yard–Carlisle
05.58 Edinburgh–Dundee	06.00 Edinburgh–Glasgow
06.00 Craigentinny & 07.40 Glasgow	06.08 Edinburgh–Stirling
06.10 Corstorphine–North Berwick	06.26 Craigentinny & 06.50 Inverkeithing
06.28 Edinburgh–Perth	06.35 ECS Craigentinny–Edinburgh
06.35 Broxburn pilot	06.38 Edinburgh–Carlisle
06.40 Edinburgh–Dundee	06.40 Niddrie–Tweedmouth
06.45 ECS Saughton & 08.02 Corstorphine	06.50 Edinburgh–Newcastle
06.48 Edinburgh–South Queensferry pilot	07.05 Suburban goods
07.13 Edinburgh–Glasgow High Street (parcels)	07.30 Edinburgh–Newcastle
07.30 Edinburgh–Dundee	07.34 Corstorphine–Edinburgh & 09.10 Dundee
07.40 Edinburgh–Perth	07.42 ECS Edinburgh–Craigentinny
07.50 Edinburgh–Corstorphine & 09.02 Glasgow	07.50 Edinburgh–Stirling
08.45 Turn mail vans via Gorgie	08.02 Corstorphine–Edinburgh
08.05 Edinburgh–Thornton	08.34 Corstorphine–Edinburgh & 10.05 Carlisle
09.00 Gorgie pilot No. 2	09.15 Edinburgh–Newcastle
09.20 Craigentinny–Edinburgh & 10.00 Glasgow	09.45 **Edinburgh–London non-stop** (2 crews)
09.53 Edinburgh–Glasgow (parcels)	09.55 ECS Saughton–Edinburgh
10.00 Edinburgh–Dundee	10.10 Edinburgh–Newcastle
12.00 Edinburgh–Carlisle	12.05 Edinburgh–Newcastle
12.06 Edinburgh–Dunbar	12.25 Craigentinny–Edinburgh & 13.00 Dundee
12.50 Edinburgh–Crail	13.04 Edinburgh–Corstorphine
13.09 Edinburgh–Dundee	13.35 Broxburn pilot
13.50 Edinburgh–Glasgow	14.00 Edinburgh–Perth
14.00 Edinburgh–Newcastle	14.05 Edinburgh–South Queensferry pilot
14.15 Edinburgh–Dundee	14.18 Edinburgh–Newcastle (meat)
14.20 Edinburgh–Newcastle	14.33 Edinburgh–Carlisle
15.00 Corstorphine ECS	15.10 Corstorphine–North Berwick
15.30 Craigentinny & 14.14 Dundee	15.53 Edinburgh–Larbert
16.00 Edinburgh–Perth	16.00 Edinburgh–Newcastle
16.02 Craigentinny & 16.35 Glasgow	
16.15 Edinburgh–Dundee	16.35 Craigentinny & 17.20 Glasgow
16.42 Haymarket–Edinburgh & 17.52 Carlisle	17.00 Suburban goods
17.35 ECS Craigentinny–Edinburgh	17.48 ECS Leith Central & 18.10 Thornton
18.08 Craigentinny & 18.45 Dundee	18.10 Edinburgh–Thornton
18.30 Edinburgh–Glasgow	18.33 Edinburgh–Berwick
18.35 Niddrie–Heaton	18.35 Edinburgh–Dundee
19.12 Edinburgh–Newcastle	19.20 Edinburgh–Newcastle (parcels)
19.35 Edinburgh–Corstorphine	19.55 Haymarket–Carlisle (Class 'C')
20.00 Edinburgh–Newcastle mail	20.05 Leith Walk–Heaton
20.15 Edinburgh–Glasgow	21.49 Edinburgh–Newcastle
22.00 Edinburgh–Newcastle	22.15 Edinburgh–Carlisle
22.20 Edinburgh–Newcastle	22.40 Edinburgh–Newcastle
23.10 Niddrie–Carlisle	23.20 Edinburgh–Newcastle

ill-conceived 'Beeching Plan' of the 1960s, so route knowledge disappeared from Haymarket route cards. The Waverley route to Carlisle, Edinburgh to Perth via the Forth Bridge, and numerous local branch lines were early casualties. However, with the closure of St. Margaret's shed, and in particular Dalry Road shed some time later, Haymarket men were soon to be seen running to Glasgow Central and Carlisle via the WCML, so it was not all doom and gloom.

The non-stop 'Elizabethan' had been abandoned by 1963, but by that time the East Coast timetable was seeing an increased number of accelerated services across the board with the Deltics playing an ever-increasing role. Steam did not, however, disappear quite as quickly as the BRB had planned, or indeed liked, since both the English Electric Type 4s and the Deltics were proving to be somewhat unreliable in service and thus, on the night sleeping car services in particular, steam continued to be the norm up to around 1965.

By then the Brush Type 4s (the Class 47s) were coming on-stream and being employed in an ever-expanding role, and, following some initial problems, reliability improved dramatically, in no small measure due to the introduction of electric train heating (ETH) and the disappearance of the dreadful steam heating boilers. Haymarket men continued to work over all the traditional, albeit contracted, routes, and the passenger express trains as of old, with all examples of the new traction.

By the mid-to-late 1970s, the Deltics were being displaced by the new High Speed Trains (HSTs) as they came on-stream, and so the ECML timetable went through yet another complete overhaul. An hourly service was introduced between Edinburgh and London, and journey times were slashed, with the best trains down to a mere 4½ hours. Haymarket-based drivers were still covering the bulk of the Edinburgh/Newcastle running. By this time, the old 'steam link' working arrangements had gone by the board, and at Haymarket, now the only Edinburgh depot, there were virtually only two large links – the Senior being the link which worked loco-hauled trains, E&GR push-pull services and the HST services, and the Junior having the bulk of the DMU operation. No longer were there any Spare link arrangements, but each of the two links carried spare turns interspersed amongst the train working turns, around which

all drivers rotated. This continued until 1984, when 64B ceased to be a train crew depot and all Haymarket men were transferred to the new Operations Centre in Waverley. 'The Glamour Boys' were gone forever!

Edinburgh drivers did not venture south of Newcastle in the final days of BR – although within the Scottish Region, Regional Railways reintroduced through workings on an out-and-home basis to Aberdeen, with young Waverley-based drivers sharing in this link and working the Class 158s over this route. The 'clock face' timetable, with a more regular service, made this entirely feasible and more importantly made for good resource utilisation.

On the privatised ECML, Edinburgh-based GNER drivers have continued to run only to Newcastle, but the Edinburgh Virgin CrossCountry drivers were soon to be working to Leeds and back via the ECML, and to Preston and back on the WCML, the latter men also having signed for the road through to Manchester Airport.

Top: Less-than-clean Class 47s awaiting their next turn of duty, which may well be night sleeping car trains. *Courtesy Jeff Hurst*

Above: The diesel shed in the 1970s with a selection of Class 27s standing outside Nos 6, 7 and 8 shed roads. These were the locomotives employed on the original Edinburgh to Glasgow push-pull workings. *Courtesy Jeff Hurst*

Left: The train which replaced the Deltics on the principal ECML high-speed services, and further cut journey times to and from London, was the most successful HST, seen here entering Haymarket station on an Aberdeen to London King's Cross service. *Courtesy John Fumeval*

8 SHED WORK

The only purpose of a locomotive depot, any locomotive depot, was to act as a central point where locomotives might be stabled between turns of duty, and where they could be refreshed, kept fit for purpose and fully prepared in time for the next duty. This, then, explains Haymarket MPD: the fact that it was nothing more or less than a central holding facility from whence locomotives of a type suitable for the train they required to work, fully serviced and in good mechanical order, could be handed over to the Operating Department at the times demanded by the working timetable. As the new (1894) shed at Haymarket grew in importance, and the allocation of engines increased in parallel, so the daily throughput of engines requiring attention increased; these being not only the allocated engines, but engines working in from other sheds and other regions. By the 1950s this had led to an onerous workload for the staff at Haymarket.

The shed work to meet this objective varied little throughout all the days of steam – but with some heavier, manual tasks gradually being eased by mechanisation of such facilities as the turntable, coaling and wheel dropping. Overall, though, the work remained arduous and labour intensive.

In order to ensure that Haymarket operated as smoothly as possible, a laid down procedure for dealing with incoming engines right through to the point where they once more were ready to go 'off shed' was established in the layout of the original 1894 shed, and was to be adhered to thereafter. This planned protocol for dealing with locomotives coming 'on shed' at Haymarket is described in this chapter.

ARRIVAL

All engines coming 'on shed' arrived from the main line at the eastern end of the depot, at the small platform outside the kit store. The kit store was latterly a much-misnamed establishment since it held very few, if any, items of locomotive kit, but was actually the store where supplies of paraffin and rape oil were held. This was where all head and tail lamps were filled with paraffin oil, gauge glass lamps with rape oil, and also where the headboards for the named trains were kept.

TURNING/COALING

The 'turntable' driver and fireman would take over the incoming engine at the kit store and run it onto the turntable where, under the instructions of the running foreman and dependent upon its next turn of duty, they would either turn the engine or run it straight across, as required. They would then take the engine up along the south side of the shed to the mechanical coaling plant, where they would replenish the tender – several tons of coal being loaded in just a few minutes and all at the push of a button. The two hoppers of the coaling plant held around 400 tons of coal and were kept topped up by wagons of coal hoisted up the southern face of the plant and tipped into the hoppers, the hoists being electrically

Class D30 No. 2495 *Bailie Nicol Jarvie* of Dundee shed is being prepared for the return working in No. 1 shed road at the east end of Haymarket. The engine positively gleams, but the tender shows signs of requiring some of the tender loving care being lavished on the Pacific in the background. This is A3 No. 2797 *Cicero*, newly delivered to Haymarket from Doncaster, standing in No. 7 road receiving the attention of the shed's cleaners prior to a Newcastle working. *Bill Lynn collection*

controlled. The coaling plant was supervised and hoists operated by a coaling plant attendant.

The mechanical coaling plant had superseded the old wooden manual hand coaling stage in 1930 and stood almost on the original site of same. In the old shed, tubs had to be filled by hand from wagons, and these tubs were then manhandled across the stage to be tipped into the waiting tenders below. Coaling by hand was time consuming and hard work. Few tears were shed when this manual operation was modernised and mechanised.

From the coaling plant, the turntable crew would then run the engine onto one of the two ash pit roads at the west end (the top end) of the shed and secure it. Each of the two ash pit roads could accommodate up to four engines.

FIRE CLEANING

At Haymarket, like many of the larger ex-L&NER engine sheds, footplate staff were not involved in fire cleaning and other associated duties, these being carried out by labourers, designated 'fire-droppers'. Here at the ash pit roads, amongst heaps of hot ashes, the fire-droppers carried out what was, without doubt, one of the most laborious and painful jobs at any steam shed.

With the Pacifics, fire cleaning was merely a case of opening the drop grate and pushing the fire down through the space into the ash pan or, in the case of the later engines, operating the rocker mechanism; but many engines still required that the fire was cleaned by the fire-dropper ladling ash and clinker out through the fire-hole door and dumping it 'over the side' using a heavy iron clinker shovel which got hotter and hotter the longer the fire took to clear. Sometimes an engine would come in with a fire so clinkered that it took hours of toil with a dart and shovel to break it up and clear it out.

But this was just the start. The fire-dropper would then have to go underneath and, with dampers fully open, push and pull the ash and clinker out of the ashpan by means of a rake, working in conditions where the ash cascading from the pan would eddy around in clouds of dust, covering everything in the vicinity, including said fire-dropper. This done, the smoke-box door would be swung open and, inevitably, the fine, abrasive char would pour out over trousers and boots; hence all fire-droppers wore bicycle clips as a matter of course. The char would then be dug out with a firing shovel and thrown to the ground, downwind of the engine to minimise the risk of it getting into one's eyes, the motion and, particularly with the Gresleys, the conjugated valve gear.

At Haymarket, the 'top end' was a satanic place despite the fact that the pits and adjacent areas were totally cleared of ash every twenty-four hours. Apart from a very short time each forenoon, it was surrounded by piles of hot ashes wreathed in clouds of white vapour – dilute sulphuric acid if truth be told. The ash pits

A visitor from Thornton (62A), D34 No. 62475 *Glen Beasdale*, **having been coaled and had the fire cleaned, moves off the ash pits on the 14th August 1958. The wagons behind contain loco coal and are standing on the ramp awaiting their turn to be run down by gravity to the coaling plant hoist for tipping into the hopper.** *Courtesy David Anderson*

A visiting B16/1 from York shed (50A), No. 61413, stands on No. 1 road at the west end of the shed having been coaled and had fire, ashpan and smokebox cleaned. The engine has not been turned to face south, so probably it was booked to work a return fast freight from Leith Walk East, working there tender-first via Abbeyhill Junction. In the background are N15/1 No. 69220 and J88 No. 68339, both denizens of 64B and both used on pilot duties.   *Courtesy David Anderson*

were also a place where preparation firemen came to seek out discarded or spare fire-irons, taking care to spit on said irons before picking them up, just in case they were, as was the norm, searingly hot.

Engines that were scheduled to undergo periodic maintenance, or with serious defects requiring heavy repair, had all the fire dropped and were removed by the shed shunt locomotive to either be stabled waiting repair, or removed to the heavy maintenance roads.

Disposal

Once the hard and unpleasant work of fire cleaning was completed, the driver and fireman forming the disposal crew would take over the engine, add some coal to the small amount of fire left in the box, fill the tender with water, and move the engine into the appropriate shed road, where it then stood waiting preparation. Engines were placed in the shed in, as far as possible, a time-order basis, this being directed by the assistant running foremen.

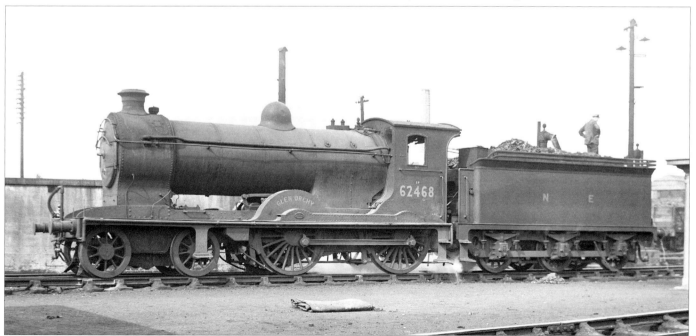

The elegant lines of Reid's classic, and extremely capable, Class D34. No. 62468 *Glen Orchy* of Thornton shed takes water at the Haymarket exit before going 'off shed' to work home. It carries its new BR number, but still has the abbreviated wartime NE on the tender. Like most of the class, this engine had a long working life of around forty-five years. Money well spent!   *Courtesy David Dunn*

D30 No. 62430 *Jingling Geordie* **of Thornton shed has just been turned to face home on the turntable at Haymarket. The next move will be to run up to take coal, and then slip back through the connection to the shed loop where the crew will re-fettle the fire for the return journey, thus avoiding the ashpits. The date is the 15th August 1951, yet the tender still bears LNER lettering. No. 62430 was withdrawn from Thornton in 1957.** *Courtesy David Dunn*

Certain foreign engines with a quick turn-round were diagrammed 'recondition only'; when these came on-shed at Haymarket they might have the fire cleaned, but smoke box and ash pans were left untouched and they might or might not be oiled. Generally, many of the engines working local services in from Fife were so diagrammed, as were some Tweedmouth freight engines.

When any work needed on such engines was complete, the disposal crews would either take them back down towards the turntable and through the connection to the shed loop, or out at the top end and into the shed loop, where the rostered crews would take over. This avoided such engines getting caught up or trapped inside the crowded running shed.

D30 No. 62430 *Jingling Geordie* **again – turned, coaled and now getting steam up in shed loop before backing down to Waverley for the return working.** *Courtesy David Dunn*

RUNNING REPAIRS

The driver who worked the engine on diagrammed working would fill out a repair card at the completion of his shift, detailing any and all defects/deficiencies, big or small, noted in running; this card was deposited with the shift chargehand running fitter, who would then delegate fitters to attend to items reported. Serious issues could see the engine stopped to enable sufficient time to be given to rectifying such defects and, if serious enough, this could also apply to foreign locomotives. Items such as leaking tubes or part of the brick arch missing generally meant that foreign engines were worked back to their home depot for attention!

Brakes became the responsibility of the brake blocker who would, as the title suggests, replace brake blocks as necessary and make adjustments to the brake rigging.

STEAM RAISING/LIGHTING UP

Once in the shed and waiting preparation for the next booked working, the engines were in the care of the steam-raisers – again labourers, but with special duties. These men would visit each locomotive on a regular basis to check that boiler water levels had not dropped to a dangerous low, and that sufficient fire was kept alight but without too much steam being raised. One or two were over-attentive and many preparation firemen had cause to swear under their breath at the steam-raiser who had over-filled a boiler with water. These men also kindled 'dead' engines off repair or boiler wash-out.

PREPARATION

Some diagrams in each link at Haymarket required that the rostered driver and fireman prepared their own engine before going off shed, generally where sufficient time existed for this duty in the train working diagram; but more often than not preparation was carried out by designated crews, generally the more junior men. The time allowed for preparation was set by national agreement, based on the heating surface of the locomotive, and all big engines were allowed one hour. This covered most of the engines being dealt with at Haymarket.

In the time available, the preparation driver had to fill all oiling points on both engine and tender, including the motion underneath. He also had to fill both lubricators and, whilst carrying out oiling duties, had to make a very detailed visual inspection of all components. When oiling was complete he would test each injector (or watch the fireman test them) and carry out a brake test.

The fireman, meanwhile, generally started outside at the smoke box, ensuring the door was air tight and properly secured, before brushing all char and ash from the front end and the running plates. Attention was then turned to the firebox and, before touching or spreading the fire, a visual inspection of the brick arch, fire bars and fusible plugs would be made. The fire would then be spread around the box, and the rear of the box, including corners, filled with coal. Exactly when the engine was booked 'off shed' would determine whether steam had to be generated quickly or whether the engine could safely stand until required. With the fire in proper shape, both

To show that not everything at Haymarket has gone the 'pigs and whistles' in the latter days of steam, Haymarket A3 No. 60090 *Grand Parade*, of Castlecary notoriety, stands on the ash pits at the top end of the shed awaiting attention from the firedroppers. *Courtesy David Dunn*

The date is the 23rd September 1961, but A3 No. 60098 *Spion Kop* is in remarkably fine condition as it stands just clear of the ashpits awaiting a turn for disposal in the shed. *Courtesy David Dunn*

injectors would be tested and the floor swept clean of any coal spillage and hosed down. The cab, tender-end, roof and faceplate were then thoroughly cleaned and oiled, and all gauges, gauge glass protectors and windows cleaned. A complete set of tools, detonators, red flags and spare gauge glasses/washers would be assembled, generally collected in the pail – which was also a mandatory requirement – along with a full set of fire irons including poker, dart and clinker shovel. The A4s would additionally be supplied with a handle for operating (opening) the 'shark jaws' doors. Two firing shovels and a footplate brush completed the kit. Sand boxes would be filled and sands tested before the task of trimming the tender began. Lastly, the tender would be topped up with water and the water scoop and operating mechanism checked.

Preparation involved a lot of hard work, and on a Pacific locomotive preparing the fire could involve two tons of coal or more being swallowed up in the big, wide firebox. Empty sand boxes, six in total, required about five pails of dry sand in each to fill them and thus the fireman, if very unlucky, might have to carry, often for quite a distance across the shed, a total of thirty pails of sand, each weighing around 60 lbs. Even if, as was the norm, sand boxes were not totally empty, filling the sands was a laborious and heavy task, detested by most firemen. There was little time to spare in the allotted hour, and preparing an engine off repair or boiler wash-out and just kindled, could require as much as an additional hour on top of the official time allowed. The running foremen always took this into consideration and would employ a spare crew to cover part of the preparation diagram when the booked men were faced with such an unpleasant task. On completion of preparation, the engine was then ready to go 'off shed' and take up its next booked working. At Haymarket, the 24-hour throughput in summer could see 150 or more engines being prepared.

Special attention was always afforded both the A4s working the non-stop 'Elizabethan' service and the stand-by diagram (normally, the 10.30 Edinburgh to King's Cross), whether the non-stop engine was the Haymarket engine or the King's Cross engine as happened on alternate days; generally, the fire of the incoming engine would be completely dropped in order that a full inspection of boiler, fire box and smoke box could be carried out. The Haymarket engine was also given a full boiler wash-out once in the week. The engines were still warm when rekindled early in the morning, but even so,

the preparation crew were allowed a full two hours in their diagram for preparation of this engine, and in fact the preparation men generally stayed with the locomotive right up until the engine had been telephoned 'off shed'.

CLEANING

In the time between being brought into the shed by the disposal crew and completion of preparation, the engine, if it was a Haymarket engine, would be thoroughly cleaned – certainly in the winter months when cleaners were available – and all engines in the allocation were cleaned on a regular basis. In summer, when cleaners were all booked out on firing duties, the passenger engines were cleaned by labourers on voluntary overtime. The three cleaning squads on rotating shifts comprised around thirty-five cleaners in each during winter months, and each squad worked under a chargeman cleaner. In summer, the chargeman supervised the labourers. Foreign engines were never cleaned – although, by exception, if say, a VIP was known to be travelling south on the 10.00 Edinburgh–King's Cross 'The Flying Scotsman', the worst of the grime would be scraped off the Gateshead Pacific allocated to the turn, and it would be turned out in a polished condition, not a Gateshead strength. This was a matter of pride at Haymarket. The King's Cross A4 on the 'non-stop' was, however, fully cleaned as a matter of course, this being reciprocated at Top Shed with the Haymarket engine.

In winter, since the cleaning squads were fully-manned, cleaners also undertook additional tasks such a polishing the brass work, painting the backgrounds of nameplates, and cleaning all steel work (buffer heads, couplings, cylinder covers, connecting rods and motion etc.) with specially supplied emery cloth.

MECHANICAL EXAMINATION

Each locomotive, generally after preparation but before going 'off shed', was given a thorough mechanical inspection by a team of highly-skilled examining fitters. These men, all of long and proven experience, had miners' safety electric head lamps fitted on their helmets and were equipped with long-shafted hammers. They carefully went around and underneath each engine, making a minutely detailed inspection of all mechanical components and sounding each with the hammer. The ring of the hammer often

Midday at Haymarket shed on the 24th July 1959, with A3 No. 60101 *Cicero*, **one of Haymarket's less vaunted denizens, being prepared to work the southbound 'Heart of Midlothian'. The preparation driver is finishing his oiling at the tender axleboxes whilst his fireman has yet to trim the tender. Behind stands a visiting A3, No. 60079** *Bayardo* **of Carlisle Canal shed (12C), which is similarly being prepared to work back home on the 14.23 Edinburgh to Carlisle passenger service.** *Courtesy Gavin Morrison*

revealed defects not visible to the eye, and these men ensured that, in so far as was humanly possible, each locomotive went into service 'fit for purpose' in all respects.

GENERAL

Shed duties in the era of steam at Haymarket had varied very little over the years from NBR days, through L&NER days and right up to BR days. The success of the operation of the shed depended on so many different men and skills. During the time each engine was 'on shed' it was attended to by drivers and firemen on turntable, disposal, shed movement and preparation duties, fire-droppers, steam-raisers, fitters, boilersmiths, examining fitters, and cleaners. They in turn were supported by shed labourers and storemen, and the labourers were instrumental in ensuring the safety of all staff working in and around the shed environment. These unsung heroes swept out the pits, shed roads and the turntable pit. They cleared up spillages of coal in the coaling plant road and in shed roads. They attended to the drains ensuring that pits never flooded, and each and every morning they shovelled the tons of hot ashes into wagons placed in the ash roads for this purpose. The chargehand (conciliation grades), otherwise known as the chargehand labourer, was responsible for the activities of fire-droppers, steam-raisers, coaling-plant attendants, general shed labourers, timekeepers, and, within his staff, the relief complement men who covered as fitter's assistants, storemen, timekeepers and chargeman cleaners as required.

Haymarket was thus a large family comprising various skills, and the public perception of express train travel – the polished engines, skilled drivers and firemen, and the glamour of such train working – was very much a façade, supported by the high levels of skill and attention of staff, the 'backroom boys' if you wish, devoted to keeping the depot ticking over like a well-oiled machine. Shed work, right up to the end of steam, was dirty, often dangerous, and was carried out in conditions which would be wholly unacceptable, if not illegal, in this twenty-first century. Nevertheless, Haymarket shed was a place of purposeful activity for twenty-four hours each day. To the uninitiated, the movements of locomotives around the shed area no doubt appeared to be chaotic, but, as described here, these movements followed a definite and planned pattern, thus ensuring that engines were stabled in time order and were presented, fit for duty and fully prepared, at the shed exit signal at the diagrammed time.

The management structure has been described at Chapter 3, and the maintenance procedures will be dealt with at Chapter 28, but the successful day-to-day running of the depot relied heavily upon the shift supervisory staff. The running foremen and assistant running foremen, on rotating shifts, had all come from the footplate; the third men were all drivers, either on 'light' duties or 'stepped up'. These men, collectively, were responsible for the provision of suitable locomotives for all booked and special duties, plus the activities of around 500 drivers, firemen and cleaners whilst on shed. Once footplate crews left the shed confines they were very much in charge of themselves, although they responded to the Operating Department requirements and orders thereof.

The rostering duties for footplate staff at such an important depot were, particularly in summer, onerous for the roster clerk and the detail of this functionary, and the role of the running foreman, have been fully described in my previous book, *Steam Days at Haymarket*.

Haymarket was run as a very 'tight ship' with good but fair discipline, and, until the advent of dieselisation, operated in an atmosphere of considerable harmony. The truth is that, particularly in summer, everyone was far too busy to do otherwise – although, it has to be conceded, in the winter months, with a large number of cleaners back on cleaning duties, there was always some nonsense or other being played out, but always within limits! The main problem over the years, especially amongst the younger members of the staff, was poor timekeeping, but this never was allowed to become a significant problem, generally being 'nipped in the bud' by the disciplinary process.

Like all steam sheds, Haymarket was a vibrant, living place, never at peace and never quiet. The shed lay under a permanent cloud of smoke haze. Engines came on shed with unfailing regularity and, after the attentions as described in this chapter, and over the subsequent few hours, were gradually worked down through the shed until they stood, once more, at the east end, prepared and ready for their next turn of duty. The shed, and the engines, lived. At any time, day or night, the shed was alive with noise. Fires roared in the bellies of the engines, the slurring clink of firing shovels on coal plates and firebox lip plates rang out as engines were prepared, injectors gave forth their whining song, blowers roared and occasionally an engine would blow off with an explosive roar. Men sang, whistled and shouted as they went about their business, and every now and then there would be the clang of the sand-pails as they were thrown away in relief. The shed drivers were almost constantly employed

Seen in final form, A3 No. 60085 *Manna* of Heaton shed runs onto the turntable at Haymarket in August 1963. There is a clear panoramic view across the east end of the shed with, from left to right, the trainman's bothy at the end of the brick building, the Chargehand Labourer's Office, Jeffrey's Brewery buildings, and behind these buildings to the right rear can just be seen the towers of Donaldson's Hospital. *Courtesy Ian Musgrave*

Sulzer Type 4 No. D178, in original green lined livery, sits at the top end, outside No. 8 road of the diesel shed. This locomotive will, in all probability, have worked into Haymarket over the Waverley route and will return the same way. Haymarket never had an allocation of these locomotives, but some Haymarket drivers were trained to drive them since they were regular performers over the aforementioned route. *Courtesy Ian Musgrave*

moving engines forward through the shed, and their warning cries (and warning whistles) rang out almost incessantly. In winter the cleaning gangs would roam the shed, seeking out the next in line for polishing, and how the Haymarket engines were polished! Boiler washing-out was carried out at the western end of No. 4 road, and the area was always wreathed in steam and running with water. All in all, the shed, at any time of day or night – but particularly during the night – was a magical, atmospheric place with the glare of fires spilling from the cabs and the smoky flames of many flare lamps flickering through the murk as preparation drivers attended to the oiling of their steeds, and all surrounded by a quite unique aroma, that wonderful *pot pourri* of hot oil, steam and smoke.

Men working on or about the locomotives had to place great faith in the provision and observance of the mandatory 'Not to be Moved' boards, placed at each end of an engine before work commenced, but nevertheless there was always the slight, niggling worry when working underneath an engine, and especially on or around the motion, that another movement might just come into contact and 'bump' the one being worked on. This was, in fact, a very rare occurrence, but nevertheless the worry was always there.

In 1963 the last few steam locomotives and long-time denizens of Haymarket began to be transferred out, one by one – going, in the main, down the short three miles to St. Margaret's. On the 9th September of that year, A4 No. 60012 *Commonwealth of Australia*, dirty, neglected and light years away from the shining from stem-to-stern Top link locomotive that it once was – and the last of the many – was prepared for the last time; as the engine moved off shed to go to Dalry Road (64C) shed, so an era, a glorious era, came to an end at Haymarket, some 121 years after the first E&GR 'Hawthorn' made an appearance at the original Haymarket shed. Another chapter closed for ever. Steam was to be no more at 64B, and in many ways the shed died. Much of the movement ceased with the disappearance of steam. The shed remained silent, as the many voices, and all the noises associated with steam traction, were stilled. The workload and many of the skills described here were

rendered redundant, having disappeared with the steam locomotive. A way of life had gone … forever!

The operation of the dieselised depot was much simpler than the steam days. The diesels came quietly 'on shed' at the east end, eschewing the journey via turntable, coaling plant and ash pits, were parked *in situ*, and shut down; and so they slumbered silently until fired into life for their next turn of duty. The shed was but a mere silent dormitory – but happily it was to survive the change. The diesels, if cleaned, were machine cleaned and never hand cleaned, and preparation simply consisted of sweeping and cleaning the interior of the cab(s) and ensuring the emergency equipment was provided. The exception was the windscreens, which were generally hand cleaned. All lubrication and mechanical and electrical inspection was carried out by the technical staff.

Gateshead A4 No. 60005 *Sir Charles Newton*, in typical Gateshead condition, sits in glorious isolation in No. 1 road in Haymarket whilst being prepared for the return working to Newcastle, which is, in all likelihood, a freight working. *Courtesy Ian Musgrave*

A sad day at 64B. The front of Haymarket shed, on 7th September 1963 in the final days of steam there, showing A4 No. 60012 *Commonwealth of Australia*, no longer a Top link locomotive and now in a very shabby and dirty condition. The shed is strangely quiet, but all the other remaining steam locomotives have already been transferred away, mainly to St. Margaret's, leaving only No. 60012. This engine was to have the distinction of being the very last Haymarket steam locomotive, and is seen here ready to take up one of its last Haymarket workings. Two days later, on the 9th, it was officially transferred out to Dalry Road (64C) shed. When No. 60012 left the shed for the last time, so an era, a quite momentous era, came to an end at Haymarket. The new order, in the shape of an English Electric Type 4, lurks in the right background.   *Courtesy W.S. Sellar*

9

EDINBURGH & GLASGOW RAILWAY LOCOMOTIVES

The NBR inherited 102 E&GR locomotives upon the amalgamation on the 1st August 1865. However, because the E&GR had absorbed the Monklands Railway Company under a separate Act on only the previous day (31st July 1865), the NBR found that a further thirty-two engines from this latter railway had also been taken onto the books. William Hurst, the Locomotive Superintendent of the NBR, had made a tour of inspection of the rolling stock and installations of the E&GR and was shocked with what was found. In his report to the directors of the NBR, he recorded that:

it has transpired that twelve E&G engines are or have long been dead, 213 wagons are known to be missing, and doubtless many more will never be seen in life. The same history applies to the Monklands, and it will be safe to write off from the aggregate number of engines of the united companies as at 1st August, 1865, fourteen engines and 450 wagons. It may be that carriages may have to be obliterated also.

Whilst no record of the actual shed allocation of E&GR locomotives has been found, it is of interest to list the locomotives built for or by the company during its existence as an independent railway from 1843 until 1865, some twenty-three years in all. Within this period, there is no doubt that Haymarket had an allocation of some of the passenger engines, and it probably had a smaller number of goods engines allocated as well.

For the opening of the railway in 1842, James Miller, Resident Engineer, appears to have been held responsible for much more than the way and works aspect of the new railway, and in 1840 he was instructed by the Board of Directors to obtain tenders for the provision of engines for the new line. In this respect Miller appears to have enjoyed considerable autonomy. The report of a visit to England to make inquiries into the merits of the locomotives in use there was read out at the board meeting dated 30th November 1840, at which Miller recommended that the company:

make trial of both the four-wheeled and six-wheeled engines and that 24 locomotives be ordered, 14 with six wheels and 10 with four wheels, with the latter coming from Mr. Bury of Liverpool and 10 of the former to be provided by English Works and the remaining four from Scottish Works.

At the meeting of the Glasgow Committee on 28th December 1840, Miller confirmed his acceptance of tenders from Bury and R&W Hawthorn as follows:

From Bury's, ten 4-wheel locomotives:
7 × 2-2-0 passenger engines	@ £1300 each
3 × 0-4-0 luggage engines	@ £1350 each
10 × tenders	@ £180 each

Price quoted included delivery at Liverpool only.

From Hawthorn's, ten 6-wheel locomotives:
7 × 2-2-2 passenger engines	@ £1370 each
3 × 2-4-0 luggage engines	@ £1430 each
10 × tenders	@ £230 each

Price quoted included delivery to Haymarket.

The Hawthorn engines were the first to arrive, before the line was actually opened. Available records suggest that only seven engines initially came from each builder, fourteen in total – but what were the 'luggage engines' and why were they more expensive? They were, in fact, what later became 'mixed traffic' engines, for it must be remembered that the E&GR was established as a 'passenger only' railway, with little or no use for 'goods' engines. Sadly, the reasons for the greater cost are unrecorded in the Minute Book. It is believed that all of the twenty engines ordered from these two builders were actually supplied, albeit not necessarily in time for the opening, but certainly soon after. Thornton, in his evidence at the trial of William Paton, stated that by 1844 the company had a total of twenty-six engines, with the Haymarket share being twelve.

The interesting and significant point is the fact that, from the earliest days of the E&GR existence, the practice of naming engines was common. The seven passenger engines from the original ten Bury locomotives of 1841 all carried the names of famous engineers or scientists; records show the names of six of these engines, with definite numbers for four, and these last four went into NBR ownership still carrying their names.

The NBR also named many of its locomotives over the years, a practice which was perpetuated right up to the grouping when the NBR handed over 122 named locomotives to the new L&NER, out of a total of only 180 from all the constituent companies. The L&NER continued this great tradition to the joy, no doubt, of loco-spotters everywhere.

Another interesting point emerges when looking at the design of the first and subsequent E&GR (and NBR) locomotives. From the earliest days, the controls, and thus the driving positions, were provided on the left-hand side of the locomotives as delivered. But, given what was happening on other railways in the UK, the assumption must be made that both the E&GR and the NBR had specified this driving position for their locomotives. Indeed, the only engines which did not fit the bill were the class of six 2-4-0 locomotives designed and built by Steel Brown at Cowlairs between 1862 and 1867. It can therefore be assumed that it was from these earliest days that the Haymarket drivers' extreme dislike of right-hand drive locomotives stemmed, and this dislike was to continue throughout all the days of steam. McKillop expressed the view that the right-hand driving position, where it existed, was chosen in order that drivers could signal to each other when passing, regarding the state of the line ahead. This is an entirely logical explanation of what might have been an early operating procedure, but the necessity of which was obviously not subscribed to by the E&GR, or its successors.

NBR 2-2-2 No. 36 was built by R&W Hawthorn in 1847 for the Edinburgh/Berwick traffic. Fitted with 6-foot driving wheels and 16 × 18 inch cylinders, the class were all soon rebuilt. No. 36 is seen at Haymarket old shed after rebuilding by Hurst at St. Margaret's in 1868 or 1869. Now fitted with a handsome Hurst copper-topped chimney and 16 × 21 inch cylinders, they proved to be reliable and fast locomotives. Immediately behind the tender is Herdman's Flour Mill, which lasted well into the 1960s. Also visible in this picture, just on the left-hand side in the rear, is the tower of Donaldson's Hospital, a school for deaf children. The crew are quite obviously very proud of their immaculately turned-out steed. *Bill Lynn collection*

The fuel for the early steam locomotives was, of course, coke, and in the lead up to the opening of the railway, the directors were inundated by offers to supply coke from many producers in the north-east of England. After careful deliberation it was decided that the E&GR Company should construct their own coke ovens in a location where there was a ready and reliable supply of good coking coal, and coke ovens were thereafter established at Falkirk, more or less equidistant from both major locomotive sheds.

One of the E&GR's most unusual and celebrated acquisitions was the purchase of a 2-2-2 well tank locomotive from the Caledonian & Dumbartonshire Railway (No. 5) in August 1862. This engine had been built initially as a 2-2-0T by Neilson's on the Adam's Patent, as a locomotive and coach combined. It ran in this formation for about one year, after which the two parts were separated and it was rebuilt as a 2-2-2T. It was renumbered by the E&GR as No. 86 in 1862, then No. 88 in 1864 and, again, as No. 13 in 1865, after which it went to the NBR as No. 312. In 1868 it was rebuilt at Cowlairs, when a solid-looking square cab was added for inspection purposes. It proved to be a very useful engine and was further rebuilt in 1882 and 1895 before being sold on in 1911. It was allocated to Haymarket through the 1870s and had its own driver at that time, one Thomas Baxter.

The rest of this chapter will review the E&GR locomotives in order of building.

1841

Ten locomotives were constructed for the company by R&W Hawthorn. These were the original engines with which the E&GR commenced their service in 1842.

The seven Hawthorn passenger engines were of 2-2-2 wheel arrangement, with 6-foot driving wheels and 13 × 18 inch cylinders, and were primarily passenger engines. The remaining three engines had a 2-4-0 wheel arrangement with 5-foot driving wheels and were designed as mixed traffic or 'luggage' engines. Only one survived, No. 2, to be taking into NBR stock (NBR No. 220).

In this same year, a total of ten engines were ordered from, and supplied by, Bury. The seven passenger engines were bar-framed with the 2-2-0 wheel arrangement and had 5-foot 6-inch driving wheels and 13 × 18 inch cylinders. The remaining three were similarly built with bar frames, but with an 0-4-0 wheel arrangement and again, they were the 'luggage' or mixed traffic engines. These Bury engines had been rebuilt to 0-4-2 tank engines by the time they went to the NBR.

Confusion reigns regarding actual numbering of these first engines. C. Hamilton Ellis, in his book *The North British Railway*, suggests the seven Hawthorn passenger engines were numbered 1–4 and 18–20, the three Hawthorn luggage engines 5–7, the seven Bury passenger engines 8–14, and the three Bury luggage engines 15–17. This suggested numbering conflicts with the (admittedly sparse) information contained within the SLS book, *Locomotives of the NBR Railway, 1846–1882*, which is probably the definitive work on this particular subject. It is known that all the Bury 2-2-0s were named, as previously described.

It is possible, however, even given the confusing information now available, to speculate as to the actual numbering. Hawthorn 2-2-2 (E&GR No. 2) was the only one of the class to pass to the NBR, being renumbered 220; and No. 9, a Hawthorn 2-4-0 'luggage' engine, is referred to in the Winchburgh accident of 1862 (see Chapter 31) and is illustrated on p. 12 – thus it is reasonable

The magnificent NBR No. 312, originally built by Neilson's in 1850 for the Caledonian & Dumbartonshire Railway as No. 5. Bought by the E&GR and numbered 86, 88 and 13 in turn, before passing to the NBR as No. 65, it was rebuilt in 1868 and fitted with this substantial square saloon for inspection purposes. Known as 'The Cab' thereafter, this proved such a useful engine that it was to be rebuilt in 1882 and again in 1895 before being sold on in 1911. In the 1870s it was allocated to Haymarket and driven by one Thomas Baxter, seen here. *Bill Lynn collection*

to assume that all ten Hawthorns, and not just seven as stated elsewhere, were delivered first, and likely to be numbered 1 to 10.

The Burys were thus possibly numbered 11 to 20, and again this fits with what is known about the Burys, since four former 2-2-0s passed into NBR hands – Nos 14 *Davy* (NBR No. 263), 15 *Rennie* (NBR No. 264), 16 *Telford* (NBR No. 265) and 17 *Galileo* (NBR No. 266).

The ill-fated *Napier*, number not referred to at Paton's trial, was a Bury locomotive of this first batch; as was *Archimedes*, again no number, but again referred to by name in evidence, and shedded with *Napier* at Cowlairs. These names fit with engineering/scientific associations. *Archimedes* was the train engine on the following 19.30 passenger ex-Glasgow which collided with the special train at Ratho on the 19th May 1844.

Haymarket had an allocation of each type, with probably eight of the Hawthorn locomotives and four Burys, totalling twelve in all. These were the main engines owned by the railway up until 1844.

1844/46

Over this period of time, R&W Hawthorn built a further six engines to order for the E&GR. These had an 0-4-2 wheel arrangement with 4-foot 6-inch driving wheels; two, Nos 25 and 26, had 14 × 21 inch cylinders, and the remaining four, Nos 27–30, had 15 × 21 inch cylinders. These were, in fact, the first engines turned out by R&W Hawthorn to have a 21-inch cylinder stroke. No. 25 was fitted with the Hawthorn Potter valve gear, and the engines were primarily constructed for freight working. Again, all had been converted to 0-4-2 tank engines by the amalgamation and were allocated Nos 255–260 by the NBR.

1846

During the year the E&GR purchased six standard bar-framed 0-4-0 goods engines with 5-foot driving wheels and 16 × 20 inch cylinders. These engines had been built by Bury, to the order of the Edinburgh, Leith & Granton Railway. All were converted to 0-4-2s and two survived to go into NBR books as Nos 261 and 267.

The E&GR also ordered six engines from R&W Hawthorn. These were 2-2-2 express passenger engines with 6-foot driving wheels and 16 × 18 inch cylinders. They were, as supplied, fitted with the Hawthorn experimental expansion link valve gear, but this proved troublesome in the extreme and they were quickly refitted with normal link motion. They were numbered 34–39 and only three passed to the NBR, as Nos 219, 221 and 222. These six engines all carried names in E&GR days. No. 36 was certainly, amongst others, allocated to Haymarket.

1847/48

The E&GR ordered four 2-2-2 passenger engines from Neilson's, with 6-foot driving wheels and 15 × 20 inch cylinders. As built, they were fitted with Neilson's patent valve gear and proved troublesome from day one. Numbered 44, 46, 48 and 49, they were rebuilt as 0-4-2 goods engines in 1852/53, at no little cost, to ease the acute shortage of this type of engine on the E&GR. All passed to the NBR being allocated Nos 243–246, but all were gone by 1868.

In the same period, the E&GR also bought six 2-2-2 engines 'off the peg' from Sharp Brothers to fill an urgent need for motive power. They had 5-foot 6-inch driving wheels and 15 × 20 inch cylinders. Numbered 50–55, the first two were to be delivered by

NBR 0-6-0T No. 39 was the Haymarket yard pilot for many years. This was Wheatley's first design of passenger tank engine to appear on the NBR. Built at Cowlairs in 1872, it was renumbered 1204 in 1913, and lasted until 1922. Seen here in Haymarket yard, Driver Hugh Dickson stands at the smokebox whilst Cleaner Bob Keppie sits on the bunker. Keppie was to become a Haymarket Top link driver in the 1940s, sharing A4 No. 60027 *Merlin*. At a later date, Andrew Manzie, another Haymarket stalwart, was to drive No. 39 in the yard, and both Norman McKillop and Charlie Scott (later to become a running foreman at 64B) fired to him on this job. *Bill Lynn collection*

NBR 2-2-2 No. 216 *Dullatur* (formerly E&GR No. 85/43) stands with the crew at the original Haymarket shed in the late 1870s. Originally one of the splendid Beyer Peacock engines built for the E&GR, it is seen here as rebuilt by Wheatley in 1873 with 6-foot driving wheels, stovepipe chimney, broad, rounded dome and cab sheets added to the original weatherboards. *Bill Lynn collection*

sea, but the remaining four came north over the newly-opened Caledonian Railway. They were rebuilt by the E&GR, and all six passed to the NBR, being renumbered 225–230.

1848

A further two 0-4-2 goods engines were delivered from Neilson's, numbered 56 and 57. They had 5-foot driving wheels and 16 × 20 inch cylinders.

This year also saw two engines emerge from Cowlairs. These were the first of an intended grand plan, as devised by Paton, to build a total of twenty. They were 2-4-0 passenger engines with 5-foot 6-inch driving wheels and 15 × 20 inch cylinders, and had Gooch valve gear. In the event, these were to remain the only two engines of the class. They were numbered 58 and 59 and named *Sirius* and *Orion* respectively, and were to be the star performers on the E&GR express passenger services for the next eight years. Both passed to the NBR, being renumbered 223 and 224 respectively, and, although considered worn out, they went on to perform sterling service until withdrawn by 1871. At least one of these engines was allocated to Haymarket for the duration.

1850

A single 0-4-2 mixed traffic engine was built by R&W Hawthorn and taken into service. Information regarding this engine is scarce and conflicting. As built, it is thought to have had 5-foot driving wheels and 14 × 20 inch cylinders. Numbered 26, it was rebuilt with 15 × 24 inch cylinders, and possibly converted to become a tank engine, at Cowlairs in 1862. It was certainly rebuilt once more in 1868. It was taken into the NBR allocation as No. 242, and scrapped in 1880.

1851

Neilson's offered the E&GR two ready-made 0-4-2 goods engines with 5-foot driving wheels and 16 × 20 inch cylinders for a mere £1,700. These were quickly purchased and worked successfully for many years. Numbered 62 and 63, they were rebuilt at Cowlairs in 1867 as 0-6-0 engines with 16 × 22 inch cylinders and renumbered 249 and 250.

1854

Two 2-4-0 locomotives were ordered from Sharp Brothers and duly supplied. They had 5-foot 6-inch driving wheels and 15 × 20 inch cylinders, and were numbered 64 and 65. The latter engine was rebuilt at Cowlairs in 1867, and the former rebuilt in 1871. No. 65 (NBR No. 232) was broken up in 1891 to provide spares for sister engine NBR No. 231, which ran on until 1894.

1855/57

During this period a total of twelve 0-4-2 goods engines, with 5-foot driving wheels and 16 × 22 inch cylinders, were constructed for the E&GR by Neilson & Co. Unusually, and peculiar to Scotland, these were built with outside cylinders, but experience quickly revealed that this was not the way forward and inside cylinders became the preferred option for future builds. Numbered 70–81, they all went into NBR ownership as Nos 283–294. Only four were rebuilt by the NBR in the late 1860s. One other, No. 80 (NBR No. 293), was rebuilt as an 0-6-0 goods engine by Wheatley in 1872 and ran until finally withdrawn in 1907.

Also within this time period, eight express passenger 'singles' were built by Beyer Peacock to the design of Charles Beyer for the

E&GR. These 2-2-2 engines had 6-foot 6-inch driving wheels and 16 × 20 inch cylinders. They had double frames but with no outside bearings for the driving wheels, which were set in the middle of the 14-foot 6-inch wheelbase. Numbered 1, 2 and 82–87, they were splendid performers from the outset and, with attractive appearance and proportions, they gave long and distinguished service on the E&GR express passenger trains. They were renumbered by the E&GR in 1862 and all went to the NBR, being allocated Nos 211–218. Wheatley rebuilt No. 85 (NBR No. 216) in 1873 with 6-foot driving wheels, but later, in 1885, Holmes restored the 6-foot 6-inch driving wheels to No. 216. Wheatley rebuilt No. 213 in 1875, and again in the 1880s, and Holmes had it rebuilt again in 1897. The remainder of the class were rebuilt by Wheatley between 1880 and 1882. They were all to be named in 1880, renumbered 801–808 in 1895 and again renumbered 1001–1008 in 1901.

It is known that Haymarket shed (both old and new) had a significant allocation of both the original and rebuilt locomotives over the years, including Nos 211 *Haymarket*, 212 *Corstorphine*, 213 *Polmont*, 216 *Dullatur* and 218 *Winchburgh*.

No. 218, carrying its second E&GR number, 57, was a 'bit' player in the 1862 Winchburgh accident. (Was there someone with a warped sense of the ridiculous who later chose the name *Winchburgh* for this particular engine, one wonders?) McKillop refers to having (he thought) fired on one of these singles as a young fireman, assisting the 16.45 Edinburgh to Hawick passenger to Falahill summit – but this is highly unlikely since most had gone by 1910, the year in which he joined the NBR. The last of class, No. 216, was withdrawn from Stirling in 1912.

1859/61

Beyer Peacock built four 2-4-0 passenger engines with 6-foot driving wheels and 16 × 20 inch cylinders for the E&GR. These were effectively a four-coupled version of the highly successful 'singles' and were numbered 4, 7, 40 and 41 by the E&GR. Cowlairs built a further three to the same design, although with domeless boilers which were slightly smaller; two of these were numbered 39 and 35 by the E&GR, and the last, No. 44 by the NBR. They were all renumbered 233–239. Drummond rebuilt three in 1881, and Holmes continued the rebuilding of the class between 1882 and 1901. Haymarket shed had an allocation of these engines.

1859/64

In 1859, Beyer Peacock commenced building the first of twelve mixed traffic locomotives with inside frames and outside bearings

to the trailing wheels, the wheel arrangement being 0-4-2. The engines – with 5-foot 1-inch driving wheels and 16 × 22 inch cylinders, inclined at 1 in 12 – closely followed Beyer's earlier 2-4-0 locomotives in design. These engines were numbered 89–100 by the E&GR. They proved to be extremely useful locomotives and Cowlairs built a further six in 1864, the latter engines having domeless boilers and, most probably, Stroudley single side window cabs, since Stroudley was works manager at that time. All engines were fitted with the Stephenson valve gear. The Cowlairs engines carried E&GR numbers 83–88 and all passed to NBR ownership, being renumbered 317–334. Haymarket was known to have an allocation, albeit small, and No. 88 was certainly allocated there.

1862/67

One William Steel Brown had taken over the reins from Paton in 1861, and William Stroudley was the Works Manager at Cowlairs. During Brown's short tenure of office in the final years of the E&GR, he had laid down at Cowlairs the first four of what were to become a very successful design totalling eight engines. These were 2-4-0 passenger engines with 6-foot driving wheels and 16 × 22 inch cylinders. These four, numbered 101–104, were quickly followed by a further two engines, Nos 105 and 106, which were completed by Brown's successor, S.W. Johnson. Renumbered 351–356 by the NBR, a further two engines, Nos 349 and 350, were completed after the amalgamation. However, contrary to E&GR and NBR practice, the engines in this class had the driving position located on the right-hand side; despite the drivers' dislike of this arrangement, the anomaly persisted for fifty years until the engines were finally withdrawn.

It is known that Haymarket had an allocation of these locomotives, including Nos 350 and 351. No. 101 (NBR No. 351) was the engine involved in the fatal collision which occurred at Manual (Bo'ness Junction) in January 1874 (see Chapter 31).

1866

A single locomotive, laid down by the E&GR at Cowlairs in the previous year, was completed by the NBR in 1866. This was a double-framed 0-4-2 goods engine, with 5-foot driving wheels and 16 × 22 inch cylinders, and was constructed largely from various parts of older engines. It was rebuilt in 1888 as an 0-4-2 tank engine. It carried the NBR No. 262.

Former NBR J36, No. 65243 *Maude*, stands at the top end of the shed, day's work done, in the 1950s. The engine was at that time without any name, although this was to be re-painted on the wheel splasher at a later date. There is an interesting arrangement attached to the fireman's window, a home-made arm rest no doubt, since crews were always seeking ways to increase comfort and window ledges on ex-NBR locomotives were uncomfortable. *Courtesy David Dunn*

10 NBR 0-6-0 FREIGHT LOCOMOTIVES

If ever clear evidence was required to prove that Haymarket was never other than predominantly a passenger shed with only peripheral freight workings, one has only to look at the relatively small allocation of freight locomotives at the shed at any given time over the years, out of the considerable number of locomotives which were entirely suited to the demands of the heavy mineral traffic available to the NBR all over the system. In the early days, the Haymarket share of freight working was minimal, with mainly local trip workings serving the shale-oil and coal industries. The Edinburgh South Suburban Railway, the 'Sub' as it was forever known to Edinburgh locomotive men, provided the connection for through wagonload freight traffic from the south, between Niddrie West and Haymarket Yard, and also for the north and west. As this traffic increased in L&NER days, so Haymarket men did then work some longer-distance freight trains such as Tweedmouth, Craiginches (Aberdeen) and Cadder (Glasgow) workings; but in the main, before the express fully-fitted goods services (Class 1 Goods) were introduced sometime after the grouping, much of Haymarket's freight work was 'round the doors' trip working. Haymarket did, however, provide locomotives and crews for several of the shunting pilots around the area, including Gorgie yards, Haymarket goods yard and, of course, the west end of Edinburgh Waverley.

In 1910 the Haymarket yard pilot (manned by Haymarket crews) was an 0-6-0 Wheatley saddle-tank, No. 39 (later No. 1204). This engine was one of eighteen tank engines built at Cowlairs in 1872. It had 16 × 22 inch cylinders and 5-foot driving wheels. The class was specifically designed as passenger tank engines and when built represented the largest tank engines on the NBR. Haymarket had a further two of the class, No. 136 (later No. 1233) and No. 405 (later No. 1215), both of which acted as west end station pilots at Waverley. These engines lasted until 1922 when they were replaced by the Holmes Class 'C' 0-6-0 tank engines, later to become L&NER Class J83. These latter engines saw out the steam era at Haymarket yard in the early 1960s. McKillop provides quite a full and interesting description of firing on No. 39 to Driver Andrew Manzie on the Haymarket yard pilot.

Some of the NBR freight locomotives allocated to Haymarket for longer or shorter periods included the following classes.

CLASS J31 (NBR CLASS 'E') LOCOMOTIVES

Eighty-eight engines, with their roots way back in the Wheatley days, were built between 1867 and 1875. All were rebuilt by Holmes between 1883 and 1900, and Reid started to further rebuild a few members of the class, but withdrawals commenced in 1911. By the grouping, fifty-one had been scrapped, with the remaining thirty-seven engines being dispersed over the NBR system and employed mainly in yard or piloting duties. The last withdrawal was in 1937. Only one is recorded as being on the strength at Haymarket and this for a very short time only:

• No. 1070.

NBR Class D29 4-4-0 No. 897 *Redgauntlet* makes a rousing start out of Waverley with the 10.05 Edinburgh/Perth/Inverness on the 1st August 1911. Although a St. Margaret's engine and diagram, the photo is of interest as it shows the Wheatley 0-6-0T which was a Haymarket engine, probably either No. 136 (later No. 1233) or No. 404 (later No. 1215), working as Waverley west end station pilot and making a shunting move with coaches on the north lines out through the Mound Tunnel. The NBR lower quadrant signals are of special interest. *Bill Lynn collection*

Surely one of the oldest train working diagrams to be allocated to Haymarket was the South Queensferry goods (the 'Ferry Goods). Here, Class J36 No. 65243 *Maude* takes this train past Hallyards Siding and across the River Almond, between Queensferry Junction and Kirkliston en route to South Queensferry.   *Courtesy W.S. Sellar*

CLASS J32 (NBR CLASS 'D') LOCOMOTIVES

Built as NBR Class 'C' locomotives in 1876/77, these thirty-two engines were employed on long-distance goods and gave a good account of themselves. Rebuilding took place between 1898 and 1903, and nineteen engines survived until the grouping. They were, however, quickly withdrawn by the L&NER, the last going in 1925. Over the years Haymarket had three engines allocated, although not all at the same time:

- 1314
- 1315
- 1343   until 1924.

CLASS J34 (NBR CLASS 'D') LOCOMOTIVES

One hundred and one Class 'D' locomotives were constructed by the NBR to the design of Dugald Drummond between 1879 and 1883, but with only ninety-three surviving to the grouping. Many were rebuilt by Holmes, and the class gave good and long service not only on main line goods but even on passenger turns. Towards their later days they were to be found mainly on colliery trip workings, being adequately suited to the light colliery branches of the time. The class became extinct in 1928. Haymarket had only three allocated over the post-grouping years:

- 565   5/23 until 6/23   Condemned
- 9553 (Duplicate list)   2/23 until 11/25
- 9434 (Duplicate list).

McKillop, however, confirms that Drummond 0-6-0s were out-based at Ratho for the Broxburn Goods and Ratho (Bathgate Junction) pilot workings between 1910 and 1919, and whilst no engine numbers are giving, it is assumed that at least another two of this class were allocated to Haymarket prior to 1923.

CLASS J35 (NBR CLASS 'B') LOCOMOTIVES

A total of seventy-six of the Class 'B' engines were constructed to the design of Reid between 1906 and 1913. The first ten were fitted with piston valves, but were later rebuilt to conform to the remainder of the class, which emerged over the years with slide valves fitted as standard. The engines were retrospectively superheated, the conversion starting in 1923. As a class they worked long-distance heavy freight trains in the earlier years, but coal haulage became their principal role in the later years. They survived into BR days and the final engine was withdrawn in 1962. Haymarket had five engines allocated at one time or another:

- 9848   /06 until 2/31
- 9850   1/39 until 6/40
- 368   2/31 until 6/32
- 9375   3/30 until 9/31
- 9058   9/30 until 3/40.

CLASS J36 (NBR CLASS 'C') LOCOMOTIVES

This class was introduced on the NBR in 1888 to the design of Matthew Holmes. In total, 168 of these extremely useful and long-lived locomotives were built between 1888 and 1900. Building was, in the main, carried out at Cowlairs, but with thirty coming from external locomotive works. They all had 18-inch cylinders. Rebuilt by Reid, they were to be found all over the NBR system (and eventually beyond), working everything from passenger to long-distance to trip trains. Twenty-six engines were loaned to the government for service in France during the First World War, and all received names relevant to the war on their return at the end of the hostilities. A further three were loaned to the Highland Railway during the same period.

Even by 1931 only one had been withdrawn, and this was as the result of an accident, but other withdrawals commenced thereafter.

The Second World War halted withdrawals, and a total of 123 of the class were handed over to BR in 1948. The final engine was withdrawn in 1967 but, happily, one was preserved and can now be seen at the SRPS Railway Museum at Bo'ness, No. 65243 *Maude* (formerly NBR 673).

Haymarket had a total of at least nine engines at one time or another, including:

- 9619   8/28 until 10/35
- 9659 (65235 *Gough*)   5/52 until 10/61
- 9668   11/35 until 5/52
- 9673 (65243 *Maude*)   6/28 until 9/63
- 9680   5/45 until 9/45
- 9687 (65258)   4/61 until 3/62
- 9711   8/28 until 8/30
- 9752   11/44 until 12/44
- 9775   11/29 until 3/39.

However, from McKillop, it is known that another of the class, No. 181 of the 1893 Cowlairs-built locomotives, was employed on the daily Haymarket Yard to St. Boswell's goods for many years and certainly, in 1910, it was the regular engine of Driver R. (Bobby) Baillie, who also spent many years on this one turn of duty with this engine. No. 715 also worked out of Haymarket shed for a period of time around 1911 and it was one of the engines involved in the collision which occurred at Queensferry junction in that year.

The Haymarket J36s were used regularly on the double-shifted South Queensferry trip working and the Broxburn pilot, another local trip working. They also worked, in lieu of Haymarket N15 No. 69220 as required, on the Suburban goods and the Prestonpans goods daily trip workings.

No. 65235 *Gough* and No. 65243 *Maude* were the last engines of the class to remain at Haymarket – although No. 65258 was transferred in for eleven months in the latter days of steam to cover for No. 65235 which had been withdrawn – before steam locomotives finally disappeared from the Haymarket scene.

CLASS J37 (NBR CLASS 'S') LOCOMOTIVES

The final and largest of the Reid-designed NBR goods engines, the Class 'S' (or 'B' depending on boiler pressure) emerged from Cowlairs in 1914. Between that year and 1921 a total of 104 were built, thirty-five coming from Cowlairs and the rest from the North British Locomotive Company's Atlas Works in Glasgow.

Haymarket had but one allocated, No. 9434 (BR No. 64552) from August 1932 until January 1939, and McKillop certainly drove this engine on Cadder freight turns. Charlie Meacher recalls that, in the period around 1935/36, No. 9434 was the regular engine on the 'Sub Goods' between Haymarket yard and Niddrie West – although the use of such a powerful locomotive on this duty was in effect 'a sledgehammer to crack a nut' situation.

J36 No. 65243 *Maude* (although the name is not being carried at this time) poses for the camera at the Royal Naval base at Port Edgar, near South Queensferry, in February 1959. The engine carries a target at its chimney showing that it is working Edinburgh District trip train E25 which is, of course, the 'Ferry Goods. The crew have rigged up a sheet to protect themselves from the cold when running tender-first, as was the norm for the outward leg of this working, since the winds down on the water side could be extremely 'snell' (bitingly cold). *Courtesy W.S. Sellar*

NBR Class 'M' 4-4-0 No. 293 being prepared at Haymarket prior to working an Edinburgh to Hyndland via Bathgate train, hardly a racing train this time, and carrying the typical NBR destination board below the chimney. *Bill Lynn collection*

NBR Class 'M' 4-4-0 No. 731 stands in Princes Street gardens, Edinburgh, in July 1902. The fireman is busy on the tender and is, in all probability, drawing coal forward whilst the opportunity presents itself. *Bill Lynn collection*

11 NBR 2-4-0 AND 4-4-0 LOCOMOTIVES: THE HURST, WHEATLEY, DRUMMOND AND HOLMES ERA

NBR (UNCLASSIFIED)

Between 1861 and 1867, Dübs and Neilson built a total of twenty-four 2-4-0 passenger engines to the design of William Hurst:

Dübs & Co. Ltd
    6 engines numbered 90–95 in 1861
    6 engines numbered 341–366 in 1865
Neilson & Co.
    12 engines numbered 382–393 between 1866 and 1867.

These locomotives were designed to replace the 2-2-2 Hawthorns of 1847 and had 6-foot driving wheels with 16 × 20 inch cylinders. Nos 90–95 were rebuilt at Cowlairs in 1874 but the main dimensions remained unaltered. In 1888 Holmes had all twelve Neilson locomotives rebuilt with larger cylinders. Holmes further modified these engines in 1891/92 with his standard rounded cab, wing-plates, chimneys and boilers, and all were also fitted with the Westinghouse brake at this time. Haymarket certainly had a small allocation of these engines in NBR days.

NBR (UNCLASSIFIED)

In 1869 the first two of Wheatley's 2-4-0 passenger engines were built at Cowlairs, Nos 141 and 164. These were inside frame engines with 6-foot 6-inch driving wheels and 17 × 24 inch cylinders, domeless flush boilers and flare-topped safety valves mounted over the firebox. They had minimal weather protection for the crew as built. In 1890 they were rebuilt by Holmes and transformed into elegant engines which, in this improved condition, were to give many years of service. Haymarket had one of these engines allocated in NBR days.

NBR (UNCLASSIFIED)

Wheatley was to build four 4-4-0 passenger engines at Cowlairs in 1873, mainly to work passenger trains over the heavy Waverley route between Edinburgh and Carlisle. Numbered 420–423, with 6-foot 6-inch driving wheels, 17 × 24 inch cylinders and fitted with the Wheatley solid bogies, they were not really up to the task. Holmes rebuilt Nos 420 and 421 in 1887 and the remaining two in 1890, and they settled down to general passenger use – with Haymarket having No. 423 allocated for a while.

NBR (UNCLASSIFIED)

In 1876 Neilson & Co. built two express passenger 2-2-2 locomotives to the design of Dugald Drummond and intended for E&GR main line working. Numbered 474 and 475, they worked out of Haymarket shed for a time. Neither was ever to be rebuilt.

NBR CLASS 'N' (L&NER D25)

Designed and built at Cowlairs under the direction of M. Holmes, these locomotives appeared in two batches of six between 1886 and 1888, a total of twelve engines in all. They were numbered 592–597 and 598–603. They were unusual for the NBR, in that they had 7-foot diameter driving wheels. They were intended for working passenger trains over the Burntisland to Aberdeen route (the Forth Bridge not having been opened at this time). After the opening of the bridge in 1890 their use was extended over a greater number of routes and they were frequently involved in Berwick/Edinburgh/Aberdeen trains.

In 1911 they were rebuilt by Reid with smaller, custom-built boilers but were not superheated. At the grouping all the engines were lined out in L&NER green livery, but only eight took up their allocated numbers. The four which did not take up the allocated numbers were amongst the early withdrawals in 1926 and received a 'B' suffix. The final remaining engine of the class, No. 9596, survived until 1933.

Members of this class allocated to Haymarket were:

- 595 (9595)   4/1887 until 3/32
- 596 (9596)   4/1887 until 9/24
- 597 (9597)   1/1887 until 10/26
- 598 (9598) 12/1928 until 10/30.

NBR CLASS 'K' (L&NER D26)

These engines, with 6-foot driving wheels, built at Cowlairs to the design of Holmes, entered service between May and October 1903, numbered 317–328. They were slightly larger than the Class 'N' engines, but otherwise were very similar in detail. The Class 'K' were employed on similar duties to the Class 'N' engines, but latterly were relegated to the Edinburgh to Glasgow services via Bathgate. They suffered from weak frames which shortened their useful lives, and by 1922 only nine engines were left. After the grouping all the remaining engines went to St. Margaret's; some then went on to Bathgate. They had gone by 1926.

No surviving records show engines of this class having been allocated to Haymarket, before or at the grouping; but they have been included in this book since it is known that Haymarket did have an allocation pre-grouping, albeit small, for use on stopping passenger services. No. 318, which was involved in the Ratho accident in 1911, was amongst engines of this class allocated to Haymarket before the advent of the NBR Atlantics displaced them.

NBR CLASS 'M' (L&NER D27 AND D28)

The original class was built by Dugald Drummond, his first 4-4-0 design, and came into traffic in three batches, each batch consisting of four engines. Nos 476–479 were delivered from Neilson & Co.

in 1876, Nos 486–489 also from Neilson & Co. in 1878, and the final four emerged from Cowlairs works in 1878 numbered 490–493. They all had 6-foot driving wheels and were designed for use primarily over the 'Waverley' route taking over from the superseded Wheatley '420' class.

As was the practice on the NBR, the engines were subjected to a rebuilding programme. In 1902, six engines, Nos 476, 478, 479, 488, 489 and 490, were rebuilt by Holmes with bigger boilers and the round cab favoured by Holmes. Only three survived the grouping to become Class D27. The remaining engines, Nos 477, 486, 487, 491, 492 and 493, were rebuilt by Reid in 1904, with the same boiler but with the standard Reid cab with a single side window. Four of these went onto the L&NER books as Class D28.

In their early days all carried geographical names relative to the locations where they worked, but the names were removed by Holmes when he became CME of the NBR.

After the grouping, all were renumbered (on the Duplicate List) as 1321–1324, 1360–1363, 1371 and 1387–1389, in order of building. In 1924 there was a further renumbering scheme, but only two engines had a zero inserted between the first two digits of their numbers, all others carried their Duplicate List numbers until withdrawal. The last two engines (D28) were withdrawn and condemned in 1926.

Those allocated to Haymarket were:

D27
- 478 (1323)   6/1877 until 9/24
- 479 (1324)   7/1877 until 12/23

D28
- 487 (10361) 10/1878 until 9/26
- 491 (10387) 1/1879 until 9/26.

NBR CLASS 'M' (L&NER D31)

The locomotives contained within this classification, forty-eight in all, were built at Cowlairs to the design of Holmes, in three separate series, but in similar form. All had 6-foot 6-inch coupled wheels.

The first series of six engines, the '574' class, entered traffic from Cowlairs, numbered 574–579, in 1884. They were non-superheated and had 17-inch (later 18-inch) cylinders.

A further series of some twenty-four engines, the '633' class followed from Cowlairs between 1890 and 1895. These were enlarged versions of the '574' class with bigger (non-superheated) boilers, an increase in coupled wheelbase from 8 feet 3 inches to 9 feet and with cylinders increased to 18 inches. They were numbered 633–642, 36, 37, 262, 293, 312, 404 and 211–218. It was from this class that the engines used by Haymarket for the Edinburgh to Dundee leg during the 'racing' days in 1885 were selected, and also by Dundee Tay Bridge depot for the Dundee to Aberdeen leg.

In 1898/99 the final batch of eighteen engines emerged from Cowlairs, with yet bigger boilers and cylinders increased to 18¼ inches. The '729' class, they were numbered 729–740 and 765–770.

In 1911 all engines in the '574' class were rebuilt by Reid to bring them into line with the '729' class, and with this latter class they formed the locomotive stock for the L&NER Class D31s.

The First World War delayed further rebuilding, but in 1918 both the '633' class and the '729' class were rebuilt to the same specification of the 1911 '574' rebuilds.

The '574' class were employed on the Edinburgh/Glasgow services and the '633' class on the Edinburgh/Perth, the Edinburgh/

Aberdeen services and the ECML passenger trains to Berwick-upon-Tweed. The final six engines of this class were built to work the heavy 'Waverley' route.

The three classes were finally displaced by the newer 4-4-0 classes and were then deployed on secondary passenger and piloting duties. From 1925 some went north to the Great North of Scotland Railway. Nos 729 and 735, both of Haymarket, were regular engines on the Rosyth Dockyard workers' train between Edinburgh and Inverkeithing and return.

The engines were extremely popular with train crews and gave sterling service over the years. Withdrawal commenced in July 1931, and by 1946 only seven of the class remained in service. They went into BR ownership with four being allocated the new 60000 numbers, but only three ever took up the new numbers. The last of the class was withdrawn from Bathgate in February 1950.

The engines of these classes allocated to Haymarket were:

- 575 (9575)   /1884 until   /23
- 579 (9579) 3/1927 until   1/30
- 637 (9637) 1/1934 until   9/35
- 638 (9638) 2/1932 until   4/34
- 639 (9639) 4/1931 until   1/34
- 642 (9642) 5/1932 until   9/28
- 211 (9211) 1/1895 until 11/23
- 212 (9212) 1/1895 until 11/23
- 293 (9293) 1/1895 until 11/23
- 729 (9729) 3/1898 until 11/23
- 730 (9730) 4/1898 until 12/29
- 733 (9733) 5/1898 until   7/26
- 734 (9734) 5/1898 until 12/29
- 735 (9735) 3/1898 until   7/25
- 763 (9763) 7/1898 until   2/25
- 753 (9753) 7/1898 until   7/25
- 767 (9767) 12/1939 until   2/40
- 768 (9768) 5/1942 until   6/43.

NBR CLASS 'N' L&NER D36 'WEST HIGHLAND BOGIES'

This class was designed and built by Holmes at Cowlairs between 1894 and 1896, for the newly opened West Highland line. The class was known from the earliest as the 'West Highland Bogies'.

Their tenure of office on the West Highland was short, and by 1904 they had been dispersed around the NBR system, being employed on minor and piloting/banking duties. Only seven engines entered L&NER ownership, but none ever carried the subsequent L&NER five digit number. The final demise of the class was unrecorded.

Haymarket had an allocation of only one engine:

- No. 1439   1/1896 until 7/23.

As a point of some interest, one engine of the class, No. 695 (9695) was extensively rebuilt by Reid, to the point that, when it emerged from Cowlairs in February 1919, it was more or less a completely new engine. This was the only Class 'N' so rebuilt, in an effort to improve what was, in effect, a very poor class of engine.

The L&NER carried out further improvements to this engine, now classed as D36, and it continued to work until 1944, but poor engine or not, in its lifetime it amassed a mileage of some 1½ million miles – only ever working from two sheds, Parkhead and Eastfield. It was withdrawn in 1943 and broken up in February 1944.

12 NBR 4-4-0 LOCOMOTIVES: THE REID ERA

The beginning of the Reid era in 1906 was heralded with the construction of a series of 4-4-0 locomotives. These were built and released into traffic in the order shown in Table 12.1.

NBR CLASS 'K' (L&NER D32) 'INTERMEDIATES'

The first 4-4-0 class designed and built in Reid's tenure of office, in 1906, set the precedent for subsequent batches of locomotives with similar features, but with two different sizes of driving wheel employed – namely 6 feet 6 inches for express passenger locomotives and 6 feet for mixed traffic (the 'Intermediates'). The earlier engines of this class were initially fitted with non-superheated boilers.

The first Class 'K' engines, numbering twelve in total and classified as 'Intermediate' for mixed traffic operation, emerged from Cowlairs works between October 1906 and January 1907, numbered 882–893; they were dual fitted with both vacuum and Westinghouse brakes. These became Class D32 in L&NER days and, from the first, largely worked long-distance express goods trains. Latterly they were to be employed on passenger trains centred upon Edinburgh, on routes both north and south from the city including the Waverley route and the ECML.

Designed and built primarily to work the express perishable freight traffic (mainly fish) originating from Mallaig, Aberdeen and the Buchan coast, they were extremely popular engines with their crews. The class proved to be good value for money and gave sterling service for over forty years. The first was withdrawn in 1947 and by 1950 a further nine had gone. The last, which had carried a BR number, No. 62451, and had been the Dunbar pilot for many years, was withdrawn from St. Margaret's in 1951.

It is believed that over the years Haymarket shed had a small allocation, but latterly only a single representative of this class remained there, and this for a very short time:

- 882 (9882)   3/39 until 6/40.

NBR CLASS 'K' (L&NER D33) 'INTERMEDIATES'

The second batch of 4-4-0 mixed traffic engines, twelve in total, emerged from Cowlairs between late 1909 and 1910 with the numbering employed following typical NBR random fashion, and being confusing in the extreme. In order of building, the numbers were 331, 864–867, 894, 332, 333 and 382–385. It has to be said that the numbering after the grouping was further confused by the L&NER when the Class D33 were again wrongly numbered.

Like the earlier build, the class was saturated as built, but under L&NER ownership they were all fitted with superheated boilers in the period between November 1925 and April 1936. This long boiler life was testament to the pure and soft quality of Scottish water, qualities which meant that boilers in Scotland had much longer than normal lives, thus slowing the need for any reboilering programme.

These engines were employed on the same duties as the earlier Class D32. Two were withdrawn in 1947 and the remaining ten were systematically withdrawn thereafter – the final engine, carrying BR number 62464, going in September 1953.

The Haymarket allocation was:

- 864 (9864)   11/23 until 4/26
- 865 (9865)   11/23 until 8/24
- 867 (9867)   6/23 until 12/25
- 894 (9894)   11/23 until 12/25.

NBR CLASS 'K' (L&NER D34) 'INTERMEDIATES' 'GLENS'

This series of thirty-two engines in total were to represent the final form of the Reid 4-4-0 'Intermediates'. All were superheated as built. Building took place in batches over the period from 1913 until 1920, the First World War impacting on the building programme. All emerged carrying the names of Scottish Glens lying within NBR territory, and were primarily constructed to meet the heavy demands of operation over the severely-graded West Highland line; immediately prior to the grouping, Eastfield Shed in Glasgow had 75 per cent of the total allocation They proved to be extremely versatile engines, much loved by drivers and firemen, and eventually were to be found all over ex-NBR territory.

All but one (withdrawn in 1946) entered BR ownership. Further withdrawals did not occur until 1956, when a further five engines were withdrawn. Thereafter, withdrawals were deferred until

TABLE 12.1	THE REID 4-4-0s				
NBR Class	**L&NER Class**	**Build Date**	**Driving Wheel Diameter**	**Boiler Type**	**Known As**
'K'	D32	1906/07	6 feet	saturated	'Intermediates'
'J'	D29	1909/11	6 feet 6 inches	saturated	'Scotts'
'K'	D33	1909/10	6 feet	saturated	'Intermediates'
'J'	D30	1912	6 feet 6 inches	superheated	'Scotts'
'K'	D34	1913/20	6 feet	superheated	'Glens'
'J'	D30	1914/20	6 feet 6 inches	superheated	'Scotts'

September 1958, but by November 1961 all but one had disappeared. No. 62469 *Glen Douglas*, when withdrawn, was partially restored to original NBR condition at Cowlairs and donated to the Museum of Transport in Glasgow to join representatives of the other pre-grouping railway companies.

With three of the other preserved engines, *Glen Douglas* worked special trains over BR lines in Scotland in the period spanning the late 1950s and early 1960s. Later, the engine was again removed from the museum and transferred to the Scottish Railway Preservation Society (SRPS) 'on loan', with a view to it being restored to running order and steamed on the SRPS Bo'ness and Birkhill railway. Regrettably, this did not happen, and *Glen Douglas*, in NBR livery, remained in the SRPS museum at Bo'ness until September 2010, when it was transferred back to the care of the Glasgow Museum, finally going on display when the new Riverside Museum of Transport opened its doors in June 2011.

Haymarket shed, whilst over the years having considerable exposure to this class as 'foreign' engines working in and out of the depot, only ever had a very limited allocation:

- 291 (9291) *Glen Quoich*   5/17 until 10/24
- 493 (9493) *Glen Luss*   4/32 until 6/40.

McKillop refers to firing No. 270 (9270) *Glen Garry* in the post-First World War period, on the Anstruther lodging turn (1919) – but this engine, according to Yeadon (and R.D. Stephen), was never allocated to Haymarket, being a Perth engine from new until 1923, when it went to St. Margaret's. He also stated that No. 270 '*was a split new engine on a split new train, the "Fife Coast Express"*' (p. 36),

but there little doubt that No. 270 did not work out of Haymarket shed – although it would regularly pass through for fire cleaning, preparation and so on before returning home, and McKillop's account is thus somewhat confusing. This service only resumed in 1919, which makes his claim of firing on it more strange, to say the least. This could not have been a lapse of memory either, since he was, as he confirms in his book, appointed a driver in 1919 and was never again to act as fireman.

CLASS 'J' (L&NER D29) SATURATED 'SCOTTS'

Reid had some sixteen 6-foot 6-inch passenger engines built between 1909 and 1912. The first six were delivered from the North British Locomotive Company's Hyde Park works in 1909, numbered 859–900. The remainder were built at Cowlairs works, emerging to traffic in the last few months of 1911, and numbered 243, 244, 338, 339, 340 and 359–362. All carried names of characters in Sir Walter Scott's Waverley novels and became known as the 'Scott' class. They were, when built, non-superheated. They all carried the names right through L&NER days and into BR days.

The L&NER carried out a programme of fitting superheated boilers to the class over the years from 1925 to 1936.

Built to work the heaviest express passenger trains over the Waverley route, they were fitted with new high-capacity tenders carrying some 7 tons of coal and 4235 gallons of water, and weighing 46 tons. They also worked express passenger trains over the rest of the NBR system, with the exception of the West Highland line. Later, as the L&NER introduced the D11/2 class and the new D49 class, so the 'Scotts' were relegated to lesser duties on stopping

Ex-NBR mixed traffic Class 'K' 4-4-0s, numbering only twelve in the class, were reclassified by the L&NER as Class D33. Here No. 62464 of Dunfermline shed has been turned to face north. *Courtesy David Dunn*

passenger trains. The first withdrawal, however, only came in 1946, and five survived to carry BR 60000 numbers, the last engine being withdrawn in 1952. The Haymarket allocation initially worked the Edinburgh to Glasgow express passenger services until displaced by the Class D11/2 'Directors'.

The engines allocated to Haymarket over the years were:

- 898 (9898) *Sir Walter Scott*   8/46 until 3/48
- 899 (9899) *Jeannie Deans*   12/41 until 4/43
- 900 (9900) *The Fair Maid*   2/32 until 4/43
                                          9/46 until 2/51
- 338 (9338) *Helen Macgregor*   10/11 until 2/28
- 339 (9339) *Ivanhoe*   10/11 until 2/31
- 360 (9360) *Guy Mannering*   8/46 until 8/49
- 361 (9361) *Vich Ian Vohr*   12/11 until 9/29.

No. 9339 *Ivanhoe* was to have quite a chequered career long after departure from Haymarket. On Monday 16th October 1939, whilst

working a train from Edinburgh Waverley to Stirling, the engine was confronted with the first bombing raid on the UK mainland in the Second World War, over the River Forth. After some indecision, the train was permitted to cross the bridge whilst the raid was still in full progress. On the 30th January 1942, No. 9339 was again in the headlines when involved in the fatal collision which occurred at Cowlairs East Junction. The engine was severely damaged in this accident (both incidents are described in detail at page 197), but was repaired at Cowlairs works and put back into traffic, surviving until January 1952.

NBR Class 'K' (L&NER Class D33) 'Intermediates'

This NBR Class 'K' consisted of twelve mixed-traffic 4-4-0 locomotives, all fitted with 6-foot driving wheels, with the design based on the 'Scott' class of 1909. They were generally similar to the earlier D32s except for certain boiler details, but were fitted with larger tenders. They were numbered, as built, 331, 864–867,

An April afternoon at Edinburgh Waverley in 1938, with NBR Atlantic No. 9509 *Duke of Rothesay*, a Dundee Tay Bridge engine on a northbound working, waiting for the 'off', whilst D34 No. 9291 *Glen Quoich*, carrying the typical NBR destination board showing the train terminates at Crail, heads the Fife Coast Express departure. This was a Haymarket working, although the engine was by this time no longer allocated there. This is an interesting photograph, since in the Yeadon Register No. 9509 was shown as being withdrawn in 1937, so either the register is wrong or the photograph is not as dated. *W. Lawson Kerr/Bill Brown collection*

ABOVE: NBR Class D29 No. 339 *Ivanhoe*, another Haymarket star, awaits departure with a Glasgow express at Waverley pre-1914. The blower is hard on and the engine is blowing off, so departure time must be imminent although the platform starting signal is still 'on'. Of interest is the old numbering of the Waverley platforms with the number being displayed at the running-on end of each of the platforms. The bulk of the new North British Hotel can be seen dimly in the left background. It is possible that the frock-coated gentleman on the platform is the Station Master, thus signifying that the train was an important one.   *Bill Lynn collection*

BELOW: Ex-NBR Class D29 4-4-0 No. 9898 *Sir Walter Scott*, another long time denizen of Haymarket, stands at Craigentinny in L&NER guise, awaiting the road 'light engine' back to the shed.   *Bill Lynn collection*

894, 332, 333 and 385, again in typical NBR random fashion. The L&NER compounded this confusion when they then wrongly renumbered the class in 1946. The engines were classed as 'Intermediates' and were saturated until L&NER days, six then receiving second-hand boilers and the other six new boilers. They worked alongside the D32s over the whole of the NBR system, and withdrawal commenced in the latter days of the L&NER.

Haymarket had the following allocation:

- 9864 (2455) (62455)   17/11/23 until   4/26
- 9865 (2465)   /11/23 until   8/24
- 9867 (2458)   18/06/23 until   4/26
- 9894 (2459)   17/11/23 until 12/25.

NBR Class 'J' (L&NER D30) Superheated 'Scotts'

A further twenty-seven engines of Class 'J' were built by the NBR at Cowlairs works in four batches over a five-year period from 1912. Two engines entered traffic in 1912, Nos 363 and 400; both were fitted with 8-inch piston valves and later became Part 1 of the class for this reason.

Fifteen more engines entered traffic between April and October 1914, as Nos 409–423, followed by another five in the summer of 1915, Nos 424–428. Five years elapsed before further engines of the class emerged from Cowlairs, when another five engines, Nos

497–501, entered traffic. All these engines became Part 2 of the class by virtue of the fact that they all had 10-inch piston valves.

Like the earlier Class 'J' non-superheated engines, the new engines continued to carry names of characters contained within the Waverley novels and thus also became known as 'Scotts'. In operation, they worked in parallel with the earlier engines, working the same types of trains.

Because they were somewhat younger, they had a longer life and withdrawal did not commence until 1945, the final two engine of the class being withdrawn together, in June 1960.

The Haymarket allocation, apart from the single locomotive No. 411, were all new engines from works and were:

- 411 (9411) (2420) (62420) *Dominie Sampson*
  6/23 until   8/50
- 412 (9412) (2421) (62421) *Caleb Balderstone*
  5/14 until   3/29
- 414 (9414) (2423) (62423) *Dugald Dalgetty*
  6/14 until   4/43
- 415 (9415) (2424) (62424) *Claverhouse*   6/14 until   6/43
- 416 (9416) (2425) (62425) *Ellangowan*   6/14 until   5/44
- 424 (9424) (2433)   *Lady Rowena*   6/15 until 11/47
- 425 (9425) (2434) (62434) *Kettledrummie* 6/15 until   9/31
- 428 (9428) (2437) (62437) *Adam Woodcock*
  8/15 until   8/55.

D29 No. 62405 *The Fair Maid*, **a Haymarket engine, gives a fair impression of being a 'single' after a visit to the wheeldrop pit in the building to the right. The engine will now sit balanced on six wheels until recalled to be united with the repaired wheel set. An unidentified A4 lurks in the background, also, it appears, waiting repair.** *Courtesy David Dunn*

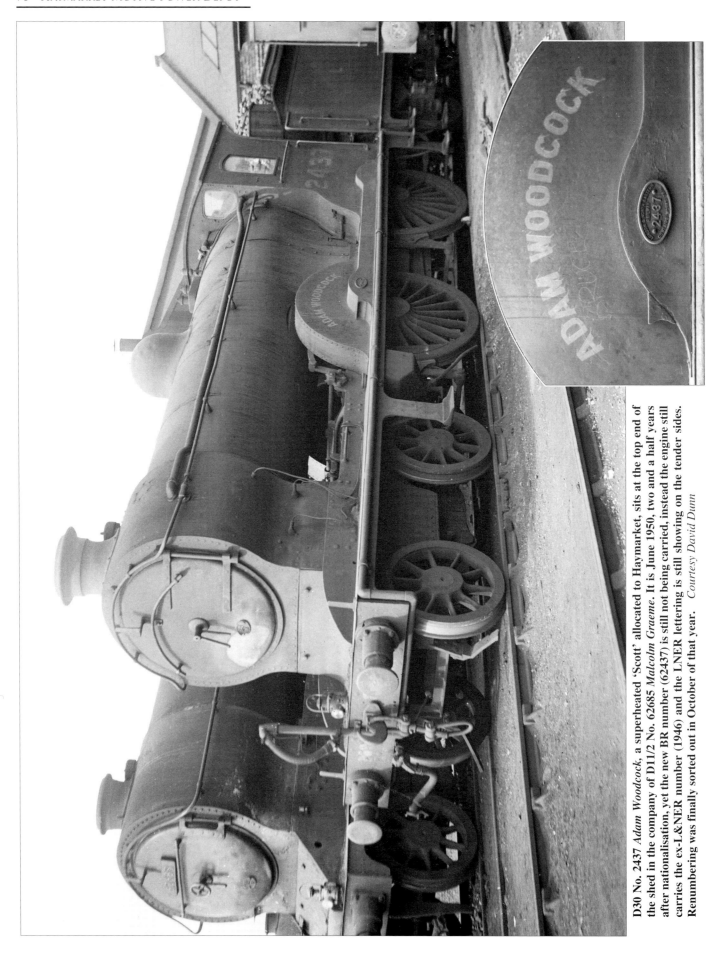

D30 No. 2437 *Adam Woodcock*, a superheated 'Scott' allocated to Haymarket, sits at the top end of the shed in the company of D11/2 No. 62685 *Malcolm Graeme*. It is June 1950, two and a half years after nationalisation, yet the new BR number (62437) is still not being carried, instead the engine still carries the ex-L&NER number (1946) and the LNER lettering is still showing on the tender sides. Renumbering was finally sorted out in October of that year. *Courtesy David Dunn*

13 THE NBR AND NER 4-4-2 ATLANTICS

NBR CLASS 'H' (L&NER C10 AND C11) 4-4-2 ATLANTICS

Designed by Reid and classed as 'H', the company placed an initial order for fourteen locomotives with the North British Locomotive Company. These were constructed at their Hyde Park works in 1906, the first emerging to traffic in the July and the remainder quickly following up to the end of August that same year. As built, they had saturated boilers and were numbered 868–881. These engines were to be classified C10 by the L&NER.

A further six engines to the same design were built by R. Stephenson & Co. and entered service the following year, numbered 901 to 906, also later classified C10.

At first the engines were not wholly popular with drivers, nor indeed were they with their firemen, given their great appetite for coal; as originally built they were reputed to be shy steaming engines. These saturated engines could worry coal supplies to some effect, and it is on record that on an Edinburgh–Glasgow–Edinburgh round trip of some 104 miles, shed to shed, some 4½ tons of coal could be consumed, which works out at about 87 lbs per mile, and this in a firebox with a grate area of only 28 square feet. This heavy coal consumption was caused in large part by the fact that there were only six cut-off positions either side of mid-gear on the Atlantic's lever reverse (74%, 67%, 60%, 52%, 44% and 34%), and the two positions located either side of mid-gear (the shortest cut-off, 34%) were not normally used because of the risk of heating problems with the link motion. Normal running was conducted with the lever in either 52% or 44%. Heavy coal consumption was thus inevitable.

In the 1908 trials between Carlisle and Preston, No. 881 *Borderer* had returned coal consumption figures of around 70 lbs per mile. Like the Gresley P2s which were to follow at a much later date, they gained the reputation of being 'miners' friends', but also like the P2s they could lift big trains without any trace of slipping. Unlike the P2s, however, the Civil Engineer of the NBR – at that time James Bell – tried to have them removed from traffic, alleging that they were causing serious damage to the track, and it was some time before the dust settled and they were finally accepted. The truth is that, despite Bell's invective against the engines, in the early days of the Atlantics the NBR track was not in a good state of repair.

It is entirely fair to say that the NBR Atlantics had a much-troubled gestation period. In an attempt to obtain unbiased professional opinion, and to get to the root causes for the trials and tribulations being experienced in their day-to-day running, both H.A. Ivatt from the Great Northern Railway (GNR) and, sometime later, Vincent Raven of the NER were requested by the NBR Board to comment on the design and operation of the Atlantics. Strangely enough, in late 1907 the controversy settled just as quickly as it blew up, without major modifications being put in hand – other than modifications to the drawbar between engine and tender – and all complaints about track damage just ceased. The Atlantics had finally been accepted and Reid was vindicated.

They could haul prodigious loads and eventually settled down to a long and useful existence, popular with their drivers if still not exactly so by their firemen. Between 1915 and 1921 all had been rebuilt with superheated boilers. In 1921 a further two new Atlantics, Nos 509 *Duke Of Rothesay* and 510 *The Lord Provost*, emerged from Hyde Park works to augment the existing fleet, both later being classified as C11 – as were the six built by Stephenson after they had been rebuilt with superheated boilers and wider cabs. No. 509 went to Dundee and No. 510 went to St. Margaret's, the latter working two trips from Edinburgh to Perth and return every day.

McKillop had little good to say about the Atlantics. Of the saturated engines he declared that they simply would not steam and they were exceptionally rough riding. John Bartholomew, Chief Motive Power Inspector, Scottish Region up to 1950, was an ex-Haymarket fireman and driver who had much experience in both roles with the Atlantics. He declared that (of a saturated Atlantic) '*one never drove or fired an Atlantic, one fought them.*' Nevertheless, many other men held the Atlantics in high regard and performed outstanding work with them. Indeed, the late John Thomas, that great and knowledgeable NBR historian, stated that their crews loved them. If they were heavy on coal, the firemen made no fuss, for to be a driver or fireman on the Atlantics meant you were somebody. Even to set foot on an Atlantic was a privilege accorded to only a lucky few. The NBR Atlantics were prodigious hill climbers and capable of taking big trains over the heavy NBR main lines, but also had a good turn of speed on the more favourable stretches of track.

The original saturated engines of the class had tenders which did not have coal cages across the front of the tender; thus coaling was essentially a time-consuming art, requiring the preparation fireman to build up a solid wall of selected large lumps of coal (known, certainly at Haymarket, as 'setters') at the front and all around the tender sides rising to cab height, behind which the maximum load of coal, and indeed over-coaling, of around 10 to 12 tons could then be safely contained and trimmed so that it could pass through low bridges and tunnels without being swept off. This excessive coaling was required as a consequence of obtuseness on the part of the Caledonian Railway who owned Aberdeen Ferryhill shed, by denying the NBR engines the facility to take coal there, despite the fact that the NBR paid rent for their all engines using Ferryhill. Thus the engines had to be coaled for an out-and-home trip of 270 miles, and there is little doubt that coal rails or not, the over-coaling was recognised by Reid to be inherently dangerous, particularly for persons working on the track and members of the public standing on platforms. Various modifications, including increasing the number of side rails and providing front cages on the tenders, were put in hand in an attempt to mitigate the risk of falling coal. The front cages came about as a result of the accident at Queensferry Junction in 1917 (see pages 192–3). McKillop gives a graphic description of this particular task of coaling an NBR Atlantic at Haymarket.

When it comes to addressing the issue of shed allocation, and specifically at Haymarket, contemporary accounts vary significantly and the exercise is somewhat of a 'black hole' since even some reliable sources contradict themselves. The works of authority are John Thomas's book, *The North British Atlantic*, Willie Yeadon's *Vol. 40* of his *Register* and McKillop's *Enginemen Elite*. The latter states quite categorically that Haymarket had an allocation of four Atlantics straight from works in 1906. Both Yeadon, in his introduction to *Vol. 40*, and Thomas suggest that at first all Edinburgh-based Atlantics were allocated to St. Margaret's shed, but that in 1908, following the move made by the NER to Haymarket a few years before, four of the St. Margaret's engines, with their crews and cleaners, were moved to Haymarket where the facilities were much more modern and space was not so much at a premium. However, the same Yeadon *Register* then indicates that the original Haymarket allocation consisted of five Atlantics entering traffic straight from works in August 1906 and made up as follows:

- 873 (9873) *St. Mungo* 8/06 until 8/23
   (Thomas does not include No. 873)
- 874 (9874) *Dunedin* 8/06 until withdrawn 1933
- 875 (9875) *Midlothian* 8/06 until 10/36
- 876 (9876) *Waverley* 8/06 until 3/23
- 877 (9877) *Liddesdale* 8/06 until 4/27.

Since it is a confirmed fact that four engines with their crews and cleaners were transferred from St. Margaret's in 1908, it is probable, given that Haymarket never, at any time, had nine Atlantics on the books, that McKillop and Yeadon were mistaken with dates. Possibly they included the four transferred from St. Margaret's in 1908 in with the two Atlantics actually allocated, but the Yeadon *Register* certainly does not reflect this 1908 transfer. R.D. Stephen, another noted and respected enthusiast of the time, states that the Haymarket allocation at the grouping was five engines and Yeadon echoes this fact. However, further research has thrown up the following information regarding the allocation of NBR Atlantics to St. Margaret's in 1907, with their allocated drivers:

- 874 *Dunedin* Driver G. Bell
- 875 *Midlothian* Driver R. Tait
- 877 *Liddesdale* Driver R. Ellis
- 878 *Hazeldean* Driver John Burns
- 879 *Abbotsford* Driver Jas. Carlisle.

This information quite possibly reflects the reality of the situation, since it is known that Driver John Ellis was latterly a driver at Haymarket and thus the four Atlantics which were transferred to Haymarket in 1908 were likely to have been:

- 874 *Dunedin*
- 875 *Midlothian*
- 877 *Liddesdale*
- 878 *Hazeldean*.

With these engines also came their allocated workings which were the heavy Edinburgh/Aberdeen turns.

With Haymarket already having No. 873 *Saint Mungo* and No. 876 *Waverley* allocated from new, this makes six engines, and not the five engines referred to by all correspondents. The five Atlantics at Haymarket at the grouping were (according to R.D. Stephen):

- 874 *Dunedin*
- 875 *Midlothian*
- 877 *Liddesdale*
- 878 *Hazeldean*
- 510 *The Lord Provost.*

This fits, since, at the grouping, from Yeadon's *Register* it appears that Haymarket transferred two of the original allocation out, Nos 873 *St Mungo* and 876 *Waverley*, receiving in return No. 878 *Hazeldean* and No. 510 *The Lord Provost*, both from St. Margaret's. Haymarket was also to receive two further Atlantics, No. 904 *Holyrood* (1/30), and No. 880 *Tweeddale* (5/33) for a short period of time. John Thomas, on the other hand, inferred that Nos 873, 904 and 510 remained St. Margaret's engines for the whole of their working lives.

However, other Atlantics then enter the scene. Probably the most complicated situation surrounds engine No. 901 (9901) *St. Johnstoun* which was to see many transfers during its life and is first shown as being allocated to Haymarket in 3/29 (this is corroborated by both Thomas and Yeadon), thereafter being shuttled back and forth with some regularity. Confusion reigns!

The Haymarket Atlantics each had two cleaners allocated to clean the complete engine in a twelve-hour shift. The tenders were attended to by the general cleaning squad. These five locomotives and their crews initially worked three daily Edinburgh to Aberdeen and return diagrams, each engine and crew having one day off every week, until the eight-hour day was introduced – after which engine changing at Dundee became the order of the day, with further switch transfers being made to give Dundee Tay Bridge an allocation of Atlantics. Even after 1919, however, two sets of Haymarket men, with their Atlantics, Nos 874 and 876, continued to work one stopping passenger train on an alternating daily basis, right through to Aberdeen, where they then lodged. This was to be their sole working for a number of years thereafter, until an Aberdeen link was established with rotating shifts (see Chapter 7). The Atlantics were to hold sway on the Aberdeen services until the Gresley A1s were finally cleared for the route in 1930, after which their star was to decline somewhat, but they remained main line passenger engines until the end.

When the 'Northern Belle' was introduced in 1933, Haymarket Atlantics and men worked this heavy train right through to Aberdeen, and this despite the presence of the Gresley Pacifics at the shed.

The first engine to be withdrawn was No. 9874 *Dunedin* in 1933, and all engines had been withdrawn by 1937. At the eleventh hour, and under instruction from Gresley himself, No. 9875 *Midlothian* was scheduled for preservation – although dismantling had started at Cowlairs, the engine was promptly rebuilt by using parts from other Atlantics, and re-entered revenue-earning service in June 1938, being allocated to St. Margaret's from where it regularly worked on Edinburgh/Perth turns of duty. With the onset of hostilities in 1939, preservation was quietly forgotten and the engine was scrapped in November 1939. It is, in retrospect, a great tragedy that no member of this outstanding and impressive class of locomotives remains today.

As a matter of interest, after scrapping had commenced, a total of eleven Atlantic tenders were sent to Doncaster where they were converted into sludge carriers to serve the various water treatment plants located at the ex-GNR water troughs, and as such they survived well into BR days. Indeed, one tender underframe – that

Haymarket Atlantic No. 9901 *St. Johnstoun* **quite appropriately takes its ease at Perth shed, Perth having been known by that name at one time. Driver James Moffat and Fireman E. Wilson look from the cab – the former went on to become an assistant running foreman at Haymarket, while the latter took his place in No. 2 link and finally drove the Class 26 diesels.**   *Bill Lynn collection*

of tender No. 9879, from *Abbotsford* – still survives to this day and is now the focus of purchase by the SRPS.

One of the earliest Haymarket crews to regularly take hold of an Atlantic were Driver R. (Bob) Ellis (ex-St. Margaret's) and Fireman J. Bartholomew in 1908, but McKillop failed to identify their allocated engine, which was likely to have been No. 877 *Liddesdale*. This was the regular engine of Driver Ellis which, after he retired, was taken over by Driver J. Shaw. Fireman Bill Stevenson, who was to become another well-known Haymarket Top link driver in his own right, fired on No. 877 for a period of time. It was whilst this engine was working the southbound Aberdeen 'Fish' in 1911 that the train ran into and killed a number of permanent way men who were working in the 'four foot' without lookout protection at Kirkcaldy. It was as a result of this accident that the Board of Trade thereafter insisted that full lookout protection should be mandatory for all persons required to work on or near running lines.

No. 874 (9874) *Dunedin* was the engine at one time allocated to Haymarket driver John Sinclair, a highly-respected Christian gentleman and elder of his local church, who also happened to be the uncle of Jimmy Swan. Sinclair inherited No. 874 from Bob Tait, who had brought it across from St. Margaret's in 1908. Swan later fired to his uncle on No. 874, and was later to become a well-known and highly-esteemed Top link driver at Haymarket in his own right. By 1917 No. 874 was in the hands of a Driver Moffat, and he and his engine were involved in the head-on collision at Queensferry Junction in that year.

No. 878 *Hazeldean* was the engine allocated to Driver Tom Henderson at the grouping, another Haymarket star, who later took his place with this engine in the joint NER/NBR Newcastle link up to, and after, the first five Gresley A1s had been allocated to Haymarket. It was this same Tom Henderson, a fearless and hard runner, who once said of the NBR Atlantics, '*They won't coup [overturn], I've tried it!*' This comment was prompted by the considerable number of complaints which had been made about the fact that the original engines tended to roll alarmingly at speed. No. 878 was the NBR engine in the 1923 'Atlantic' trials referred to hereinafter. It was Henderson who worked the first Up-direction run of the non-stop 'Flying Scotsman' out of Waverley on 1st May 1928.

The allocation of NER engines and drivers to work the ECML joint express passenger trains between Edinburgh and Newcastle was the cause of much friction between the two companies, with the NBR drivers at Haymarket clamouring to claim a share of these workings. In the dying days pre-grouping, No. 510 *The Lord Provost* (by then renumbered 9510) took part in much-belated trials between Edinburgh and Newcastle, held in October 1922; these were run in order to determine whether the NBR Atlantics were capable of hauling trains in excess of 380 tons over the route, in a bid to break this NER monopoly of East Coast train workings. The redoubtable Driver Sam Bruce of St. Margaret's was at the controls on both runs. On the first run, on the 23rd October 1922, with 380 tons behind the tender and with three permanent way speed restrictions plus a 5½ minute stop for water at Alnemouth, Bruce ran into Newcastle only 4 minutes late. On the return journey there was a need to make a water stop at Berwick.

A stop for water was required on both days of the trial running, since the tender was not fitted with a water scoop, but the trials proved quite conclusively that the NBR Atlantics were more than capable of hauling the immense loads involved and running to time. The load provided for the second trial with No. 9510 consisted of thirteen East Coast Joint Stock (ECJS) bogie coaches plus the NER dynamometer coach, totalling 400 tons. In the course of one of the runs, No. 9510 lifted this train from a standstill at the Innerwick Up Home signal on the 1 in 210, then 1 in 96, rising gradients on Cockburnspath bank. During the two trials No. 9510 returned an average coal consumption of 72 lbs per mile. The outcome of these trials was that three NBR Atlantics, Nos 9510, 9877 and 9878, were fitted with tender water scoops and the Raven cab-signalling equipment; and two, Nos 9877 and 9878, driven by Driver J. Shaw and Driver T. Henderson, were thereafter integrated into the NER Newcastle link at Haymarket. No. 9510 was transferred from St. Margaret's and became the dedicated spare Newcastle engine, although her regular driver, the very same Sam Bruce who had partaken in the trials, declined the offer to transfer with his engine and remained at St. Margaret's.

No. 9878 also took part in the later 1923 trials held by the L&NER, between Newcastle and Edinburgh in competition with NER Class 'Z' Raven Atlantic No. 733 (Gateshead shed) and GNR Large Atlantic No. 1447. Whilst these tests were somewhat inconclusive, No. 9878 put up a very good performance. The driver was the aforesaid Tom Henderson, the fireman was Jock Todd, who was later to become an Edinburgh-based locomotive inspector. No. 9878 *Hazeldean* was driven at 52% cut-off throughout the trial period and proved to be the most economical of the three 'Atlantics' over all runs, recording the lowest coal consumption per drawbar-hp-hr.

The NER driver of No. 733 was Harry Potts of Gateshead shed (later to also become a locomotive inspector) who was also very much on home ground. On the final test run with the heavier special train weighing 403 tons, No. 733 returned a marginally better overall performance. The GNR Atlantic was, surprisingly, outclassed, being disadvantaged by the effects of having boiler fittings reduced in size to fit the restricted NBR loading gauge.

The story goes that, when No. 9878 was returning home after the completion of the trials, Henderson, annoyed at what he considered unwarranted interference by the officials-in-charge in his having been instructed to avoid blowing off and to work with a shorter cut-off during the trials, said to his firemen '*get these valves blowing mate, there's nae pounds per mile this time.*'

As a matter of some interest, it has been suggested in other publications that the NER had their own supply of coal for their engines in the 1923 trials which was of a far superior quality to that used by the NBR at Haymarket. Accordingly, it was alleged that the work of the NER Atlantic during the trial was in all probability skewed because of this, and had the same coal been used by all engines, the outcome might have been slightly different. This contention must be viewed with some suspicion. The performances of Nos 733 and 9878 were almost equal in all respects, and the 1922, 1923 and 1925 trials were conducted by Gresley himself. Indeed, John Thomas records in his book *The North British Railway, Vol. 2*, that in the 1922 trials, Scottish coal from Fordel-mains, Glencraig and Greenrigg collieries was supplied in equal amounts to No. 9510's tender and that in the later 1925 trials, where No. 878 again took part, the coal supplied to all participating engines was English coal from Maria E. Wylam and Addison collieries. It is therefore most unlikely that the locomotives taking part in the 1923 trials were each supplied with different coal.

THE NER CLASS 'Z' (L&NER C7) ATLANTICS

The NER Class 'Z' Atlantics were constructed to the design of the then new CME, Vincent Raven, who, following on from the success of the Worsdell Class 'V' two-cylinder Atlantics, took the opportunity to introduce a new, three-cylinder version. Fifty locomotives of this class were constructed between 1911 and 1918, the first twenty emerging from the North British Locomotive Company's works in Glasgow, numbered 706, 709, 710, 714, 716–721, 722, 727, 728, 729 and 732–737. Ten were saturated and the last ten were superheated.

The next ten engines, built in Darlington works, were numbered 2163–2172. The remaining twenty engines were also constructed at Darlington, numbered 2193–2212.

Up to the grouping, four NER Atlantics of Class 'Z' (C7) were allocated to Haymarket from new, specifically to work Edinburgh–Newcastle East Coast trains with NER train-crews who were also allocated to this depot. The booked working for the engines involved only two passenger trains to Newcastle and return daily, with an unbalanced 'Mondays Only' turn; the spare engine capacity was available for any special workings arising. In respect of NER locomotive matters, Haymarket was at that time little more than a sub-shed of Gateshead, and remained so up until 1923. In that year one C7 was transferred away; the NBR Atlantics with their own crews were integrated into the former NER Newcastle link and began to work the East Coast Joint express passenger trains through to Newcastle. After this link took delivery of the first A1 Pacifics in 1924, the remaining three NER Atlantics began to be used more widely across the ex-NBR territory by Haymarket crews; all locomotive matters thereafter fell very much under the single control of Haymarket shed. The C7s were, however, notoriously weak on the banks and even their regular NER crews used to say that '*a "Z" could smell a bank long before she came to it.*' Accordingly, Cockburnspath to Grantshouse in the Up direction and St. Margaret's to Waverley in the Down direction, quite frequently proved to be their nemesis when working alone on a heavy train.

By the Second World War, Haymarket was left with just one example of the C7 class, No. 2193.

The Haymarket-allocated engines were:

- 714   7/11 until 3/39 (transferred to St. Margaret's)
- 2193   12/14 until 4/43 (transferred to St. Margaret's)
- 2194   12/14 until 3/39 (transferred to Gateshead)
- 2204   6/15 until 3/23 (transferred to Gateshead).

No. 2205, although not allocated to Haymarket, was a Tweedmouth-based engine that was the spare engine for Haymarket should any of the regulars be out of service for any reason. The Haymarket engines and No. 2205 were, for some unrecorded reason, fitted with bell-shaped whistles instead of the normal NER organ whistle.

After the grouping, Haymarket drivers, and in particular the Senior Spare drivers, had a wide exposure to the ex-NER Classes C6 and C7 locomotives, particularly over the ECML, and they continued to be used on relief trains and general passenger working with great success. However, as previously recorded, the right-hand driving position did not exactly meet with the approval of the Haymarket drivers. In addition, the engines were particularly difficult to work on during both disposal and preparation duties – the C7s in particularly. Again, McKillop made it quite clear in his writings that he had little time for the NER Atlantics.

14 THE GNR 4-4-0 LOCOMOTIVES

In 1911 Henry Ivatt, CME of the GNR, had his final design of 4-4-0 locomotives, totalling fifteen in all, constructed at Doncaster. These were classed as '1321's, along with the seventy locomotives constructed between 1898 and 1909. Numbered 51–65, the fifteen engines were fitted with Schmidt superheaters from new and were also fitted with piston valves. They had 6-foot 7-inch driving wheels and were fitted with inside Stephenson valve gear.

At the grouping in 1923, the L&NER classified these final fifteen engines as D1s. By 1925 the L&NER (GN Section) no longer had any use for these engines, and the whole class were transferred to the Scottish Area, eleven in total being allocated to Haymarket shed. This transfer required that they were modified with cut-down fittings to meet the NBR loading gauge. On being transferred they displaced a variety of ex-NBR 4-4-0s, including the whole D31 class.

They were never in any way very popular with the ex-NBR drivers and were nicknamed 'Ponies' early on. They were found to be very rough, with uncomfortable and draughty cabs, they had the universally disliked right-hand driving position, and they suffered from many mechanical and steaming problems. This gave rise to poor utilisation and erratic performance, and they were all mostly confined to either secondary passenger services or piloting duties. The Fife allocation of these engines was used primarily on Engineer ballast train working.

Nevertheless, when in service some exceptional performances were recorded by the Haymarket allocation. R.D. Stephen is on record as stating that the 'Ponies' did some able work when piloting on the Aberdeen road. Similarly, C.J. Allan recorded some quite outstanding runs on both the East Coast and the Aberdeen roads with Haymarket men in charge of both train engine and a 'Pony' as pilot. But McKillop condemned the engines out of hand – although, quite uncharacteristically, he then somewhat contradicted himself by describing a southbound trip on a heavy Aberdeen to Edinburgh express of 430 tons, which was worked by an NBR Atlantic with a D1 as a pilot. The Atlantic (not identified) had the misfortune to throw a motion bar at Burntisland and the crew of the 'Pony' got stuck-in to no little effect; this small pilot engine hauled the train and pushed the incapacitated Atlantic single-handedly up the 1 in 70 gradient from Inverkeithing to the Forth Bridge and on safely to its destination in Edinburgh. The driver of the 'Pony' was none-other than McKillop's pal, Jimmy Swan, then a Spare link driver. Despite this exceptional piece of work, McKillop considered that their efforts at piloting were '*more a hindrance than a help on the various roads where their efforts in assisting passenger trains proved futile.*'

Strangely – although in retrospect, perhaps not – McKillop got himself embroiled in a three-way exchange of views in the then *Trains Illustrated*, a publication for which he wrote articles on occasions; his disagreements were with no less a personage than

Ex-GNR Class D1 No. 3063 stands on the original 50-foot turntable whilst her crew struggle to turn her, sheer brute strength being the order of the day. An NBR Atlantic stands at the shed in the left background whilst the old sand kiln is clearly seen in the right background. The date is pre-1930. *Bill Lynn collection*

Ex-GNR Class D1 No. 3051 stands adjacent to the coal stack just outside the top end of the shed. Largely unpopular and unloved during their stay at Haymarket, nevertheless these engines did some sterling work piloting heavy express trains on both the Edinburgh to Aberdeen route and also on the ECML to Newcastle. *Bill Lynn collection*

C.J.A. himself and another heavyweight, R.H.N. Hardy (writing as 'Balmore'). C.J.A. recounted some remarkable work carried out by the D1s. 'Balmore' similarly recalled good work by the engines, but McKillop, unrepentant to the last, rubbished these views, declaring of the engines, *'they were useless.'*

Seven engines were returned to the Southern Area between 1930 and 1932, and were initially stored at Doncaster. Withdrawals commenced in 1946, with a total of seven lasting into BR days and two Scottish engines being renumbered in the BR 60000 classification. The final engine to be withdrawn was No. 62209 from Stirling shed in 1950.

Haymarket had the following allocation:

• 3051 (2202)	1/25 until 3/43
• 3053 (2204)	12/26 until 12/30
• 3054 (2205)	5/27 until 9/41
• 3055 (2206)	9/25 until 12/28
• 3057 (2208)	4/34 until 3/36
• 3058 (2209)	6/45 until 6/46
• 3060 (2211)	6/25 until 4/29
• 3061 (2212)	9/25 until 12/33
• 3063 (2214)	7/25 until 8/37
• 3064 (2215)	6/25 until 11/42
• 3065 (2216)	6/25 until 11/36
	5/38 until 1/42.

A D11/2, No. 62691 *Laird of Balmawhapple* of Haymarket shed, in full cry as she roars past the shed at the head of a stopping passenger train on the Down North Main line. *Courtesy David Dunn*

15   THE L&NER 4-4-0 LOCOMOTIVES

CLASS D11/2: THE SCOTTISH 'DIRECTORS'

After the grouping in 1923, the newly established L&NER required additional 4-4-0 type locomotives in the Scottish Area to supplement the already extremely capable, but ageing, ex-NBR locomotives described earlier – and the need was immediate. Consequently, Gresley recommended new engines based upon the design of the Great Central's Class D11 'Directors' – but suitably modified to meet the more restrictive loading gauge applying north of the border – and that the construction should be undertaken by two independent engineering contractors. Boiler fittings were reduced in height, with consequential changes to the fine looks that the 'Directors' enjoyed. The one modification which was not carried out was a change-over of the driving position from the right-hand side of the cab to the left, as favoured by the NBR drivers; this omission became a continuing source of irritation to the Scottish drivers, despite the fact they had been presented with otherwise extremely competent engines.

The builders chosen in December 1923 were Armstrong Whitworth & Co. of Newcastle and Kitsons & Co. of Leeds, with each contracted to build and supply twelve engines. The twenty-four engines, classed as D11/2, were all delivered to traffic by November 1924, numbered 6378 to 6401. Although they were delivered with deep valances over the coupled wheels, these valances were quickly removed during 1925/26.

All of the engines carried names from the Waverley novels, just like the earlier 'Scotts', and were capable of doing all and any work allocated, from express passenger working to fitted freights. They did some excellent work on the Edinburgh/Glasgow and Edinburgh/Aberdeen lines, displacing the 'Scotts' on the latter route. Apart from the 'wrong' driving position, they were well-liked by both drivers and firemen. For a while, individual locomotives were allocated to specific drivers on the Glasgow and Aberdeen workings.

Up until the arrival of the A1 Pacifics, the Haymarket Class D11/2 engines also took over the heavy 07.35 Edinburgh to Aberdeen passenger working, for so long the preserve of the Atlantics, generally accompanied by a D49 or D1 as a pilot engine. By the mid-to-late 1950s, however, the Haymarket-allocated engines were relegated to ECS workings in the main, but they did enjoy some main line

Haymarket D11/2 No. 62685 *Malcolm Graeme* **stands on the ash pits at the top end of the shed in 1955, waiting to have the fire cleaned. The front end of the framing reveals evidence of a 'rough shunt' at some earlier time. In the right background, an unidentified B1 is receiving attention from the firedroppers and is in the process of having its smokebox cleaned, a most unpleasant task indeed.** *Courtesy David Anderson*

forays during the summer months when they were pressed back into service on passenger workings.

McKillop believed that the free-running capabilities of the 'Directors' were adversely affected when the sight feed displacement lubricators were replaced by mechanical lubricators, but, be that as it may, they were undoubtedly excellent engines in their own right and did much good work in the passenger links.

During the period of BR ownership many of them spent long spells in temporary storage, being taken back into service as demand required. The first withdrawals came in 1958, and by 1962 the final engine of the class had been withdrawn.

Those allocated to Haymarket over the years were:

- 6381 (2674) (62674) *Flora Mcivor*   8/24 until 8/43
- 6383 (2675) (62675) *Colonel Gardiner*   8/24 until 8/43
- 6383 (2676) (62676) *Jonathan Oldbuck*   8/24 until 8/43
- 6384 (2677) (62677) *Edie Ochiltree*   9/24 until 4/57
- 6385 (2678) (62678) *Luckie Mucklebackit*   9/24 until 4/57
- 6386 (2679) (62679) *Lord Glenallan*   12/40 until 4/57
- 6390 (2683) (62683) *Hobbie Elliot*   4/43 until 9/58
- 6391 (2684) (62684) *Wizard of the Moor*   4/43 until 8/45
- 6392 (2685) (62685) *Malcolm Graeme*   4/43 until 1/62
- 6397 (2690) (62690) *Lady of the Lake*   /34 until 7/61
- 6398 (2691) (62691) *Laird of Balmawhapple*
                                              4/43 until 11/61
- 6399 (2692) (62692) *Allan Bane*   4/43 until 11/59
- 6400 (2693) (62693) *Roderick Dhu*   12/27 until 11/61
- 6401 (2694) (62694) *James Fitzjames*   11/24 until 11/59

CLASS D49: THE 'SHIRES'

An order was placed with Darlington works in 1926 for a total of twenty-eight new engines only, the construction of the tenders being allocated to Doncaster works. Of the total class, the engines fell into three completely separate designs (Parts 1, 2 and 3).

The Class D49/1 numbered twenty, and these were designed with piston valves driven by Walschaerts valve gear. The Class D49/3 were six in total, and were fitted with Lentz poppet valves and oscillating cams also driven by Walschaerts valve gear. The final two of the initial build, classed as D49/2, had Lentz poppet valves fitted, which were rotary-cam operated.

The Class D49/1s were all given shire county names, as were five of the further 1928 build of eight. The remaining three carried the names of the northern counties of Westmorland, Cumberland and Northumberland.

In 1932 there was a further build of Class D49/2 engines, and these were all named after famous English hunts. In 1933 another order was placed for a further twenty-five 'Hunts'.

As a class they numbered seventy-six in total. Over the intervening years they were the subject of many changes, often on an individual basis, and the tenders allocated varied widely in origin and fitments.

The Haymarket allocation were to be common-user engines from the outset, working over all routes covered by 64B; these workings ranged from express passenger trains over the East Coast to and from Newcastle, to fast freight workings on the Aberdeen road. They were also used as pilots on the heavy East Coast expresses and did sterling work in their time. Latterly they were largely confined

Haymarket D49 No. 62719 *Peebles-shire* **stands forlornly at the top end of the shed, in the company of one of the two allocated J36s, while the corridor tender of an unidentified Haymarket A4 lurks in the right background.** *Courtesy David Dunn*

to local passenger workings and empty stock movements, suitable work becoming more difficult to find as the DMUs took over many of the passenger train services. They were generally economical machines whilst working – but, strangely, in the L&NER coal and oil consumption tables for 1937 the Scottish D49s were recorded as having an annual average coal consumption of 60.7 lbs per mile. This appears excessive, but the figure must be taken in the context of the statistics not taking the weight of the trains being hauled into consideration. The figures would have been more meaningful had they been based on ton-miles.

Many fine runs behind D49s have been reported upon over the years, but one run of some significance is well worthwhile mentioning here as testament to the capacity of a 'Shire' for sheer hard work. The date was the Thursday before Easter, Maundy Thursday, in 1937, with Norman McKillop, at that time a Senior Spare driver at Haymarket, and his fireman, J. Sellars, who by the author's time at 64B was a driver in his own right in No. 3 link. The engine was No. 249 (later No. 62713) *Aberdeenshire*, on the second portion of the 13.20 King's Cross to Edinburgh Waverley from Newcastle. Now, owing to a mix-up at Newcastle Central, the Pacific for the regular train went out with the lighter of the two portions, leaving the 'Shire' to cope with thirteen coaches, all heavily laden, weighing 412 tons tare/435 tons gross. Booked stops were made at Alnemouth and Berwick-upon-Tweed, and two conditional stops were also taken up at Dunbar and Drem. Despite their best efforts with a train way above the load for a D49, a few minutes were lost in running and the running time from Newcastle to Edinburgh excluding station stops was 141½ minutes. Remarkably, the engine maintained a speed of 46½ mph up the 5-mile, 1 in 200 gradient from Reston to Grantshouse. This was an exceedingly strenuous task for a D49, and speaks volumes about McKillop's calibre as a driver. Both C.J. Allen and O.S. Nock were travelling on the train and both timed the run,

quite independently, with C.J.A. complaining about 'slow running', when, in fact, adverse distant signals contributed to some of the lost time. The shortcomings of timing from the cushions!

Strangely, No. 249 was not a Haymarket locomotive but was allocated to Dundee Tay Bridge from new until 1950; it had, no doubt, been 'borrowed' for the day.

The last of the class, 62712 *Morayshire*, was withdrawn on 3rd July 1961, but happily it has been preserved and is regularly to be seen in steam on the Scottish Railway Preservation Society's Bo'ness and Birkhill Railway.

The Haymarket allocation at various times over the years was:

Class D49/1
- 253 (2702) (62702) *Oxfordshire*   6/43 until 11/47
- 264 (2704) (62704) *Stirlingshire*   12/27 until 10/45
- 265 (2705) (62705) *Lanarkshire*   3/43 until 11/59
- 266 (2706) (62706) *Forfarshire*   1/40 until 4/57
- 270 (2708) (62708) *Argyllshire*   1/28 until 1/35
- 277 (2709) (62709) *Berwickshire*   3/43 until 1/60
- 281 (2711) (62711) *Dumbartonshire*   3/43 until 3/49
- 246 (2712) (62712) *Morayshire*   3/44 until 3/48
- 306 (2715) (62715) *Roxburghshire*   3/43 until 11/47
- 309 (2717) (62717) *Banffshire*   2/31 until 12/43
- 311 (2719) (62719) *Peebles-shire*   3/43 until 11/59
- 320 (2721) (62721) *Warwickshire*   6/43 until 3/48
- 2754 (62754)   *Rutlandshire*   7/29 until 12/33
- 2758 (62758)   *Northumberland*   8/43 until 1/58
- 2759 (62759)   *Cumberland*   8/43 until 12/46
- 1760 (62760)   *Westmorland*   8/43 until 12/46
Class D49/2
- 269 (2743) (62743) *The Cleveland*   1/51 until 5/60
- 365 (2768) (62768) *The Morpeth*   11/42 until 1/43.

The longest serving D49/2 allocated to Haymarket, No. 62743 *The Cleveland* stands at the top end of the shed in the company of an unidentified D49/1. *Courtesy David Dunn*

Haymarket A3 No. 60037 *Hyperion*, wearing the BR blue livery and in immaculate condition, heads the 12.00 noon 'Queen of Scots' Pullman train as it sets out on its journey from Edinburgh to London. The train started from Glasgow Queen Street at 11.00 and No. 60037 has taken over at Waverley. The train is running past the entrance to Craigentinny carriage sidings with the engine well linked up. A magnificent sight!   *Bill Brown collection*

16 L&NER PACIFICS: THE GRESLEY A1S AND A3S

Haymarket received its first allocation of Gresley A1 Pacifics in 1924, from the early batch constructed by the North British Locomotive Company in Glasgow. Thus was the soon-to-be-familiar, and altogether glorious, sound of the syncopated inequality in the beats of the Gresley three-cylinder locomotives – caused by the irregular crank spacings (127°, 113° and 120°) – and the distinctive 'ring' of the lightweight nickel alloy forged side rods and motion, the 'Gresley knock', first introduced to Scotland.

The allocation numbered five in total:

- 2563 *William Whitelaw*[1]   delivered new 7/24
- 2564 *Knight of the Thistle*[2]   delivered new 7/24
- 2565 *Merry Hampton*   delivered new 7/24
- 2566 *Ladas*   delivered new 7/24
- 2567 *Sir Visto*   delivered new 8/24.

These five Pacifics, after a period of running-in on the E&GR main line, quickly replaced the ex-NBR and ex-NER Atlantics on the Newcastle workings. They were immediately allocated, on a 'one engine–one man' basis, to the Haymarket Newcastle link:

- 2563   Driver Tom Henderson (ex NBR)
- 2564   Driver A. Davidson (ex NER)
- 2565   Driver T. Smith (ex NER)
- 2566   Driver J. Shaw (ex NBR)
- 2567   Driver Tom Roper (ex NER).

Driver R. Shedden took over the running of No. 2566 when Shaw retired.

The engines were thus single-shifted, and the four regular Newcastle workings were:

13.15 Edinburgh to Newcastle and corresponding return service
13.50 Edinburgh to Newcastle and corresponding return service
19.45 Edinburgh to Newcastle and corresponding return service
23.05 Edinburgh to Newcastle and corresponding return service.

In order to introduce a day shift turn, and also a 'lighter' turn of duty, the link also worked the 07.35 Edinburgh to Glasgow and return.

The Scottish Area A1s did not at first perform well in terms of annual coal consumption, the 1937 figures showing an average consumption of 71.75 lbs per mile. By 1938 this was up to 73.3 lbs per mile and by 1939 had increased to 76.01 lbs per mile. As stated in Chapter 13, this figure would have been more meaningful if it had been based on ton-miles run and not train miles run.

The A1s were initially confined to the Newcastle and Glasgow routes, but in March 1927, No. 2563 *William Whitelaw*, still with the original 180 psi boiler, made a test run to Carlisle and back with a 400-ton train, with Driver D. Smith and Fireman A. Moffatt of Carlisle Canal in charge. This trial run was less than successful owing to poor coal and engine mismanagement by the Carlisle Canal crew, with a coal consumption figure of 89.6 lbs per mile being returned; but a further trial was arranged for the 26th February 1928 with No. 2580 *Shotover* (by this time newly rebuilt to A3) and with the same Canal crew in charge. This trial was successful, with the coal consumption having been reduced to around 58 lbs per mile, and was to lead to an eventual allocation of four A3s at Carlisle Canal shed.

In 1928, following the success of non-stop workings between Newcastle and London King's Cross, it was decided that the summer 10.00 Edinburgh to London King's Cross should be run non-stop and that the train should be worked by crews from Gateshead and King's Cross depots. However, following pressure by Sir Ralph Wedgewood, the then Chief General Manager, it was agreed to involve Haymarket crews in this working as well. This led to some convoluted diagrams, particularly for the Gateshead crews. For this working, Haymarket was to receive three North-Eastern Area engines and give up three of its own allocation in return. This led to a most confusing transfer arrangement, with Gateshead and the North-Eastern Area losing out all round.

A.C. Stamer, Assistant CME, had selected three North-Eastern Area engines for the non-stop working on 5th April 1928, Nos 2573 *Harvester*, 2580 *Shotover* and 2569 *Gladiateur*, all A3s and by now fitted with corridor tenders. This reflected the original plan to use only Gateshead and King's Cross crews and engines on the non-stop working. But after it was determined that Haymarket crews should also share in the work, it was decided that Haymarket locomotives should be used instead, and to facilitate this arrangement the three Gateshead engines were to be transferred to Haymarket, complete with corridor tenders, in exchange for three Haymarket A1s.

Nos 2573 and 2580 from the North-Eastern Area were eventually sent north, arriving at Haymarket by late April, but Gateshead had decided to hold on to No. 2569 as long as possible, until, finally, Gresley himself had to intervene and instruct Gateshead that the transfer should take place. No. 2565 *Merry Hampton* was sent south in exchange. However, No. 2569 in going north, ran hot *en-route* and had to be worked back to Gateshead. No. 2565 was, as things turned out, to be the only Haymarket engine to go south, but was only to remain there until July of that same year when, proving of

---

1   No. 2563 was to be renamed *Tagalie* from 02/08/41 when the original name was allocated to A4 No. 4462, formerly *Great Snipe*.

2   No. 2564 was later renamed *Knight of Thistle* (12/34), allegedly following concerns expressed by the Lord Lyon's Office in Edinburgh, an allegation which was entirely refuted later. The renaming then made the name wrong for both the locomotive and the horse it was named after, and indeed *Knight of the Thistle* was correct and totally in order. The new name made no sense whatever, but it was never corrected. Indeed, *Knight of the Thistle* was merely an abbreviated title for '(Knight of) the Most Ancient and Noble Order of the Thistle'. Now, what a name plate that would have made! Incidentally, the GWR got it right in 1908 with 'Star' class No. 4012, without any ensuing controversy.

Haymarket A1 No. 2566 *Ladas* makes a smoky departure from Glasgow Queen Street with a stopping passenger train back to Edinburgh in February 1937.   *W. Lawson Kerr/Bill Brown collection*

little use in the North-Eastern Area being vacuum-fitted only, it was returned to Haymarket.

It was then decided by the powers-that-be to prepare two of the original Haymarket engines for non-stop working. Nos 2563 *William Whitelaw* and 2564 *Knight of the Thistle* were thus fitted with corridor tenders – the former receiving the tender from the erstwhile No. 2569, which was then returned to Gateshead *sans* corridor tender, and the latter receiving the tender from No. 2573 *Harvester*, which in turn was also then returned to Gateshead shed with a vacuum braked tender. The Haymarket non-stop engines for the 1928 inaugural workings were, therefore, Nos 2563, 2564 and 2580.

Gateshead, however, had lost two Westinghouse-fitted corridor tenders and inherited two vacuum-fitted ordinary tenders now paired with Nos 2569 and 2573. Since Gateshead had diagrams requiring Westinghouse brake fitted engines, to now have only one locomotive (No. 2565) which was vacuum-fitted, plus two vacuum-only tenders, left a big void in their available fleet of suitable engines and led to heated, and protracted, correspondence with Doncaster before the situation was finally resolved. A quite bizarre affair all round!

In Scotland attention now turned to the Aberdeen road, over which loading problems had long required the use of double heading – problems which had been exacerbated by the introduction of the sleeping car services. In 1928 a trial run was made with No. 2573 *Harvester*, supplied by Gateshead for the purpose, purely for clearance trials, but it was not until 1930, after the LM&S had

completed bridge-strengthening north of Montrose, that the full route was cleared for the Pacifics and three were transferred from Haymarket to Dundee Tay Bridge shed, the numbers being 2565 *Merry Hampton*, 2566 *Ladas* and 2567 *Sir Visto*. This transfer was made possible by the fact that in 1930 Haymarket received a further allocation of three of the new A3s then being put into traffic from Doncaster:

- 2795 *Call Boy*
- 2796 *Spearmint*
- 2797 *Cicero*.

No. 2795 *Call Boy* and No. 2796 *Spearmint* became regular performers, and indeed real stars, on the summer non-stop workings between Edinburgh and London King's Cross, and were kept in true Haymarket condition for this working. However, quite inexplicably, No. 2797 *Cicero* never participated in this working although it was an entirely competent member of the class.

In 1934/35 Haymarket received an allocation from the final batch of nine A3s built at Doncaster, namely:

- 2500 *Windsor Lad*   delivered 7/34
- 2502 *Hyperion*   delivered 7/34
- 2505 *Cameronian*   delivered 10/34
- 2506 *Salmon Trout*   delivered 12/34
- 2508 *Brown Jack*   delivered 2/35.

On a fine spring afternoon in 1958, A3 No. 60098 *Spion Kop* takes water at Leuchars Junction whilst working an Edinburgh to Aberdeen express. Although Leuchars was a scheduled stop for almost all express passenger services, the taking of water was most unusual. It is probable, however, that, with the platform starting signal remaining obdurately at danger, some delay for whatever reason is being incurred and, with the engine most likely working through to Aberdeen, the crew have decided to fill up the tender here to save time at Dundee Tay Bridge where taking water was a painstakingly slow process.   *Courtesy W.S. Sellar*

By the spring of 1935, Haymarket had an allocation of A1/A3 Pacifics numbering ten in total.

A3 Pacific No. 2744 *Grand Parade* was transferred from King's Cross to Haymarket in July 1937 and later, in 1939, Haymarket received No. 2556 *Ormonde*, No. 2747 *Coronach* and No. 2598 *Blenheim* in exchange for three A4s.

No. 2744 was, however, to be damaged beyond repair in the December 1937 Castlecary collision and was removed to Doncaster. There, a new A3, sufficiently advanced in construction, replaced the original No. 2744 and, fitted with a new tender (No. 5331), entered

service in April 1938, being allocated to Doncaster shed. The story behind this replacement is interesting, since the construction of new A3s had ceased – with the final engine of the class, No. 2508 *Brown Jack*, being delivered to traffic in 1935. In all probability, when No. 2744 had been examined at Haymarket after recovery from the accident and decreed to be beyond economic repair, this information would have been passed to Doncaster where the construction of a replacement locomotive was immediately set in motion. This replacement would have used frames from the spare frame float, a spare boiler, and much from the pool of other

A3 No. 60041 *Salmon Trout* heads a Glasgow to Edinburgh express past Haymarket shed on 29th September 1957. Notice both the variety of, and the different liveries on, the coaches forming the train. In the left background is the familiar bulk of the cenotaph coaling plant and the big water tower alongside the shed proper. The train is running on the Up North line, diverted from the South lines owing to engineering work.   *Courtesy David Anderson*

spares – so that, when No. 2744 finally arrived in Doncaster in April 1938 the replacement was all but complete. The original 2744 was stripped and all reusable equipment recovered and put back into the general pool of spare parts. It was to be 1950 before No. 2744 returned to Haymarket.

In 1941, in keeping with the policy being adopted throughout the L&NER, all Scottish A1/A3 locomotives were transferred to Haymarket in order to concentrate the maintenance regime required by the Gresleys at a single location where the expertise and modern maintenance facilities existed. The A3s and A4s continued to be given general repairs at Doncaster but, although the railways were a reserved occupation, much of the available labour was 'directed' labour, where engineering staff from other disciplines were drafted in and had to be retrained in the specialised work of maintaining railway locomotives. This initiative was, in all likelihood, partly responsible for the (premature) withdrawal of the P2s as we shall see.

At the end of the Second World War, regular manning of A3s by No. 2 link drivers was quickly reverted to at Haymarket. The drivers in No. 2 link were allowed to choose an engine on the basis of two men to one locomotive, an exercise well described by then No. 2 link driver, Norman McKillop, in *Enginemen Elite*. However, McKillop also stated elsewhere that it was the regular manning of engines which led to the success of railway operation on the ECML in Scotland during the war. This is somewhat erroneous, since all engines at Haymarket, other than the A4s, eventually became 'common user' engines during the war years. Regular manning was not reintroduced until about 1946/47, when the shed LDC, on which McKillop sat as a staff representative, was involved in consultation regarding regular manning at the invitation of the then Shed Master of the day, Mr. G. Lund. It was to be under the latter's stewardship, and with No. 1 link sorted out with the A4s, that the aforesaid No. 2 link got the pick of the A3s, with McKillop opting, as is widely known, for No. 60100 *Spearmint*.

Whilst the A1/A3 engines had been mostly held in high regard by the crews at Haymarket, the drivers greatly disliked the right-hand driving position on the earliest of the A1s (as they had with the NER Atlantics and other NER engines over the years) and it became quite a point of dissension. Following trade union representation at the highest level in 1950, and as a direct consequence of the catastrophic derailment with No. 66 (2565) *Merry Hampton* (a right-hand drive engine) at Goswick in 1947, Nos 60064/65/66/67 (ex 2563–7) were transferred to the Eastern Region whilst, in exchange, Haymarket took possession of A3s Nos 60090 *Grande Parade*, 60096 *Papyrus*, 60097 *Humorist* and 60098 *Spion Kop*, all with left-hand drive. The remaining right-hand drive engines were, however, soon to be rebuilt with a left-hand drive position, since the spread in use of colour light signals, now firmly located on the left-hand side of the line in the direction of travel, demanded this conversion for ease of the drivers' signal sightlines.

Commencing on the 18th October 1954, week-long trials were initiated to test the feasibility of the No. 2 link A3s and their crews working the 10.05 Edinburgh Waverley–London St. Pancras 'Waverley' express, from Edinburgh right through to Leeds via Ais Gill, instead of changing engines at Carlisle Citadel station. Haymarket A3 No. 60087 *Blenheim* made the run on the first day, returning with the corresponding northbound service on the following day. The trials were successful but the Scottish Region motive power officers of the time were neither willing to upset the carefully planned and well tried regular manning arrangements then existing in No. 1 and 2 links at Haymarket, nor were they prepared to accept the costs for the considerable amount of additional route learning which would be involved (all Senior Spare men at Haymarket would have been required to add the 'Settle and Carlisle' route through to Leeds to their route card, and what route cards they would have been). The scheme was never followed through, although the Leeds A3s did, at a later time, work through to the

The last of the production A3s, No. 60043 *Brown Jack*, by now sporting a double chimney, restarts the 14.36 Edinburgh to Carlisle stopping passenger train away from Galashiels station in April 1960. *Courtesy W.S. Sellar*

Scottish Region – but to Glasgow St. Enoch, on the 'Thames Clyde' express. However, as an interesting aside, the engine allocated to work the 10.05 'Waverley', certainly through the 1950s, was always fully coaled-up on leaving Edinburgh in order to be able to work onwards through to Leeds from Carlisle if the need ever arose, and there was a standing instruction to this effect at Haymarket at that time.

By 1956 the Haymarket allocation of A3s stood at fifteen in total, consisting of:

- 60035 *Windsor Lad*
- 60037 *Hyperion*
- 60041 *Salmon Trout*
- 60043 *Brown Jack*
- 60057 *Ormonde*
- 60087 *Blenheim*
- 60089 *Felstead*
- 60090 *Grande Parade*
- 60094 *Colorado*
- 60096 *Papyrus*
- 60097 *Humorist*
- 60098 *Spion Kop*
- 60099 *Call Boy*
- 60100 *Spearmint*
- 60101 *Cicero*

When the A3s were reclassified downwards to become Class 7P6F locomotives through only having a tractive effort of 32,910 lbs, which was below the 35,000 lb bench mark for Class 8P, the new Peppercorn A1s (Class 8P) were allocated to Haymarket No. 2 link. Perversely, there were only five Peppercorn A1s ever allocated to Haymarket, whilst No. 2 link had twelve turns. Following the decision to leave No. 1 link permanently with fourteen diagrammed turns, which thus required the seven A4s to be allocated to it, the sixth engine in No. 2 link was thereafter an A3. No. 60096 *Papyrus*, certainly during the author's time at 64B, was the allocated sixth engine, working turn for turn with the higher-rated 8P locomotives round the link. The reality was that Haymarket drivers were quite prepared to have an A3 on any diagram, including those calling for a Class 8 engine, since they generally coped without any problems – especially after receiving the improved draughting arrangements. The only occasions a Class 8 would be allocated, if at all possible, was to work the two Edinburgh to King's Cross night sleeping car services which, in summer, loaded up to – and sometimes exceeded – the maximum tonnage for a Class 8 engine. This was, however, not always possible and Class 7P engines, including the A3s, were not unknown on these heavy workings … and they always performed up to expectation!

Overall then, at one time or another, Haymarket had a great number of A1/A3 class engines 'on the books' and, with the final

A gleaming A3, No. 60087 *Blenheim*, breasts the climb round the Edinburgh South Suburban line (the Sub) at Morningside Road, heading the 12.40 Niddrie West to Aberdeen Craiginches Class 'C' express freight train on 21st April 1961. *Courtesy W.S. Sellar*

The last production A3 to be built, No. 60043 *Brown Jack*, stands in its final form with Kylchap exhaust arrangement and German 'trough'-style smoke deflectors. These modifications gave the ageing A3 fleet a new lease of life and saw them once more take over the working of many of the principal East Coast expresses, which they did with absolute competence. *Courtesy David Dunn*

allocation of fifteen in the mid-to-late 1950s, this was to be the single largest allocation of A3s to any shed in BR.

It is essential that, in considering not only the A1/A3s, but also all the Gresley Pacifics and the other big Gresley engines which followed from the Doncaster stable – the V2s, V4s and P2s – personal preferences and opinions are laid to one side, and the engines be considered quite objectively, right across the spectrum. Thus, to be absolutely honest, these locomotives, good as they were, had been saddled, right from the outset, with what was undoubtedly to prove to be the Achilles heel of the three-cylinder designs, the Gresley conjugated valve gear, and a suspect middle big end. How this inherent problem was to be later dealt with, and largely mitigated, is discussed later in Chapter 28, but at this point it is enough to say that the A3s and A4s were later to receive a new lease of life, which saw some spectacular performances being returned, time and time again, right up to the demise of steam.

A3 No. 60043 *Brown Jack*, now in final guise, starts the 'Berwick Slow' train out of Edinburgh Waverley. This three-coach train ran all stops to Berwick-upon-Tweed, hardly a taxing load for such an engine. *Courtesy W.S. Sellar*

17 L&NER PACIFICS: THE GRESLEY A4S

Haymarket was not included in the initial depots to be allocated the new A4 Class, these being just four in number and allocated between Gateshead and King's Cross for the 'Silver Jubilee' working. Following the success of this service, there was a subsequent plan to run a similar high-speed service (nine hours) between Aberdeen and London, and on 26th September 1936 No. 2511 *Silver King*, with Driver Dron of Gateshead at the controls, worked the 'Silver Jubilee' train-set plus dynamometer car from Newcastle to Edinburgh and return, to the timings which had been prepared for the proposed Aberdeen service.

The plan to run to Aberdeen was quickly shelved thereafter, but a new streamlined service was introduced between Edinburgh and London King's Cross from the 3rd July 1937, named 'Coronation'. A few days previously there had been an 'Invitation Run' for the press, using the same train-set, between Edinburgh and Newcastle and return, with Driver J. Binnie and Fireman M. Brand, both of Haymarket, on the footplate of No. 4491 *Commonwealth of Australia*, and the 125 miles were run in the southbound (Up) direction in 112 minutes, and on the return (Down) journey in 114 minutes.

When the 'Coronation' entered revenue-earning service on 3rd July 1937, crews from three sheds, Haymarket, Gateshead and King's Cross, were to be involved in the working – but, like the non-stop, only Haymarket and King's Cross A4s were used to run the trains. Once again the crew diagrams were somewhat convoluted, with the Haymarket men working the Up 'Coronation' to Newcastle on Mondays, Wednesdays and Fridays, where they were relieved by King's Cross men. The Haymarket men then travelled forward to York on Mondays and Wednesdays, as passengers on the 19.10 Newcastle to Bristol 'mail', in order to lodge. They then, on the following Tuesday and Thursday, relieved the King's Cross men at York and worked the Down 'Coronation' through to Edinburgh. On Fridays, the Haymarket crew lodged at Gateshead after relief, and returned to Edinburgh on the Saturday working of the 09.32 semi-fast. From 7th March 1938, a Newcastle stop was inserted into the Down train and, thereafter, the Haymarket crews worked the Up train to Newcastle and returned with the Down service on an out and home daily basis, completely eliminating the need to lodge away.

On the inaugural run, No. 4491 *Commonwealth of Australia* worked the northbound service, with Gateshead Driver Dron taking it from King's Cross to Newcastle and Gateshead Driver Hutchison bringing it on to Edinburgh. No. 4489 *Dominion of Canada*, driven by Haymarket driver D. McGuire with Fireman Wilson, worked the southbound train, with Driver Burfoot of Top Shed taking the train forward from Newcastle. It has been recorded elsewhere that Driver Binnie of Haymarket, who ran the 'Invitation Run' referred to above, drove the first southbound service train. The fact is that, owing to a link reorganisation, he missed out and took over the working on the following week instead. No. 4491 *Commonwealth of Australia* ran forty-eight of the first fifty-one turns of this new train,

amassing an incredible 19,000 miles in high-speed service, and a further 4,000 miles in balancing workings.

As a matter of interest, Ross Dougan, a St. Margaret's man who had come to Haymarket as a driver in 1925, was the first Haymarket Senior Spare driver to drive the 'Coronation'. Ross went on to be a running foreman at Haymarket in the 1950s.

Following problems experienced during the winter period, when coal supplies ran out on a southbound journey, the coaling up of the engines for the 'Coronation' service became the focus of special attention at Haymarket until such times that suitable tender modifications could be put in hand to ensure maximisation of available coal space.

Also in 1937, the A4s took over the non-stop running of the 'Flying Scotsman' for the first time.

The first A4 to be allocated to Haymarket was No. 4483 *Kingfisher* in December 1936, which by the summer of 1937 had been joined by Nos 4484 *Falcon*, 4485 *Kestrel*, 4487 *Sea Eagle*, 4488 *Union of South Africa* and 4491 *Commonwealth of Australia*, giving a total allocation of six engines.

By the following March a further four engines were allocated, Nos 4490 *Empire of India*, 4492 *Dominion of New Zealand*, 4497 *Golden Plover* and 4486 *Merlin*. There was considerable movement of A4s in the late 1930s, with some staying only a short time at each depot. For instance, No. 4484 *Falcon* was transferred out in March 1938, and No. 4483 *Kingfisher* had been transferred away twice, and back twice, by May 1939. Other A4s which saw service at Haymarket during this time were No. 4482 *Golden Eagle* and No. 4462 *William Whitelaw*.

By July 1938 the Haymarket allocation of A4s had peaked at ten, but in 1941 the allocation settled at seven and was to remain thus until the early 1960s. The final allocation consisted of:

- 60004 (4462) *William Whitelaw*
  (formerly *Great Snipe* until 5/6/41)
- 60009 (4488) *Union of South Africa*
  (originally *Osprey* from April to June 1937)
- 60011 (4490) *Empire of India*
- 60012 (4491) *Commonwealth of Australia*
- 60024 (4483) *Kingfisher*
- 60027 (4486) *Merlin*
- 60031 (4497) *Golden Plover*.

On 31st August 1939, all three L&NER streamliner services – including the 'Coronation', the only train in which Haymarket played an active part – were withdrawn prior to the outbreak of war. The 'Coronation' had, in its years in service, made a total of 1,084 runs, and of these, two Haymarket A4s were the only engines to have exceeded in excess of 100 appearances at the head of this train, No. 4490 *Empire of India* (125 runs) and No. 4497 *Golden Plover* (104 runs).

A4 No. 60012 *Commonwealth of Australia* powers the 10.00 Edinburgh to Glasgow 'fast' past Haymarket Central signal box on a grey February morning in 1955. In the left background can be seen the shed's east sidings where the wagons of loco coal were stored pending transfer to the coaling plant sidings, plus the empty 3-plank and 5-plank wagons for ash disposal. Also put there were 'dead' engines awaiting fitters attention, with a B1 (smokebox door open) and an unidentified A1 so stabled. The 10.00 was a Top link turn in 1955, hence the A4. This morning departure also coincided with the departure of the 10.00 Aberdeen, a No. 2 link turn with an A1, and a race as far as Saughton Junction was the norm – but the Aberdeen appears to be well behind on this occasion.   *Courtesy David Anderson*

The enamel plaque presented by members of the Royal Navy to A4 No. 60024 *Kingfisher*, depicting the badge of HMS *Kingfisher*, is being unveiled at a small ceremony at Haymarket shed on 21st October 1954. *Kingfisher* was at that time allocated to Top link drivers A. (Tony) McLeod and W. (Bill) McLeod (unrelated). In the picture, from right to left are, Driver Bill McLeod, Driver Tony McLeod, Mr G. Lund, ADMPS, Edinburgh, and the Naval representative, Lt. A.F. Mortimer. *Courtesy Mr Peter Lund*

During the early years of the Second World War, regular manning of the A4s at Haymarket was perpetuated insofar as was possible, unlike the A3s which became common user almost immediately. After cessation of hostilities, Haymarket quickly reinstated the regular manning, with the Top link (No. 1 link) having six A4s allocated to twelve drivers – the remaining A4, No. 60012 *Commonwealth of Australia*, working in No. 2 link. This arrangement was perpetuated until the mid-1950s (see Chapter 15).

When the new afternoon express service, 'The Talisman', was first introduced on Monday, 17th September 1956. The honours went to No. 1 link at Haymarket, with Driver Tommy Smith and his beloved A4, No. 60031 *Golden Plover*, working the first southbound service out of Waverley. This same A4 had been chosen in September 1947 to take part in trials with Thompson's new A1 No. 60113 *Great Northern* (rebuilt from the first Gresley Pacific) between Edinburgh and Dundee. By this time No. 60031 had had the inside cylinder diameter reduced to 17 inches.

In 1960, which was supposed to be the last year of steam on the non-stop 'Elizabethan', No. 60027 *Merlin* – a long time star of Haymarket, with the longest spell of non-stop running over the past years – again hit the headlines. In this year the engine worked the longest consecutive spell of forty-six non-stop turns, with a further thirty-one to follow before the end of the season; in total it worked an incredible seventy-seven non-stop runs in a single season – a testament to the TLC lavished on the Haymarket A4s.

No. 60009 *Union of South Africa* was to have the distinction of being the last A4 to work a special train out of King's Cross station on the 24th October 1964. Happily, thanks to the generosity and foresight of one man, John Cameron, one of the best Haymarket A4s, No. 60009 *Union of South Africa*, can still be seen gracing the main line stage, now in preservation and gloriously wearing the final form of double chimney and BR Brunswick Green livery. This engine famously, and most appropriately, took pride of place in the centenary celebrations of the Forth Railway Bridge in 1990.

Some Haymarket A4s were specially targeted for additional embellishments post-war. No. 4486 *Merlin* had previously held the dubious honour of not only being renamed three times in a single day, but also renumbered, during a routine visit to Doncaster plant in August 1944. What transpired would have been quite an extraordinary event at the best of times, but in wartime it was bizarre in the extreme. The occasion was to celebrate the arrival on the Board of the then newly-appointed director of the L&NER, Fitzherbert Wright. During a visit by Wright and his family to Doncaster on the 10th August 1944, No. 4486 was, in turn, numbered, named and photographed – first 1928 *Brigid*, then 1931 *Davina* and finally 1934 *Bryan* – in honour of Wright's three children, each having their name and year of birth displayed on the engine.

Happily, the second occasion was far more appropriate. On 26th May 1946, and now as No. 27 *Merlin*, the engine was worked light from Haymarket shed to Donibristle, where it was taken through a rail connection into sidings where ne'er a Pacific had ever previously strayed, inside HMS *Merlin*, the Admiralty Shore Establishment at Dalgety Bay, in Fife. There the Captain of HMS *Merlin* presented two beautifully enamelled cast plaques depicting a merlin in flight, the badge of the Naval Establishment, which thereafter adorned each side of the engine. The driver on the day was the regular driver, Bill Stevenson, accompanied by his opposite number, Bob Keppie, and their respective firemen.

In 1953, No. 60009 *Union of South Africa* was also to receive a special adornment, when a Bloemfontein newspaper proprietor presented a stainless-steel plaque with the depiction of a Springbok elegantly engraved thereon. The plaque was not to be affixed to the side of No. 60009 until the 26th April 1954, when it was in Doncaster for general repair.

The last of the Haymarket trio to be so embellished was No. 60024 *Kingfisher* when, at a small ceremony at Haymarket shed on the 21st October 1954, another naval officer, Lt A.F. Mortimer, presented a pair of diamond-shaped enamelled plaques, similar to

A4 No. 60011 *Empire of India* slips off-shed and is crossed onto the Up South Main at Haymarket Central Junction, prior to going down to Waverley station on the 26th August 1956. Given the amount of coal on the tender, it may be working the non-stop 'Elizabethan', but it is more likely that this is the stand-by engine for the non-stop, now going to take up its own booked working on the 10.30 Edinburgh to London (the 'Junior Scotsman'), and the reversed headboard is that for 'The Flying Scotsman' which is the booked back-working from Newcastle. Whatever, it is surprising that the running foreman has allowed the engine to go off-shed without the tender having been properly trimmed. In the centre rear of the photograph there is a fine panoramic view across the front end of the shed. An A3 waits at the shed exit signal to follow No. 60011 down to the station, whilst an A1 and a J38 sit dead, waiting fitters' attention, in the east yard sidings.   *Courtesy David Anderson*

Haymarket A4 No. 60012 *Commonwealth of Australia* stands dead at the head of two engineer's 'Grampus' wagons in east shed sidings while waiting repair. The signal box in the upper background is Coltbridge Junction, on the ex-Caledonian Edinburgh Princes Street to Leith North branch. *Courtesy David Dunn*

BELOW: A4 No. 60024 *Kingfisher* stands alongside stablemate Peppercorn A2 No. 60530 *Sayajirao* outside the front of Haymarket shed in the early 1950s. The date is before 21st October 1954, since 60024 has not yet received its commemorative diamond-shaped enamel plaques. *Author's collection*

those presented to No. 60027 but depicting the badge of HMS *Kingfisher*, which were, again, to be fitted to the sides of the engine. The unveiling was attended by Top link drivers A. (Tony) McLeod and W. (Bill) McLeod, who ran No. 60024, and Mr G. Lund, Assistant Motive Power Superintendent, Edinburgh.

The Haymarket A4s also achieved the distinction of bettering the average annual mileage for the whole class which, over a working life of twenty-five to thirty years, was calculated at around 58,000 miles per year. The Haymarket engines were running an annual average of 62,000 to 66,000 miles per year, a not insignificant betterment.

The A4s, given the same remedial treatment as the A3s (as described at Chapter 28), were also given a new lease of life after the heady days of non-stop running. On the 8th September 1962 a new 3-hour express train service was introduced between Glasgow and Aberdeen consisting of two trains each weekday in each direction. This service was handed over to the new NBL Type 2 diesel electric locomotives. These were to prove an unmitigated disaster from the outset, with woeful performance and availability, and so the Gresley A4s, now displaced from the ECML, were pressed into service on these prestige trains. Not all the ex-LM&S enginemen at Perth and Glasgow Balornock (St. Rollox) totally mastered these engines, but the Aberdeen Ferryhill crews, long used to Gresleys, took to them like a duck to water and ran this tightly-timed service with great success.

The ex-Haymarket A4s transferred to this working from 1st July 1964 were Nos 60004/9/12 (to Aberdeen Ferryhill) and Nos 60027/31 to Glasgow St. Rollox. No. 60011 had also been transferred to Ferryhill but was almost immediately withdrawn. No. 60024 was transferred to Ferryhill in May 1965, and this high profile working was to be entrusted to these A4s, supplemented by a further nine from south of the border, until 1966, when No. 60024 was the final ex-Haymarket A4 to be withdrawn.

ABOVE: Haymarket A4 No. 60004 *William Whitelaw* waits for the road out of Craigentinny carriage sidings up to Waverley, with the empty stock for the onward train working, probably an Aberdeen turn, in June 1961. The engine is in sparkling condition with, strangely, a light blue background to the nameplate (a new innovation at Haymarket). The tender is filled with nice, hard, quality coal and the fireman can look forward to an easy time ahead. *Courtesy W.S. Sellar*

BELOW: Sunday, 23rd August 2009, and preserved ex-Haymarket A4 No. 60009 *Union of South Africa*, by now nearly seventy-four years old, is still working main line special trains. Seen here heading an SRPS special at Linlithgow station, still sporting Haymarket shed plate and with Haymarket allocation painted on front. *Courtesy Ian Musgrave*

18 L&NER LOCOMOTIVES: THE GRESLEY P2S

The P2 2-8-2 locomotives, sometimes referred to as the 'Gresley Enigma Variations', numbered but six in total, each with its own unique peculiarities. Designed specifically for the Edinburgh/Dundee/Aberdeen services which conveyed either restaurant cars or sleeping cars or both – posing a heavy train consist over a very difficult road – it was intended that the P2s would eliminate the need for piloting with two locomotives and two crews to work these heavy trains, thus saving an engine and crew.

These were, despite their imposing look, perhaps the most controversial locomotives ever designed by Gresley, and for somewhat strange reasons. The new, heavy trains being worked between Aberdeen and Edinburgh comprised of, quite basically, two services in each direction per day, the daytime trains carrying the through portion of the 'Flying Scotsman', and the evening/night service 'The Aberdonian' which was a sleeping car service. Hindsight indicates that the perpetuation of piloting, even with the demand for additional resources, may still have proved a cheaper and equally effective alternative, although it should be conceded

that it was unlikely that piloting of A3/A4 locomotives would have been accepted from a structural loading point of view. However, the running of the booked train in two portions, or a booked relief train on diagrammed paths, would have achieved the same end result without incurring the costs of building the six unique locomotives. It is worth noting that the London to Aberdeen sleeper services did become two complete trains in later years. Nevertheless, the engines were built, and from the outset they could easily cope with prodigious loads between Aberdeen and Edinburgh – 600 tons being set as the trailing load over the route. In many ways, in particular with the allegations of high coal consumption, plus their ability to lift big trains effortlessly, the P2s had many similarities to the earlier NBR Atlantics discussed in Chapter 12.

The first of the class, No. 2001 *Cock o' the North*, ran several preliminary trials between King's Cross and Peterborough before coming north. On the 18th June 1934 it was loaded up with a trailing load of 649 tons, consisting of nineteen coaches plus the dynamometer car, from London to Barkston and back. A speed of

P2 No. 2002 *Earl Marischal,* **fitted with double smoke deflector plates, stands at the head of a southbound express at Montrose. The massive proportions of these magnificent engines is seen to advantage.**   *JohnThomas/Bill Brown collection*

No. 2003 *Lord President* stands on the turntable at Dundee Tay Bridge. The P2s were elegant locomotives, particularly those fitted with the Bugatti front end. *Bill Brown collection*

70 mph was easily attained on the Down run, although a high-speed trial was not the intention, and on the 1 in 440/264 rising gradient on Stoke Bank, the summit at Stoke was topped at 56½ mph with this big train. On a second trial, a maximum speed of 87½ mph was recorded when descending Stoke Bank. The engine was brought to Scotland in the following month.

In December 1934, with the cooperation of André Chapelon, No. 2001 was taken via the cross-Channel 'Night Ferry' to France, and there underwent a series of controlled tests at the French locomotive testing station at Vitry-sur-Seine. The tests proved unsatisfactory, with the engine running hot on several occasions and with the power outputs being largely undistinguished. On controlled road trials to Orléans, however, excellent figures for both coal consumption and water evaporation were returned, but the poppet valves required constant attention. On the whole, the L&NER gained very little as a consequence of these not inexpensive trials, and No. 2001 proved to be, at best, a very mediocre performer. The reference to coal consumption during these trials has been purposely highlighted for reasons which will become obvious.

The allocation of the P2s to Haymarket, and their variations in design, were:

- 2001 *Cock o' the North*   delivered 31/07/34.

  This engine had a double chimney, single smoke deflector plates, and was fitted with an ACFI feed-water heater and Lentz rotary cam-operated poppet valve gear. From September 1937, No. 2001 received an A4-type front end and was refitted with Walschaerts valve gear. The feed-water heating apparatus was also removed.

- 2002 *Earl Marischal*   delivered 9/06/35 but quickly transferred onwards to Dundee on 22/06/35.

  This engine was fitted with Walschaerts valve gear from new. It also had a single set of smoke deflector plates, which, in service, proved to be ineffective in clearing drifting exhaust; thus, from April 1935, it re-entered service fitted with a second pair of smoke deflectors in front of the original plates. This modification proved to be an entirely satisfactory arrangement, although it did little from an aesthetic point of view. In October 1936 it was released ex-works fitted with an A4 'Bugatti-styled' front end.

- 2003 *Lord President*   delivered 06/36 and transferred on to Dundee 4/09/36.

  This engine was fitted with a Bugatti-type (A4) front end and Kylchap draughting arrangement.

- 2004 *Mons Meg*   delivered 07/36.

  This engine had a manually-operated by-pass valve to divert exhaust steam away from the blastpipe. The valve was of the butterfly type and proved troublesome due to carbonised oil causing it to stick. In 1937 it was fitted with a manually operated plug-type valve, but this was largely ignored by drivers and thus, in 1939, the arrangement was replaced by an automatic control, working off the reversing shaft, which opened the valve when the cut-off was increased to 38% or longer.

- 2005 *Thane of Fife*   was delivered straight to Dundee shed from new, from where it worked until withdrawal.

  This engine was unique in having only a single blast pipe and chimney.

- 2006 *Wolf of Badenoch*   delivered 09/36, transferred to Aberdeen 16/11/36, and returned to Haymarket on 23/10/42.

  This engine had a longer firebox with a combustion chamber.

That the engines could competently haul the big trains was never in any doubt, but on the sinuous Edinburgh/Aberdeen line this performance was being obtained at a cost. It has been recorded that, because of the line curvature, the longer four-coupled rigid (overall) wheelbase of 37 feet 11 inches, as against the 35 feet 9 inches of the A3 Pacifics, and the provision of only a pony truck at the front, gave rise to overheating of the big-ends, with consequential crank pin problems on the coupling rods. There has been some considerable doubt expressed over the years as to whether the curvature of the Aberdeen road did in fact actually cause the problems with the crank pins, or whether the problem lay in the design of the front pony truck. This was the same swing-link pony truck mechanism Gresley had used on his K3 class engines, and on which class this design had already exhibited similar problems, both with lubrication and springs, resulting in crank pin damage. This very same problem thereafter also manifested itself on the V2s. This, then, must beg the question as to whether the curvature of the line was to blame, or was this factor somewhat of a red herring put about for ulterior reasons?

The known problem with the pony truck is something which could have been redesigned and engineered out of the equation, as it had been on the K3s and was to be on the V2s, had the will to do so existed. Indeed, during the Vitry trials in France, no less a person than the great André Chapelon had identified that the design of the leading pony truck was resulting in No. 2001 being very hard on the track, since the first coupled axle of the rigid wheelbase encountered any change in direction of the track too roughly, and he told Gresley so. He had particularly noticed this inherent weakness at the great junction at Montlouis, which had been taken very harshly during one of the trial runs. This was a valid criticism from a respected locomotive engineer, and it emanated from a railway system, the SNCF, where big, eight-coupled passenger locomotives were doing sterling service on difficult routes, but without any similar problems.

Whilst McKillop considered No. 2001 to be '*a great hulking boor which trundled and swung her bulk round in elephantine, ungraceful jerks, trumpeting protest from the tortured length of her rigid driving wheels,*' it was said by O.S. Nock – who had had the opportunity to ride extensively on both Nos 2001 and 2002 whilst in service in Scotland – that, whatever might have developed later, in the early days these engines rode smoothly and comfortably with an easy buoyancy, and a total lack of anything in the way of lurching and jolting which would have suggested that the engines were reacting unkindly to line curvature.

In an article by E.H. Livesey for the Institution of Mechanical Engineers publication *The Engineer* in 1939 regarding footplate trips made with the P2s on the Edinburgh to Aberdeen route with Haymarket crews, the author stated:

I was beginning to note the riding, which I had been looking forward to judging, on my first run on an eight-coupled engine in this country. I had wondered how an engine with a long rigid wheelbase – 19 feet 6 inches (coupled wheelbase) – would behave on this much-curving route, and was pleased to find its action easy. It took the bends quite sympathetically, though I could only feel them as it was still dark, and I could not judge their magnitude well.

This article was written in connection with a footplate trip on No. 2004 *Mons Meg*, on the 03.57 'Early Aberdeen' sleeping car train north from Edinburgh ('The Aberdonian') in about 1938/39. No mention of trundling, ungracious jerks or the like!

However, a biographer of Sir Nigel Gresley did go so far as to say that the P2s did damage the track and spread the gauge and this was again claimed by no less a personage than C.J. Allan in his book *The London & North Eastern Railway*. What would have been the reality of the situation had this been true? Well, had the riding of these engines caused problems with the road bed, such as spreading the gauge or causing misalignment, then there is little doubt that the Scottish Area Civil Engineer (L&NER) would have had them immediately excluded from the route, probably for all time, thus sounding the death knell for the 'Mikados' between Edinburgh and Montrose. But the line north of Kinnaber Junction right into Aberdeen was owned by the LM&S Railway Company, over which the L&NER only enjoyed running rights; had there been the least suspicion of track damage or gauge spread over the curves which abound on this section, then all hell would have been let loose, with the P2s being banned from north of Montrose forthwith.

There is, unlike the earlier furore surrounding the NBR Atlantics and the alleged track damage they caused, no record of any concerns over damage to the permanent way between Edinburgh and Aberdeen by these six engines. The author, therefore, concludes that McKillop's criticism was considerably overstated given the evidence – or, rather, lack of same – and must therefore be balanced against McKillop's own personal dislike of these engines.

Regarding the allegation of high coal consumption, McKillop's generality that the P2s burned at least 112 lbs of coal per mile must also be considered in context. That was an excessive consumption for any engine and something which would have had the engines quickly sidelined by crews. However, McKillop conveniently forgot to mention that the A1s (and the 'Shires') based at Haymarket were returning average coal consumption figures well in excess of 60 lbs per mile around the same period. It must, in fairness to the locomotives, be pointed out that this figure for coal consumption was based on train-miles run, as stated previously, and would have been significantly more relevant, and accurate, had the calculation been based on ton-miles run, particularly in the case of the P2s. The high coal consumption also points to the considerable under-utilisation of the locomotive fleet pre-war.

The fact is that the first in the class, No. 2001 *Cock o' the North*, when running in the trials with King's Cross Top Shed crews, had evoked no response, or any criticism whatsoever, regarding excessive fuel consumption, even when being thrashed along; and as already discussed, the road trials in France had produced excellent results.

On trials in Scotland sometime later, No. 2001 did earn a name for being particularly heavy on coal, since, on controlled road tests between Dundee and Edinburgh, with a trailing load in excess of 500 tons, it had returned a coal consumption figure of around 104 lbs per mile (when corrected for non-traffic purposes, it was 92 lbs per mile). McKillop made much of the fact that No. 2001 ran out of coal at Dalmeny during the return leg on the first of the runs – where the signalman's store of coal had to be raided to get the engine home – as an indication of just how heavy the engines were on coal; but the root of that particular problem lay in the fact that the engine had not been fully coaled before the trial began, plus the driver on the day was well-known as being 'heavy

P2 No. 2002 *Earl Marischal* **passes Aberdeen Ferryhill Junction with a southbound fish train out of Aberdeen Guild Street and bound for London on a dull day in May 1938. The train is a heavy one and maximum effort is being expended by the 'Mikado' in getting the load underway. The fire is certainly being stirred up in readiness for an unbroken climb of eight miles round the Aberdeenshire coastline.** *C. Lawson Kerr/Bill Brown collection*

No. 2005 *Thane of Fife* **leans into the curve at Craiginches with a southbound express.**   *F.R. Hebron/Bill Brown collection*

handed'. However, this all occurred during the time No. 2001 was still fitted with the Lentz rotary cam poppet valve gear arrangement, and this exceptionally high coal consumption figure could possibly (and quite probably) be put down to the developing wear in the poppet valves; this wear had been a constant source of trouble from new, and perhaps the bad name No. 2001 was then gaining tended thereafter to reflect on the class as a whole. To exacerbate the already problematical situation, the ACFI feed-water heater required exhaust steam to heat the water before it entered the boiler; thus, to work efficiently, the locomotive had to be worked with the regulator open continuously. This patently was just impossible on the Edinburgh to Aberdeen road, and thus the ACFI equipment was in itself wasteful and pointless.

Geoffrey Lund, who became a technical inspector in the Locomotive Running Superintendent's Office in Edinburgh in 1943, and was Shed Master at Haymarket from 1944 until 1947, had some experience of the P2s, and No. 2001 in particular. He considered that with the rotary valve gear, the cylinder design was such that it had a very high clearance volume, almost twice that of an A4 – and that this factor, combined with the rapid-opening exhaust valves and the Kylchap draughting, caused the smokebox vacuum to peak so high as to pull holes in the firebed; he concluded that this had much to do with the excessive coal consumption being recorded. Unsurprisingly, F.H. Eggleshaw, the Locomotive Works Manager at Doncaster Works, had made much the same prediction before No. 2001 had even left the plant.

At the time, certainly within the L&NER, these were the first passenger engines to be turned out with a grate area of 50 square feet – but, since the advent of the A1s/A3s, crews were no longer unused to firing locomotives with large and wide grate areas (41.25 square feet), and this should not have posed a significant problem to the firemen. The 50 square feet grate area could, under certain conditions, result in disproportionately heavy coal consumption, partly due to the greater area requiring to be kept fed with coal, thus perhaps contributing to the P2s reputation for being 'miners' friends'. Again, whilst actual coal consumption was not a problem that was commented upon during the Vitry trials, the grate area and the L&NER-type half-trap firedoor had allegedly caused problems to both the British and French firemen, in their being unable to keep the back corners of the box sufficiently fed with fuel.

Chief Locomotive Inspector James Cunningham of Edinburgh, one time fireman on the P2s at Haymarket, in conversation said that as a young fireman on No. 2001 he would finish each shift soaked in perspiration and thinking that each turn was the hardest work he had ever done. With his own dry sense of humour, he said, '*aye, the lassie had a bonnie appetite.*' All evidence appears to point to the fact that it was only No. 2001 herself which had a 'bonnie appetite' for coal and a big part of the reason was the inability of the fireman to not only keep the firebed fed with coal, but to maintain a sufficiently thick firebed to stop it being drawn into holes by the sharp exhaust. It is probable that this also held true in the Vitry trials.

There must be little doubt then that No. 2001, as first built, was, and became even more so, an increasingly extravagant engine in

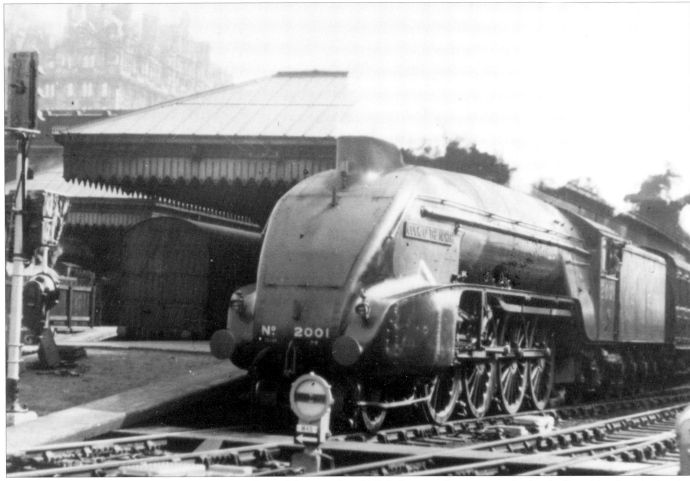

No. 2001 *Cock o' the North*, now rebuilt with Bugatti front end and Walschaerts valve gear, at the head of an Aberdeen train at Waverley, awaiting the 'right away'.   *C. Lawson Kerr/Bill Brown collection*

terms of coal consumption during the time it ran in the original form and was the 'black sheep' of the class. However, after rebuilding with normal Walschaerts valve gear, No. 2001 settled down to give much the same results as the remainder of the class.

Other drivers known personally to the author, and who had fired and driven the P2s, all commented on the fact that they tended to be somewhat heavier on coal than, say, an A3; most agreed, however, that the coal consumption did increase proportionately with the way they were driven, and that with full regulator/short cut off working, they were definitely more economical. Driver D. Anderson, who had been involved in the Castlecary collision and to whom the author later fired, had, as a Senior Spare driver, handled most, if not all the P2s and was at the controls of No. 2006 *Wolf of Badenoch* on the occasion when O.S. Nock rode with him on the 'Early Aberdeen'. Anderson considered them to be fine engines, but best worked with full regulator and driven expansively or, as he said, '*on the reverser.*' '*This saved the fireman many a wet shirt.*' Anderson was actually well-known at Haymarket as a driver who made careful use of the reverser and avoided resorting to extremes in his manner of driving.

It has been said elsewhere that the 50 square feet grate was excessive, almost beyond the capabilities of a fireman to hand fire, and wholly unnecessary. One of the regular firemen who worked on the P2s, firing to Top link driver R. Shedden whilst they were at Haymarket, was J. Hardisty. By the author's time at 64B, Hardisty was a driver who for medical reasons had been accommodated on

the shed shunt J88. He was, nevertheless, a fund of information and spoke highly of the P2s and their ability to handle any train thrown at them. He also considered that, due to the slightly larger grate area, the fireman's work was constant, but depending upon how they were being driven, generally it was in no way over-onerous. All in all, as a fireman he had liked them well enough.

Perhaps, as suggested by other commentators, they should have been fitted with mechanical stokers – though the experiments with the later 9Fs showed up the inherent problems with this apparatus – but the same commentators appear to then ignore the fact that the later Peppercorn A1s and A2s had, what else … but 50 square feet grate areas. From the author's personal experience the A1s and A2s never proved difficult to fire, although, in terms of coal consumption, the A1s could have their moments. The reality is that, if a fireman could cope with a grate area of 41.25 square feet, as fitted to the A3s and afterwards to the A4s, V2s and the Thompson derivatives, then there was little difference made by a grate area which was slightly less than 9 square feet more. The author's personal view is that the arguments surrounding the grate area on the P2s were, and are, somewhat spurious, since firemen, including the less experienced cleaner/firemen at Haymarket, himself included, had little or no problem on the Peppercorns.

Oliver Bullied was probably right on the mark when he said that they were 'extravagant' engines since, in service in Scotland, he considered that they were not being put to the proper use they were designed for. The diagrammed working between Edinburgh,

Dundee and Aberdeen meant that there was a lot of spare time 'on shed' at all three depots, with poor mileages being run each day. As an example, the Aberdeen P2 diagrammed to work the 19.10 'Aberdonian' south to Dundee then had a 12-hour lie-over at Dundee until worked back home to Ferryhill. This meant that the engine only ran some 142¼ miles every 16 hours – and this was appalling under-utilisation with an unquestionable, and considerable, stand-by loss in fuel. Had through-engine working with the P2s been maintained between Edinburgh and Aberdeen, better locomotive utilisation would have been the result, with, it is suspected, much improved coal consumption figures. However, to Dundee the P2s went, quite unnecessarily, to satisfy the demands of the Dundee train crews that they be involved, and this was to prove a big mistake. The result of this limited working, involving engine changing at Dundee, and with locomotives having the very large grate area, meant a lot of the coal was being burnt through misuse rather than in train working and, inevitably, a lot of unburned coal remaining in the firebox after completion of the run. Indeed, had the Peppercorn A1s been confined to the same limited daily use as the P2s, the reality is that they too would have reflected a very high overall coal consumption. All things considered, the P2s were unfairly condemned, in terms of coal consumption, when the root of the problem lay in the limited train miles they were working in an average day.

Despite McKillop's harsh words about the P2s, they did do some sterling work whilst in Scotland. Another Haymarket Top link driver, James (Jimmy) Swan, in correspondence with Gresley's biographer, F.A.S. Brown, conceded that, even with trailing loads of 600 tons or more, he never found a P2 refusing to start, no matter how steep the gradient – even at the locations where there was a 'hole' at the start of several very steep climbs. In the Up direction, there was the heavy start out of Aberdeen up to Cove with gradients of 1 in 96 and 1 in 88, with the line running along the sea cliffs above the North Sea where storms and flying sea spray were frequently encountered. At Stonehaven, a conditional stop, there was another long and hard six-mile climb averaging 1 in 106; at Montrose the gradient was 1 in 88, with 1 in 111 on a severely curved gradient up to Usan. Dundee Tay Bridge up to the Tay Bridge proper was, at the most severe point, 1 in 66, and this was followed by a 4-mile lift averaging 1 in 104 from Ladybank up to Lochmuir over the shoulder of Falkland Hill. Through Thornton there was a stiff climb up to Randolph Sidings and finally, from Inverkeithing there were the two miles of 1 in 70, through two tunnels, up to the Forth Bridge. In the Down direction, the problems were similar.

The P2s could always tackle these big banks, plus the plethora of lesser climbs – of which there were many between Edinburgh and Aberdeen – with ease, and Swan considered them the ideal engines for the terrain encountered on this most difficult of roads. Nock has stated that in his footplate travels on the first two engines, each being worked by two allocated crews only, the success in their running depended totally on the skill and attention of these crews. Variations in working by the two different drivers resulted in detectable changes in engine performance, particularly in regard to coal consumption. One of the regular drivers who used full regulator and short cut-off regularly returned a lesser coal consumption than that of his counterpart who seemed reluctant to use a wide open regulator, and ran with longer cut-offs, with consequential adverse effects on economy.

A debate which has raged for well nigh on sixty years has centred upon exactly why the P2s were rebuilt. At the time rebuilding took place it was wartime – and whilst the class consisted of only six engines, they were, as proven on the Aberdeen road, very strong locomotives capable of hauling immense trains. The engines, as built and with plenty of working life left, could usefully have been transferred to the southern end of the ECML with the less demanding geography and geometry of the route, and where 600- to 800-ton trains out of King's Cross were the wartime norm. Their huge tractive effort could have been usefully employed on these lines where the longer wheelbase would not have encountered the same problems as found on the Aberdeen road. This alternative employment must surely have been well worth a trial. However, even accepting that they were a small and quite unique class, the re-engineering of the swing-link front pony truck – or, as Lund had suggested, the fitting of a knuckle joint between the driving and third (and even fourth) pairs of coupled wheels – at a far lesser cost to rebuilding, plus their potential for sheer hard work, must surely have been presented as an option which would have come down heavily on the plus side during the difficult war years.

Given the evidence now available, it is clear that Thompson had already decided that they should, come what may, be rebuilt; partly to demonstrate his thoughts on what form a new standard L&NER Pacific locomotive should take, partly because they were a non-standard class of only six engines, and undoubtedly due to his anathema towards all things Gresley. His trials with W1 No. 10000, the rebuilt 'Hush-Hush', in the early summer of 1943 on Haymarket P2 diagrams in Scotland, appeared to prove, to him at least, that a six-coupled engine could carry out the work of the P2s between Edinburgh and Aberdeen quite effectively – although the results were, in reality, skewed by remarkably (for Scotland) good weather and consequently, good, dry rail conditions and light winds. Not surprisingly, given the favourable weather conditions, no slipping was encountered by the locomotive during the trials. It also appeared that Thompson chose to ignore completely the fact that the P2s had an 80-ton axle loading whilst the W1 only had 66 tons. These were important factors which were to see his rebuilds come to grief on many occasions in years to come because of their high propensity for slipping.

This supposition that the P2s were doomed, come what may, is not quite such a far-fetched opinion as it might at first seem, since there are several very significant factors which point to the possibility of such an ulterior motive. Consider: Thompson, now CME of the L&NER and a very senior company officer, had, through trials, determined that the A3s and A4s (being six-coupled locomotives) were perfectly capable of running these heavy trains, but did he actually disseminate this information to the L&NER Board? It is a fact that Thompson, a difficult man and a very poor man-manager, through his high-handed attitude towards, and his treatment of, the three area locomotive superintendents, did very little to promote any inter-departmental harmony whatsoever, and nowhere did this reveal itself more than in his dealings with the P2s.

The Shed Master at Haymarket in the early war years, T.C.B. (Terry) Miller, was under strict instructions not to utilise the P2s on any working south of Edinburgh, although this did happen on a few occasions. Whilst this decision has been ascribed to a L&NER management directive to ensure that no member of the 'great and good' should have reason to complain about shortcomings in the working of the high-profile Edinburgh/Aberdeen services which were widely used by such persons, one cannot help but wonder if the directive was in fact manipulated to fit in with Thompson's own plans, since he was already satisfied in his own mind that six-coupled engines were completely adequate for the running of these trains. It would appear the senior management was unaware of this fact.

The whole affair has more than a whiff of underhand machinations, pointing fairly and squarely at Thompson and his efforts to ensure that it would never come to light just what a valuable asset to the operators on the East Coast the P2s might have proved on the big wartime trains. Confined to the route north of Edinburgh, where they had displayed mechanical problems and were not entirely popular, there would always be a tenuous argument for replacement through rebuilding, citing 'poor availability' as the reason. On the ECML, the P2s would undoubtedly have shone, blowing Thompson's plans to use them as his 'guinea pigs' out of the water!

Geoffrey Lund related the efforts he made to prepare a suitable memorandum to prove why the P2s need not be rebuilt, having identified the cause of a series of mechanical failures in 1943 as being due in five out of eight cases to superheater elements blowing out of the header, the result of being improperly expanded at Cowlairs and mostly due to the 'directed' labour force of inexperienced (non-railway) fitters, plus poor quality control. In doing so, he was at that time unaware that E.D. Trask, then Locomotive Running Superintendent at Edinburgh and his immediate superior, had already written several strong letters of protest to Thompson, regarding the proposed rebuilding, to the point where Trask was warned off by no less a person than Arthur Peppercorn himself, to stop trying to thwart Thompson's plans. The proposed rebuilding caused a significant furore north of the border, a response that could hardly be construed as the opinions and actions of practical running staff faced with seriously problematical locomotives. These men, all highly-experienced locomotive engineers in their own right, were in the front line of having to manipulate the provision of motive power to meet all the demands of the operators at a most difficult time, but Thompson was quite unsympathetic. The die was most obviously cast!

The argument still goes on, largely unabated. However, the pros and cons are well entrenched in history and the whole truth will probably never now be known, although it has been a question which has exercised many learned minds over the years.

Thompson used their much-vaunted weaknesses in the motion and bearings, as experienced on the Edinburgh/Aberdeen line of route, as a reason, and thereupon built his case for their rebuilding. Re-engineering never entered the equation! No. 2005 was the first to be withdrawn, and was sent to Doncaster for rebuilding to become the new Class A2/2. The remaining five engines were subsequently withdrawn from service between January and August 1944 and similarly rebuilt in what must be one of the greatest acts of corporate vandalism – particularly during wartime when raw materials, and all motive power resources, were at a premium. The results were to prove to be less than competent engines!

One of Haymarket's mixed traffic Class V2s, No. 60816, at work on the Waverley route as it heads the 12.00 Edinburgh to Carlisle passenger train at Fushiebridge on 23rd May 1959. The train is made up of a motley array of coaching stock that poses no load at all for the V2. The fireman (Haymarket Passed Fireman John (Jock) Smith) is taking things easy despite the 1 in 70 rising gradient, while a Kamikaze pigeon flies through the exhaust. The V2s always excelled on this most difficult of routes. *Courtesy W.S. Sellar*

19 L&NER LOCOMOTIVES: THE GRESLEY V2S AND V4S

THE CLASS V2 LOCOMOTIVES

The other equally famous, and the most highly respected, Gresley locomotives allocated to Haymarket were, of course, the Class V2 2-6-2 mixed traffic engines, with an allocation of around nine or ten being the norm. These engines – widely known as 'Green Arrows', after the first of the class so named – with their 6-foot 2-inch driving wheels, were ideal for most of the roads worked over by the Haymarket men, and in particular the difficult Edinburgh to Aberdeen route. Whilst the P2s had struggled to gain respect on this route, the V2s were immediately loved, and with some workings over this route they were much preferred over the very competent Gresley Pacifics. They were equally at home with express passenger trains, express fully-fitted freight trains and the heavy unfitted freights, all of which abounded well into the latter days of BR. When 'off the beat' they could indeed be mediocre performers (albeit a joy to hear) since they had to be thrashed along, but, with valves well set up, they could competently tackle anything that might be thrown at them. Many of the common-user V2s at other depots suffered from the inherent weaknesses of the conjugated valve gear, compounded by inadequate or irregular maintenance, but the Haymarket allocation were afforded the same level of maintenance as the Pacifics and could generally tackle anything. They were eminently suited to the severe conditions abounding on the Waverley route, and could be seen working turn for turn with the A3s between Edinburgh and Carlisle. As an engine which could stand the hard slog for mile after mile on heavy roads, with big trains, whilst maintaining optimum steam and water levels, they had no equals.

The class numbered some 159 in all. Twenty-five were built at Doncaster, with the bulk of the class being built at Darlington.

Two of Haymarket's allocated Class V2s outside the front of the shed. No. 60816, in BR lined black livery, has been prepared and is awaiting departure time – whilst No. 60959 appears to be dead and waiting, or undergoing, fitters attention. *Courtesy David Dunn*

They were later quite justifiably to be classed alongside the LM&S Black Fives as '*the engines that won the war.*'

The V2s, as built, had the same swing-link design of pony truck which had proved a weakness on the P2s. In the immediate post-war period, the riding of the pony trucks on the V2s began to prove troublesome, culminating in a series of derailments – the worst of which was the V2 working the down 'Aberdonian' at Hatfield in July 1946, closely followed by the V2 working an evening Newcastle to London King's Cross express, at Marshmoor on 10th November that same year. These incidents followed previous wartime derailments with V2s at Newark and Thirsk, and focused attention on the V2 pony trucks and their riding characteristics. Peppercorn had the class converted and fitted with a modified pony truck as used by Thompson, based on the Stanier 8F design but with alterations to the springing, and the problem was resolved.

At Haymarket their availability and performance was always of the highest, and over the years the Haymarket allocation of V2s was to be somewhat fluid, with a maximum of fifteen being allocated in the early war years, a reflection on the increased level of wartime traffic that Haymarket was having to cope with. Latterly the allocation settled down to be around nine engines. As a class they could be found covering Top link turns, with the drivers there quite happy to have a V2 working in place of the allocated Pacific, particularly on the Perth and Dundee turns.

Over the years various locomotives of the class were allocated to Haymarket for longer or shorter periods of time. Unfortunately, whilst the *Yeadon's Registers* proved to be most valuable sources of information regarding allocation/transfers, the information in *Volume 4* proved to be at odds with the reality of the situation at Haymarket in the author's days (the mid-to-late 1950s); he has thus relied on his own experience and depot knowledge to list the mid-1950s allocation which varied little until the last years.

V2s allocated over the years were:

4784 (60816)	4819 (60848)	3665 (60953)
4790 (60819)	4853 (60882)	3667 (60955)
4795 (60824)	4865 (60894)	3670 (60958)
4798 (60827)	4891 (60920)	3682 (60971)
4805 (60834)	4898 (60927)	3684 (60972)
4807 (60836)	3658 (60931)	3685 (60973)
4815 (60844)	3653 (60951)	3692 (60980).

The mid-1950s allocation of V2s at Haymarket, and lasting more or less until the final days of steam were:

- 60816
- 60819
- 60824
- 60827
- 60920
- 60927
- 60951   (from new 7/42)
- 60957
- 60959.

As will be discussed in the following chapter, Haymarket did lose five V2s for the winter season in 1957/58 and then four for the winter season of 1958/59, but these engines were transferred back to the Haymarket allocation at the end of each of these seasons. Thus the transfer was temporary – albeit, it has to said, still unfortunate.

THE CLASS V4 LOCOMOTIVES

There was, however, one further 2-6-2 class of mixed traffic locomotive, numbering but two in total, designed by Gresley just before his death. These two were the Class V4 engines:

- 3401 (1700) (61700)
- 3402 (1701) (61701).

Only one engine, No. 1700, had an association with Haymarket, and that relatively short.

Known as Gresley's 'Unfinished Symphony' – he had planned further engines of the class, but there is no evidence to indicate just how many were ever intended, although a class of ten locomotives has been mentioned elsewhere – they were built as lightweight but powerful mixed traffic engines, with a high route availability (RA4) covering around 85 per cent of all the L&NER route miles. From the start they proved to be most successful, versatile and well liked engines. Indeed, whilst stationed at Aberdeen Kittybrewster, No. 1700 actually ventured, with complete success, onto the RA3 Deeside line.

The V4s were once appropriately referred to as '*Rolls Royce engines designed to do a Ford car's work.*' However, it was wartime, and changing operating and maintenance conditions demanded a simpler design capable of mass production and of being maintained by a less skilful workforce at running sheds, and the V4s were fitted with the conjugated valve gear – these were factors which were to mitigate against them. Strangely, Gresley must have been aware of what a fine all-round and extremely competent mixed traffic locomotive Stanier had produced for the LM&S in the Black Five. This was a design which ticked all the boxes: two cylinders, simple and easy to maintain and a powerful workhorse to boot, but one which was equally capable of running express passenger trains. Why Gresley stuck to three-cylinder designs, fitted with his controversial conjugated valve gear, for a smaller, mixed traffic engine, and had not followed the lead set by Stanier in the changing climate, must forever remain somewhat of a mystery, particularly in a time where suitable materials were becoming difficult to source. It is an intriguing thought as to just exactly what a Gresley equivalent of a Black Five might have been.

Thompson was quick to exploit the high maintenance requirements of these two engines, this time not without good reason, and thus as an expanded class, he quite properly decided against building any more but went on to build his own B1 locomotive instead. However, although targeted, the two locomotives in the class survived in their original form well into BR ownership, unlike the P2s, giving good service to boot, and were popular with crews; but by the end of 1957 both had been withdrawn.

It is worth considering that if the V4s had been built, or rebuilt with only two cylinders, just what difference that would have made to what were extremely capable and versatile machines.

No. 1700 (61700) *Bantam Cock* was briefly allocated to Haymarket for about six weeks in 1941, and again for twenty months in 1942/43. Little is known about the performance of this locomotive whilst at 64B, although both engines of the class were highly thought of by both Eastfield and Aberdeen Ferryhill men, proving to be very useful and strong machines. It is only as a consequence of a significant derailment (see page 198) that we know Haymarket were using No. 1700 regularly on the Perth road to good effect, on both passenger and fast freight train working.

20 L&NER LOCOMOTIVES: THE THOMPSON 4-6-2 PACIFICS

A2/1 CLASS

In 1943, to the design and order of Edward Thompson who had succeeded Gresley as CME of the L&NER, the final four of Gresley's Class V2 2-6-2 mixed traffic engines were to be built not as 2-6-2s, but rather as 'Pacific' type engines at Doncaster, very much along the same lines of the rebuilt P2 engines. Authority for building came in August 1943. The four new locomotives emerged from Doncaster between May 1944 and January 1945, and were soon nicknamed 'the ugly quartet'. All four locomotives were initially unnamed, but after a lapse of around three years all were named in true L&NER style, with three carrying names previously carried by NBR Atlantics and the fourth being given a name with proud Scottish connotations. They were initially numbered 3696–3699, but quickly renumbered 507–510 under the general renumbering scheme.

After a brief allocation to the North-Eastern Area, one engine was transferred to Haymarket, later to be followed by a further two. These engines worked both express passenger and freight trains all over the system, turn and turn about with the other Gresley Pacifics and V2s allocated to Haymarket – but whilst generally liked well enough, they never proved to be the equal of either class.

The Haymarket allocation was:

- 3696 (507) (60507) *Highland Chieftain*   12/49 until 7/60
- 3698 (509) (60509) *Waverley*   3/45 until 8/60
- 3699 (510) (60510) *Robert the Bruce*   3/49 until 7/60.

All were condemned and cut up at Doncaster works between August 1960 and February 1961.

Interestingly, No. 60507 *Highland Chieftain* was paired with tender No. 5672 which had been originally allocated to A4 No. 4469 *Sir Ralph Wedgewood*. This latter locomotive was completely destroyed by enemy bombs during a raid which badly damaged York shed on 29th April 1942. The tender, although damaged, was repaired. Until the end, the tender carried the stainless steel strip along the bottom edge, although this was kept painted over.

A2/2 CLASS

As described in Chapter 18, between January 1943 and December 1944, Edward Thompson carried out a most incomprehensible act, given it was wartime, by withdrawing the six 2-8-2 Class P2 engines from service. This was apparently done, and justified, under the banner of 'standardisation'. As discussed, some problems had been encountered with these engines when working in Scotland, but the longer wheel-base would have been more readily at home on the level and much straighter track existing on the southern end of the ECML, and their immense power a boon, particularly given the weight of East Coast expresses being worked out of King's Cross at the time. It was not to be!

The six P2s disappeared into Doncaster works, to emerge some time later as rather hideous-looking Pacific 4-6-2 engines. Still with three cylinders, but with the Gresley conjugated valve gear abandoned and now fitted with divided valve gear, they were classed

One of the two V4 class locomotives, No. 61700 *Bantam Cock*, awaits turning on the turntable after working in from Glasgow. This engine was allocated to Haymarket for two short periods. *Author's collection*

as A2/2; all (eventually) were to again carry the fine Scottish names as given when new as P2s. Despite Thompson's anathema for many of the works of his former chief, and in particular the conjugated valve gear, this valve gear was not, in fact, the major weak point of the Gresleys, as oft recorded; rather, the problem lay with the design and performance of the middle big end, a fact revealed by no less a personage than Stuart (E.S.) Cox when he was Personal Assistant to Stanier on the LM&S and had been remitted by Thompson to give best professional engineering advice. The engines, as rebuilt, apart from being ungainly and indeed ugly in the extreme, were never anything other than mediocre performers thereafter; they certainly could not hold a candle to the remaining Gresleys, including the V2s, in terms of overall performance. Given the propensity for the Thompsons to lose their feet, one driver at Haymarket commented that '*thae engines wid slip on Portobello sands.*' Enough said indeed!

They never found favour thereafter with the Haymarket men, and in 1949 all were transferred away from Haymarket, with few tears being shed at their passing!

No. 2005 *Thane of Fife* was the first to enter traffic in January 1943, the remainder following between May and December 1944. All returned at some point to Haymarket – some only for a very brief time – where they worked passenger and freight trains all over the system. However, they were never really liked in their rebuilt guise (but neither had they, it must be said, been altogether popular in their original condition) and they never equalled the performance of the Haymarket Gresley A3 and A4 engines.

The Haymarket allocation consisted of:

- 2001 (501) *Cock o' the North*   9/43 until 10/44
- 2002 (502) *Earl Marischal*   9/49 until 11/49
- 2003 (503) *Lord President*   3/45 until 4/45
                                5/45 until 5/48
                                5/48 until 11/49
- 2004 (504) *Mons Meg*   11/44 until 1/50
- 2005   *Thane of Fife*   4/43 until 12/49
- 2006 (506) *Wolf of Badenoch*   4/44 until 11/49.

All were withdrawn from service between 1959 and 1961.

A2/3 CLASS

The building of thirty new Standard 'Pacific' class locomotives, with 6-foot 2-inch driving wheels to the design of Thompson was approved in April 1944, followed by a later authorisation, in the October of that year, to build a further thirteen. In the event, only a total of fifteen of the new engines were constructed before Thompson retired, and the new CME, A.H. Peppercorn, had the remaining order cancelled and replaced by an order for another 'Pacific' class locomotive of his own design.

The Thompson engines were built between May 1946 and September 1947 and were initially classified as A2, but from April 1947 they were reclassified as A2/3 in order to make way for the proposed new Peppercorn A2 class. The Thompson locomotives were numbered 500, 511–524.

The Scottish Region allocation was to be but a single engine, and this was allocated to Haymarket. It carried out similar duties to the other Thompsons, but generally was one of the better performers, frequently covering for the regular engines in the Top links when required.

The single Haymarket engine was No. 519 (60519) *Honeyway*, allocated there from 2/47 until 10/61; in its short life it ran up the highest mileage of all the class. The engine was withdrawn (from St. Margaret's) and cut up at Doncaster in December 1962.

The sole representative of Thompson's A2/3 class allocated to Haymarket, No. 519 *Honeyway*, lifts the 14.36 Edinburgh Waverley to Carlisle stopping passenger service up the gradient past Niddrie North Junction on 17th October 1955. This engine was possibly the most popular of Thompson's otherwise mediocre Pacifics allocated to 64B. Niddrie North Junction signal box can be seen on the left behind the overbridge which carried the Lothian lines over the Waverley route. To the right of the locomotive can be seen the tail-end of a freight train making its way along the Lothian lines, a most useful route avoiding the main lines in a busy part of Edinburgh. *Courtesy W.S. Sellar*

21 L&NER LOCOMOTIVES: THE THOMPSON B1s

Edward Thompson, although second in command to Gresley, was not the automatic choice of the L&NER Board to succeed him; the L&NER Chairman, Sir Ronald Matthews, had actually approached the LM&S Board to enquire whether they might be agreeable to releasing R.C. Bond, the then Works Superintendent at Horwich, to take over the role of the CME at Doncaster. The enquiries met with little success and ultimately Thompson was appointed. When he took over the reins following Gresley's untimely death, one of his first actions was to cancel the building of any further V4 mixed traffic engines to Gresley's design, but his main aim was to get rid of Gresley's conjugated valve gear.

Having successfully stopped the building of a further ten Class V4 locomotives, he then pursued construction of his own design for a mixed traffic locomotive – the two-cylinder 4-6-0 with 6-foot 2-inch driving wheels, a locomotive which was based on Stanier's LM&S Black Five, a well proven mixed-traffic locomotive with moderate-sized driving wheels. The new B1 was to use many standard Gresley features such as boiler, K2 class cylinders and V2 class driving wheels. Boiler pressure was 225 p.s.i., and total weight of engine and tender was 123 tons 3 cwt. The B1, as built,

was considered by most to have been Thompson's most successful design, although with a route availability of RA5 it was a less versatile machine than the V4. Thompson had planned to build at least 310, and obtained authority to do so, although he only saw twenty-four completed before his retirement in June 1946. Building was carried out in batches – in-house at Darlington and to a lesser extent at Gorton, and also by the North British Locomotive Company in Glasgow – over the period between December 1942 and 22nd April 1952, with a final total of 410 being built. The numbering and renumbering which followed was complicated in the extreme.

Destined to be forever in the shadow of the Pacifics and V2s at Haymarket, nevertheless the B1 proved to be a very competent engine and was to become no stranger to named trains carrying headboards. In Scotland, both Haymarket and Eastfield B1s carried the headboard 'The Queen of Scots' as of right, being diagrammed for this working over a number of years between Edinburgh and Glasgow. The B1s as a class were well enough liked by Haymarket crews and did sterling work, particularly over the Waverley route. However, as the mileage increased after General Repair, so the riding deteriorated, and at around 50/60,000 miles they became

Haymarket B1 No. 61178 stands on the ash pits, along with a second B1 and an unidentified A4 bringing up the rear. The ash pits appear to be overdue clearing out. *Courtesy David Dunn*

Another light and shade portrait taken within the shed confines in 1963. A1 No. 60159 *Bonnie Dundee,* **now less than bonnie and in unkempt state, and with its days at Haymarket now numbered, waits patiently for its next turn of duty in April 1961.** *Courtesy Ian Musgrave*

somewhat lively at the rear end, giving crews a rough ride – but this was an inherent problem with most, if not all, two cylinder 4-6-0s.

The Haymarket allocation varied across the years, with the following locomotives of the class being at 64B for a longer or shorter period of time. From the mid-1950s, the allocation settled to around ten.

- 8303 (61002) *Impala* — 11/43 until 11/44
- 8380 (61007) *Klipspringer* — 5/44 until 6/60
- 1019 (61019) *Nilghai* — 8/48 until 10/48
- 1025 (61025) *Pallah* — 8/48 until 10/48
- 1072 (61072) — 9/46 until 3/48
- 1076 (61076) — 9/46 until 9/62
- 1081 (61081) — 10/46 until 9/63
- 1178 (61178) — 6/47 until 9/63
- 1219 (61219) — 12/57 until 9/62
- 1221 (61221) *Sir Alexander Erskine Hill* — 10/47 until 9/63
- 1244 (61244) *Strang Steel* — 10/47 until 6/60
- 1245 (61245) *Murray Of Elibank* — 10/47 until 9/63
- 1260 (61260) — 3/57 until 4/60
- 1261 (61261) — 3/57 until 1/59
- E1292 (61292) — 3/48 until 7/48
- 1333 (61333) — 8/48 until 11/48
- 1355 (61355) — 9/54 until 1/59
- 1404 (61404) — 11/50 until 1/59.

Scrapping of the class commenced as early as November 1961, but all of the Haymarket complement of B1s were to be transferred out – the final four, Nos 61081, 61178, 61221 and 61245 going with the final mass exodus of steam from 64B in September 1963.

An interesting aside about the B1s was that whilst the build was recognisable as having Doncaster origins, many bemoaned the fact that, with the single downward curve of the footplate at the cab, the elegant ex-GN 'S' curve had been lost. Around 1956, frequent instances of corner cracking at both the cab-end and the front-end of the footplate were arising, and to help cure the problem Cowlairs works fitted a strengthening plate in each corner, thus increasing the radius of the corner appreciably; of course, the Cowlairs painters followed this curve when lining out the engine and, lo and behold, the elegant 'S' curve was reintroduced, at least on the engines maintained by Cowlairs, and is clearly displayed in the photograph of No. 61178 on page 131.

22 L&NER LOCOMOTIVES: THE PEPPERCORN 4-6-2 PACIFICS

THE A2 CLASS

When Thompson retired on 30th June 1946, he was succeeded by Arthur Peppercorn as CME. Peppercorn immediately decided that the final fifteen Class A2 locomotives of the authorised thirty planned by Thompson should still be built – but to a revised, and improved, design.

Whilst the final Thompson engines were being completed, there were inevitably further amendments to the proposed Peppercorn engines, and the result was that it was not until late 1947 that Doncaster laid down the frames for what would be, more or less, a completely new design of locomotive. The number to be built had by that time also been increased to twenty.

Strangely, at the design stage it was decided to abandon the double-chimney Kylchap arrangement and revert to single chimneys for the new A2s, which were to be fitted with self-cleaning smokeboxes. This decision was perhaps based on the problems of soft exhaust beating down and inhibiting the driver's sighting, but more likely it was based on mere aesthetic grounds (a desire to return to the Gresley clean-line design).

In the event, only fifteen engines were completed within a nine-month period, Nos 525–531 (60525–60531) and Nos 60532–60539. The remainder of this particular order was then cancelled. By the time the final engine of the initial build was under construction, someone, and most probably Peppercorn himself, had had second thoughts about abandoning the Kylchap exhaust arrangement and

A1 No. 113 *Great Northern*, the Thompson rebuild of Gresley's very first A1 class Pacific, No. 4470, runs through Princes Street Gardens, Edinburgh, at the head of the 10.00 Edinburgh to Aberdeen express whilst on comparative trails against A4 No. 31 *Golden Plover* of Haymarket depot in September 1947. During the trials, No. 113 was found to be prone to slipping and here, quite unusually for a level location, the sanders are working full bore as the engine accelerates the train of around 400 tons out through the Gardens. No. 113's stay was short, the performance less than happy, and the Haymarket men were glad to see the back of it.   *Bill Brown collection*

No. 60539 *Bronzino* emerged with a double chimney as new. In 1949, five of the new A2 class were to be retrospectively fitted with the Kylchap arrangement and double chimneys, Nos 60526, 60529, 60532, 60533 and 60538.

Because of the continuing reliability problems being experienced in Scotland with the Thompson A2/2 class (formerly the P2 class), in 1949 five new Peppercorn A2s were drafted in to assist with the summer service demands. In November of that year, the A2/2s were transferred away and Scotland ended up with a total of eleven A2s, six of which worked out of Haymarket. Here they were used on principal express passenger duties, particularly on the Aberdeen line where their 6-foot 2-inch driving wheels were admirably suited for quick, sure-footed starts on the many gradients encountered on this route. Apart from No. 60529 *Pearl Diver* (which was fitted with the Kylchap exhaust arrangement), they were not first preference to replace the allocated engines in the two top links when this need arose, although this did inevitably take place, but otherwise they were well enough liked.

The first of these engines were withdrawn in 1962/63, but the last engine, No. 60532 *Blue Peter*, survived, and was preserved in 1966.

The Haymarket allocation were:

- E529 (60529) *Pearl Diver* new   2/48 until 10/61
- E530 (60530) *Sayajirao* ex New England 1/50 until 10/61
- 60534 *Irish Elegance* ex York   11/49 until 11/61
- 60535 *Hornet's Beauty* ex York   11/49 until 10/61
- 60536 *Trimbush* ex New England 11/49 until 11/61
- 60537 *Batchelor's Button* ex Aberdeen   1/51 until 11/61.

THE A1 CLASS

This classification had featured large in Thompson's aspirations for standardisation, although, happily, none but the one sad rebuild of the unfortunate Gresley A1, No. 4470 *Great Northern*, ever appeared, classed as A1/1 and numbered 113. This locomotive did make a foray north of the border, when it was transferred to Haymarket on 2nd September 1947 for trials at what was one of the most pro-Gresley sheds on the L&NER and where Thompson's Pacifics were later to be largely unwelcome. The trials consisted of tests against A4 No. 31 *Golden Plover*, one of the two A4s which had had the inside cylinder reduced to 17 inches diameter; each engine worked, on alternate days, the 10.00 Edinburgh to Dundee service, returning with the 14.43 Dundee to Edinburgh train. The trailing load northbound was 390 tons and southbound 360 tons. Under trial running, No. 113 returned slightly better coal and water consumption results than the A4, but the smoke deflection arrangement was found to be useless, slipping an inherent problem, even during actual running, and riding was less than smooth and comfortable; serious problems were envisaged even then, with the cylinders becoming loose because of line curvature and as the mileage increased. Indeed, lack of adhesion appears to have been an extremely significant problem, apparent in two photographs included within this chapter; No. 113 can be seen accelerating the 10.00 Aberdeen through Princes Street Gardens on two different days, with all the sanders working, and this on a piece of line which is completely level. Use of sand in this area was largely unknown, and perhaps says a lot about this rebuild. The trials ended somewhat

Another view of No. 113 *Great Northern* on trials, again working the 10.00 Edinburgh to Aberdeen express through Princes Street Gardens, Edinburgh. Once more, adhesion appears to be a problem since the sanders are again in full use. *Bill Brown collection*

No. 2 link A1 No. 60162 *Saint Johnstoun*, pride of both Driver Willie Bain and Haymarket shed, and in normal pristine condition, accelerates an Edinburgh to Aberdeen express, probably the 14.15 departure, past the top end of the shed (immediate left). An unidentified A4 fitted with corridor tender sits in the shed loop. In the far background, and through the haze of smoke drifting over from the shed, can be seen the bulk of the Castle Rock and Edinburgh Castle.   *Courtesy David Anderson*

On 9th September 1959, Haymarket A1 No. 60152 *Holyrood*, a No. 2 link engine, is reversing down to Waverley on the Up North Main line and is just about to pass under the 'Caley Brig' carrying the Edinburgh Princes Street to Leith North suburban line over the ex-L&NER main lines to the north and west. The signal box is Coltbridge Junction, of typical Caledonian Railway design. The engine is quite irregularly carrying a Class 'B' stopping passenger train headlamp display – the lamp should be on the centre bracket above the buffer beam indicating a light engine movement. It is probable that the engine is en route to work the 16.00 Edinburgh to Perth service, always a Class 'B' train, and the fireman, to save himself the trouble at Edinburgh, has already set the appropriate headcode.   *Courtesy David Anderson*

unsuccessfully for No. 113 – whilst the Scottish Area locomotive officers had been keen to run further tests, the engine was required elsewhere and lasted only eleven days, before being transferred back south of the border to Top Shed on the 13th September 1947. Whilst at Haymarket, amongst the footplate staff No. 113 was much unloved and unwanted – and sadly, but not unexpectedly, the predicted loose cylinders were to plague its remaining career.

Following Thompson's retirement in June 1946, Peppercorn, on taking up the reins at Doncaster, had the designs for the Class A1 locomotives, as prepared by Thompson, quietly shelved. What has been referred to elsewhere as '*the brooding influence of Thompson*' at Doncaster, was gone forever. These final Thompson designs, it must be said, had been progressed somewhat tardily by the Drawing Office staff during his last days and had been the subject of much covert (alternative) modification. The new drawings for the Peppercorn A1s were thus readily completed, and authority was given in October 1946 to build sixteen of the new Peppercorn locomotives. This was followed by an order for a further twenty-three engines in May 1947 (approved in October 1947). The L&NER directors had agreed that the new A1 class should be streamlined from the outset and had factored in an additional £500 to the cost of each locomotive – but, post-nationalisation in 1948, the new Railway Executive very quickly cancelled this requirement. In early 1948 the design was quickly further amended to have all locomotives built with the Kylchap draughting arrangement as standard.

A total of forty-nine engines were constructed: Nos 60114–60129 and Nos 60153–60162 were built at Doncaster works, with Nos 60130–60152 being built at Darlington works. The first engine, No. 60114 *W.P. Allen*, entered traffic on 26th October 1948. The Haymarket allocation of five locomotives was delivered as new over the period between 1951 and 1953. Three of the five allocated locomotives, Nos 60152, 60160 and 60161, were each thereafter transferred, on two separate occasions, 'on loan' to the ex-LM&S Glasgow Polmadie shed. It has been suggested that this somewhat unusual transfer was supposed to be part of a proposed locomotive exchange, with three Polmadie-based 'Princess Coronations' coming to Haymarket for evaluation. Because of loading gauge (kinetic envelope) problems on the ECML, this balancing element of the transfer never took place, but what an exciting prospect that would have been! The A1s were never very popular with the Polmadie men – but one thing they did all agree, and comment most favourably upon, was the fact that the A1s were all, when compared with their beloved 'Duchesses', considerably lighter on consumption of both coal and water.

The five Haymarket engines, classified as 8P from the outset, were allocated to dedicated crews in No. 2 link; these five replaced all the Gresley A3s except for one (60096 *Papyrus* in the mid-1950s, which by this time was only classified as 7P) that made up the sixth engine in the link. The seven A4s were allocated to the fourteen-turn Top link diagram. All the engines worked express passenger services to Newcastle, Glasgow, Perth and Dundee within that link. One of the principal express freight workings, the southbound 10.45 Aberdeen to London (Smithfield) 'meat', was a regular turn in No. 2 link, highlighting the importance placed on this traffic. The single A3, Class 7P or not, was never bested by the other five engines in the team whilst working in No. 2 link.

One engine, the last in the class, No. 60162 *Saint Johnstoun*, was allocated to Driver Willie Bain, then in No. 2 link; both he and No. 60162 gained much fame for the high standard of cleanliness, and indeed the positively gleaming condition in which the engine was always turned out, and which he maintained throughout the 1950s whilst he was paired with this engine. The five engines were well liked, although they could be rough and never rode with the smooth action of the Gresleys.

Good as the A1s were, they were heavier coal burners and did suffer from inherent riding properties. It is interesting that the non-stop working, post 1950, was never handed over to the new A1s. The transfer of corridor tenders would not have been an insurmountable

A1 No. 60162 *Saint Johnstoun*, now in less than immaculate condition, heads an Aberdeen Craiginches Up freight past Haymarket shed. The train is probably the Aberdeen–London (Smithfield) 'meat', an express freight service and a long-time diagram of Haymarket No. 2 link. The train will be re-engined at Waverley for onward working. *Bill Brown collection*

A fine panoramic view across the eastern suburbs of Edinburgh, as A1 No. 60162 *Saint Johnstoun*, in very dirty condition and a far cry from her prime, heads a stopping passenger train, possibly off the Waverley route, past Craigentinny carriage sidings towards the final destination, on 29th June 1961. *Courtesy W.S. Sellar*

problem despite the fact the A1s were fitted with a steam brake; but the A4s were the main-line greyhounds, and, ageing or not, were to see the running of this premium service out until the end.

Withdrawal of the class commenced in October 1962, and by the 19th June 1966 all had gone after an average working life of no more than fifteen years.

The Haymarket allocation was:

- 60152 *Holyrood*   7/49 until 6/53
- 60159 *Bonnie Dundee*   11/49 until 9/63
- 60160 *Auld Reekie*   12/49 until 9/63
- 60161 *North British*   12/49 until 9/63
- 60162 *Saint Johnstoun*   12/49 until 9/63.

In retrospect, the *raison d'etre* behind the allocation of the five, and only five, A1s to Haymarket is unclear, and indeed is open to question. There were twelve diagrammed turns, requiring six Class 8P engines, in No. 2 link, yet only five Class A1, 8P engines were allocated. During the time that No. 1 link consisted of twelve turns, there was one 'spare' A4 which was used to cover this 'hole' in No. 2 link, but when No. 1 link became a fourteen-turn link, the A4 was no longer available, and an A3 was drafted in.

The confusing situation regarding power classification and allocated work was further compounded when the engine diagrams, as issued by York HQ, are examined. In 1958, the diagram for the 22.15 Edinburgh Waverley to Carlisle, always a heavy train, indicated that it was a Class 8 engine working, yet the 22.15 Carlisle was allocated to No. 4 link (the Carlisle link) at Haymarket, who rarely

saw Class 8 engines; thus this train was regularly worked by A2, A3 and even V2 engines, and, it must be said, worked successfully!

Whilst the A1s were entirely competent engines, Haymarket was primarily a Gresley shed and it seems that it might have been more sensible to have given Gateshead shed these five Class A1 engines, since they already had a large allocation of A1s; the eight Gateshead A4s, Nos 60001/2/5/16/18/19/20 and 60023, could then have been transferred to Haymarket. The Gateshead A4s always appeared to be run down and generally were only seen on secondary duties much of the time; thus it would have made sense to have concentrated all the A4s on only two ECML sheds, King's Cross Top Shed and Haymarket, where the expertise, resources and the will to maintain the Gresleys in top condition, both mechanically and externally, already existed (see Chapter 17). The Haymarket A4s had proved that they were on top of any and all work allocated to them. No. 2 link at Haymarket had no need for any further engines fitted with corridor tenders, and thus the Gateshead engines would have fitted the bill admirably, and with a couple of A4s (and Class 8 engines to boot) or so as spare. An interesting thought indeed!

A split-new Class A1, built by the A1 Steam Locomotive Trust, costing around £3 million and taking nineteen years to actually construct by an undaunted group of volunteers, entered railway service in 2008. This of course is No. 60163 *Tornado* and it is altogether an engineering triumph – true to the original designs, but with modern equipment such as air brake pumps, additional water capacity and the latest rail safety electronics necessary to meet modern railway operation. Just one comment: '*well done, looks great … but pity about the name!*'

23 OTHER STEAM LOCOMOTIVES

Locomotives allocated but not otherwise mentioned previously, or engines of other classes not allocated but that were regular or casual visitors, are discussed hereunder.

HAYMARKET ALLOCATED

At the grouping, the Haymarket allocation of only some thirty-four engines included three Class C15 saturated 4-4-2 tank engines fitted with 5-foot 9-inch driving wheels. Built to the design of Reid, they were not actually built by the NBR at Cowlairs as might be expected, but were built under contract by the Yorkshire Engine Company at Sheffield. Known throughout their long life as 'Yorkies', and totalling thirty in number, they were built for the purpose of working suburban and branch line passenger services in and around Edinburgh and Glasgow, and were to be found spread around the ex-NBR system. The Haymarket allocation was but three, Nos 1 (9001), 25 (9025) and 141 (9141), which were used primarily on the Edinburgh/South Queensferry/Dunfermline local services. By 1932, all had been transferred away.

There were also a further four Gresleys allocated, consisting of the V1/V3 2-6-2 tank engines Nos (2910) 67610, (2915) 67615, (2916) 67616 and (2920) 67620. These were used mainly on local passenger workings such as the Edinburgh Suburban, the Edinburgh/Stirling/North Berwick/Musselburgh/Peebles routes and the Edinburgh to Hyndland via Bathgate passenger services. No. 2916 was transferred to St. Margaret's in 1942, leaving Haymarket with a final allocation of three engines. By the late 1950s, these three locomotives were largely relegated to empty coach (ECS) workings and were even to be seen deputising for N15/1 No. 69220 on the 'Sub Goods' on the odd occasion.

The remaining engines allocated were a mix of ex-NBR tank locomotives. They included two Class J88 0-6-0 tank engines, Nos 68328 and 68339, utilised on the 'Shed Shunt' turn and the 'wee Gorgie pilot' turn respectively, the former being three-shifted and the latter double-shifted. When No. 68339 was withdrawn in 1961, it was replaced by J88 No. 68335 as the 'wee' pilot. Two Class N15/1 0-6-2 tank engines were allocated, No. 69169 working the treble-shifted Gorgie pilot (the 'big Gorgie pilot'), and No. 69220 being the regular engine on the early-shift Suburban Goods to and from Niddrie West and the late-shift Prestonpans Goods – both Edinburgh District trip trains working out of Haymarket yard. N15/1 No. 69169 was withdrawn in February 1959 and replaced, at different times, by sister engines Nos 69211 and 69150 until the end of steam at Gorgie in 1962.

Haymarket V1 No. 67610 stands at the top end of the shed in February 1958. By this time, the three V1/V3 engines had been deposed from their regular passenger workings by DMUs, and were mainly to be seen on ECS workings in and around Edinburgh Waverley. Interestingly, an ex-Caledonian Railway 0-4-4 passenger tank engine, No. 55165, complete with stovepipe chimney, lurks in the background. *Courtesy W.S. Sellar*

Four Class J83 0-6-0 tank locomotives completed the Haymarket steam allocation, with two being allocated permanently to the Waverley west station pilots, Nos 1 (No. 68481) and 2 (No. 68470) turns. No. 68457 covered the three-shifted shunting turn in Haymarket yard, whilst No. 68474 acted as shed coal pilot – but on two shifts only. These J83s lasted in service until the early 1960s.

The unique 'Hush-Hush' 4-6-2-2 locomotive, No. 10000, fitted with the high-pressure (450 p.s.i.) Yarrow water-tube boiler, first came to Haymarket in February 1930 for various test running and clearance trials, and in the course of these worked across the Forth Bridge. The most important of these trials, which was given little or no publicity at the time, was a return trip from Edinburgh to Perth, on Sunday, 23rd February; on the return leg of this trial, No. 10000 worked a train of thirteen coaches plus the L&NER dynamometer car, weighing 406 tons in all, up the 6-mile-long Glenfarg bank, with its ruling gradient of 1 in 74. This was a vast load for any engine on such a steep gradient. Little information was given out regarding these tests, other than they were 'highly satisfactory'. This same engine was later used on the non-stop 'Flying Scotsman' service on one return trip only, on 31st July/1st August 1930.

The same engine, in its rebuilt guise as W1 No. 10000, returned in 1942 and was again allocated 'on loan' to Haymarket, and for a brief time only, from 27th May until 11th June; this was on a trial basis, being employed on the P2 Aberdeen diagrams. This locomotive was now basically an A4 but with a different wheel arrangement. Edward Thompson had arranged the test to ascertain whether a six-coupled locomotive could, in fact, handle the heavy Aberdeen sleepers which were then the principal trains worked by the P2s. The W1 worked the P2 diagram for this period of time and at the end was considered to have performed satisfactorily.

Other locomotives which stopped for a while before passing on included several of the ex-GER B12s, generally known as 'Hikers' by the Scottish crews. These worked out of Haymarket until they were transferred onwards, via St. Margaret's, to the ex-Great North of Scotland Aberdeen Kittybrewster shed. In fact Haymarket had an allocation of four such locomotives:

- 8500 (1500)   12/41 until 3/43
- 8503 (1503)   12/41 until 3/43
- 8511 (1511)   2/42 until 3/42
- 8521 (1521)   2/42 until 3/42.

Whilst at Haymarket, the two long-standing members of the class were not at all disliked and did some sterling wartime work.

HAYMARKET VISITORS

Before and after the grouping, the NER allocation of Atlantics shedded at Haymarket was supplemented by regular appearances of Worsdell Class R 4-4-0s, which were also used on the Edinburgh/ Newcastle services. Certainly, post-grouping, the Senior Spare link drivers at Haymarket would have taken the controls of these engines on many occasions, as well as the Class V and Class Z Atlantics. McKillop gives a detailed description of life in the Spare link and driving the NER Atlantics in his book *Enginemen Elite*. Another NER visitor to Haymarket was the NER Atlantic No. 2212 which was fitted with Uniflow cylinders to the design of Dr Stumpf, the locomotive being thus universally known as 'Stumpy'.

Early in 1923, the first of the Raven Pacifics, No. 2400, put in an appearance at Haymarket and, thereafter, the Ravens made

The NBR remained very much to the fore at Haymarket throughout the days of steam, and here is Class J88 No. 68339, the 'wee Gorgie pilot', standing in the shed loop in February 1955. *Courtesy W.S. Sellar*

Ex-NBR Class N15/1 No. 69169 stands at the top end of Haymarket shed, out of steam. This engine was for many years Gorgie No. 1 pilot or, as known at 64B, the 'big Gorgie pilot', covering the three-shifted, seven-day working at that location. Normally only coming 'on shed' to take on coal or for maintenance purposes, it is likely that No. 69169 is awaiting a boiler wash-out on this occasion.   *Courtesy David Dunn*

NER Class V Atlantic No. 705 (designed and built by Wilson Wordsdell in 1903) is seen at Gorgie Junction whilst turning before going 'on shed' at Haymarket in July 1926. The engine has just brought in the relief to the Down 'Flying Scotsman' (the 'Junior Scotsman') to Edinburgh from Newcastle and is being turned on the Gorgie triangle, being too long for the 50-foot turntable then provided at Haymarket shed.   *R.D. Stephen collection/Courtesy NRM*

ABOVE: A long-time Haymarket trip working was the 'Sub Goods', which conveyed traffic from Haymarket Yard to Niddrie West and return every weekday morning via the Edinburgh & South Suburban Railway. N15/1 No. 69220, another long-time denizen of Haymarket shed, was the regular engine employed on this working and is seen here topping the climb and entering Morningside Road station in March 1955. *Courtesy W.S. Sellar*

Ex-LM&S 4-4-0 compound No. 40921 of Perth South shed pays a visit to Haymarket on 20th April 1955. This engine worked into Edinburgh Waverley regularly during this period. Here it has been turned to face north, coaled and fire cleaned, and is ready to be prepared for the return trip home later in the day. Behind, in the murk, lurks a D11/2 Director and the corridor tender of one of the seven Haymarket A4s. *Courtesy W.S. Sellar*

regular visits. Whilst there is no evidence forthcoming to prove or disprove that Haymarket-based drivers ever handled these engines, on the balance of probability it is most likely that the men in the Spare links would do so on a fairly regular basis, since the engines regularly worked over the ECML north of Newcastle.

In January 1921, following a quest by the NBR to fill a perceived need for an 0-8-0 freight locomotive for the heavy coal train workings between Fife to Aberdeen, the GWR offered 'on loan', for trial running, an 'E' group Class 28XX locomotive, No. 2846, to work a test train over the heavy incline between Bridge of Earn and Glenfarg on the Perth main line. No. 2846 was shedded at Haymarket overnight on the evening of the 10th January 1921 before the trial running. The actual working of the trials was undertaken by the GW crew who had accompanied the engine north. The trials proved the worth of an eight-coupled locomotive, with No. 2846 lifting a train of 552 tons (twenty-nine loaded 16-ton wagons plus two brake vans) over the test stretch in the scheduled time. The engine failed on a third test run with a train of 643.5 tons, but this was in near blizzard weather conditions which had developed.

Further test runs were planned, using an NER Raven Class T3 three-cylinder 0-8-0, but these particular trials had to be postponed until the August of that year as a consequence of the 1921 coal strike. On 25th August 1921, T3 No. 903 was brought north from Darlington and again was shedded temporarily at Haymarket. On Sunday, 28th August, No. 903 went to Bridge of Earn to make four test runs. On the third run, the engine lifted a train weighing 754 tons 16 cwt up to the summit at Glenfarg in only 31 minutes. The fourth run was abandoned in the light of this quite prodigious effort. However, Mr Fraser, the then Chief Civil Engineer, vetoed the use of the Class T3 eight-coupled engines on NBR metals, although he conceded the use of the NER Class T2 two-cylinder 0-8-0 engine, one of which was put to use in revenue-earning service between Thornton and Aberdeen.

Later, in July 1923, an ex-Great Central 2-8-0, No. 1185, entered revenue-earning service in Scotland, where it proved to be superior even to the NER engines; as a result, some ten ex-ROD engines of this class, out of a total of 125 purchased from the War Department by the L&NER, were in revenue-earning service on ex-NBR lines by 30th August 1924.

Post grouping, in about 1924, Haymarket received an allocation of four ex-NER Class J24s, only one of which, No. 1858, was superheated. A total of ten came to Scotland to supplement and cover duties carried out by ex-NBR Class 'C' engines (J36s), and this they did with no little success. Not entirely liked by Haymarket drivers because of the right-hand driving position, it was conceded that they had a far superior engine steam brake then their NBR counterparts and were very strong engines.

In around 1927, Haymarket was to see visiting, on at least two occasions, the ingenious Reid MacLeod geared turbine condensing locomotive of 1910, as rebuilt by the North British Locomotive Company in 1924 and trialled on the E&GR main line, amongst others, at that time. This locomotive used a conventional boiler to supply superheated steam to two-stage expansion turbines driving through gearing on the road axles. The locomotive was carried on two composite eight-wheeled bogies and weighed 135 tons, but only had a maximum power output of 1000 bhp. It was never to do any revenue earning work, but did show what might have been with a direct turbine drive distinct from electrical transmission.

A rare visitor to Haymarket in the late 1930s was an Ivatt GNR Atlantic, No. 4452, which is recorded as being on shed in July 1939. These engines were unusual visitors 'over the border' since they were 'out of gauge' on the ex-NBR lines, owing to the height above rail level of both the boiler fittings and the cab. Nevertheless, one of the class, No. 1447, had boiler fittings and cab cut down and was sent north to work in trials against an NBR Atlantic and an NER Atlantic, but nothing more ever came of the experiment. Later, a booster-fitted GNR Atlantic, No. 4439, also appeared at Haymarket to undergo tests, but such appearances turned out to be rare indeed. Engines of this class did, however, undergo commercial repairs in Scotland after the First World War, and generally ran to and from their home depots with the dome cover removed, to ensure they did not foul the restricted NBR loading gauge.

V3 No. 67620 is in fine condition, sitting at the top end of the shed. The date is the 1st January 1956 and, like the rest of Scotland, this engine and the J88 behind are having a welcome break. *Courtesy W.S. Sellar*

One of Haymarket's least popular denizens over the winter period of 1957/58 was BR Standard 6MT (Clan class) No. 72006 *Clan Mackenzie*, seen here standing in the shed loop. This was one of four 'Clans' that were transferred in during October 1957 to replace five Class V2s which had been sent to St. Margaret's for the heavy winter sugar beet traffic, but from the word go they stood little chance of acceptance. It can be seen from its fine polished condition that the Haymarket cleaners, at least, were not permitted to neglect their charges. *Authors collection*

Haymarket, as previously discussed, was very much pro-Gresley from the early 1920s when the first A1s arrived, right through until 1963 when steam was finally deposed at 64B. Haymarket enginemen were by nature very conservative when it came to locomotives and the Haymarket allocation of steam locomotives over the years displayed this conservatism. Yes, the crews handled, with considerable competence, many other types of locomotives, generally from other depots; so, for instance, the ex-NER B16 4-6-0 mixed traffic engines (in original form and as rebuilt) from Heaton and Tweedmouth sheds were regular visitors and were regularly handled by the drivers in No. 5 link (the goods link), and Nos 6 and 7 Spare links, as were 'foreign' K3s. Ex-LM&S 5XPs (Jubilees) came in regularly from Perth, along with the ubiquitous Black Fives from both Perth and Eastfield sheds. Standard Fives, again from both these depots, also regularly worked into Haymarket in the 1950s, with Nos 73005–73009 from Perth, and Nos 73105, 73108 and 73109 from Eastfield being almost daily visitors, and these were, in turn, driven by Haymarket men. Other unfamiliar engines turned up on odd occasions, such as ex-WD 2-8-0s from south of the border and, at least twice, ex-LM&S 'Princess Coronations' came visiting. Ex-LM&S Compounds were also visitors, albeit infrequent visitors, to Haymarket, working in from Stirling or Perth. Usually they worked into Edinburgh Princes Street and went to Dalry Road shed – but at least one, No. 40921 from Perth South shed, was to be a fairly regular visitor around the mid-1950s and was photographed on shed on 20th April 1955.

In the summer of 1961, No. 46251 *City of Nottingham* (Crewe North) made an impromptu, but necessary, visit after working

a fully-fitted freight train of vans from Shawfield (Glasgow) to Slateford. En route, it was unfortunate enough to suffer the indignity of a hot driving-wheel axlebox and, since this was beyond the capability of the maintenance facilities at Dalry Road shed, down to Haymarket it came, via the Dalry Middle/Haymarket West connection, and straight to the wheel-drop pit. Duly attended to, No. 46251 left for home metals the following day. Another red 'Coronation' Pacific, No. 46244 *King George VI* (Carlisle Upperby), came visiting in 1962, when it worked the overnight sleeper service from Inverness to Edinburgh, between Perth (06.25 departure) and Waverley. It subsequently came to Haymarket LE for disposal and preparation but how, or what, it worked home to Perth is unknown! It is known that at least one 'Coronation' Pacific worked south over the Waverley route at some time, since there was an instruction in a supplement to the L&NER General Appendix, requiring that the sidescreens on the ex-LM&S 8Ps be folded inwards whilst passing through certain locations, including Bowshank Tunnel. But none of these 'foreign' locomotive classes were ever taken onto the Haymarket booked allocation. They were merely visitors, and visitors they remained.

However, in the late autumn of 1957, October to be precise, the Haymarket way of life was to be disrupted, albeit briefly, when four Standard Class 6MT 4-6-2s, the 'Clan' Pacifics, were transferred and became Haymarket locomotives for a while.

Post nationalisation there was much discord between the then Railway Executive (RE) and the British Transport Commission (BTC) regarding what the future choice of traction should be. The BTC wanted both electric locomotives and diesel locomotives as the future traction for main line work – but the RE, despite the fact that steam was disappearing around the world, wished to stick with steam traction until full electrification could be achieved, and this policy was personified in Robin Riddles, the Executive Member with responsibility for Mechanical Engineering. Riddles won the day and he was, perhaps unwisely as it turned out, given *carte blanche* to develop a new Standard breed of steam locomotives with the aim of providing machines with the twin aspirations of ease of maintenance and economy. Riddles proposed a list of thirteen different classes, which was refined down to twelve in the final analysis. Being Crewe-trained, he naturally leaned strongly towards the continuation of ex-LM&S basic design principles despite the fact that other constituent company locomotives were, at that time, setting up sparkling performances, day in and day out, and with plenty of useful life left. Riddles' strategy of making one main works each responsible for the design of one class of Standard locomotive fooled no-one, since the reality was that each of these works had to dance to the ex-LM&S tune! In short, the quest for standardisation was to overrule any logical thinking on just how, and where, these new steam locomotives might be usefully employed, especially as the building programme was undertaken immediately after a total in excess of 1,500 entirely new locomotives had just been built (post 1948) to former company/region designs and to which Riddles was now to add a further 999 Standard locomotives.

Some of the Standard locomotives, it must be conceded, were good, the Standard Fives (merely LM&S Stanier Black Fives in a new guise) being good all-round performers, as were the Standard Class 4MT 2-6-4 tank engines (although, again, these were merely the excellent Stanier/Fairburn 2-6-4 tanks in a new guise). The 9Fs were an exceptional breed, but never appeared at 64B, and they had a very short and expensive life indeed – but not before setting up some spectacular high-speed running on express passenger trains on the southern end of the ECML. The Class 7MT 'Britannias' were well enough received on the former Eastern Counties lines and did some good work elsewhere, although they were by no means universally liked, and could even be found working over the Waverley route into Haymarket in the last days of steam. 'Britannias' also worked into Haymarket from Perth from about 1961, but whilst it has not

been possible to find a record of a Haymarket crew actually working this class of engine, such a working was most highly probable – and it is just as likely that these engines, like the Class 6MT, would not have been held in particularly high regard by the Haymarket men (see below).

Other Standards did well enough in certain, but not all, hands, but many others were, as a class, totally unnecessary, and represented a waste of scarce and extremely valuable capital, thus gaining for the nationalised railway the dreadful reputation which continued to haunt it right up until privatisation. Into the ranks of the questionable, and totally unnecessary, Standard designs fell the Class 6MT 'Light Pacifics' (the 'Clans'). Twenty had been authorised for construction, but (happily) only ten were ever built. It was clear from the earliest days that there would be little useful work for them since BR already had more than a sufficient number of excellent Class 6MT engines. The 'Clans' were, quite incredibly, designed as a potential replacement for, amongst other Class 6MT locomotives, the ex-L&NER V2s, but in truth they never at any time came anywhere near to matching the versatility and outstanding performance of the V2s. They were, quite simply, never in the same league. However, they were on the BR books, not exactly popular, and work, any work, had to be found.

The 'Clans' in their entire (short) working life were never called upon to undertake any really demanding work, and they spent the bulk of their days spread between Carlisle Kingmoor and Glasgow Polmadie (with a generation of Polmadie firemen cursing them), carrying out duties which were often menial in the extreme. They were transferred around, getting as far as East Anglia at one point, and being transferred away just as quickly. Although there was at least one foray (16th June 1956) on to the West Highland line by No. 72001 *Clan Cameron* (a route for which the Clans were actually designed), they never took up service on that line. On that day No. 72001 worked a special train in connection with the gathering of the Clan Cameron at Achnacarry Castle, through from Glasgow Queen Street to Fort William.

And so, in the fullness of time, Haymarket drew the short straw, and in October 1957 took delivery of four 'Clans': Nos 72000 *Clan Buchanan*, 72002 *Clan Campbell*, 72005 *Clan Macgregor* and

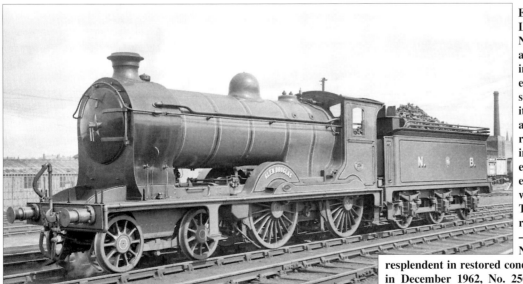

Ex-NBR Class 'K' No. 256, later L&NER and BR Class D34, No. 62469 *Glen Douglas*. After a useful life of forty-six years in revenue-earning traffic, the engine was withdrawn from service in October 1959. Happily it was scheduled for preservation, and was taken into Cowlairs for restoration and repainting back into original NBR livery. In the early 1960s it, and three other examples of preserved steam, were brought out of the Glasgow Transport Museum and steamed, running a series of special trains – and it is in this connection that No. 256 is seen here at Haymarket, resplendent in restored condition. Finally withdrawn (again) in December 1962, No. 256 was returned to the Glasgow Museum of Transport in September 2010, where it is now once more on display at the new Riverside Transport Museum in Glasgow, opened in June 2011. *Courtesy David Dunn*

Haymarket shed east yard invaded! The date is sometime in 1960 and the point of interest is, of course, the famous Caledonian Railway Single, No. 123, making one of several visits to 64B during the period that this engine, and others, had 'escaped' from the Glasgow Transport Museum and were employed on a series of special train workings in the Scottish Region. General 'wandering' by enthusiasts around Haymarket was generally frowned upon but on this very sunny day, the gods were smiling, and so was the Shed Master, John Banks, who can be seen on the far right-hand side, walking, apparently quite unconcerned, towards the General Office. In the picture, from left to right, are Thompson A2/1 No. 60509 *Waverley*, Peppercorn A2 No. 60534 *Irish Elegance*, CR No. 123, V2 No. 60801 and English Electric Type 4 diesel electric locomotive No. D260, the first of twelve to be allocated to Haymarket. *Courtesy David Anderson*

72006 *Clan Mackenzie*. This, in all conscience, was bad enough, but Haymarket then lost five V2s which were in first-class order to St. Margaret's for the winter seed potato and sugar beet seasonal traffic. At the time this reason was accepted without question, but looking back it can be questioned just why the 'Clans' were not transferred directly to St. Margaret's, thus avoiding the additional counter-transfers involved, since they were 6MT engines just like the V2s. It is more than suspected that Management, knowing very well their shortcomings, decided not to risk their exposure to what was extremely high-value, vulnerable and time sensitive traffic which demanded the highest levels of locomotive performance, hence the convoluted transfer process.

From the first morning when the first of the 'Clans' (No. 72000) appeared in the shed, they were immediately disliked, by both drivers and, especially, firemen, not to mention the cleaners. The one-piece cabs were draughty and dirty to work in, the LM&S-type firedoor with large oval opening and sliding firedoors was an anathema to Haymarket firemen and made the work of firing very hot and uncomfortable in the extreme. They were ostensibly transferred in to work over the Waverley route, but were soon found to be inordinately heavy on water, mediocre at steaming and sluggish in running; very soon the universal dislike at Haymarket turned to sheer hatred and every opportunity was taken to avoid the four engines. By April 1958 they were gone, with a big sigh of relief all round, but in October 1958 two were again transferred in for the winter season. By 1959 they had gone for good. At a depot where the whole allocation of engines was ex-NBR/L&NER in origin, maintained in tip-top condition and well looked after, the 'Clans' stood little chance, even though they were afforded the same high levels of attention. They were, as a class, built by a frustrated steam engineer who, as CME of the Railway Executive, had been allowed to proceed with his ideas for steam traction, even though this was not what the railways of the 1950s actually required, particularly with

the 1955 Modernisation Plan soon to be tabled. The Standards, by and large, were in fact becoming obsolete as they were being built, and their building was nothing other than the height of folly when dieselisation was already knocking at the door. This ineptitude of the RE/BRB was to be seen yet again in the following years, during the dieselisation programme, more of which later.

Other locomotives which visited Haymarket during the late 1950s/early 1960s included, strangely enough, one Colwick-based Thompson Class L1 2-6-4 passenger tank, No. 67769. It was one of the class fitted with 'limousine doors' – that is, a full-height side door with a droplight window, opened and closed by a leather strap in the manner of the coach windows of the day. This was fitted because of many complaints from footplate staff about these engines being exceptionally draughty to work on. The engine was bound for minor works attention at Cowlairs. Whence it came is not known, but it spent an overnight at 64B before being worked light to Glasgow the following morning.

Preserved Caledonian Railway single No. 123 also graced Haymarket on several occasions, and made one unscheduled visit after it had worked a special train from Stirling to Edinburgh in 1959. It required attention to a heating axlebox, and was quickly attended to, prepared, and took up the booked return working. No. 123 attracted a lot of attention from the older fraternity at the shed and there was some keen competition as to who would have the privilege of preparation and delivery back to Waverley. During the period when the preserved locomotives from the Transport Museum in Glasgow were out on loan and in steam, working special trains around the Scottish Region, ex-NBR Class D34 No. 256 *Glen Douglas* also put in an appearance at Haymarket on more than one occasion.

Post-dieselisation, foreign locomotives, but not foreign classes of locomotive, still came to Haymarket for refuelling, and thus it was much of a muchness with what had gone before.

24 HAYMARKET AND THE NON-STOPS

Surely the most famous named train to run anywhere in the UK or, indeed, worldwide in the period from 1928 until 1962 (but omitting the war years) was the Edinburgh/London non-stop express which ran under three different titles and carried three different headboards within these years. It did exactly what the commonly given nick-name suggested. The train ran the 393 miles between London King's Cross and Edinburgh Waverley in either direction without any intermediate stop. The other unique element of this working was that it remained the domain of Gresley Pacifics throughout its life, despite the advent of more modern and more powerful L&NER Pacifics.

Haymarket's claim to fame was, in no small measure, justified by the part which locomotives and crews based at the depot played in the running of this non-stop express passenger train, in every summer timetable, beginning on 1st May 1928. The departure of both the original southbound service and the northbound service was at 10.00. The train was, of course, 'The Flying Scotsman'. Until 1928, the southbound working of the 10.00 'Flying Scotsman' from Edinburgh had, from away back in 1862, been the preserve of the NER Gateshead crews, but with the introduction of non-stop through-running between the two capitals, Haymarket men were to be given a share in working the northern half of the journey; this arrangement continued until the non-stop service, now dieselised and worked by 'Deltics', was finally withdrawn at the end of the 1962 summer timetable.

Initially it was intended that the non-stop train be worked by two sheds only, King's Cross and Gateshead – Haymarket having been, before the grouping, and in respect of the working of East Coast express passenger trains, effectively a sub-shed of Gateshead – with NER engines and crews working the services. As has been discussed, the NBR crews eventually won a right to share in these workings, and by 1928 the ex-NBR drivers in the Newcastle link had gained considerable experience of the Gresley Pacifics. As a consequence of this, and with some pressure from the then Chief General Manager, Sir Ralph Wedgwood, this new non-stop working was eventually to be shared by four Haymarket crews, four King's Cross Top Shed crews and six Gateshead crews – an extremely important step by the L&NER management towards total integration of engine workings on the East Coast route. It brought former GNR, NER and NBR enginemen into a common partnership which would have been impossible by mere interpenetration workings; it was, in reality, the catalyst which finally broke down the NER prejudices against the Gresley Pacifics. This working, however, gave rise to a very complicated set of enginemen's diagrams, with the Gateshead men being required to lodge at either end on a regular basis, involving three nights away from home at a time. This non-stop working was to continue until the advent of the Second World War.

Post-war, non-stop working was reintroduced once more from 1948, thus the non-stop ran every summer between 1928 and 1962, but excluding the nine-year gap between 1938 and 1948 – firstly as 'The Flying Scotsman' then, in 1949, retired, and renamed 'The Capitals Limited', and finally, having been further renamed once again, in the Coronation year of 1953, as 'The Elizabethan'. Post-war, however, the working was confined to Haymarket and King's Cross Top Shed crews only. On the non-stop turns, the Haymarket men lodged in the Kentish Town hostel in London; but in Edinburgh, since there was no railway hostel, the King's Cross men were lodged in private bed and breakfast accommodation.

Another Haymarket stalwart, Top link driver James (Jimmy) Paterson being congratulated by Mr W. Arnott, Station Master, Edinburgh Waverley, and Mr G. Lund, ADMPS Edinburgh, after bringing the first northbound run of the new non-stop express, 'The Elizabethan', into Edinburgh with Haymarket A4, No. 60024 *Kingfisher*, a few minutes before time on the 29th June 1953. No. 60024 was to be a regular performer on the non-stop over the remaining years the train ran. Driver Paterson's own engine in No. 1 link at Haymarket was No. 60009 *Union of South Africa*, another noted performer. *Courtesy Mr Peter Lund*

For the inaugural run in May 1928, Haymarket turned out A3 No. 2580 *Shotover* – driven by no less a personality than Tom Henderson of NBR Atlantic fame, with Fireman Robert McKenzie – to work the first southbound train as far as York; relief by Driver Day and Fireman Gray of King's Cross taking place on the move via the then new, and quite unique, corridor tender. Haymarket depot was also instrumental in providing the first headboard, as per standard NBR practice, on the Up train, displaying in black lettering on a white background the legend 'The Flying Scotsman', and thus was born the use of headboards on selected principal express passenger services on the L&NER, a practice which was to spread throughout BR.

On this first southbound run, the Haymarket crew had to contend with heavy mist along the Southern Uplands (this was without doubt the infamous 'east coast haar' which affects the eastern seaboard of southern Scotland each year on a regular basis) and 4 minutes were lost in running, although all lost time was eventually recovered by York and the arrival in London was one minute early. The excellence of the Gresley Pacifics was never better demonstrated than by the coal consumption figures released for this first run – inclusive of lighting-up and preparation, the average consumption worked out at a mere 34.02 lbs per mile.

On the northbound run, the train was hauled by No. 4472 *Flying Scotsman* itself, with Driver Pibworth and Fireman Goddard of King's Cross being relieved by Gateshead men Driver Blades and Fireman Morris. This latter crew had to contend with a hot tender axle-box in the latter stages of the journey, with the fireman playing water on the box to ensure they could make Waverley. In the event, the train arrived safely and 12 minutes early.

However, this non-stop working commenced during the time of the quite scandalous cartel entered into between the Joint West Coast and East Coast Companies (the 1896 Agreement), which was thereafter to inhibit the speed of all Anglo-Scottish services; as a result, 'The Flying Scotsman' was tied to a quite ridiculous 8½-hour schedule which was to plague this working until the summer of 1931.

In the first 1928 season, No. 2580 *Shotover* and A3 No. 2563 *William Whitelaw*, the latter having exchanged tenders with No. 2569 *Gladiateur* in order to gain a corridor tender, alternated for the whole of the season, except for one brief spell when No. 2573 *Harvester* was pressed into service.

In 1929, Haymarket used only three engines for the whole season, namely Nos 2563 *William Whitelaw*, 2464 *Knight of (the) Thistle* and 2566 *Ladas*, the latter engine taking the corridor tender from No. 2565 *Merry Hampton*.

In 1930, the first trip of the season was marked by engines allocated to King's Cross Top Shed working both the northbound and southbound services, No. 2746 *Fairway* taking the Down train and No. 4472 *Flying Scotsman* working the Up train. Thereafter, Haymarket again used only three engines for the remainder of the season, Nos 2563 *William Whitelaw*, 2796 *Spearmint* and 2795 *Call Boy* – the latter being the star performer, running a total of twenty-eight consecutive trips. This was, without any shadow of a doubt, testament to the exceptionally high standards of maintenance existing at Haymarket at that time. The 1930 season was also notable in that the high pressure 'Hush-Hush' compound No. 10000 made one return trip (31st July/1st August) on the 'The Flying Scotsman', this was completed successfully but was never to be repeated.

In 1931, the last season of the tedious and artificially-slow running times, Haymarket used but two engines for the whole season, namely Nos 2795 *Call Boy* and 2796 *Spearmint*.

1932 saw the ending of the East Coast/West Coast agreement, with the running times reduced to 7½ hours. Haymarket again depended on two engines only for the whole season, Nos 2563 *William Whitelaw* and 2795 *Call Boy*. On the first southbound run of the new season, the train was headed by No. 2795 *Call Boy* driven by A. (Sandy) Davidson with Fireman James Collins, both of Haymarket, and the run was completed in 7 hours 27 minutes at an average speed of 56 mph.

1933 saw the exceptional reliability of the Haymarket engines continue, with again only two engines alternating for the whole season, Nos 2795 *Call Boy* and 2796 *Spearmint*.

In 1934 Haymarket again used only the two stars, Nos 2975 *Call Boy* and 2976 *Spearmint*, both of which continued to dominate the non-stop service.

1935 saw a further 15 minutes being pared off the timings. Haymarket yet again, and with almost regular monotony, relied on Nos 2796 *Spearmint* and No. 2795 *Call Boy* for almost the whole season. This monopoly was to be finally broken on the 15th August, when the almost-new No. 2508 *Brown Jack* was given the corridor tender from No. 2563 *William Whitelaw* and pressed into non-stop service.

1936 was the last year in which A1s and A3s were to be used on the non-stop workings. Thereafter, the ten 1928-built corridor tenders were transferred to the new A4s. For this new season, No. 2795 *Call Boy* opened the batting for Haymarket, with No. 2976 *Spearmint* again taking a lion's share, and No. 2975 *Call Boy* making its final non-stop appearance on the last Down working.

1937 saw the A4s begin to monopolise the non-stop scene for the first time, with running time further reduced to the even seven hours, but not before A3 No. 2750 *Papyrus* put in the final appearance for the class. Haymarket, as was now the norm, chose to rely on only two A4s for the early part of the season, Nos 4484 *Falcon* and 4485 *Kestrel*, but with a third A4 – No. 4492 *Dominion of New Zealand* which had been transferred to Haymarket at the beginning of July – also taking an active part in this running and actually working, in total, sixty-two turns, of which fifty-two were consecutive.

In 1938, two completely new train-sets were introduced, fitted with electric air-conditioning equipment and thus posing a heavier trailing load for the locomotives. Haymarket, quite unusually, used four A4s for the season, Nos 4482 *Golden Eagle*, 4487 *Sea Eagle*, 4490 *Empire of India* and 4491 *Commonwealth of Australia*.

In 1939 the season was cut short by one week because of the escalation of hostilities in Europe, and this was to be the last year of non-stop running for a long nine years. Haymarket used the same engines as for the 1938 season, but with the exception of No. 4491 *Commonwealth of Australia* which was replaced by No. 4484 *Falcon*.

The running of this non-stop service over the ten years prior to the Second World War saw exceptional feats by the A1s, A3s and, latterly, the A4s involved, and by their crews. The level of care and maintenance at Haymarket was, without doubt, quite remarkable and nowhere did this manifest itself more than in the years when only two Haymarket engines maintained the running for the whole season. This is not meant to dismiss, or denigrate in any way, the equally very high standards existing at King's Cross Top Shed, but nevertheless the Haymarket performance was quite in a class of its own. The exploits of Nos 4492 *Dominion of New Zealand*, co-opted as it was in 1938 for use on the new 'West Riding Limited' service,

It is February 1930 and locomotive No. 10000 (the 'Hush-Hush'), Gresley's high-pressure 4-cylinder 4-6-4, or, more properly, 4-6-2-2, fitted with Yarrow water-tube boiler with a working pressure of 450 p.s.i., stands in the shed loop at Haymarket. The engine was in Scotland and temporarily allocated to Haymarket in order to undertake a series of loading trials, and on Sunday, 23rd February worked a train of thirteen coaches plus the L&NER dynamometer car (406 tons) up the six-plus miles of Glenfarg bank on a ruling gradient of 1 in 74. Various other loading trials were conducted on the Edinburgh–Perth line of route, but little or no publicity was given to the event.

The photograph is also of interest for the background. To the extreme right can be seen the original Haymarket manual coaling stage, seldom photographed; but more interestingly, the scaffolding structure just above the engine cab shows the preliminary supports for the construction of the new concrete coaling plant, construction of which was already underway and which would be brought into operation later in the same year.   *R.D. Stephen collection/Courtesy NRM*

Magnificent *Merlin*! Haymarket Top link A4, No. 60027 *Merlin* was always an outstanding performer, but was to excel itself in the summer of 1960 when it ran an incredible seventy-seven turns on the non-stop 'Elizabethan' between Edinburgh and King's Cross, forty-six of which were consecutive runs. Here the engine is seen to perfection, in sparkling, but normal, Haymarket condition, standing outside the shed and prepared for the next turn of duty, on the 2nd March 1958. *W. Hermiston/Transport Treasury*

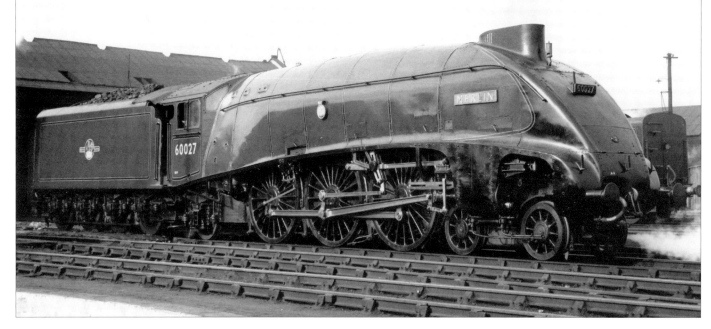

to be followed on the same service by No. 4491 *Commonwealth of Australia*, and after which No. 4491 went on to work the 'Coronation', might just have suggested that Haymarket was, by and large, underpinning all the new streamlined services around that time. But even better days were to follow in the post-war years! Such performances must have been quite an eye-opener for the detractors of the Gresley conjugated valve gear.

June 1948, the year that the nationalised British Railways came into being, saw the restoration of the summer non-stop working of 'The Flying Scotsman', with No. 60034 *Lord Faringdon* working the first northbound service, whilst Haymarket's No. 60009 *Union of South Africa* worked the first southbound service. On the 12th August of that same year, however, in a repeat of a similar occurrence some 102 years before, severe thunderstorms following a prolonged period of heavy rains across the southern uplands of Scotland, and specifically high up in the Lammermuir Hills, caused the many small hill streams to become raging torrents – in particular the Eye Water, down beside which the railway ran between Grantshouse and Reston. The ECML crossed this stream no less than seven times over this section of the route and, once again, every one of these seven bridges was swept away by the floods. At the height of the floods, the water of the Pease Burn, another stream lying to the northern edge of the hills, was running down through Penmanshiel Tunnel, the water level being within a few feet of the tunnel crown. This storm was described as a 'meteorological holocaust', when an estimated 400 million gallons of water, the equivalent of a rainfall of over 6 inches, fell in a very short period of time on ground which was already at saturation point. The severe flooding also caused several culverts to collapse. Initially the complete line of route was cut in thirteen places and was totally closed between Newcastle and Edinburgh. By the 24th August the route had been restored

between Tweedmouth and Newcastle, and the non-stop working had been rearranged and reinstated, but running over the Waverley route as far as St. Boswells, thence via Kelso to Tweedmouth, to rejoin the ECML there. Whilst this route was only some 15.9 miles longer, it posed far more severe gradients and in terms of time, it added around 70 minutes to the running time, all north of Lucker troughs. Water supplies were thus perceived to be a likely problem and the amended working arrangements as issued included out-of-course booked stops to be made at Hardengreen Junction for rear-end assistance for the ten-mile 1 in 70 slog up through the Moorfoot Hills to Falahill summit in the Up direction, and at Galashiels for water in both directions.

At this point, what actually happened with the rerouted train, and involving whom from Haymarket, becomes a bit confused when the various accounts are considered. There is absolutely no doubt that the requirement for these extra stops, in what was billed as a non-stop service, irritated many of the Top link drivers at Haymarket. It is also without doubt that most, if not all, of the Top link men of the time were first-class enginemen in their own right and capable of producing outstanding performances when required. It must be remembered that, with the rapid promotion from firing to driving owing to the introduction of the eight-hour day away back in 1919, many of the young drivers then promoted were now manning the top links whilst still relatively young men.

According to the RCTS book, *Locomotives of the LNER*, Part 2A, Driver Bill Stevenson had No. 60028 *Walter K. Whigham* on the southbound run on the 24th August and, having worked out a strategy in advance, he passed Hardengreen at speed, ran through Galashiels without stopping for water and ran on to uplift water at Lucker troughs after 96 miles of hard running, and with around 2000 gallons still remaining in the tender. He handed over to the

TABLE 24.1   RECORDED NON-STOP RUNS DURING THE DIVERSION OF 1948

		UP DIRECTION			DOWN DIRECTION	
Tuesday	24/8	60028 *Walter K. Whigham*	Stevenson			
Wednesday	25/8			60028 *Walter K. Whigham*	Stevenson
Thursday	26/8	60028 *Walter K. Whigham*	Stevenson	60027 *Merlin*	McLeod
Friday	27/8			60029 *Woodcock*	Stevenson
Saturday	28/8	60029 *Woodcock*	Stevenson		
Thursday	2/9			60029 *Woodcock*	Stevenson
Monday	6/9			60029 *Woodcock*	Swan
Tuesday	7/9	60029 *Woodcock*	Swan	60012 *Commonwealth of Australia*	McLeod
Wednesday	8/9			60029 *Woodcock*	Swan
Thursday	9/9	60029 *Woodcock*	Swan	60031 *Golden Plover*	McLeod
Saturday	11/9	60012 *Commonwealth of Australia*	Swan		
Wednesday	15/9	60022 *Mallard*	Swan		
Thursday	17/9	60029 *Woodcock*	Swan		
Friday	18/9	60012 *Commonwealth of Australia*	McLeod		

King's Cross crew just north of York and the 408.65 miles over the extended route to London King's Cross were run non-stop, creating the longest non-stop journey in the world. Drivers Stevenson, Swan and the McLeods (Bill and Tony), all of Haymarket shed, then proceeded to repeat this performance a further sixteen times, with a total of nine runs in the Up direction and eight runs in the Down, over the remainder of the summer timetable.

This is confirmed by O.S. Nock in *The Gresley Pacifics*, although he records that Stevenson had No. 60029 *Woodcock* on the first day. Then, strangely for Nock, he records that Stevenson had No. 60028 *Sea Eagle* on two other occasions, this despite the fact that No. 60028 had been renamed *Walter K. Whigham* in the previous October. These aberrations apart, after the initial record-breaking run by Stevenson, Haymarket drivers went on to repeat this exceptional feat a further sixteen times, leaving little room for doubt that enginemanship of the highest order was required, and that Haymarket men rose to the challenge quite magnificently. This has been further confirmed more recently, by Peter Coster of the Gresley Society. The recorded non-stop runs are shown in Table 24.1.

Some more recent evidence supplied has, however, suggested that the last non-stop run via the borders deviation was not on the 18th, as oft recorded, but actually occurred on the 21st September, the last day of the service, when an on-train recorder, a Mr Alan Robinson, confirmed that a further north-bound (Down) non-stop run was made by the train, hauled by Haymarket A4 No. 60024 *Kingfisher*, although the driver on this occasion was not identified.

In *Enginemen Elite*, McKillop records that the honour for the first of these longest non-stop runs was down to Jimmy Swan with No. 60029 *Woodcock*, on the 7th September 1948. Cecil J. Allan in *The Railway Magazine* (April 1949) also credits Swan with this record on this day, having no doubt been given the information by R.I. Nelson, and claiming Swan ran non-stop in the both the Up and Down direction four times.

Here then, are three reputable sources saying one thing, and a driver (and author) who was at Haymarket at the time, saying something else. Nelson was a great pal of McKillop's and had, no doubt, obviously been given the story from that source, from whence it was passed on to C.J. Allan.

It would appear that history, and the facts, are confused to say the least. However, there can be little or no doubt that this feat was achieved by drivers other than Swan, although McKillop does not acknowledge this point; thus, if the non-stop runs were made on eighteen separate occasions by different drivers, then the first run most likely would have been much earlier than the 7th September, since the summer timetable finished on the 21st. Had McKillop detailed the other drivers who managed to run non-stop, then more credence might have been paid to his assertions, but he chose to leave the honour solely with Swan, another one of his close friends it has to be said. In fairness, however, Swan is recorded with the greatest number of non-stop runs (seven) over this circuitous route through the Scottish Borders. On balance, and considering all the facts, there is little doubt that the O.S. Nock/RCTS/P.J. Coster account is the more accurate.

In his book *Nigel Gresley: Locomotive Engineer*, F.A.S. Brown, who corresponded with Swan, merely records that a major share of the credit for these non-stop runs was due to the foresight and careful driving of Swan. Whatever the facts of the matter, there is little doubt that this was engine driving of the highest order since, after taking water at Lucker, the Haymarket crews had to nurse the water supplies until Danby Wiske troughs were reached, some 100 miles to the south. Credit for this success must also be paid to the King's Cross crews who came through the tender at, or around, Tollerton on the Up run, since they also had to manage the water supplies carefully until the troughs at Scrooby were reached, the previous 'dip' having been at Danby Wiske troughs, some 74 miles to the north – particularly when a full tank had not been achieved there, as sometimes was the case. They had also to deal with the more tightly-timed sections of the run. Equally, it was only by the dint of some exceptional and careful work by the King's Cross men on the Down working, to ensure sufficient fuel remained to meet the demands of this 70-minute longer than usual leg of the journey, that the Haymarket crews were able to repeat this feat on the northbound journey no less than seven times.

Haymarket No. 1 link and No. 2 link drivers were, however, well noted for their dedication to their craft and, with seeming indifference, they regularly ran the 125 miles between Edinburgh and Newcastle without lifting water at Lucker (76 miles from Edinburgh). Indeed, in 1951, when the troughs at Lucker were being renewed, not one Haymarket crew took on water between

Newcastle and Edinburgh over the whole period of time that the troughs were out of use. This was not a problem with the A3s and A4s, but it could be a 'touch and go' situation with an A1 or A2 and called for the most careful engine management.

Beginning in 1949, the non-stop working was renamed 'The Capitals Limited' and was re-timed to depart before the 10.00 'Flying Scotsman' which then retained its booked stops. In the year of Queen Elizabeth's coronation, 1953, the non-stop working was renamed once again, and became 'The Elizabethan'. Haymarket driver Jimmy Paterson, with A4 No. 60024 *Kingfisher*, had the honour of working the first northbound run of this new service into Waverley.

1960 was supposed to see the end of steam on the non-stop. However, circumstances dictated that this prediction would be somewhat premature. As described in Chapter 17, in 1960 No. 60027 *Merlin*, very much the star of Haymarket Shed, ran a total of seventy-seven non-stop turns, forty-six of which were consecutive runs, setting an incredible performance – which only served to highlight just what magnificent engines the A4s actually were, given proper care and maintenance. In doing so, *Merlin* fully deserved the soubriquet bestowed upon it by enthusiasts, 'Magnificent *Merlin*'. With modified middle big ends, and other modifications including the fitting of the Kylchap exhaust arrangements and double chimneys, the A3s and A4s were transformed and went on to prove just how good they could be.

Steam reappeared on the non-stop working in 1961 and, in the summer of that year, the steam-hauled 'Elizabethan' went out in a blaze of glory with Haymarket A4s Nos 60009 *Union of South Africa* and 60024 *Kingfisher* sharing much of the last season's running with, quite appropriately, King's Cross A4s Nos 60014 *Silver Link* and 60022 *Mallard*.

Nos 60031 *Golden Plover* and 60028 *Walter K. Whigham* worked the Up and Down trains respectively on the first day of the summer timetable, with Nos 60022 *Mallard* and 60009 *Union of South Africa* working the trains on the last day of the service. Some exhilarating

final runs were recorded with net running times of not more than 369 minutes being very much the norm.

On one of the last Up runs, No. 60009 *Union of South Africa* passed Grantham some 10 minutes late, but after the mandatory slow through Peterborough, the King's Cross crew 'let her go' to good effect and the train arrived in King's Cross some 5 minutes early, the 105.45 miles from Grantham having been reeled off in only 93 minutes. The working and performance of the A4s on both the non-stop and other workings have been well documented by other commentators.

So that icon of exceptional steam locomotive working and performance, the non-stop London/Edinburgh express over the East Coast route, passed into the annals of history, and with it, sadly, the glory days at Haymarket. The great days of Gresleys were not, however, quite finished, as they went on to put up some spectacular performances on the three-hour Glasgow to Aberdeen services. But their remaining days at Haymarket were now numbered.

The non-stop working in 1962 was entrusted to what else but the new Deltics, but a station stop had to be inserted at Newcastle to allow for a crew change-over, it being considered that having the second crew riding in the rear cab throughout would be unacceptable owing to the high noise levels. However, even with a footplate change at Newcastle, the working continued to be in the hands of King's Cross Top Shed and Haymarket crews. The non-stop was thus no more, and 'The Elizabethan' was withdrawn from the end of that 1962 season.

Accelerated timings, additional trains, reduced journey times and high-speed running became the norm as first the Deltics, followed in turn by the magnificent High Speed Trains, the HSTs, and finally the electrically-hauled 225 trains, took the speed of express passenger trains over the ECML to a level way beyond the reach of steam power. The outstanding performances put up in the heyday of the Gresley Pacifics were consigned to history – and to the memories of those lucky mortals who, like the author, are fortunate enough to have experienced those 'glory' days.

An interesting photo. Here Top Shed A4, No. 60015 *Quicksilver*, **fresh from working the Down 'Elizabethan', has been appropriated by the running foreman at Haymarket, in response to an SOS from Edinburgh Control, to provide assistance to a failed Sulzer Type 2 locomotive working a Glasgow to Edinburgh Parcels train. The A4 is seen here, running tender-first on the Up South Main line opposite the shed, hauling the failed diesel and train, en route to Waverley.** *J.Simpson/D. Spaven collection*

25 THE DMU DAYS

Despite some dabbling, and it can be described as no more than that, by the LM&S and Southern railway companies with diesel electric traction as a possible replacement for steam, at nationalisation it was the Diesel Multiple Unit (DMU) which was to start making inroads into what had been steam operated lines – in particular the rural and suburban lines. In Edinburgh, the Gloucester twin-car DMU sets (Class 100) built in 1955 started to appear, and in 1956 the Swindon six-car DMUs made their first appearance.

With the gradual phasing out of individual traction units (locomotives) and the replacement by multiple unit trains, much of the attraction and romance of railways disappeared. The DMUs were considered by many footplate men to be nothing but glorified trams, but with considerably less appeal. Initially the Gloucesters appeared to take over many of the local passenger services worked by Haymarket shed (and the other Edinburgh sheds), including the

North Berwick, Musselburgh and Galashiels via Peebles lines. These units, consisting of a power car and a trailer car, were fitted with two BUT (AEC) 150 bhp engines, with cardan shaft and freewheel to four-speed epicyclic gearboxes, and further cardan shafts to the final drive. They were soon followed by the Metro Cammell twin-car sets (Class 101) fitted with similar engines and transmission. At first the DMU diagrams were incorporated into Nos 3 and 4 links' diagrams at Haymarket, since both these links had been allocated much of this local work under steam. During the weeks (three in each link) when drivers were manning the DMUs, their firemen were rostered 'spare'. This situation existed until Leith Central depot, where all the DMUs in the Edinburgh area were stabled and maintained, was established as a proper Promotion, Transfer & Redundancy Depot for train crews, and coded 64H by BR at the end of 1959.

The new order arrives. The first of the new Swindon six-car DMU sets for the Edinburgh Waverley to Glasgow Queen Street services makes an appearance in August 1956. After a period of driver training they gradually entered revenue-earning service from January 1957, bit by bit supplanting steam workings over the route in the course of the next two to three years. Finally becoming Class 126, they remained in service until May 1971, when the new push-pull sets with Class 27 diesel electric locomotives front and rear took over the running of the Edinburgh and Glasgow route. *Courtesy Scotsman Publications*

On the Edinburgh and Glasgow main line, the Swindon-built DMUs were introduced from 1956 in a rolling programme. These train-sets were of six-car formation with compact buffet facilities provided. Each motor coach was fitted with two BUT (AEC) six-cylinder horizontal engines producing 150 bhp. From 7th January 1957 they were introduced on the route alongside the normal steam-hauled services, and gradually superseded steam completely. Towards the end of the 1960s the limitations of the Swindon (now Class 126) sets were becoming clearly obvious and they no longer measured up in terms of either speed or comfort. For various reasons, but mainly to obtain improved timings, it was decided to again revert to locomotive power when replacing them, and after a series of trials with both a single Class 37 locomotive in a push-pull formation followed by a Class 47 with the same trial formation, it was ultimately decided to utilise specially converted Class 27/1 and Class 27/2 locomotives in push-pull formation with six Mk II coaches to replace the ageing DMUs.

Over the years after closure of Leith Central as the main Edinburgh DMU depot, Haymarket fell heir to a wide selection of DMUs. These consisted of, in no particular date order:

- Class 101   Metro-Cammell two-car units
- Class 120   Swindon six-car units
- Class 122   Gloucester RC&W single car units. Nos SC55000, SC55002, SC55005, SC55007, SC55011 and SC55015.
  These worked on the Edinburgh/Dundee services until, initially, SC55007 was converted to a 'Sandite' unit, followed in course by the conversion of the reminder

- Class 104   Birmingham RC&W (short stay only)
- Class 107   Derby works three-car units. Total fleet of twenty-six transferred from Hamilton, but condemned out of service on arrival at Haymarket. Later repaired and put back into service except for three units which were converted to 'Sandite' trains
- Class 108   two-car units from Midland Region
- Class 117   two-car units originally allocated to Western Region but transferred to Haymarket from Hamilton.

Scotland was, thankfully, spared the 'Pacer' twin-car units (Class 140), but not before three Class 143 units had been transferred from Heaton to Haymarket, intended for the Bathgate services. Some extensive trial running was carried out on nights on the Edinburgh/Fife Circle lines, at which the author was the official Operating Department representative, accompanying Edinburgh Traction Inspector L. Gracie. These units were of BR design, incorporating body parts and equipment as used on the standard Leyland National bus. They had under-slung Leyland engines, delivering 200 bhp with mechanical transmission, and had a top speed of 75 mph. They were, quite simply, dreadful, and could barely cope with the severe gradients whilst running empty, let alone attaining 75 mph, or anywhere near. During the trials the screeching of flanges on rails as the test set made its way round the curves of the Fife coast was appalling. They were also trialled elsewhere in the region but with no success. Following their return south, Haymarket took allocation of a further three two-car Class 101s for the Bathgate service.

A Class 101 two-car DMU heads for Edinburgh from the Fife circle, over the Forth Bridge in the summer of 1969.   *Courtesy Ian Musgrave*

Haymarket Class 122 No. SC55000 undergoes attention in the workshops on 11th June 1983. Built by the Gloucester R.C.&W. Co. in 1958, this was a single-car DMU equipped with two BUT (AEC) six-cylinder horizontal engines rated at 150 bhp. The car provided sixty-five seats and the unit weighed 36 tons tare. This was one of six allocated to the Scottish Region and worked between Edinburgh and Dundee. This particular unit was converted to a 'Sandite' unit, followed in turn by the conversion of the remaining five of the class. *Courtesy Gavin Morrison*

The 'Sprinters' did, however, descend upon Scotland. The Class 150/2 (Sprinters) and Class 156 (Super Sprinters) were introduced into the Scottish Region, mainly for local train working, with an allocation coming to Haymarket in 1987 and 1988 respectively.

Haymarket received six units initially, 150255/257/258/259/283 /284 and 150285. They were two-car units, a power car and a trailer car, and were fitted with Cummins engines of 285 bhp, Voith transmission and Gmeinder final drives. They were restricted to a maximum speed of 75 mph. The 150s were pretty basic, but the Class 156s were somewhat of an improvement, albeit not exactly brilliant. They were employed mainly on Edinburgh/Fife Circle/ Dundee services.

The Haymarket allocation of Class 156 Super Sprinters also included the six sets dedicated to working over the West Highland line. These were specially fitted with 'Storno' radios, to address the new requirements for working over the Radio Electronic Token Block (RETB) system of train signalling as was now employed on this line of route. These sets continue in service today serving the Glasgow/Oban/Mallaig route and the Far North of Scotland lines from Inverness, but are no longer allocated to Haymarket.

Finally the Class 158s arrived. These 'Express Sprinters' entered service in 1989 and took over the running of the Edinburgh/ Glasgow route on 17th September 1990, initially replacing the ageing Mk III push-pull sets. These units were in two-car formation, equipped with 350 bhp Cummins NTA855RI turbo-charged and inter-cooled engines, with one engine on each vehicle. Transmission was by Voith TR211RZ units driving two axles by Gmeinder final drives and they had a maximum speed of 90 mph. Built by the now long-gone BREL at Derby, they were of aluminium construction, with swing plug, bi-parting, power-operated doors, seating for 66/70 persons in each car and were also air-conditioned. They were designed to run in two-, four- or six-car formation.

Not without many teething troubles, not least of which was a problem with the under-slung engines moving on the mounting frames, the two-car 158 sets eventually settled down to fairly ordinary service on this and other main routes in Scotland. It was a lesson learned the hard way when it was discovered that they were not entirely suitable for running in the harsh winter conditions likely to be experienced on the Edinburgh/Glasgow/Inverness line – when, in such conditions and upon the driver applying the brakes for the Carr Bridge station stop in the southbound direction, his train then ran on for well over 2000 yards past the station, with speed unchecked. The powdered snow being blown up had gathered on the brake discs and formed a solid coating of ice. With no friction to provide heat, the brakes had quite simply ceased to function. This led to urgent instructions being issued to drivers to carry out regular running tests with the brakes in such adverse weather. Another case of the wrong type of snow!

In 1991, Dr John Prideaux, the then Director of the BR InterCity network, decided that the impressive performance of the InterCity 225 electric trains, so successfully introduced on the ECML services to replace the ageing HSTs, should be exploited to demonstrate that further considerable savings in the already good sub-five-hour journey times then existing between King's Cross and Edinburgh, were possible. A working party of engineering and operating officers of the Eastern and Scottish regions (the author included) were remitted to prepare a comprehensive engineering/operating plan to permit an InterCity 225 train to run non-stop between London King's Cross and Edinburgh, with the target being a run in under four hours. A comprehensive plan with suggested timings was duly prepared – which with many of the speed relaxations requested involved a maximum line speed of 140 mph wherever possible. The result was a record-breaking non-stop run of 3 hours 26 minutes with a specially prepared train-set consisting of only five Mk IV coaches and a Class 91 electric locomotive.

As part of the 150th anniversary of the Edinburgh & Glasgow Railway (1842–1992) celebrations, the then General Manager of the Scottish Region, Cyril Bleasdale, not to be outdone, decided that there should be a record-breaking high-speed non-stop run over the flagship route between Glasgow and Edinburgh, using two two-car Class 158 units coupled. It fell to the author to be Officer-in-Charge of this train. Haymarket provided the two units, Nos 158708 and 158710, both with specially-strengthened cardan shafts and modified fuel pumps, but with no other modification. A few days before the special run, and to ensure that the train would be able to stop safely within the braking distances then provided on the E&GR, from what was still an unknown quantity in terms of maximum speed, arrangements were made for the modified units to be run on high-speed braking tests on the ECML between Edinburgh and Drem. These tests were entirely satisfactory and thus, on the morning of Wednesday, 6th May 1992, this special train with the invited guests, press and representatives of Haymarket maintenance team on board, crewed by Glasgow-based driver Archie Anderson and Jesus Hernandez as conductor, ran non-stop over the 47.1 miles in 32 minutes and 9 seconds start-to-stop, reaching an impressive maximum speed of 107 mph en route. The highly-respected railway commentator P.W.B. Semmens took the official timings. Both 158 sets were thereafter restored to normal condition and returned to traffic. The congratulatory letter from the General Manager and the detailed timings are included here.

The General Manager was suitably impressed, but in reality it was somewhat of a hollow victory, for, when conducting the much earlier trial running over a period of Sundays in the early 1980s in connection with the possible push-pull workings using DVTs instead of a locomotive at each end, the team was regularly running this route with six Mk III coaches, hauled by a Class 47 diesel electric locomotive, with its greater power output and acceleration, in just a few seconds over 30 minutes, and on one Sunday in just under 30 minutes, but that was well before Cyril's time!

THE PRESENT DAY

The initial Haymarket allocation of Class 158s was fifteen two-car units, but as at January 2009 there was an allocation of fifty sets allocated to ScotRail and a further ten sets sub-leased, giving Haymarket the largest single Express Sprinter fleet in the UK. The allocated sets are numbered sequentially from 158701 to 158736 and 158738 to 158741. Units No. 158701 to 158725 are based at Inverness and four of these units are named:

- 158702 *BBC Scotland – 75 years*
- 158707 *Far North Line 125th Anniversary*
- 158715 *Haymarket*
- 158720 *Inverness and Nairn Railway*.

The 158 fleet are now at 'mid-life' and are undergoing a refurbishment programme.

A wintery scene in 1993, with the south wall of the amenity block on the left side. In the yard sidings stand, from left to right, two Class 150 sets coupled and, in the adjacent road, a Class 108 DMU set. *Courtesy Ray Murison*

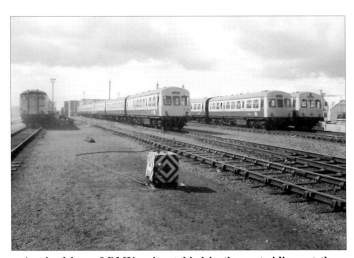

A mixed bag of DMU units stabled in the east sidings at the shed. *Courtesy Jeff Hurst*

At a much later date than it's record-breaking run, and now in First ScotRail livery, Class 158 No. 158710 stands in Platform 13 in Waverley station. The destination indicator is not properly set.   *Courtesy Ray Murison*

SCOTRAIL Edinburgh & Glasgow Special
GLASGOW - EDINBURGH

		6 May, 1992	
Date		6 May, 1992	
Formation		2 x class 158	
Nos:		158 708/710	
Load: No/empty/full(tons)		4/151/155	

Dist.	Sch	Actual	Speeds†
Miles	mins	m s	mph
0.0 GLASGOW (QUEEN ST)	0	0 00	–
1.4 Cowlairs		2 44	30
1.8 Cowlairs Box	3	3 13	54
3.1 Bishopbriggs		4 29	75
6.2 Lenzie	6¼	6 38	93
11.4 Croy		9 51	101
12.8 Dullatur		10 40	104
15.4 Castlecary		12 11	105
17.2 Greenhill Upper Junc	13	13 13	103
18.3 Bonnybridge		13 50	107
21.7 Falkirk (High)	15	15 44	90#
24.6 Polmont Junc.		17 33	–
24.9 Polmont	17	17 44	101
27.1 Bo'ness Junc.		19 03	106
29.6 Linlithgow	20	20 26	106/104
32.6 Philipstoun		22 03	107
34.6 Winchburgh Junc.	23	23 17	105/95#
36.4 Broxburn Junc.		24 24	98
38.7 Newbridge Junc.		25 46	107
39.0 Ratho		25 57	104
43.8 Saughton Junc.		28 40	107
45.3 Haymarket C. Junc.		29 32	*102*
46.0 Haymarket	30	29 59	65#
47.1 EDINBURGH (WAVERLEY)	32	32 09	–

\# *Speed restrictions.*

† *Figures in italics are averages from previous timing point.*

P W B Semmens MA CChem FRSC MBCS MCIT

DIRECTOR SCOTRAIL
RECEIVED
DATE   - 8 MAY 1992

Archie Anderson,
Driver,
Glasgow Queen Street
Copy to:
Donald Macpherosn
Harry Knox
George Steele

Jesus Hernandez
Conductor
Glasgow Queen Street

SCOTRAIL

ScotRail
ScotRail House
58 Port Dundas Road
Glasgow G4 0HG
Telephone 041-335 3355
Fax 041-335 2008

15th May 1992

Dear Harry

<u>RECORD RUN - 6TH MAY</u>

I enclose a copy of the timings as recorded by the Timekeeper for the record run between Glasgow and Edinburgh. I thought you would like to know what was achieved on the day and my thanks to you for the part you played in this successful record breaking run.

Cyril Bleasdale

CYRIL BLEASDALE
DIRECTOR, SCOTRAIL

A division of British Railways Board

RIGHT: The dreadful Class 143s, with No. 143016 standing in the shed. These three sets came to Scotland for the then new Bathgate and Fife Circle services, but following running trials on the Fife lines they were deemed to be unsuitable and were returned from whence they came, very quickly. *Courtesy Ray Murison*

LEFT: Class 170 No. 170402 in NX ScotRail livery. *Courtesy Ray Murison*

A Class 158 'Express Sprinter', No. 158701, newly delivered in early 1990 and bearing BR ScotRail livery, stands outside the shed. *Courtesy Ray Murison*

Class 170 in First ScotRail livery. *Courtesy Ray Murison*

BELOW: **Class 158 No. 158741 in NX ScotRail livery, but additionally bearing the logo of First Group, stands outside the shed roads at Haymarket.** *Courtesy Ray Murison*

In 1999 the first Class 170 'Turbostar' three-car DMUs started arriving, initially being included in the National Express ScotRail fleet and from the outset they were allocated to Haymarket. The franchise was subsequently won by the current train operator, the First Group, running as First ScotRail. With a change of ownership, the Class 170 fleet allocated to Haymarket has grown to fifty-nine sets. These 170s run all the major express routes north and west of Edinburgh and are currently running the Edinburgh to Glasgow route on a 15-minute frequency throughout the main part of each weekday and Saturday.

The Class 170s were built by ADTranz/Bombadier Transportation Services. They have an aluminium body shell and are fitted with six-cylinder, 428 bhp, turbo-charged diesel engines and have a maximum operating speed of 100 mph. Like all traction and rolling stock, the owners are one of the private train leasing companies, in this case Porterbrook Leasing.

From introduction in 1999, the 170s were the first of a new breed of rail unit built to fully comply with the new Rail Vehicle Accessibility Regulations 1998. The 170 fleet was delivered in build stages, with the fourth-stage sets being upgraded in many ways. Improvements include cross-feeding, on-board diagnostics, CCTV, PIS and a different type of train data recorder equipment.

Haymarket currently operate and maintain four main types of three-car Class 170 units, namely:

- 170 Express 40 units Nos 170401–170434 and 170450–170455
- 170 Suburban 6 units Nos 170456–170461
- 170 PTE 9 units Nos 170470–170478
- 170 Ex-Hull 4 units Nos 170393–170396

The 170s offer a greater degree of comfort and have better customer facilities than the 158s. Their introduction on the E&GR services saw patronage rise significantly and with the present 15-minute interval service throughout the main period of the day, there is, without doubt, improved customer satisfaction with the service both in terms of comfort and punctuality. The 170 Express units also run the Edinburgh/Glasgow/Aberdeen/Inverness services, whilst the 170 Suburban sets operate on the Bathgate and Fife services. The 170 PTE units operate mainly in the former Strathclyde PTE area, whilst the Ex-Hull sets share the running of the Highland main line. There is, it must be said, a lesser degree of customer satisfaction with these trains on the longer journeys to the north, with an ongoing litany of complaints regarding lack of passenger comfort and overcrowding.

Trials are currently being undertaken with two units which have been fitted with a more powerful MTU power unit which gives greater acceleration and will reduce journey times in consequence. It is likely that a proportion of the fleet will eventually be so modified.

Haymarket based Type 4 locomotive No. D265 stands alone at the temporary fuelling facility created in the shed loop at the top (west) end of the shed. This temporary facility was to last into the late 1960s.   *J. Simpson/D. Spaven collection*

26 THE DIESEL ELECTRIC LOCOMOTIVES

Dieselisation on BR was to have a chequered career. Scarcely anywhere in the world did diesels supersede steam without extreme pitfalls and with no little pain, but the BR transition was to prove to be quite probably the most painful of all.

BR dieselisation came about as a consequence of a 'panic' decision by the then BTC in 1957 to implement a rapid replacement of steam by diesel traction, in an attempt to stem the flow of fast-diminishing traffic levels and to reduce operating costs. Thus BR dieselisation did not evolve through a predetermined strategy, based on a dispassionate study by mechanical, electrical and motive power engineers, as should have been the case, but rather, dieselisation was wished upon the engineers and the operators as a result of extremely obscure deliberations and aspirations by senior BTC management. In short, it was the story of the 'Standards' all over again!

Main line diesels were thereafter to be ordered 'off the drawing board' in a most haphazard manner and with only the haziest ideas of what exactly they might, or might not, be able to do, and what was likely to be the most economical way for their effective utilisation. The essential prerequisites of analytical study: exploration, inspiration and solution by approximation to determine the evolution of a comprehensive motive power strategy were entirely and, as came to be regretted, erroneously ignored.

The result was a flawed decision to have five types of diesel locomotive, Types 1, 2, 3, 4 and 5. Within these types a considerable number of different manufacturers thereafter obtained orders, which inevitably led to:

a) a lack of prototype testing,
b) protracted teething troubles,
c) long periods of unproductive investment,
d) a bewildering variety of variations in possible weight and power, and
e) the introduction of traction not fit for purpose.

The reality of the whole Modernisation Programme was that, with so many different, non-standard classes of diesel locomotives being ordered and taken into ownership without any apparent rhyme or reason, the disproportionately high costs had to be offset by wholesale scrapping of steam. Perfectly good steam locomotives, many of which were nearly new, for example the aforesaid Standards, went to

Times they are a'changing. Here, in May 1961, two BRCW Type 2 Sulzer 1160bhp diesel electric locomotives stand at the top end of the shed, coupled in multiple. The near locomotive is D5304, the other unidentified. The 'Sulzers' ran in multiple on both Edinburgh to Aberdeen freight and passenger services, and here they have just arrived on shed and been shut down, their crew walking nonchalantly away with no fires to clean or ash pans and smokeboxes to empty. Oil lamps still reign supreme, however – note the tail lamp. *Courtesy Ian Musgrave*

An unidentified Haymarket Class 40 working a southbound Aberdeen to Edinburgh express across the Forth Bridge. The Class 40s were allocated to Haymarket from the late 1950s, primarily to work the Aberdeen road services, but they were not particularly popular with drivers as it was claimed that they had no power in reserve whatsoever. *Courtesy Ian Musgrave*

the scrap heap to pay for successors which were to be, by and large, less productive, less reliable and less effective, and were themselves in some cases to be scrapped after just a few years of service. This aspect of the Modernisation Plan was somewhat of a shambles and a financial disaster, and quite properly led to questions being raised (yet again) about the quality of senior BR management. Haymarket was but one depot on the receiving end of this misguided strategy!

Because of the chaos which beset the dieselisation plans, regional and local management were faced with problems quite unlike anything they had ever faced before, and a situation which was to change the way of life for every man in the locomotive department for all time. Not only had the fitting staff (mechanical) to be retrained to deal with diesel traction and the relatively precision engineering associated therewith, but they had to be able to deal with every one of the many new builds which were coming on stream, each with their own peculiarities. Suitable accommodation for the new traction had to be found or built, and this had to be done, in Haymarket's case, at a main line steam shed which was still operating a fleet of steam locomotives. Steam-age fitting staff had no electrical maintenance experience, and whilst, initially, the electrical side of the new traction was looked after at main works, it became imperative that running sheds should have qualified electricians on the complement. At Haymarket, this turned out to be not so much of a problem, because of the pool of time-served electricians available from the heavy electrical engineering industry located within Edinburgh, with firms such as Bruce Peebles and Ferranti.

The reality of the emerging situation, desperate as it was, was that the blame for much of the reported unreliability of most of the diesel locomotive classes lay fairly and squarely at the door of the BRB and not with the manufacturers. Competent day-to-day maintenance was often conspicuous by its absence, and frequent stoppages for minor issues quite often unnecessarily led to major stoppages – such as diesels being left standing out in the open during winter months waiting attention for minor problems and suffering frost damage and cracked crankcases in consequence. The shambles of the dieselisation project as embarked upon by the BRB unfortunately, and most unfairly, did little to enhance the reputation of those private manufacturers who had been caught up in it.

HAYMARKET: DIESEL ELECTRIC LOCOMOTIVES

In 1959, Haymarket began to take delivery of new main line diesel electric locomotives, primarily BRCW 1160 bhp Sulzer Type 2s in the number range D5300 to D5305, quickly followed by D5306 to D5313. These were initially stabled at Leith Central (64H) whilst suitable accommodation was being provided by the partial reconstruction of the old steam shed at 64B; driver training in the new traction was carried out from Leith Central.

At Haymarket, as well as the partial modernisation of the running shed, some of the other important prerequisites for diesel operation were being installed – namely four new 4,000 gallon diesel oil fuel tanks which were provided on the north-west corner of the depot just off Roseburn Street, along with a custom-built, but temporary, fuelling facility in the shed loop (west). Facilities for the reclamation of used lubricating oil and a general expansion of the stores were also put in hand.

Following driver training, which initially covered Nos 2, 3 and 4 passenger links, the Type 2s began to enter service, generally working in multiple. By June 1960, freight diagrams were established which called for sixteen Type 2s working in multiple (eight pairs) to work between Edinburgh and Aberdeen. It must be recorded that the performance and reliability of the Type 2s was not of the best, and often, steam had to deputise at short notice. It must also be highlighted that, in order to ensure some degree of reliability and performance, these locomotives were being worked in multiple, that is, two locomotives being employed on workings but with one crew, work which any of the Haymarket Pacifics or V2s, and even lesser engines, could, and did, cope with ably and economically on their own!

Two English Electric 350 bhp diesel electric shunting engines were allocated to take over the duties of the two Waverley west end pilots, thus deposing the two long-serving J83s, the numbers being D3560 and D3561, later replaced by D3738 and D3739. A single NBL diesel hydraulic 240 bhp 0-4-0 shunting locomotive, D2751, took over as the Haymarket yard pilot, displacing the long-serving J83. However, the 350 bhp shunting engines were to bring their own problems in that the short wheelbase would not actuate the track circuits in Waverley station, which is where they were

solely employed, and thus, until resignalling in the 1970s, these locomotives each had to run permanently coupled to a fitted 'hyfit' wagon.

March 1960 saw the completion of the new facilities, and the Type 2s were now becoming a familiar sight 'on shed' at Haymarket. By this time the fleet had been expanded to include Nos D5314–D5317, D5320–D5323, D5325–D5327, D5332–D5335 and D5343–D5346.

In 1960 Leith Central received 'on loan' an English Electric Type 4 for crew training purposes, and in April 1960 Haymarket received, again 'on loan', EE Type 4s Nos D256–D259 from York. These went into service on both the ECML and the Edinburgh to Aberdeen road and remained at Haymarket until the first of a new permanent allocation were received, Nos D260–D266, all fitted with Clayton boilers. It was intended that Haymarket would eventually work diagrams calling for an allocation of twelve Type 4s, and thus a further, but surprisingly larger, allocation was forthcoming sometime later, numbered D357–D368. The Type 4s, as supplied, were way too heavy, significantly underpowered and were not in any way inspired performers, particularly in the early days, and barely ever equalled the ability of the Gresleys which they replaced.

It must also be recorded, however, that Haymarket depot was becoming recognised as the best within BR when it came to maintenance and availability records. The availability of the Haymarket Type 4 fleet, despite being considered only just fit for

English Electric Type 4s Nos D263 and D365, both allocated to Haymarket, awaiting refuelling on a rather murky Edinburgh morning. *Courtesy Ian Musgrave*

purpose by their crews, was being maintained at 90 per cent and above, which was way superior to anywhere else, with the general average being just below 70 per cent.

Throughout 1961 the Type 2s continued to be unreliable, and although Edinburgh to Aberdeen workings had been turned over to Type 4s, steam continued to make frequent appearances, deputising for failed diesel electric locomotives. Indeed, such was the concern at the poor availability and reliability of the main line diesel fleet that all the night express trains over the ECML continued to be steam-hauled. By February of that year, Haymarket had, theoretically, only three diagrammed ECML workings left for their Pacifics, but the reality of the regrettable situation pertaining was that steam was proving to be the only reliable standby for the ailing diesel fleet; thus the Pacifics were still very much to the fore, both then and for some time to come.

In the summer of 1961, much of the gloom lifted at Haymarket as the first of the English Electric Napier Deltic-engined Type 5s came on stream, thereafter universally known, and loved, as the 'Deltics'. Such was the impact that these engines, twenty-two in all, went on to have on high speed train performance on the ECML, that a full chapter (Chapter 27) has been dedicated to them later in this book.

By early 1962 the BRCW Type 2s were, conversely, now deputising for the non-availability of the EE Type 4s on the Edinburgh/ Aberdeens, but they were soon to be relegated to the Waverley route

and express freight duties, working as single engines. The Type 4s finally took over the Edinburgh/Aberdeen express passenger workings in their entirety, but the drivers were soon complaining that they had 'absolutely nothing in hand' whilst working over this difficult route. Nevertheless the fish trains and other high-speed freight turns over this route were also turned over to the Type 4s, thus increasing the already impressive weekly mileage figures for the class. During this time the author had the opportunity to cab-ride on the Type 4s on several occasions with the 10.00 Edinburgh– Aberdeen service as far as Dundee and return, with Haymarket No. 3 link drivers Andrew Fraser and Peter Robertson. Both were scathing in their comments regarding capability and performance, and the general opinion at the time, and on every trip, was, 'it's just a matter of fully opening the throttle and letting her find her own level, for after that, she's got absolutely nothing in reserve.' They were all, without exception, uninspiring trips with a little time frequently dropped in either direction. The climb out of Dundee Tay Bridge revealed the lack of tractive effort very clearly.

In 1962, Haymarket was also allocated a small number of the quite dreadful (and destined to be very short-lived) 900 bhp Clayton diesel electric Type 1 Bo-Bo (Class 17) locomotives, numbered D8554, D8555 and D8556. These were found work on the Fife/ Grangemouth cement workings but were quickly rendered non-available, waiting modification after modification, and thereafter the reliability in service was to be abysmal; even when they did work,

North British Locomotive Company diesel mechanical 0-4-0 shunting locomotive No. D2751 displaced the J83 which had been the long-serving Haymarket yard pilot. It is seen here, obviously acting as coal pilot, standing on top of wagons in the coal road at Haymarket in wintery conditions in April 1962. *Courtesy Ian Musgrave*

Sulzer Type 4 No. D153 stands in front of Sulzer Type 2 No. D5300 at the back of Haymarket in February 1962. D153 was allocated to Haymarket from new, as seen here, for traction training, and during this time worked to and from Perth. Tenure was, however, to be of short duration and D153 was transferred out within a few weeks. *Courtesy Ian Musgrave*

their performance was extremely poor and with an extremely high failure rate. They were, however, well-liked by their crews – but only in respect of the design of the centre cab, which gave good all-round sighting, a high degree of comfort and excellent tea-making facilities. The crews were just as equally unimpressed by both the poor performance and the high failure rate. The first three were followed some time later by a further five, D8573–D8577. By 1968/69 the whole class had been largely either stored or dumped across the system, and by 1971 all but one, No. D8568, had been scrapped.

Also in February 1962, Haymarket was allocated, for a short time only, one BR/Sulzer Type 4, D153, mainly for crew training purposes, as this class of locomotive was by that time regularly working on the Edinburgh/Carlisle route. Whilst at Haymarket, D153 occasionally worked the 07.40 Edinburgh–Perth and back with the 12.05 to Edinburgh for training purposes, but this was by no means a regular working and was undertaken to provide 'hands on' driving out on the road. These locomotives, now known as Classes 45 and 46, made irregular forays into Haymarket, but were

A Type 1, the 900 bhp (Class 17) Clayton No. D8558, allocated as new to Haymarket in March 1962. Although the design of the centre cab, with comfortable driving positions and all-round sighting, was liked well enough, the engines proved to be an abject failure with abysmally poor availability and a high failure record. *Courtesy Ian Musgrave*

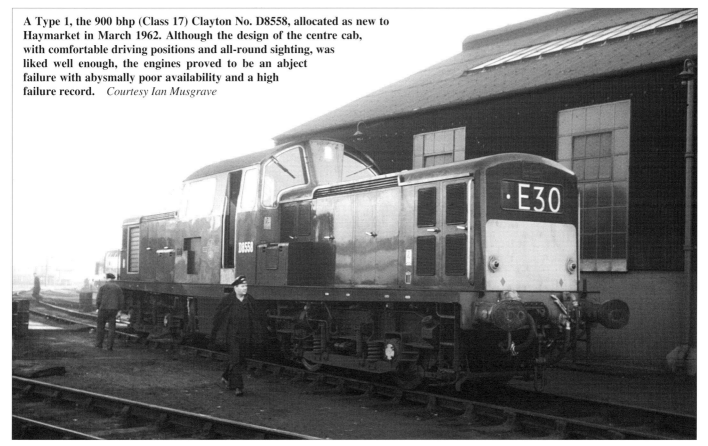

not worked by Haymarket crews on any regular basis; maintenance of traction knowledge for these classes amongst Haymarket drivers was thus difficult, to say the least. Like the EE Type 4, these Sulzer-engined locomotives were far too heavy (138 tons) and, despite being rated as 2,500 bhp locomotives, they were also underpowered and had a chequered career on the Edinburgh to Carlisle road.

Whilst steam and diesel had been coexisting at Haymarket in 1963, although not exactly peacefully, in September the big clean-out of steam commenced. The Gresley and Peppercorn Pacifics went, in the main, to St. Margaret's; by October of that year the final twelve steam locomotives had gone, A4 No. 60012 *Commonwealth of Australia* being one of the last engines to leave.

In October 1963, however, the Scottish Region strategic plan for the future of traction was revealed, which meant that St. Margaret's (64A) and Dalry Road (64C) would be closed completely as running and maintenance sheds. All main line diesel locomotives would be concentrated on Haymarket (64B), all diesel railcars allocated to Leith Central (64H) and the residual freight diesel locomotives and steam allocated to a new traction depot located at Millerhill Yard. This plan also required the relocation of train crews from the two depots facing closure. The closures duly took place in 1967. Nevertheless, despite the grand strategies, Millerhill was never to be anything more than a fuelling/servicing facility and staff booking-on point, with all diesel maintenance continuing to be carried out at Haymarket.

Until the mid-to-late 1970s Haymarket had an allocation of 109 diesel electric locomotives, comprising the following classes:

- Class 08
- Class 20
- Class 24
- Class 25
- Class 26
- Class 27
- Class 40
- Class 47
- Class 55.

The Class 17s had long disappeared by that time – without, it must be said, any tears of regret.

Haymarket maintained eight Class 25 diesel electric locomotives fitted with Sulzer six-cylinder 6LDA-28-B engines rated at 1250 bhp, with GEC control equipment and four AEC 253AY traction motors. The Class 25s were allocated to Bathgate shed for a period of time in the early 1970s to work block trains of spent blaes from Livingston to Glasgow Shieldhall, and these engines were run light in two rakes of four, from Bathgate to Haymarket, every Saturday for inspection and maintenance, returning late evening on the Sunday.

Haymarket also took delivery of twenty-two Class 27 BRC&W 1250 bhp Bo-Bo locomotives, some of which were specially converted for push-pull working for the new Edinburgh/Glasgow push-pull operation and classed as 27/1 (twelve) and 27/2 (ten); they were shared between Eastfield and Haymarket and were numbered 27101–27012 and 27203–27212. This new push-pull service was introduced in May 1971 to provide what was described at the time as 'the best ever service', with the journey times being reduced by 12 minutes and providing a 43-minute running time. It has to be said that, from the outset, this push-pull working would undoubtedly prove to be the least successful initiative for many years within the Scottish Region, with, over the years of operation, locomotive

A stranger in the camp! No. 46040 at the top end of the shed, having accessed Haymarket via the Waverley route. Haymarket shed did not have an allocation, although Haymarket crews worked these locomotives over the aforesaid route as required. *Courtesy Gavin Morrison*

performance and reliability being largely below par. The schedule was demanding in the extreme. The 27s were being required to run at the limits of their capacity (90 mph) for some eighteen hours per day, and thus locomotive failures were frequent. These failures then called for manipulation of the already tight cyclic diagrams of the sets, and one (unfortunately all too regular) consequence of this rearrangement was that the locomotives working the last services of an evening from Glasgow to Edinburgh, when utilising rearranged sets, frequently ran out of fuel around Philpstoun or in the Winchburgh cutting. Many an evening, the author, as Area Manager, Bathgate, or one of his traffic inspectors, was called out in order to obtain and arrange assistance for the train so failed. It became the habit not to go to bed until well after midnight during 'on call' weeks!

Locomotive failures also led to significant problems. In one instance, just after the service was introduced, the leading Class 27 locomotive of the 17.15 Glasgow to Edinburgh train failed immediately before departure time. A Class 37 was quickly commandeered from Eastfield and coupled in front of the failed locomotive. Haste, and failure to carry out a brake continuity test, meant that the rear locomotive was making air (the trains were air-braked) and keeping the brakes off throughout the train, whilst the 37, now switched to passenger-air setting, but with the intermediate brake pipes coupled but cocks left closed, was the train engine. The Class 37 was being driven by an Eastfield conductor since the regular train (Haymarket) driver did not have Class 37 traction knowledge. A running brake test of a sort was carried out at the top of Cowlairs incline (it turned out that the driver had partially applied the engine brake), but approaching the first stop at Falkirk High the train brake application was totally ineffective (since it applied on the locomotive only) and the train overran the station by a significant distance, coming to a stand inside the Falkirk Tunnel.

ABOVE: **The unloved Class 17s. Nos D8560, D8615 and D8614, no doubt waiting repair (the normal state), in Haymarket east yard sidings, standing against an independent snowplough. A Class 37, D6850, not allocated to Haymarket, brings up the rear.** *Courtesy John Furneval*

ABOVE: **Class 20 No. 20224 stands with an unidentified Class 20 at the top end of the shed awaiting its next turn of duty.** *Courtesy Ray Murison*

LEFT: **A Class 26, No. 26034, heads a train for Perth out of Platform 2 at Haymarket. In the foreground is the Duff Street connection, diverging to the right-hand side and connecting with Slateford Junction and the WCML. This line is now electrified with 25Kv OHLE.** *Courtesy John Fumeval*

Haymarket east yard on Sunday, 2nd September 1979 with 27204, 40007 and an unidentified 350 bhp shunter stabled 'waiting repair'. The Class 27 is showing signs of a 'tight squeeze' somewhere along the line. Behind the pile of coal (for the steam crane) stand two three-car DMU sets, one in BR standard livery, the other in the livery of the Greater Glasgow PTE.   *Courtesy Gavin Morrison*

A considerable delay was then incurred and an official inquiry followed. The Class 27 push-pull trains were themselves soon to be replaced by a newer form of push-pull operation.

It has to be pointed out in all fairness, however, that these Class 27/1-operated push-pull trains proved very useful on the not-infrequent occasions when a train failure occurred on the E&GR main line. With the capacity to have one locomotive in 'Air Pass' mode maintaining the air brakes on the push-pull set, the other locomotive could be changed over to run in 'Vac Pass' mode if necessary, thus creating vacuum to maintain and operate a brake on a failed train. A very handy option this proved to be over the years.

No tears were shed, however, when in 1979 the E&GR push-pull operation was replaced by Mk III coaching stock with a modified Mk II Driving Brake Second Open (DBSO) at one end, ahead of one FO, four SOs and a Class 47 locomotive permanently coupled at the other end (normally at the Edinburgh end of the train). The push-pull operation with the 47s was also to be later extended to operate between Glasgow Queen Street and Dundee/Aberdeen.

Initially a total of twelve locomotives were specially converted for, and dedicated to, this new push-pull operation, but were all to be allocated to Haymarket. The locomotives, classified as 47/7s, were:

- 47701 *Saint Andrew*
- 47702 *Saint Cuthbert*
- 47703 *Saint Mungo*
- 47704 *Dunedin*
- 47705 *Lothian*
- 47706 *Strathclyde*
- 47707 *Holyrood*

- 47708 *Waverley*
- 47709 *The Lord Provost*
- 47710 *Sir Walter Scott*
- 47711 *Greyfriars Bobby*
- 47712 *Lady Diana Spencer*.

With the extension of push-pull working to Aberdeen, a further four Class 47s were converted to become Class 47/7, namely:

- 47713 *Tayside*
- 47714 *Grampian*
- 47715 *Haymarket*
- 47716 *Duke of Edinburgh's Award*.

Another locomotive was converted at a later date, when a 'rogue' Class 47, which had proved troublesome on the Western Region, was taken into main works and converted for push-pull operation. It emerged as 47717 (unnamed) and was allocated to Glasgow Eastfield depot for the duration.

Four of these new push-pull sets were in use by 1980, but serious stability problems in the Falkirk High Tunnel had meant that the introduction of the full service had to be delayed whilst essential tunnel repairs were effected. All services had to be run via Falkirk Grahamston, and the new timetable was therefore not introduced until the 8th December 1980, and with a slower timing schedule. This proved to be a very successful operation with high set availability and punctuality in performance. Best timings between the two main cities over the E&GR were between 47 and 49 minutes with these sets. The operation was marred by only the

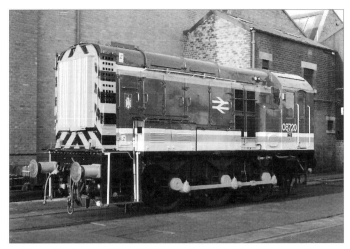

Class 08 shunter No. 08720 stands resplendent in new livery outside the shed, having been completely repainted in BR colours. On the bodyside front door panel, above the shunter's step, can be seen the Haymarket depot logo. *Courtesy Ray Murison*

one tragic accident, which occurred at Polmont (see Chapter 31) in 1984 and called into question for some time thereafter the safety of push-pull working. The E&GR push-pull operation was finally superseded by the introduction of the Class 158 Express Sprinter units, although not without more teething troubles and problems with poor build quality.

Class 47s were now being widely used from Haymarket, and proved to be good performers and more reliable than the earlier main-line diesel electric locomotives, although they could have their moments. The main advantage was the introduction of electric train heating (ETH) and the ability of the 47s to generate sufficient

power for both this purpose and traction power, although official ETH ratings had to be published to ensure that, as a consequence of the high ETH demands inherent in sleeping-car stock, the locomotives themselves were not overpowered when working big night trains.

The diesel years generally were to be largely marked by poor equipment, poor design and frequent locomotive (and DMU) failures. The root cause of the problem lay in what was stated at the beginning of this chapter: the provision of locomotive types which, whilst perceived to be entirely suitable, were in fact proving not to be fit for the purposes of the work on which they were being employed. During this time, it sadly became accepted that the serious shortage of motive power caused by exceptionally high number of locomotives 'waiting repairs' became just another cross that the hard-pushed operators had to 'grin and bear', whilst watching traffic, both passenger and freight, bleed away from rail to road. The blame lay not with the maintenance depots like Haymarket, which were stretched to the limit, but with the 'powers that be' and their ill-considered dieselisation initiative.

As one small example of the hand-to-mouth existence the operators had to contend with in regard to locomotive shortages, in the latter part of the 1970s, Bathgate, having been closed as a traction depot, became dependent upon Millerhill for its daily motive power – Class 26s in the main – and at that time the British Motor Corporation (BMC) and later British Leyland Truck and Tractor Division factory was in full swing. Additionally, Bathgate had become a centre for the distribution of new cars, worked inwards daily in train loads which were serviced by Millerhill depot. Bathgate also dispatched, every day, through-loaded continental rail traffic by means of a daily Glasgow Sighthill to Harwich Parkeston Quay via Bathgate air-brake express freight service. For one whole week, with diesel locomotive availability at an all-time low, and

Two Haymarket Class 47s fitted for push-pull working. Nos. 47711 *Greyfriars Bobby* and 47712 *Lady Diana Spencer* stand outside the east end of the depot on 25th July 1981, newly-painted and the first of the class to carry the large logo and numbers. *Courtesy Gavin Morrison*

Millerhill concentrating all its efforts on providing motive power for the coal mining industry, not one wheel turned at Bathgate. Over 4,000 new cars (inward) were delayed in transit (sitting in Millerhill yard) and valuable outward rail traffic from British Leyland, worth many thousands of pounds in freight revenue, went over to road. Desperate times indeed!

Generally, however, advances in rail traction technology marched on and the remarkable HSTs were supplanting the Deltics on the East Coast. The HST sets (soon to be classified 254s) consisted of fixed formation, ten-car units with a driving power car at each end. Each power car was equipped with a Paxman Valenta twelve-cylinder, supercharged and intercooled engine supplying 2,250 bhp. The transmission consisted of four Brush fully-suspended traction motors driving through a cardan shaft with flexible couplings and single reduction gearing. The eight intermediate Mk III coaches were bar-coupled, providing extremely comfortable first and second class accommodation with full restaurant and buffet facilities. The sets also rode very smoothly at high speed and were to transform the ECML services, both in terms of journey time and comfort.

The Class 254s were, in reality, nothing more than extremely up-market, high-speed diesel electric multiple units, but with power cars as opposed to underslung power units – and in Edinburgh were to be serviced and stabled at Craigentinny, although Waverley station was also utilised for overnight stabling. The HSTs took over all daytime train working on the East Coast with only the night trains continuing to be diesel locomotive hauled. Aberdeen and Inverness were also to become stabling and (limited) maintenance points for the HST sets running right through from King's Cross. Thus fewer and fewer locomotives were entering service from Haymarket shed, and the need for light locomotive running was reduced. Consequently, the depot became little more than a booking-on and off point for the complement of drivers allocated there, who then had to travel to the point at which they would take over their train working.

The HSTs, although prone to engine problems, generally have given good and reliable service on the ECML; some thirty years

on, they continue running in 2011, refurbished and re-engined, turn and turn-about on the ECML with the newer electric 225 trains, and still covering the London King's Cross to Aberdeen and Inverness through services.

Unlike its traction, however, the privatised ECML and its two train operating companies has seen casualties with both companies 'going under'. The ECML services are, in 2011, once more back in the public domain under the temporary ownership of the government and operated by a provisional holding company, East Coast, pending refranchising.

Provision of a new operations centre in Edinburgh Waverley in May 1984 saw all train crews and guards being concentrated centrally within the station. From that date, Haymarket ceased to become a Promotion, Transfer and Redundancy Depot as defined in the National Agreements, leaving the depot for maintenance purposes only.

By the middle of 1985 Haymarket had twenty-five DMU sets allocated; with the Classes 17, 25 and 55 now gone, the somewhat depleted diesel electric locomotive fleet included:

- 13 × Class 08   Nos 08421/515/701/710/718/726/730/755 /761/763/764 and 781
- 12 × Class 20   Nos 20202/212/213/216/217/218/219/220 /221/222/223/224 and 225
- 33 × Class 26   Nos 26001/002/003/004/005/006/007/008 /010/011/014/015/021/023/024/025/026 /027/028/029/031/032/034/035/036/037 /038/039/040/041/042/043 and 046
- 15 × Class 47/7 Nos 47701/715.

Of these locomotives, Class 26/0 Nos 26001–26007 were fitted with slow speed control for working merry-go-round coal trains.

In the following year, all the Class 47/7s were transferred away to Eastfield, then the older DMUs were gradually withdrawn, and eventually Haymarket lost its diesel electric locomotive fleet. The wheel had turned full circle and, as discussed at Chapter 25, DMUs were to dominate life at Haymarket thereafter.

A Haymarket Class 47/7, No. 47712 *Lady Diana Spencer*, heads an Edinburgh-bound E&GR push-pull set into Platform 3 at Haymarket station. The original NBR buildings and canopies are still *in situ*, but the station was to be completely modernised in 1982/83. *Courtesy John Furneval*

27   THE ENGLISH ELECTRIC NAPIER DELTICS

This unique class of twenty-two diesel electric locomotives rightly demands a chapter to itself, for they were to transform performance on the ECML and take it to previously unknown heights.

In the mid-1950s the English Electric Company had built a prototype diesel electric locomotive (DP1, named *Deltic*) for the purpose of trial running and evaluation to demonstrate its potential to possible customers, but primarily to the BRB, running over the London Midland, Eastern and Scottish regions of BR. The name was adopted by the fact that this very powerful and trend-setting diesel electric locomotive used the famous Napier Deltic power units that had been so successfully used in the Royal Navy motor torpedo boats (MTBs) during the Second World War. The Napier Deltic engine was an eighteen-cylinder, opposed piston, water-cooled, two-stroke diesel engine. The cylinders were arranged in three banks of six, each bank containing a crankshaft and forming an inverted equilateral triangle. Each locomotive had two such

The Deltics arrive in Edinburgh. Type 5 D9000 is seen here, just released to traffic in March 1961, stabled temporarily at Leith Central. This locomotive, the first of twenty-two ordered by BR, and allocated to Haymarket, had been held back at the English Electric works waiting to be fitted with an experimental flashing warning light (positioned between and above buffers) and whilst waiting clearance at EE was struck and damaged by the works pilot engine. When repaired, D9000 reached Edinburgh in March 1961, but was quickly stopped 'out of traffic' when fractures were found on the bogie transoms and rubbing plates were found to be working loose. All of the Deltics which were showing these problems were returned to EE for repair, and D9000 eventually emerged in April, fully fit, and located at Haymarket shed. The original livery in which they entered traffic was by far the most attractive of all the colour schemes applied to these engines during their revenue-earning service lifetime.   *Courtesy Scotsman Publications*

engines fitted, each engine being coupled to its own generator. They were rated at 3,300 bhp.

From the outset, and on the assumption that modified locomotives based on this ground-breaking prototype would eventually enter service with BR, it was planned that a preventative maintenance and heavy repair regime would be the norm; this allowed the adoption of a system of engine removal and replacement, since the engine layout made it well nigh impossible to work on them *in situ*.

Meanwhile, the Government White Paper of 1956 on Transport Policy confirmed that priority was to be given to the electrification of the West Coast Main Line, with any electrification hopes for the ECML, between London and Leeds initially, receding well into the 1970s. G.F. Fiennes, Line Traffic Manager of the Eastern Region, had then prepared a financial case for a ten-year 'holding operation', using powerful, high-speed diesel electric locomotives based on the 3,300 bhp-rated prototype *Deltic*. This financial case also demanded that the new class of locomotives would need to be utilised more intensively than any other BR class of locomotive, and thus reliability was a prime consideration.

This prototype locomotive was constructed to generous proportions and was run experimentally within the LMR and ER from around 1956 onwards. Trial running on the NER revealed the fact that it actually fouled the BR loading gauge and kinetic envelope in many places, particularly in Scotland, and could not be run between Newcastle and Edinburgh because of fouling problems at Morpeth. It eventually came to Scotland via the WCML and Carlisle, and worked here between the 8th and 18th June 1959, returning south by the same circuitous journey. It was used on Haymarket turns for a few of those days on a trial basis, and W. (Bill) Nairn of Haymarket Top link was one of the relatively few drivers (and the only Edinburgh-based driver) who took hold of this locomotive whilst on trial in Scotland. He had been sent on a driver training course at the Deltic Training School in London and afterwards drove the prototype on trial running over both the ECML (to Berwick) and on the Edinburgh/Aberdeen road. The new locomotive proved its ability by lifting a 450-ton train from a stand at the Up intermediate block signals (IBS) on the 1 in 96 rising gradient between Innerwick and Grantshouse. The prototype locomotive was, however, always in the ownership of English Electric and it was never intended that it would enter revenue-earning service with BR in its prototype guise. It was eventually gifted to the Science Museum in London before being later transferred to the National Railway Museum in York for preservation.

After other very successful trials, the Eastern/Scottish Regions jointly placed an order for, initially, twenty-three (later revised to twenty-two) of these Type 5 locomotives, but in a redesigned format. They were for use over the ECML, and it was intended that they should replace a total of fifty-five Peppercorn, Thompson and Gresley Pacifics. The building costs for these twenty-two locomotives were immense, so much so that initially the BRB intentionally censored details. In fact, the English Electric Company's quotation in early 1958 for the twenty-two locomotives, including spares and maintenance, was £3.41 million (£59m at current-day equivalent prices), or £155,000 (£2.7m) per locomotive. This offer was accepted by the BRB in May 1958, and a delivery date of October 1959 was agreed for the first locomotive, with two being delivered each week thereafter.

The building contract also contained an agreement that locked English Electric into a maintenance contract for five years, and was interesting in the extreme. Once in traffic, for years one to four

Deltic No. D9000, fresh out of the English Electric factory, stands outside the fitting shed in 1961. It is fitted with the flashing staff warning light (centre) which was quickly removed and was never carried by any other member of the class. *Courtesy Ian Musgrave*

BRB would pay English Electric £720 (£12,500) per locomotive per month – and in the fifth year this amount was reduced to £600 (£10,250) per locomotive per month. As planned, under this contract English Electric would maintain the locomotives, including engines and generators, on the agreed fixed-price basis and would construct a number of spare engine units to enable engines to be taken out and swapped over on a regular basis for maintenance purposes, for the reasons described earlier.

However, owing to the many variations to the originally agreed design as demanded by BRB, the delivery dates slipped a whole year and the second locomotive – but the first to be delivered – D9001, was not to be delivered into traffic until December 1960. It was just as quickly withdrawn since EE had identified an inherent problem with fracturing of the bogie transoms. This fault was found to exist across the whole class and, despite remedial action at the time, was to persist until 1966 when the problem was finally resolved. The first locomotive, No. D9000, had suffered minor collision damage whilst still at English Electric and was not to appear until February 1961. This locomotive was fitted with the experimental, centrally-mounted, flashing warning light above buffer height, but this was removed soon after delivery. The latter engine initially went to Leith Central for stabling and crew training purposes before entering traffic from Haymarket later in the year.

The locomotives in this class were to be afflicted with many problems over their years in service. BRB had insisted on the use of the Spanner Mk II steam-heating boiler against best advice from EE, and, like all other main line diesel locomotives, this was to prove their Achilles heel; the Deltics were to be plagued with boiler failures until all locomotives of the class were finally modified for electric train heating (ETH). Indeed, in a six week period around August 1961, there were no less than thirty-eight boiler failures, thus locomotive failures, on the night sleeping car services between Edinburgh and London. Pistons and cylinder liners also gave problems and required many modifications.

By the middle of 1964, availability of the Deltic fleet was running at around 88.5 per cent with the actual Napier diesel engines achieving 97 per cent of their gross possible running hours. Engine changes could be carried out in only eight hours and engine overhauls were fixed at 4,000 hours, which equated to an annual requirement. However, BR stipulated that the Deltics should be free of overhaul commitments for the duration of the summer timetable and this, in turn, led to an unwelcome concentration of overhauls in the March to May period. However, on engines overhauled after October 1963, design improvements embodying strengthening of cylinder liners and improved Mk 3 pistons led to an increase in available running hours, with a 6,000-hour service interval being introduced. In fact, with the agreement of BR, English Electric left four nominated engines in service for 8,000 hours, on a trial basis, with the target being a 10,000-hour service period by 1965/66 season. 'Repair by replacement' was proving its worth in no small way!

It was intended from the outset that the locomotives would be assigned to three depots only – Finsbury Park (London), Gateshead (Newcastle)and Haymarket (Edinburgh) – which indeed they were for the whole time whilst on ECML high-speed working. From these depots they worked one fairly complicated but comprehensive cyclic diagram. The initial 1962 cyclic diagrams, introduced in April of that year, had twenty-two turns requiring the whole fleet of twenty-two locomotives to be in operation, and which saw each locomotive achieve on average 1,000 miles every 24 hours. These locomotives were all initially fitted with water scoops to enable the steam heating boiler water supply to be replenished when running, but the apparatus was later removed.

By early 1962, the full Haymarket allocation of Type 5s was completed, eight in all, and although primarily diagrammed for ECML express passenger working, one Haymarket Deltic was regularly employed on the 17.15 Edinburgh to Glasgow train, a heavy commuter train, returning with the 20.00 ex Queen Street. Availability was to be good despite the recurring problems. The eight Haymarket locomotives engines were, like the Haymarket

A4s which preceded them, returning high utilisation results, each averaging 153,960 miles per annum in service, while the operating cost for the Scottish engines were as low as 8 pence per mile (Period 12, 1975). In comparison, neither the Finsbury Park nor the Gateshead locomotives ever came near to matching this performance, these having a combined annual average mileage of 138,740 miles per annum. The Deltics went on as a class to dominate the high-speed services on the ECML from 1962 until their withdrawal in 1981/82, having by then been superseded by the equally successful Class 254 HSTs.

In the 1962 summer timetable, which came into operation from the 18th June, the principal Edinburgh–King's Cross express services were given accelerated timings, calling for six-hour running between the two termini. The timetable was specifically prepared to ensure the availability of Type 5 locomotives at all times, and it worked!

Train working from the 1962 timetable fell into three categories for Type 5 haulage:

1) Fully accelerated limited load express trains
   11 coaches/385 tons
2) Secondary express trains   13 coaches/455 tons
3) Sleeping car trains or equivalent   15 coaches/530 tons.

The six-hour timing was, in effect, a reproduction of the pre-war 'Coronation' timings, but with heavier loads, and applied to 'The Elizabethan', 'The Flying Scotsman' and the afternoon 'Talisman'. Between Edinburgh and Newcastle, in each direction, 116 minutes were allowed for the 125 miles, an average speed of 64.4 mph. The 'glory days' were back again, but for what was to be a very short

When the Deltics held sway at Haymarket. The quite unique bulbous noses of 55009 *Alycidon* and 55021 *Argyle and Sutherland Highlander* can be seen to some effect as the locomotives rest from their labours. *Courtesy Gavin Morrison*

Monday, 18th June 1962, and exactly 100 years to the day since the very first run of the 10.00 'Scotch Express' – later to become the world-famous 'Flying Scotsman' – over the East Coast Main Line between Edinburgh and London King's Cross. In this photograph, Deltic locomotive No. D9000, having only just been named *Royal Scots Grey* by the commanding officer of that regiment that same morning, pulls out of Edinburgh Waverley at 10.00 'on the dot', at the head of the new, accelerated 'Flying Scotsman'. Driver D. Duncan of Haymarket is at the controls for the first leg of the journey to Newcastle, and the train will go on to run to London King's Cross in a few minutes short of six hours, attaining a top speed of 101 mph en route. *Courtesy Scotsman Publications*

time indeed. At this juncture it is worth noting that the 116-minute Deltic schedule puts into perspective the many recorded runs made over this section by the Gresleys of 110 to 114 minutes and under on a fairly regular basis in steam days.

The choice of Monday, 18th June 1962 for the commencement of the first day of the summer timetable and the accelerated services was a happy coincidence, since the very first run of the London to Edinburgh 'Scotch Express', later to become the world-renowned 'Flying Scotsman', pulled out of King's Cross station at exactly 10.00 on June 18th 1862, some 100 years before. Prior to departure of the new, accelerated (6-hour) service, and to mark the centenary of this famous named train, D9000 of Haymarket depot was named *Royal Scots Grey* by the then Colonel of the Regiment, Brigadier J.E. Sweetenham DSO, at Waverley Station. On the inauguration run which followed, the Up 'Flying Scotsman' from Edinburgh was then worked by the newly-christened D9000 *Royal Scots Grey*, under the control of Haymarket driver D. Duncan, accompanied by Edinburgh traction inspector Bob Mitchell in the cab. The Lord Provost of Edinburgh, Sir John Greig-Dunbar, flagged the train off at 10.00 'on the dot'. Newcastle was reached 4 minutes early and the train went on to finish in King's Cross 6 minutes early despite signal 'slows' en route. A maximum of 101 mph was recorded on Stoke Bank.

After some track improvements and the easing of some severe curves on the ECML, the Deltics went on to work trains to an even further accelerated timetable when they ran the 393 miles in 5½ hours. In the course of the summer timetable in 1963, the twenty-two Deltics ran an aggregated 1 million miles in the twelve

weeks and repeated this prodigious feat again in the 1964 summer timetable.

Even with the greatly accelerated timings in place, the locomotives had the capacity to run hard but with some spare capacity in hand. There is on record a trip with the Up morning 'Talisman', the 08.00 Edinburgh to King's Cross on the 22nd July 1964, when, after an on-time arrival at Newcastle, a defective coach had then to be detached. The train ran forward, hauled by D9013 *The Black Watch* of Haymarket depot, leaving Newcastle some 32 minutes late. King's Cross was reached 3 minutes early, passing Darlington to the final stand in King's Cross being reeled off in only 2 hours 57 minutes, an average speed of 80 mph pass to stop. D9013 was always regarded as one of the better runners.

In May 1964, Inverness got its first sight of a Deltic when D9004 worked the Edinburgh–Inverness sleeper train north for the purposes of receiving its name, *Queen's Own Highlander*. After the naming ceremony it worked back south as far as Perth on the same day, on the 17.45 'Royal Highlander'.

In the late 1970s, when weekend diversions via the West Coast main line were the norm for all the ECML sleeping car services, the author can recall, as Area Manager at Bathgate, the heart-stopping moments experienced in the midnight hour as the huge Down East Coast/Inverness 'Highland Car Carrier' – which regularly loaded up to twenty or, on occasions, even twenty-two GUVs and Sleeping Cars and was always Deltic-hauled – had to be slowly set back over scotched and clipped, but otherwise unlocked, facing crossover points at Mid Calder Junction for the purposes of single line working. One night in particular will remain with him forever,

TABLE 27.1   NAMED DELTIC LOCOMOTIVES AT HAYMARKET

D9000 (55022) *Royal Scots Grey*[a]	from	3/61 to 5/79	but with 3 months on loan to Finsbury Park
D9004 (55004) *Queen's Own Highlander*	from	6/61 to 5/79	
D9006 (55006) *The Fife and Forfar Yeomanry*	from	8/61 to 5/79	
D9010 (55010) *The King's Own Scottish Borderer*[b]	from	9/61 to 5/79	
D9013 (55013) *The Black Watch*	from	10/61 to 5/79	but with 3 months on loan to Finsbury Park
D9016 (55016) *Gordon Highlander*	from	11/61 to 5/79	but with 5 months on loan to Finsbury Park
D9019 (55019) *Royal Highland Fusilier*	from	12/61 to 5/79	but with 4 months on loan to Finsbury Park
D9021 (55021) *Argyll and Sutherland Highlander*	from	5/62 to 5/79	but with 7 months on loan to Finsbury Park

NOTES
a) D9000 was renumbered 55022 because the computerised TOPS system could not cope with three zeros.
b) D9010 was the first of the class to accumulate 2 million miles in traffic.

when the clip fell off the point-blades just as No. 55013 started to move over the points, fortunately without incident.

After they were supplanted by the High Speed Trains (HSTs) in the late 1970s, the Haymarket Deltics were then transferred to York shed and there were used extensively between York and London on secondary passenger workings, and during that time were followed by a large band of very enthusiastic supporters. The small number of the class meant that they had a very limited future, since it was not an economic proposition to maintain so few non-standard locomotives. They were initially classified as Type 5 locomotives, but later were to be reclassified and renumbered for TOPS purposes as Class 55s. The early 1980s saw the first withdrawals. The others continued to operate with only limited maintenance, until, one by one, they finally broke down; it was engine failure which was to see their final demise in January 1982.

A total of six locomotives were preserved after withdrawal and several have been restored; these, happily, can now be seen on

main line running on special trains. The Deltic had quite a unique sound and, on being opened up, two columns of whiter-than-mist exhaust would erupt from the roof, whilst the engine note, a moan increasing in pitch, would rise, then fall, before becoming like the bellow of some demented animal as the pent-up power of the engines was unleashed. Who could ever forget the sight and sound of a Deltic starting off, or running at 'full chat'?

At Haymarket, a total of eight Deltics were allocated from new, and eventually named after famous Scottish Regiments. Interestingly, the Scottish Region was initially holding out for its allocation of locomotives to carry names from the Waverley novels and Scottish history (shades of the NBR Atlantics, Scotts, D11/2s and A1s) but pressure was brought to bear and, reluctantly, the regional management finally accepted that names of Scottish regiments would be acceptable. The named locomotives were as shown in Table 27.1.

Five Haymarket locomotives went on loan to Finsbury Park.

Haymarket Deltic No. 55013 *The Black Watch*, in rather drab BR blue livery, stands at the east end of the depot on 21st April 1981 waiting its next turn of duty. By this time the major ECML passenger services were being worked by HSTs, with the Class 55s being reduced to night sleeping-car services and secondary ECML duties. *Courtesy Gavin Morrison*

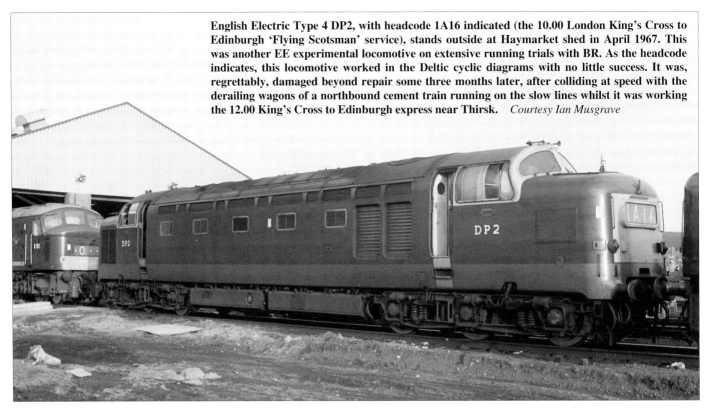

English Electric Type 4 DP2, with headcode 1A16 indicated (the 10.00 London King's Cross to Edinburgh 'Flying Scotsman' service), stands outside at Haymarket shed in April 1967. This was another EE experimental locomotive on extensive running trials with BR. As the headcode indicates, this locomotive worked in the Deltic cyclic diagrams with no little success. It was, regrettably, damaged beyond repair some three months later, after colliding at speed with the derailing wagons of a northbound cement train running on the slow lines whilst it was working the 12.00 King's Cross to Edinburgh express near Thirsk. *Courtesy Ian Musgrave*

These were locomotives which had already been converted to dual-braking and were to ensure that Finsbury Park had sufficient air-braked locomotives with which to operate the new 1968 coaching diagrams involving air-braked Mk II passenger coaches whilst their own locomotives were being dual-brake fitted. During this time Haymarket was loaned:

- D9001 (55001) *St. Paddy*
- D9003 (55003) *Meld*
- D9009 (55009) *Alycidon*
- D9012 (55012) *Crepello*.

In the final analysis, whilst the Deltics did everything they were designed to do, and did it well, the reality was that as a class they were extremely expensive machines, not only from the initial purchase cost, but also the cost of the ongoing maintenance contract with English Electric, costs incurred through the many modifications and, of course, running costs. However, it was to be a great number of years before the true costs of their total operation were finally revealed.

As a class – and despite good availability which was a credit to the staff at the three depots involved – they had been plagued with problems throughout their service life and had individually incurred very considerable down time in main works, either at Doncaster or Newton-le-Willows. Indeed, in the first twenty years, each locomotive in the class had incurred an average of 3.33 years in works, with two of the class having each spent an aggregated time of over four years in works. Sadly, whilst they had quite radically revolutionised ECML running, they were never to be the commercial success which EE (and BR) had hoped for.

At least one of the class was involved in a serious accident. On the night of 8th May 1969, D9011 *Royal Northumberland Fusilier* was at the head of the Down 19.40 London King's Cross to Aberdeen night sleeping car train, the 'Aberdonian', and in the charge of a

Gateshead crew who had only taken over at Newcastle. On the approach to Morpeth and the 40 mph permanent speed restriction applying round the notorious Morpeth curve, the driver had allowed himself to become distracted, and the train entered the curve way too fast, at a speed of approximately 80 mph. The locomotive and first van negotiated the curve and remained on the tracks but the reminder of the train went into a rolling derailment to the left-hand side; five passengers and a travelling ticket collector were killed outright, with a further 121 passengers suffering serious injuries.

English Electric went on to produce another prototype diesel electric locomotive, rated at 2,700 bhp and designated a Type 4, numbered as DP2. This locomotive, incorporating many new features of locomotive design, was also loaned to BR for comprehensive testing in regular revenue-earning traffic; eventually it was working turn for turn in the Deltic diagrams, and thus was a regular visitor to Haymarket.

DP2 proved to be a straightforward, rugged, powerful but simple design which was reliable … and fast. The BRB decision to go with the Brush Sulzer Type 4 as the preferred design was regretted by many and proved to be a most questionable decision in later years. An impressive performer, DP2 was to come to a sad end near Thirsk, on the ECML north of York, on the 31st July 1967 whilst working the Down 12.00 King's Cross to Edinburgh express passenger service. Running at line speed on the Down Fast line, DP2 ran into the tank wagons of the 02.40 Cliffe (Kent) to Uddingston (Glasgow) cement train, whilst they were actually in the process of becoming derailed – the latter train proceeding north-bound on the parallel Down Slow line. The wagons, derailing to the right, fouled the Down Fast just as DP2 was approaching, and the driver had little or no warning before he sideswiped the derailing cement empties. Seven passengers in the express were killed and a further forty-five received serious injuries. DP2 was so badly damaged that it was eventually scrapped, and a bold experiment came to a sudden end.

28 LOCOMOTIVE MAINTENANCE

When describing the various locomotive allocations over the years, and the sterling work that these Haymarket locomotives were giving, it is only proper that due credit is given to the band of skilled men who maintained them, particularly during the years when a large number of Pacific classes were allocated.

Mention has been made of the fact that NBR drivers were, by necessity, fairly competent self-taught engineers who could cope with many of the day-to-day repairs required, but behind them were the highly-skilled fitters and other workshop grades who carried out the heavier tasks, the routine examinations and the heavy repairs. The NBR locomotives were, in the main, simple in design and robust in construction, facts which may explain why Walter Chambers, then Chief Draughtsman of the NBR at Cowlairs and later CME for a short period, had a hand in preparing an eight-volume work

Atlantic No. 510 *The Lord Provost* **in a somewhat undignified pose,** *sans* **tender and rear-end to the sky, undergoes repair in the shear legs at Haymarket in pre-grouping days.** *Bill Lynn collection*

entitled *Modern Railway Working*, published by the Gresham Publishing Company in 1912 – volumes which addressed not only locomotive maintenance and repair, but the complete British railway operating practices. Chambers' contribution, a detailed description of locomotive repair and maintenance contained in Volume 5, Part 4, Section III, was to be the bible for NBR locomotive maintenance practice thereafter, and interesting reading it makes.

A mechanical foreman, the equivalent of the locomotive foreman in NBR days, and assistant to the shed master in later days, oversaw all maintenance and running repair activities in both the workshop and running sides of the shed. Three shift chargehand fitters, on rotating shifts, supervised all locomotive examination and running repairs by examining fitters, fitters and fitters' assistants, whilst scheduled exams and heavy repairs were undertaken by the workshop fitters under the control of another chargehand fitter. A number of apprenticeships were awarded each year, and so Haymarket was to be fortunate, with a pool of time-served and certificated young fitters with inside knowledge of the peculiarities of the steam locomotive regularly coming through to back up the older, more experienced staff. Such was the care lavished on the Pacifics that one fitter on each shift was solely employed on checking and setting locomotive lubricators, with particular care being afforded the non-stop A4s. The boilermakers and boiler-wash-out staff reported to the shift chargehands. Finally, every engine, before leaving the shed to take up a main line turn, was examined by an examining fitter, one of a highly-skilled body of men, well versed in locomotive engineering.

As discussed in earlier chapters, the Gresleys and the three-cylinder locomotives fitted with the conjugated valve gear proved to be a different kettle of fish in terms of maintenance compared to earlier engines. The locomotives fitted with the conjugated valve gear, and particularly the A3s, A4s, P2s and V2s, required careful and frequent attention to ensure best results, and the fitting staff at Haymarket did this with great success. The performance out on the road was testament to the almost loving care lavished on the locomotives in their care.

This conjugated valve gear assembly suffered from excessive wear in the working parts, with the all-too-frequent consequences of overheating, and not infrequent collapse of middle connecting rod big-end bearings and heating of axle box bearings; it also posed a particularly serious, and continuing, worry for the shed running and maintenance staff. The 2-to-1 lever in these larger engines was located in front of the cylinders, just below the smokebox door, and upon which the joints were grease lubricated. Smokebox char inevitably got mixed in with the grease, forming what was nothing less than a grinding paste, and thus the pin-joints and knuckles were subjected to more or less continuous wear. This was a constant headache for the maintenance staff, and whilst the problems were well within the competence of shed fitters to cope with unless the resulting damage required wheels and axles to be sent to main works for attention, it nevertheless placed a heavy burden of maintenance work on Haymarket shed. This problem was by far and away a

This 2-4-0 passenger locomotive was built by the E&GR at Cowlairs as No. 39, to the design of Beyer Peacock. It was re-numbered No. 211 by the NBR. Re-built by Holmes in 1886, it remained in service until 1914. In the Drummond days, it carried the name *Dunbar*. Seen here at Haymarket shed with the shear legs in the background, it is a very elegant locomotive. *Bill Lynn collection*

much more serious problem on the Pacifics, because of the intensive diagramming, than with the V2s for instance, and this undoubtedly was a significant factor in taking the decision to concentrate all the Pacifics at Haymarket.

In 1941, in keeping with L&NER policy, all Scottish Area A1s and A3s were transferred back to Haymarket. The importance of this centralisation was reflected in the number of 'Gresley Men' who subsequently took control of the depot in the following years, men like J. Hutchison, T.C.B. Miller, E.D. Trask, G. Lund, J. Murray, F. Bishop, W.G. Cherry and J.W. Banks, all men with a sound knowledge of the conjugated valve gear and the vagaries thereof!

In BR days, locomotive maintenance on the Eastern and Scottish regions was to be carried out on the basis of planned preventative maintenance in compliance with a schedule known as Circular MP11, which was a 64-page document covering almost every component part of all locomotives on BR. Thus the Haymarket Pacifics and V2s were required to have a regular 'X' day examination. At Haymarket, this took place every 12/14 days and boilers were washed out at this time. South of the border, this exam was carried out every 6/8 days because of the poor, or hard, water supplies available there. The soft Scottish water enabled this period to be almost doubled at Haymarket. A full examination was carried out

at this time, brake blocks were renewed and any worn items such as split pins were also renewed. After this examination, the engine had to be examined by either the mechanical foreman or Shed Master, before going back into traffic.

Fusible plugs were renewed every 7/9 weeks. Middle big-ends were taken down every 10/12,000 miles and coupling rods and motion were taken down every 20/24,000 miles. A 'No. 6' examination was carried out at every 30/36,000 miles when the valves and pistons were removed. Although not a requirement of a No. 6 exam, at Haymarket the conjugated valve gear was also dismantled at this time with all pins and bearings being renewed as required. This meant that the subsequent valve setting was carried out with the 2-to-1 gear in correct working order.

Mention was made in Chapter 15 about the problems with middle big-ends and the conjugated valve gear. Thanks to the work of K.J. Cook, who took over as CM&EE at Doncaster in 1951, the vagaries and inherent problems with the conjugated valve gear and propensity to suffer from middle big-end problems were to be largely laid to rest. Cook, a Great Western man and Swindon-trained, introduced to Doncaster the use of optical equipment (supplied by Taylor, Taylor and Hobson) to align axle boxes, wheels, coupling rods and cylinders along the longitudinal centre-line of the locomotive, and

Haymarket D11/2 No. 62685 *Malcolm Graeme* had by this date fallen on hard times and been relegated to act as stationary boiler for washing-out purposes. Much neglected, the engine is seen at the top end of Haymarket shed. This was not to be the engine's final role, however, because it was then moved over to Edinburgh Princes Street station where it languished in a siding, hidden from general view, acting as stationary boiler for the prestigious Caledonian Hotel before finally being condemned in February 1962. *Courtesy David Dunn*

with each other, during general repairs. Optical alignment, however, brought its own peculiar headaches and overheating of the right-hand driving wheel axle boxes continued to be an ongoing problem. Optical alignment meant that standard spare axle boxes could not be used, since each individual replacement axle box had to conform to the dimensions appertaining to the last alignment at Doncaster. This problem was partly addressed by a spare pair of driving axle boxes, unique to that engine and conforming to the alignment, accompanying each engine as it returned from main works repair. Experience revealed that potential for failure of driving axle boxes occurred at around 40,000 miles, so it was decided that, since the spare axle boxes were available in the stores in any case, the driving axle boxes would be replaced at the No. 6 examination and this led to a dramatic improvement in reliability. Cook also largely resolved the weaknesses in the Gresley middle big-end by fitting Swindon marine-style big-end brasses which had a thin white-metal surface right around the brass bearing with short lubricating pads, and by having the bearings machined to far more accurate tolerances of approximately 10–12 thousands of an inch clearance between journal and brasses, with a high quality finish.

The Haymarket machinists could produce this laid-down accuracy of finish when brasses were remetalled, this being done at the shed, so that there was no need for the depot to comply with the instruction that all brasses should be returned to Doncaster works for remetalling and machining. Incidentally, Haymarket, right to the final days of steam, continued to carry out No. 6 examinations (36,000 miles) in-house, such was the high calibre and availability of the fitting staff employed at the depot, unlike the sheds at the southern end of the ECML which latterly had to rely on Doncaster works to carry out this work.

Maintenance continued to be of the highest quality until the final days of steam, and the mileages being run annually by all Haymarket Pacifics was testament to this attention.

Class 27 No. 27018 awaiting a boiler test in No. 10 road.
Courtesy Ray Murison

With dieselisation came new and unique problems on the maintenance front. Steam fitters and their methods were often unacceptable on machines where more finesse was required. The fitters were sent on training and conversion courses for each class of diesel electric locomotive allocated and this is where the younger men were to shine. They took to the new forms of traction quickly and soon became skilled diesel fitters. However, diesel electric locomotives required electricians and there was a considerable period of unrest in the early 1960s as this new breed of craftsman took up residence. Most came from outside the industry and, regrettably and a sign of the times, brought many of their restrictive trade practices with them, something unheard of at Haymarket. The appointment of an electrical foreman gradually brought a semblance of order to the depot.

Initially, and certainly into 1963, the various manufacturers of

With the arrival of main line diesel locomotives, a suitable fuelling point had to be provided at Haymarket and, as a temporary measure, a make-do-and-mend facility was created in the west end of the shed loop, adjacent to the main line. Here, Type 4 Sulzer No. D178, which has worked into Edinburgh via the Waverley route in March 1963, is refuelled for the return working, which is likely to be the night Waverley-route sleeping train service. This 'temporary' facility was, in fact, to remain in use for several years. *Courtesy Ian Musgrave*

Class 47/7 stands on jacks in No. 9 road, with bogies removed. In the upper right corner can be seen what was the original Mechanical Foreman's Office – a lasting link with steam days when this was the new machine shop. *Courtesy Ray Murison*

diesel electric locomotives were heavily involved in the day-to-day maintenance, modification and improvement of their products; thus service engineers from Sulzer, English Electric and, later, Brush became a normal and extremely welcome part of the Haymarket scene as 'troubleshooters'. In many cases the service engineers oversaw the work of the depot fitters and electricians in these early days of the new forms of traction, and an extremely valuable contribution they made.

Despite all the trials and tribulations of dieselisation, maintenance at Haymarket was to prove better than at many other depots, a point reflected in the availability and annual mileages being returned by

the Haymarket diesel electric passenger locomotives. Regrettably, some of the inherently poor designs proved to be beyond even the most skilled fitters and electricians. Diesel maintenance was initially conducted to a laid-down set of examinations which were time-based – for example daily, weekly, monthly, three-monthly exams – but engines were maintained on the basis of engine-hours run.

After the implementation of the computerised TOPS system in the early 1970s it became possible to maintain an accurate record of mileages run by each locomotive; the maintenance regime was thus altered to become a mileage-based system as opposed to the set time-based exam and routine maintenance periodicity described above.

Sadly, defects and failures were high, placing a severe strain on the resources at the depot, but these problems were met with the traditional *savoir faire* which set Haymarket apart from many other depots. It is, however, a pleasure to be able to record that with the conversion to multiple units, the maintenance at Haymarket thereafter continued in the best traditions of the 'golden years' and even today is recognised as being of the highest quality.

The current First ScotRail fleet continues to be given mileage based exam/maintenance, as follows:

Class 158
- Fuel point exam: 1200 miles +100/-200 (fuel, coolant, oil levels and toilet tanking)
- Balanced A exam: 7000 miles +/-700 miles.

Class 170
- Fuel point exam: 1500 miles +100/-200 (fuel, coolant, oil levels and toilet tanking)
- Balanced A exam: 10,000 miles +/-700 miles
- Balanced B exam: 20,000 miles +/-700 miles.

The interior of what was the 'new' steam-era machine shed, now Nos 10 and 11 roads, on 28th July 1984, with 26001 under repair. In steam days, the wheeldrop pit was situated immediately in front of the two wheel sets, but basically the shed is 'as was'. *Courtesy Gavin Morrison*

29 TRAINING AND COMPETENCY OF DRIVERS AND FIREMEN

As recorded away back in Chapter 1, a telling statement was included in the report of the legal proceedings in connection with the Ratho fatality in 1844 (see Chapter 31), in which the competency of railway footplate-men in general was called into question. In the preliminary comments in the aforesaid report into the trial of William Paton, there was indeed a damning assessment of engine drivers:

Men are employed about the Railways who are utterly incompetent to the duties assigned to them. Men, after a short experience of firing, are set to drive locomotives, trusted with the safety of hundreds, yet both careless and ignorant, not only to the very responsible position in which they are placed, but grossly ignorant of the powerful machines entrusted to their charge. And this is done to decrease the working expenses of the companies. Whilst they lavish extravagant salaries on their higher officials, they will not, in too many cases, pay decent wages to respectable and thorough-bred engineers, but taking men from the barrow, or the plough, to whom 16s. or 18s. per week is high pay, they place such parties to drive locomotives.

After some comments regarding the powers of the Board of Trade and their role, the remarks as published finish:

In conclusion, we say that there must be a Public Board to examine and grant certificates of qualification to engine drivers – that no person be allowed to drive a locomotive without such certificate and that an independent public officer be appointed to oversee the working of every railway.

These were no idle throwaway statements; nor, if one is objective, were they unjust criticism, but were perfectly true statements based

on hard fact, regarding the state of railway operation at the time. They were, in addition, a good indicator of the problems faced by not only the Edinburgh & Glasgow Railway Company, but also all the new railway companies, since the railway was indeed an entirely new industry with no base of experience to draw upon. The Lord Advocate's recommendations did obtain an overseer of all railways in the shape of Her Majesty's Railway Inspectorate, and a valuable role they were to play in coming years – but it was to be a long, long time, some 150 years plus in fact, before certification of competence as opposed to certified competence, not only for drivers but for every member of staff employed in a safety-critical role on the railway, became a reality.

Early engine drivers were, in truth, little more than self-trained artisans. If a company was lucky, men with experience of colliery or factory boilers might be enlisted, but much of the driving experience was to be gained by trial and error, often considerable error, and continued to be exactly so for several years afterwards. Even in the great days of steam – unlike the continental railways where drivers were workshop-trained, mechanically qualified, and proven to be fully competent in all aspects of locomotive engineering and management – in Britain drivers picked up their expertise through the long apprenticeship of cleaning, firing and eventually driving locomotives. And every depot had its own particular black sheep!

On firstly the E&GR, and later the NBR, things were no different; but, artisan or not, every driver of the day did become, by necessity and through practice, a first class engineer who could, and did, tackle running repairs with the utmost confidence. Gland packing, renewing trimmings, packing injector steam keys and even attention to small ends and big ends – short of dismantling them – were jobs regularly undertaken by drivers on their own engines. This was, however, work undertaken by sheer self-preservation,

Class 150 No. 150255 stands in No. 9 road undergoing attention. This set appears to have just been fitted with a small snowplough. *Courtesy Ray Murison*

No. 1 road (underframe wash) looking east. *Courtesy Ray Murison*

A retirement get-together for Edinburgh drivers. Standing left is R.H.N. Hardy, whilst standing fourth from right is Geoffrey Lund, Assistant District Motive Power Superintendent, Edinburgh. Seated third from right is former driver Norman McKillop ('Toram Beg') of Haymarket, and on his immediate right is his close friend R.I. Nelson, the noted Edinburgh publisher. *Courtesy Mr Peter Lund*

since promotion on the NBR was not automatic and the locomotive foremen of the time had the ultimate say on whether a man continued in service, or was sacked. Poor performance, carelessness or an engine showing signs of mechanical neglect, or even something as minor as a small blow of steam from a gland, was a sure path to unemployment!

But a quite dramatic event occurred at Haymarket in 1919. Led by a group of enlightened younger drivers, including Norman McKillop, an informal series of meetings to discuss all things locomotive was established. These meetings at first took place in the open shed amongst the engines and outside working hours, normally on a Sunday. These keen 'railwaymen' – and the term is used quite intentionally, for they all, to a man, did have a keen interest in what was their chosen way of life – met on a regular basis and the meetings quickly became more and more popular as interest in the idea grew apace. The purpose was a forum for the two-way flow of information, and where problems could be aired in the knowledge that a) it was an informal get-together, and b) honest answers, based on experience, would be forthcoming, without any risk of 'official' wrath being incurred or having to toe the party line.

Management initially, and for some time thereafter, took no active interest, neither did they provide any assistance – but, more importantly, they never at any time sought to discourage the initiative. They clearly saw the benefits of such a forum and, just as important, it was not costing the company any money whatsoever. The mutual improvement movement had been established at Haymarket, as it was at other sheds up and down the country.

It must be said at this juncture that 'Mutual Improvement' was not the brainchild of Haymarket footplate staff. Whilst the origins of this movement are perhaps a little unclear, it is most likely that credit, certainly in Scotland, can be placed at the door of one John Farquharson McIntosh – the noted J.F. McIntosh, Locomotive Superintendent of the Caledonian Railway and based at St. Rollox in Glasgow. McIntosh, an ex-driver himself, not only designed and had built what were amongst the finest engines of their day, but ever conscious of the fact that his drivers had one significant weakness – the lack of proper mechanical training – introduced 'Mutual Improvement' classes at St. Rollox in the closing years of the

nineteenth century. Held out of working hours and with attendance purely voluntary, McIntosh attached great importance to this initiative and he conducted many classes himself whenever possible. Theoretical and practical lectures were given by experts, and the students were taken on shed visits and given practical problems to solve. Up to ninety men attended the classes at any given time and a substantial improvement in the quality of candidates presenting themselves for driving was soon to be seen. It was not long before the NBR staff at Cowlairs were lobbying Matthew Holmes for similar classes.

Mutual improvement at Haymarket thus followed on this great tradition but, unlike the Caledonian Railway example, it was to be very much a 'self-education' process, established by drivers themselves, for the benefit of all footplate grades who were interested. It provided a more structured learning process about managing the locomotives they operated, and covered instruction, discussion and education, not only in the locomotives themselves, but also all the appropriate rules, regulations and working arrangements. The mutual improvement class (MIC) became a focal point at Haymarket, not just for tuition on all things locomotive, but it was expanded into an extra-mural activity where friendships were made and social activities arranged. The mutual improvement movement gained momentum, and over the years became much more formalised and structured throughout the whole railway industry, providing a valuable training ground for all footplate staff who were 'engine daft' and who wished to establish a good grounding in personal competence for themselves in their chosen career. Mutual improvement, from its humble beginnings, went on to feature large in BR self-training and improvement policy, with, at Haymarket, new facilities and accommodation being provided specifically for this purpose.

Thus the experienced men at Haymarket tutored the less experienced, through discussion and practical hands-on sessions, on the know-how of effective firing and driving techniques, and even Top link drivers took an active part. It is recorded that the great Tom Henderson, of NBR Atlantic fame, took one of the first classes, speaking from an engine cab to the assembled gathering. His subject was the vacuum brake and its working, at that time very much an unknown quantity to the men at Haymarket; Henderson took the group on a step-by-step account of driving and braking a locomotive working a vacuum-fitted train from Edinburgh to Aberdeen. It was not unknown for the motion of a 'dead' engine to be partially dismantled to prove, or disprove, a theory. On some occasions even fitters entered, or were persuaded to enter, into the spirit of mutual improvement.

The beneficial consequences of mutual improvement at Haymarket were never more evident than when the first Gresley A1s arrived in 1924 and the Haymarket men quickly became exponents of full regulator/short cut-off working, as preached by Gresley himself. These were the same men who had, up to that time, driven NBR and NER Atlantics and who were not in the first prime of youth. The results were there to be seen, and with the passing-on of experiences, and experiments in driving and firing these new engines, Haymarket was to develop into very much a pro-Gresley institution. The mutual improvement movement was the catalyst which raised up, and continued to maintain, the high quality of enginemanship there, generation after generation, throughout the great years of steam.

THE STREAMLINER DAYS

The point has been made in print by noted commentators elsewhere, that the L&NER (and indeed, the LM&S) management adopted a cavalier and unprofessional attitude when it came to both the provision of proper staff training and suitable signalling infrastructure when venturing into the realms of the high-speed Streamliner services. One commentator went so far as to suggest that the LM&S Board and management were 'spineless' and unworthy of their footplate staff for this 'failure'!

The particular point about lack of high-speed training has been echoed in other publications and by other railway commentators, but the truth of the matter is that the advent of the Streamliners,

and accelerated timings, did not in fact actually require drivers to drive at speeds previously unknown, or not previously experienced by them, but merely to maintain such speeds over some longer distances. Certainly, even in the author's time at Haymarket, and with the Haymarket Top link working through to York over the very fast Northallerton/York section on the non-stop services, the question of lack of high-speed training never raised its head.

Regarding the whole issue of 'high-speed' training, fine words indeed, but the question to be asked is really '*was there any validity in this implied criticism?*' Having made an issue of this 'problem', the same commentators thereafter offered no sensible suggestions whatsoever as to how this training might actually have been achieved, but left the following questions totally unanswered:

- What format might the 'high-speed' training have taken?
- Who was, or might have been, competent to carry out this training?
- More importantly, how was the would-be trainer himself to be trained to then carry out this initial training? This, particularly, is a chicken and egg situation indeed!

The issue of a perceived lack of 'high-speed' training was in fact a bit of a nonsense, raised in the main by amateur commentators who little understood the realities of railway operation.

Quite simply, the drivers trained themselves, and each other, through the medium of the mutual improvement movement as they did for any other footplate matter. Gresley had spread the gospel of full regulator/short cut-off working with his engines, and most of the drivers put this into practice. There were the misfits who went their own way, but they were few and far between. The reality was, the drivers involved in 'high-speed running' were never themselves concerned, nor did they ever consider that they had been short-changed by their superiors. The issue of high-speed running had arisen well before the Streamliners ever made an appearance – one

A 2-2-2 passenger locomotive, No. 211 built by Beyer Peacock for the E&GR in 1861, the engine was rebuilt by Drummond 1880/2. Named *Haymarket* in 1880, it is seen here standing on the turntable at the new Haymarket shed. It was withdrawn in 1910. *Bill Lynn collection*

A fine head-on shot of D30 No. 62442 *Simon Glover* of Thornton shed, accelerating away from the Haymarket station stop with a Fife stopping passenger, passing Haymarket Central Junction on a fine summer evening. The fine lines of this well-loved ex-NBR class of engine can be seen to advantage from this angle.   *Courtesy David Dunn*

has just to re-visit the heady days of the 'Railway Races' of 1885 to see this. Just what training had any of the participating drivers from all the companies received? The simple answer! No training, just long experience and an extreme confidence in machine, infrastructure and in their own ability.

Drivers not only imparted their knowledge and experiences through the MIC, but also did so on a daily basis. Firemen were frequently invited to take the regulator, particularly the older hands, and so, when passed out for driving, these young men were then entirely competent to put themselves in the left-hand seat and run any and all trains to time. This practice started in the early days of young careers and the author, even at the early age of 17 or 18 years as a passed cleaner, was given the opportunity to 'take hold' of engines under the supervision of his driver.

The safe progress of train running, irrespective of speed, was, and still is, vested in the system(s) of signalling employed and the driver's route knowledge. In terms of signalling, whether it is 'route' or 'directional' signalling as used in the UK (where the signals indicate to a driver exactly where he is routed), or 'speed' signalling as employed on the Continent and elsewhere (where signals indicate the safe permissible speed), it matters not, the signals determine operational safety. The block signalling systems employed in the 1920s/30s were by that time well-proven and robust fail-safe systems. In terms of signal-spacing, a series of documented braking curves were compiled, based on the correlation of line speed, gradient and braking capacity; as a result, when spacing signals, and according to the physical conditions on the ground, the necessary 'Service Braking Distance' (SBD) could be provided between the distant signal and first stop signal – so that when a 'shut' distant had been encountered the fastest, and heaviest, trains could be safely brought to a stop before reaching the home signal. Every new signal was also 'sighted' by a signal sighting committee, consisting of signal engineers, operating inspectors and locomotive inspectors, who checked each signal to ensure optimum sighting by drivers.

With accelerated running, the situation could, and indeed did, arise – as on the track-circuit-block areas north of York fitted with two- and three-aspect colour light signals – where SBD for 90 mph running was to be rendered deficient in some instances, and where signalling changes to meet the demands of the faster schedules (for example, the provision of a fourth aspect) could not be effected overnight. As a consequence of these higher line speeds and resulting deficiencies in SBD, there were only two practical courses of action available to the operators in order to mitigate the risks associated with the high-speed services:

- imposition of a lower permanent maximum line speed restriction, or,
- as a longer term solution, provision of a fourth aspect, or repositioning the existing two-aspect colour light distant signals to provide the required SBD.

It must be recorded here that the NE Area signalling system between York and Northallerton was fully converted to full four-aspect colour light signalling by March 1938, thus permitting reversion to full high-speed running (90 mph).

However, despite the initial signalling deficiencies and the limited options to address the problem, it is an undisputed fact that the Streamliners did operate successfully and safely. This fact can be attributed to one other essential and important skill as mentioned above, the driver's route knowledge – which was, and still is, the real strength of the professional driver. What is route knowledge? Quite simply, it is the ability of a driver to know every detail and idiosyncrasy of a line of route; drivers know where they are at every point of the journey and will know where every signal is, and at what point they will first see it, night or day, in clear or foggy weather. As a result, locations where shortages of SBD arose because of higher line speeds quickly became common knowledge amongst drivers across the shed, any shed, and were widely discussed. Drivers, armed with this information, then used 'sighting distance' (that is, the distance at which the distant signal first came into to view) as an adjunct to SBD, thereby creating for themselves an increased braking distance by adding the sighting distance to the available SBD.

The importance of good route knowledge was proved over and over again. The main experience of 'high-speed' running available to Haymarket drivers prior to the introduction of the A3s and A4s was driving over the E&GR main line, at that time the fastest route worked by the shed, but where 80 mph was a high speed – yet these same men, without any special training, and with the advent of the A4s, were suddenly producing runs where the magic 100 mph was being attained and even exceeded on the Edinburgh/Newcastle route, on a regular basis, confident that they were in complete control and could do so without incident.

On the southern part of the ECML, several King's Cross Top Shed senior drivers fell into this same category, indeed their names were almost household words. They regularly pushed their engines well beyond the laid down speed limits imposed when running demanded, and with complete faith in their own abilities. This was, of course, all before the 'dead hand' of Health and Safety, and 'radar guns' replaced common sense. Today, most, if not all these most experienced footplatemen would be classified as 'Drivers at Risk' and have had their names recorded on a register of drivers requiring special attention (the Drivers At Risk Register), if they had not already been removed from the footplate.

It was to the credit and professionalism of the drivers, signalmen, and of the 'backroom' signalling and safety 'experts', that safety in operation was never at any time compromised during all the heady days of the Streamliners. There was not, contrary to what has been inferred in print elsewhere, a less than professional approach to the issues of high-speed running. The 'problems' were quite properly, and safely, addressed! It should be noted that the author considers himself to be competent to offer this opinion since he was the Regional Signalling and Safety Officer for the Scottish Region in BR days, and as such was closely involved in provision of Special Instructions and the redesign of signalling infrastructure to accommodate many of the high-speed running initiatives being demanded at that time.

It should also be added as a rider that, in all training given in diesel electric traction, and indeed later with electric traction, there was never any element of this training which addressed high-speed driving, even though when it came to the Deltics, and later the HSTs and electric 225 sets, very-high-speed running was an everyday requirement. Why? The answer has already been given above and, it must be said, many of the drivers involved from the Edinburgh end had formerly been Haymarket passed firemen.

THE DIESELISATION ERA TO THE PRESENT DAY

The onset of the diesel era brought its own inherent problems with driver training. Not only were men whose roots were steeped in steam required to be completely retrained in a new and unique form of traction, but each man had to be trained in every single class of diesel unit or locomotive upon which he might be called upon to work. With steam locomotives, a driver was a driver was a driver, and was expected to be able to step onto any type of steam locomotive, quickly familiarise himself with it and drive it, without any special familiarisation or training. Not so the diesels, and every driver was required to undergo a three-week-long basic diesel training course, followed by a single week's conversion course for each and every different diesel type. All training involved the men thereafter being examined and certified as competent to drive each individual class. This then required that suitable records were prepared so that roster clerks, who previously only had to check on a driver's route card, had now to check on individual driver's traction knowledge as well. All this brought problems, not least with the men in the senior links who thought they were too old to learn 'new tricks'. Haymarket, with its big Spare links, managed training very efficiently and, all in all, things went remarkably smoothly – but at a cost, and indeed a cost which no one has ever quantified, or factored into the real costs of a grossly mishandled modernisation programme.

However, all that has been said must, of course, also be considered from the reality that the long apprenticeship leading to locomotive driving quickly ceased-to-be with the demise of steam, and very quickly thereafter the old guard of locomotive men were themselves to retire. With an 'in-house' succession list no longer existing, replacement drivers were having to be recruited 'off the streets' – firstly by BR, and thereafter by the many train operating companies who followed – requiring the need for a structured and formalised training system. Thus there are, at the present time, extremely robust requirements addressing the selection and training of drivers. There are several pieces of EU legislation governing this, and the EU has set the minimum age limits for train drivers as eighteen years for domestic services and twenty years for international services. In the UK, however, twenty-one years has been set as the minimum age for all drivers, based on an assessment of risk. Within the UK

A panoramic view of the shed from the east in the 1980s. From left to right: a Class 40 and a Class 26 stand in the yard sidings, waiting repair. In the next road stands the breakdown train with a Class 08 partially obscured, and next to that are two DMU sets – again probably waiting repair – and a single-car (Class 122) DMU. Immediately behind is the new Admin/Amenity block which also housed the Haymarket Diesel Training School on the upper level. *Courtesy Ray Murison*

railways, Rail Industry Standard RIS 3751 TOM sets down the requirements for 'Train Driver Selection'. Group Standard GD/RT 3451 addresses 'Train Movement Staff Suitability and Fitness Requirements' and sets down the medical parameters entrants have to meet, and so it goes on, with a proper auditable trail for selection and training.

When selected for training, a variety of training methods are employed, with an ever-increasing reliance on the use of state-of-the-art simulators. The train operating companies are now particularly attracted to the use of simulators since every possible permutation of events in train operation can be replicated without actually requiring real-time line capacity. Simulators are particularly useful in training would-be drivers where experience in differing examples of freight train dynamics (drawbar pull/braking and gradients) can be introduced to great advantage and without risk. Driver training is now a long process taking, from start to completion, up to a year, and involving both theoretical classroom training and practical handling under supervision. Most train operating companies now make much use of training simulators.

After completion of training, new drivers have the support of mentor (instructor) drivers where they are then further monitored and coached by more experienced drivers when they finally take control 'out on the road'. Training is all very well, but the one thing that cannot be taught, and must be acquired through experience is, of course, 'Route Knowledge' and the handling characteristics of the train on the road on the day, hence the need for additional support in the early stages. Drivers are also thereafter subjected to a regular review of continuing competence.

It is also worth mentioning that in all the days of high-speed running with steam, the incidence of signals being passed at danger (SPADs), whilst it occurred, was never a significant problem. However, with the advent of the new traction and despite the provision of modern three- and four-aspect colour light signals, and routes fitted with the BR Automatic Warning System (AWS) – as the old guard of steam men retired, so the incidence of SPADs reached epidemic proportions, spawning many studies and causing much soul-searching amongst the professional operators. Much of the cause could be put down to 'human error' and, indeed, inexperience, but the incidence of the 'disregard' category of SPAD was alarming in the extreme. This, in part, was addressed by the adoption of 'defensive driving' procedures where the driver of a train approaching a signal displaying a 'stop' aspect, was required to stop some 20 metres on the approach side of the signal. However, a more recent mitigation measure opted for in the UK was the provision of the overlaying of a Train Protection Warning System (TPWS) on the existing AWS, as a 'stop-gap' measure, where the equipment will react if the driver does not. The UK rail industry is now, however, committed to implementing the EU (UIC) preferred option of the European Railways Train Management System (ERTMS), a fully automatic control system which effectively overrides the driver's actions should the equipment sense that his response to given adverse indications or speed is inadequate or inappropriate. Trial operation with ERTMS has now commenced in Wales, but as a system-wide concept, with the immense financial commitment required, and given the current track record of Network Rail, the author, for one, is not holding his breath! Until that day, drivers' route knowledge will remain the main weapon in a driver's armoury.

E&GR push-pull set powering away from platform 4 in Haymarket station bound for Glasgow, with the Driving Brake Second Open (DBSO) leading. This vehicle is a modified Mk II BSO coach which has been provided with a driving cab. The driver sits on the right-hand side in this photograph – left-hand driving position. *Courtesy John Fumeval*

30 HAYMARKET ON FILM

Haymarket locomotives (and crews) were to feature in several films at one time or another. One of the earliest appearances was in the original 1935 Hitchcock production of an adaptation of John Buchan's great novel *The 39 Steps*, starring Robert Donat as the hero, Richard Hannay. As originally filmed, the hero's arrival at Waverley station featured engines from 64B – a 'Director' No. 6338 *Captain Graigengelt* piloted by a D29 No. 9338 *Helen Mcgregor*. St. Margaret's men also had a role to play, when the departing train – which was actually the 4.03 pm Perth (distinguishable by its Pullman car in the coaching set) hauled by D49 No. 281 *Dunbartonshire* – was filmed. Hannay's subsequent abandonment of the train on the Forth Bridge also involved Haymarket men. Sadly, in the editing process, the film as prepared for general distribution had nearly all the railway (locomotive) scenes cut, and these cuttings can now only be seen on the video referred to below.

The remake of this same film classic in 1958, starring Kenneth More, was to once more involve Haymarket men and Top link locomotives. Over a period of four Sundays in the late August/early September of that year, two special train-sets were given over to the film makers, and both No. 60012 *Commonwealth of Australia* and No. 60027 *Merlin* appeared in the finished article, as did, very briefly, No. 60162 *Saint Johnstoun*. The scene starts with No. 60012 running into the South Main (platforms 10 and 11) at Edinburgh Waverley, complete with the 'Talisman' headboard. There is then a fine shot of No. 60027 *Merlin*, starting away, with cylinder cocks roaring, from Waverley, with Top link driver Tom Fell (one of the two regular drivers) at the controls. The is followed by some fine shots of what has become, once again, No. 60012 *Commonwealth of Australia*, running on to the Forth Bridge with black smoke billowing and the engine blowing off as the communication cord was pulled. With true artistic license, the hero is then seen hanging on to the outside of the non-working side of the still-moving train on the bridge proper, as an Up express hauled by No. 60162 *Saint Johnstoun* rushes past, an impossible event in real life.

The actual Haymarket crews who finally appeared in the film were not identified, but all the crews associated with the train operation over the period of filming received an interesting handshake as a big 'thank you' from the film company – each driver getting £10 (two five-pound notes), and firemen getting £5. The notes were the then-new issue by the Bank of Scotland, featuring, on the reverse side, the Forth Bridge. A nice touch indeed!

Just as interesting, if indeed not more so, is the footage from both of the above films which dropped on to the cutting-room floor, was later retrieved, and eventually issued on a railway-interest video (*Steam on 35mm, No. 3*, 1995), and includes a truly magnificent slip by No. 60027 as it starts way from Waverley, but with this omitted in the final editing.

Earlier in the 1950s, a rather pleasant quasi-documentary film was made called *Waverley Steps*, which displayed life over a 24-hour period in Edinburgh. The film starts with a shot of No. 12 *Commonwealth of Australia* working northbound on the East Coast; it is seen running past Seton level crossing, with Bill McLeod of Haymarket Top link at the controls and a young fireman – sadly, name now unknown – as his mate. Further shots were taken with the engine (but now, mysteriously, No. 27 *Merlin*) approaching Waverley station up through the Calton South Tunnel and then running light through the gardens and on to shed at Haymarket, with the same crew. The crew both had brief speaking parts, but then the film followed the fireman going home and, after looking at many other aspects of Edinburgh life, finishes with the same fireman reporting for nightshift – once more with some spectacular night shots of No. 27 coming 'off shed' at Haymarket, with cylinder cocks roaring and a violent slip thrown in for good measure. There is also some interesting footage of Waverley east-end as well as Edinburgh trams. It is understood that the young fireman involved left railway service shortly thereafter, to follow a new career in acting.

One cannot leave the film stars of 64B without mentioning that very famous British Transport Films production entitled *Elizabethan Express* which was made in 1953/54. This documentary film revolves around the working, and follows the journey, of the non-stop 'Elizabethan', the 09.30 from London King's Cross to Edinburgh. The film features Top Shed A4 No. 60017 *Silver Fox* (with a blow in the cylinder cocks), with Driver Bob Marrable and Fireman Rollie Rufnell, also of Top Shed, being relieved en route, via the corridor tender, by Haymarket's other famous McLeod, Tony, and his (passed) fireman, Mungo Scott. This, despite the rather dated and banal commentary, is surely one of the best steam railway films ever, a product of the genius of Edward Anstey, who ran the BT Films unit with great success for many years.

Haymarket A4 No. 60012 *Commonwealth of Australia* was given some further exposure in the 1960 film *Carry on Regardless*, with the usual 'Carry On' actors on the Forth Bridge. The engine can be identified, albeit with reversed numbers (the film was obviously reversed). There is also a very (very) brief glimpse of A4 No. 60024 *Kingfisher*, and although other A3s and A4s appear, they are too far away to be identified.

Finally, another long-time stalwart of Haymarket was to appear in a film, long after its official retirement. Class J36 No. 65243 *Maude*, built by the NBR at Cowlairs and entering traffic in 1891, came to Haymarket in June 1928 and remained there until September 1963. Finally withdrawn in July 1966 from Bathgate shed, the engine was sold to the Scottish Railway Preservation Society in November 1966 and, in restored condition and under various guises, was again steamed on the Bo'ness & Birkhill Railway. In 2000, it made several appearances in the Carlton TV film *The Railway Children*, directed by Catherine Morshead, running on the Bluebell Line in Sussex, where No. 65243 was on loan at the time, and carrying the original NBR number, 673.

The 1958 film *The 39 Steps*, starring Kenneth More, was shot, in part, on the Forth Bridge and employed two special train-sets, hauled by Haymarket A4 Pacifics with their crews, over a period of four Sundays in the August/September of that year. The dramatic scene where the hero flees from the train after pulling the communication cord on the bridge is being shot by the film crew. A BR traffic inspector is in the centre background, and to the right behind the camera crew can be seen the lookout man, identified by his distinctive arm band. The leading man, Kenneth More, stands in the group on the far right.   *Courtesy Scotsman Publications*

31 ACCIDENTS AND INCIDENTS

A locomotive depot the size and age of Haymarket has inevitably over the years had its fair share of accidents and incidents, attributed to both its engines and/or men – some minor, but some which at the time made headline news and were, in themselves, a catalyst for altered working practices. Recounted below are some of the noteworthy events, and the author has, as a retired professional railway operator, added his own opinions based on both practical experience and to reflect how accident investigation has moved on apace. These are, it must be stressed, his own opinions.

RATHO: 1844

On the 19th May 1844, a cattle and spirits dealer named Thomas Cooley, who had been on business in Glasgow, missed the 17.00 passenger train from Queen Street to Edinburgh. Owing to further business commitments, he needed to get back to Edinburgh that evening and so he ordered a special train to take him there through the station staff in Glasgow Queen Street. Eventually, a train of sorts, consisting of a single coach, was provided and Cowlairs shed sent down the only engine in steam, a Bury four-wheeler, *Napier*, the boiler and firebox of which were leaking badly. It should be noted that each E&GR locomotive was required to have, whilst in traffic, two engine lamps (a head lamp and a tail lamp), a gauge-glass lamp and a driver's hand lamp. *Napier* was sent into traffic minus all lamps. No guard was provided on the train, which eventually set off with only Driver Richard McNab, his fireman and Mr Cooley on board. The small train staggered on its way, stopping frequently to raise steam and fill the badly leaking boiler. By the time it reached a point between Ratho and Gogar, it had taken well over three hours to get there and, inevitably, it was caught up by the following 19.30 passenger train from Glasgow to Edinburgh hauled by sister engine *Archimedes*. In the darkness, and with no lights showing on the standing special, the 19.30 train ploughed into it, killing the unfortunate Mr Cooley.

Driver McNab and William Paton, Superintendent of Locomotives on the E&GR, stood trial in Edinburgh on the 3rd and 4th November 1844, the driver being charged with neglect of duty for going out without lamps, and Paton indicted on a charge of culpable homicide, in having sent out an engine in such a poor state of repair. We have already heard Robert Thornton's evidence regarding the appalling state of *Napier* when inspected by him at Haymarket shed following the accident (see Chapter 2). In April 1845, McNab was sentenced to nine months imprisonment whilst Paton, by virtue of a reasoned plea regarding the engine situation then existing on the E&GR, narrowly escaped transportation and was instead, sentenced to twelve months imprisonment.

WINCHBURGH: 1862

On 13th October 1862, relaying was being undertaken on the Up line between Edinburgh and Glasgow (E&GR nomenclature was Up to Glasgow and Down from Glasgow) and all trains were thus required to pass over the Down line between Linlithgow and Winchburgh Junction. In keeping with the procedures of the time, a light engine was used as a pilot engine (the equivalent of the latter-day pilotman), and this engine followed the last preceding train through the section. Thereafter, and until it returned, no other train could proceed in that same direction, the line then being clear for movements from the end at which the pilot engine stood. The pilot engine was No. 9, one of the original Hawthorn 2-4-0 'Luggage' engines, from Haymarket depot, which was deputising on that day for one of the smaller Beyer Peacock 0-4-2s, No. 88. Entry to the single line was controlled by pointsmen situated at the crossovers at each end of possession. The Scottish Central Railway's 18.00 passenger train from Edinburgh to Stirling, having set back through the crossover to the Down line at Winchburgh Junction, was to follow an E&GR ballast train – worked by Beyer Peacock 2-2-2 No. 57, also of Haymarket depot, newly overhauled and painted, and on a running-in turn – carrying, in a coach and a wagon, the dayshift platelayers who were now making their way home to Polmont and Falkirk. Both these trains were thus to run in front of the pilot, No. 9, through to Linlithgow.

However, at Linlithgow, the inexperienced pointsman, in the failing light, saw the biggish engine and a flash of brass as the ballast train (No. 57) passed, and mistaking it for the pilot engine (No. 9) he then gave clear road to the 17.00 Glasgow to Edinburgh express which was running on time at Linlithgow. The Glasgow to Edinburgh train, running at speed under clear signals, met the Scottish Central train head-on in the long, deep Winchburgh cutting. The engine of the E&GR express train had wide sandwich frames, but the smaller tank engine on the other train was narrow and telescoped into the express engine. Cylinders were broken and the boilers sprung on both engines. The E&GR locomotive's motion was disrupted and the Central engine's tank became displaced, killing the fireman. Both enginemen on the express were killed and the coaches of both trains were reduced to matchwood. Eleven passengers died at the scene and a further four died overnight in Edinburgh Royal Infirmary. Twenty-one passengers were seriously injured, the Edinburgh-bound train being exceptionally busy, conveying a full load of passengers travelling home from the Falkirk Tryst (market).

Mr Latham, the General Manager of the E&GR, and Mr Thomson, the Traffic Superintendent, were both prosecuted by the Lord Advocate, being charged with culpable homicide and culpable neglect of duty. There was considerable unease at this prosecution, and who was being prosecuted, and the E&GR was able to prove that the arrangements for emergency single line working worked perfectly safely, and that this occasion had arisen through the unfortunate pointsman having mistaken the ballast engine for the pilot engine. After eight hours of legal debate, the Lord Advocate stated that he would not press for conviction and the case was, quite properly, thrown out.

Incidentally, the Beyer Peacock 2-2-2 No. 57 (which until that same year of 1862 had been numbered 87) was in 1880 to be named *Winchburgh*, and one cannot but think that a warped sense of humour was abroad when this name was chosen!

BO'NESS JUNCTION, MANUEL: 1874

At around 07.10 on 27th January 1874, a mineral train consisting of twenty-one wagons arrived on the branch from Bo'ness. Nine of the wagons had to be detached and left on the westbound siding at Manuel. Despite the rule governing time-interval working which was in force, and which prohibited the fouling of the main line 15 minutes prior to the passage of a passenger train, the signalman at Bo'ness Junction, with the agreement of the yard inspector, allowed the mineral train to cross over and detach. However, the engine of this train was required for another passenger turn, and thus the signalman then permitted the train to run out onto the Down line. The 06.35 express passenger train from Edinburgh to Perth conveying through 'Highland' coaches for Aberdeen and Inverness from King's Cross, was hauled by 2-4-0 No. 351 (formerly No. 101 of E&GR) with 6-foot driving wheels and built at Cowlairs to the design by W. Brown Steel. The engine was running tender-first and was under the control of Driver Robert Allan with Fireman Sutherland, both of Haymarket shed.

The morning was clear and fine, but both the preceding Glasgow express and the Perth were running late. At Manuel, the Down Home signal was lying clear and the Perth train, making up lost time, was approaching at line speed. By the time Driver Allan saw the Bo'ness Junction Down Home signal at danger it was far too late. He had only time to sound the whistle for brakes and shut

the regulator before the collision. The fireman jumped but was seriously injured. Driver Allan and fourteen passengers were killed immediately and two girls later died of injuries received. Of the two horses in the horse box, one was killed outright and the other had to be destroyed.

One of the issues that Colonel Yolland, the Inspecting Officer, closely questioned was the fact that No. 351 was running tender-first. Wheatley, in his evidence, at first stated that he was at a loss to understand why this was so (but the reason was most likely to be down to the obtuseness of the Caledonian Railway, who owned the turntable at Larbert and regularly made a point of keeping NBR locomotives waiting to turn), however he finally conceded that there was no reason why No. 351 could not have been turned at Haymarket shed, after working the earlier turn on the newspaper train.

Another element contributing to this accident was the signalman himself, merely nineteen years old and seven weeks in the job! The NBR management had a lot to answer for regarding employment and training of safety-critical staff.

ELLIOT JUNCTION: 1906

This accident, whilst not directly involving Haymarket, has been included because, a) it reveals the realities of footplate life at the turn of the century, and b) it is referred to later in this chapter for comparison purposes and to illustrate how the legal system had changed. Incidentally, all these Aberdeen turns, including the working referred to in this accident, were transferred to Haymarket with the NBR Atlantics just two years later.

In 1906, a St. Margaret's driver was involved in a serious collision which resulted in fatalities at Elliot Junction on the Edinburgh

Haymarket V2 No. 60927 in a spot of bother in Princes Street Gardens in June 1958. The tender is 'off all wheels' and has not only caused quite a lot of damage to the track on the North Up line but has also come into contact with the stone retaining wall before coming to a stand. The breakdown gang weigh up their options before tackling the task of re-railing. The driver and fireman as onlookers are no doubt pondering just what they will say in their respective reports. *Courtesy W.S. Sellar*

to Aberdeen main line, between Dundee and Arbroath. The date was the 28th December and Driver George Gourlay with Fireman Robert (Bob) Irvine were rostered to work the 07.35 express from Edinburgh to Aberdeen and return. This was still in the days where the 12-hour working day was the norm, and so the rostered work on this diagram was book-on 06.35 for the 07.35 Edinburgh Waverley to Aberdeen, and return with the 13.25 from Aberdeen, being relieved at 18.00 at Edinburgh. On the day in question, Gourlay had NBR 4-4-0 No. 324 of the NBR 'K' (later L&NER D25) class, as designed by Holmes and put into traffic in 1903. The train consisted of four NBR six-wheeled coaches and one ECJS eight-wheeled coach. At this juncture, it is worthwhile to record, in light of what transpired later, that the cab was the standard NBR single side-window cab. Northwards from Dundee, the train was running very late owing to snow, with severe blizzard conditions pertaining, and eventually could get no further than Arbroath. After considerable further delay at Arbroath, Gourlay was instructed to run round his train and work it back to Edinburgh, tender first!

The local operators had not covered themselves in glory and a whole chain of serious errors of judgment had been made before the accident. There were complete block and telegraph failures between Arbroath and the signal boxes to the south, and time interval working had been put in place. Single line working had also been instituted over the Down line between Arbroath and Elliot Junction because a freight train, which was propelling part of its train (in a snow storm) had derailed on the Up line. The line to the turntable at Arbroath was occupied and the turntable pit covered in snow, thus No. 324 could not be turned. It was to be a concatenation of these individual events which set the trap for Gourlay. He had been given the right away from Arbroath, just 15 minutes after a slow passenger train for Dundee East had departed (under time interval working) and, in the severe weather conditions existing and running tender-first, with his forward view partially obstructed by the coal, he failed, in the atrocious weather conditions pertaining, to properly control his train – with the result that it collided with the rear of the preceding passenger train which was standing in the platform at Elliot Junction.

Unfortunately, but with the tacit agreement of an inspector, Gourlay was given some brandy after the collision by a well-meaning person or persons. At the inquiry which followed, however, allegations were made by members of the public that before the train left Arbroath, Gourlay appeared to be under the influence of alcohol, allegations not supported by the railway staff who had seen and spoken to Gourlay prior to the accident. The doctors who were called to examine Gourlay after the accident gave conflicting evidence, but the general consensus was that he was not rendered unfit, though alcohol had been taken. The one doctor who thought he might be drunk was unaware that Gourlay, by the time the examination was carried out, had consumed a tumbler-full of neat brandy, given by the aforesaid person. Not one, but two, locomotive inspectors who subsequently saw and spoke to Gourlay after the accident were quite definite that he showed no signs of being under the influence.

It is interesting to note that, as reported in *The Scotsman* dated Monday, 22nd April 1907, the Crown authorities had decided that the question of alcohol was not to be included in the case against Gourlay, since there were, quite properly, serious doubts as to the validity of doing so.

However, at the public inquiry, it was the chairman, Major J.W. Pringle, who insisted that the question of Gourlay's sobriety or otherwise should be brought into the public arena, by querying whether Gourlay's neglect of orders and want of caution – the charges which were laid by the Crown – were, as he delicately (and mischievously) put it, '*accountable by the bemusing effects of alcohol*'. Pringle, whilst he was critical of the actions taken by the local staff on the day – given the derailment, block signalling failures, lack of line protection and the severe weather – nevertheless concluded that Gourlay, who had been described by his locomotive superintendent as a careful and reliable driver who had worked royal trains, had erred that day and was rendered unfit through alcohol, and thus was found to be wholly responsible for the fatal collision.

COMMENT

Viewed from the twenty-first century, the accident inquiry and conclusion reached in respect of this incident must be considered as seriously flawed. The working conditions were horrendous to say the least. Twelve-hour days being the norm, plus the fact that a train could then suffer many hours of delay without relief being provided, speaks volumes about the total lack of what now is quite simply 'duty of care.' That Gourlay (and his fireman) had to hang about in the most severe cold weather, in a cab which provided little shelter, for some considerable period of time, and then be asked, nay instructed, to work tender-first, some 76¼ miles back to Edinburgh in blizzard conditions, and with time interval working and single line working both in place, was simply wrong, and would now be totally unacceptable.

The question of alcohol was tenuous in the extreme. The giving of brandy was recommended by an operating inspector, since Gourlay, aged sixty years and who, once he had been freed from the wreckage, was found to have had his face scalded, would have been in extreme pain and shock after the accident and was, in all likelihood, somewhat hypothermic. He was, therefore, given some brandy to drink as a medicinal measure and thereafter showed signs of having done so, thus rendering the allegation of drunkenness before the accident extremely unsafe in the extreme, since it was based on much hearsay evidence; it is obvious that the Crown was well aware of this pitfall when they chose not to include it in the indictment. Indeed, in reading through the evidence contained in the Accident Report, it becomes quite clear that the unfortunate Gourlay was very much ignored, from a medical attention point of view, after the accident and was left hanging around in a shocked and injured condition.

Time interval working, despite all the safeguards added over the intervening years, was eventually abandoned by BR in the late 1980s, even as an emergency measure, simply because it was perceived as inherently unsafe and carrying an unacceptably high risk of collision/accident. Even by 1906, time interval working had been exposed as an unsafe method of working by the then Board of Trade in the many inquiries held into accidents where this working had been in place. No real consideration was given to the risks posed by this method of working on the day, particularly with regard to the other unusual and quite exceptional dangers posed by severe weather, equipment failure and train congestion. The local operators had played leading roles in the ensuing disaster and had failed to comply with the basic train warning and protection procedures demanded by the *Rule Book* in such circumstances. In this context, the station master and general management of the Joint Lines were widely condemned, but these individuals never stood trial.

There was considerable public and legal disquiet regarding the fact that Gourlay had been found guilty by Major Pringle at the public inquiry and thus there was little prospect of a fair trial ensuing in the court of law. The shortcomings of the staff and management of the Joint Lines had been fully recognised, and well aired in the press of the day – but it was Gourlay, and not they, who was to go into the dock. Today, with possible legal proceedings pending, Pringle would have been debarred from questioning Gourlay in a public inquiry.

Just for a moment compare this accident, and the way Driver Gourlay was treated, with the Morpeth accident of 1984 as described later in this chapter. Here, alcohol was a proven and relevant factor. Today, Gourlay would surely have been given the benefit of the doubt. As it was, he was jailed for five months for his role in the accident at Elliot Junction. However, the jail sentence provoked a furious public outcry and, on Saturday, 23rd March, over 1,500 persons attended a public meeting in the Synod Hall, Edinburgh, to protest at the way Gourlay had been treated. Quite uncharacteristically, the NBR Board joined in; only two days earlier they had petitioned the Secretary of State for Scotland for the remission of the remainder of Gourlay's sentence. Gourlay served three months of his sentence; the company paid his wages whilst he was in jail and also arranged employment for him on his release. Gourlay was, sadly, a victim of his time.

GLASGOW QUEEN STREET (HIGH LEVEL): 1911

On 12th August 1911, NBR Class 'M' 4-4-0 No. 575, of Haymarket shed, was booked to work the 13.05 passenger express from Edinburgh Waverley to Glasgow Queen Street under the control of Driver Forrester. The normal train consist of ten coaches had been made up to twelve coaches on that busy Saturday afternoon, a load of 277 tons, and representing an overload of 11 tons for this class of engine. The driver had his work cut out to run time with this heavy train, although booked to run non-stop between Haymarket and Glasgow. Several minutes were, however, lost in running, and the driver was injudicious enough to run through Cowlairs platform at a speed of around 25 mph, instead of the regulation 3 mph.

The circulating area behind the buffer stops in Queen Street station was thronged with people when, at a few minutes after 14.10, the Edinburgh train burst out the tunnel and ran into Platform 3 at an excessive speed, to collide with the buffer stops. The crowds ran for safety as No. 575 mounted the buffer stops, *sans* tender, and came to rest sitting right across the circulating area with the front buffer beam and smokebox inside the refreshment room. The front bogie was torn off with the impact and the driving wheels were sunk deep into the platform, whilst escaping steam and water added to the infernal scene. Very fortunately there were no serious casualties, although seven passengers on the train were slightly injured – but the NBR came very close on that day to dispatching Glasgow's Lord Provost, Sir Archibald McInnes Shaw, who had been seeing a friend off and was standing in the circulating area as the train struck.

The driver, Forrester, claimed he had steadied his train to a speed of no more than 4 mph at Cowlairs station signal box, leaving some 60 lbs of air in the train pipe. When he attempted to make a further brake application at the first ventilation shaft in the tunnel, he got no result whatsoever. Immediately applying sand, he put the engine into reverse and had the fireman screw on the tender handbrake, but without any appreciable reduction in speed.

A C&W examiner, who had been standing on the platform end as the train came out the tunnel, witnessed someone screwing on the tender handbrake, and noted that no brake blocks were touching the wheels of the train, except for the brake van. However, on examining the train immediately after the collision, he found all brake blocks tight on, on every wheel.

After recovery of the engine, all Westinghouse brake gear was stripped off and fitted to another engine. It functioned as designed and Forrester was left to shoulder the blame for allowing his train to get away on the incline.

RATHO (QUEENSFERRY JUNCTION): 1911

Late in the evening of the 18th December 1911, an Up goods train from Broxburn to Niddrie West (the Broxburn pilot), with Holmes Class 'C' 0-6-0 No. 715, had been shunting at Queensferry Junction. The engine was then uncoupled from its train to go and take water at Ratho station. The signalman (Paterson) intended that the engine should cross to the Down Main line via the trailing crossover to the east of the signal box. Driver Cruikshank (Haymarket depot) misunderstood the arrangements, however, and, standing on the Up line, he took the signalman's handsignal as an authority to proceed wrong direction, via the Up Main to the sidings at Ratho station, although the points there were still set for the main line.

Paterson, on seeing the engine run past his box, assumed that it was on the Down Main and, re-setting the crossover points, he accepted the 20.20 express passenger train from Glasgow to Edinburgh, from Bathgate Junction. Meanwhile, engine No. 715 had overrun the Ratho station siding points by some 131 yards when the driver saw, firstly, the Up Main line signals lying off, followed by the headlights of the approaching express. He quickly reversed his engine and put on steam. His fireman, H. Hulse, quickly abandoned ship, but Cruikshank stuck to his engine.

The express, consisting of seven eight-wheeled coaches and with a horsebox in rear, was hauled by a Holmes Class 'K' 4-4-0 (1904), No. 318, driven by Driver Hotchkiss and running at around 50 mph. It struck the tender of No. 715 with a tremendous impact and, with both engines interlocked, came to a stand along the Up Main line. The coaches followed into derailment and became detached from the tender, but fortunately remained upright and there were no injuries. No. 318 was of the same class as that of the unfortunate Driver Gourley at Elliot Junction in 1906, referred to above, and was severely damaged.

Major Pringle, the Inspecting Officer who chaired the subsequent inquiry, laid the blame fairly and squarely on Paterson, Guard Imrie, Driver Cruikshank and Fireman Hulse for behaving in an extremely casual and irresponsible manner, so much so that they all appeared not to take any particular notice of what they were doing and what exactly was going on at the time in question.

RATHO (QUEENSFERRY JUNCTION): 1917

Yet again at this location, on the evening of 3rd January 1917, a train of empty coaches from Dalmeny arrived on the Down Branch line at Queensferry Junction behind Class 'J' superheated 'Scott' No. 421 *Jingling Geordie*, which was running tender-first. The engine was then required to run round its train.

The track layout at Queensferry Junction was as follows: a double junction diverged from the Up and Down Main lines to the Branch and provided a passing loop facility as the Up and Down Branch lines, before converging to form the Branch single line.

The procedure then used for the movement was, to say the least, peculiar, since it required the branch train to come up the Down loop. The engine was then detached and had to run forward to gain the Down Main line, where it was then required to run wrong direction to cross over to the Up Main via the Main to Main trailing crossover, which was facing for this movement. The engine was then again required to run wrong direction via the Up Main to Up Branch and on to the single Branch line, and then reverse back to couple to the train on the Down Branch.

At 16.31, the signalman (Philp) had accepted the 16.15 Down express passenger train from Edinburgh to Glasgow; at 16.35, No. 421 arrived on the Down Branch with its train. Although Philp had, quite correctly, assumed that No. 421 would wait for the signal after uncoupling, the driver, Ramsay of Haymarket, unbelievably took the lack of any instruction from the signalman as permission to proceed and thus drove his engine forward on to the Down Main line, bursting the loop points in the process. Here, on the Down Main, he encountered the express, running at around 60 mph. The express, consisting of nine modern NBR bogie coaches with a single NER coach in the rear, hauled by NBR Atlantic No. 874 *Dunedin* of Haymarket shed and driven by Driver Moffat, also from Haymarket, was running at line speed and the ensuing head-to-head collision was extremely destructive, killing twelve passengers and causing serious injury to a further forty-four. The enginemen on No. 874 were almost completely buried in coal which spilled forward from the tender (which led to the retrospective fitting of front cages on the Atlantic tenders). Both drivers did however survive, although seriously injured, so much so that the public inquiry had to be delayed until they were both well enough to be questioned. No. 421 was driven back a full 97 yards after the impact and its tender was damaged beyond repair. No. 874 suffered broken main frames with the front framing being bent right back to the cylinders and the front bogie completely destroyed. It took some 28 hours to clear the main lines for traffic.

Major Pringle of HMRI, who chaired the inquiry, laid the blame fairly and squarely at the door of both Signalman Philp and Driver Ramsay, although he also had some harsh words to say about the method of rounding the branch trains, as employed by the NBR at Queensferry Junction, where wrong direction running was involved. The NBR Operating Superintendent, incredibly, had been totally unaware of this practice, but to his credit had it abandoned immediately and replaced by a far safer method.

HAYMARKET STATION: 1924

On the Monday, 28th July 1924, the 18.41 Inner Circle suburban passenger service from Leith Central (18.50 ex-Waverley station) took up the booked stop at Haymarket station. This train, on that day and because of Trades holidays, was made up of eight Victorian four-wheeled coaches and a six-wheeled brake van, weighing 98 tons, instead of the normal robust suburban bogie stock, and was hauled by ex-NBR Class C15 No. 133. There was, however, some delay incurred at the station whilst a large party of tourists – who had spent the day at St. Andrews and who had alighted at Platform No. 1 to travel via the suburban to Newington station – were entrained, regrettably, as it turned out, in the rear coaches. Whilst the Circle train was thus standing in the platform, it was struck heavily in the rear by the 18.54 Edinburgh Waverley to Port Edgar (South Queensferry) passenger train, travelling at a speed of approximately 10 mph. This latter train consisted of four coaches (102 tons) hauled by an ex-works saturated 'Scott' Class D29 No. 9338 *Helen Macgregor*, of Haymarket shed, running tender-first. The driver was

a young James Swan of Haymarket, later to become a respected Top link driver there, with his fireman, John Ross, also of Haymarket. Swan, at the controls of No. 9338, had misread the signals at the entrance to Haymarket Tunnel and also missed the warning bell inside the tunnel entrance. Conditions in the tunnel were poor and hindered by exhaust smoke, steam and damp conditions. Although the D29 struck the rear of the Suburban train at a relatively slow speed, because of the frail nature of the coaching stock on this train on the day, severe telescoping of coaches seven and eight occurred. Five passengers were killed, and a further fifty-four injured although the rear six-wheeled brake composite itself withstood the shock of the collision.

CRAMLINGTON: 1926

During the General Strike of 1926, on the 10th May, the 10.00 'Flying Scotsman' from Edinburgh to London King's Cross, hauled by Haymarket A1 Pacific, No. 2656 *Merry Hampton*, with Top link Driver R. Shedden at the controls, became derailed at Cramlington after striking miners had deliberately removed a rail from the Up Main line. The train consisted of nine bogie coaches and a triple kitchen-car set. Driver Shedden was an ex-NBR man who, having just been stepped-up into the Haymarket Newcastle link, was still route learning between Edinburgh and Newcastle; consequently, he had an ex-NER conductor driver accompanying him. Fortunately, because of the troubles, the train was proceeding slowly at this location, but nevertheless the locomotive overturned to the left and the train followed into derailment. Both drivers were uninjured, but one of the two volunteer firemen on the footplate was severely scalded and two passengers suffered injuries. This was a case of deliberate sabotage which could have had the most tragic consequences. Sadly, the striking miners and their families stood around and cheered and jeered at the derailed train and the unfortunate passengers as they were being helped out. Happily, the perpetrators were later apprehended and nine miners were later jailed after their trial at Newcastle Assizes, for their incredible stupidity.

NORTH BELTON LEVEL CROSSING: 1929

This accident is included since it concerned the non-stop 'Flying Scotsman', a train and working with which Haymarket men were closely involved at the time. At around 17.55 on the afternoon of Tuesday, 14th May 1929, an unladen 4½-ton four-wheeled flatbed Leyland lorry was being driven towards North Belton Farm, near Dunbar. The access road to the farm required that a level crossing over the ECML be negotiated, this crossing being a private (occupation) level crossing, fitted with 13-foot-wide gates which opened away from the railway. By law (*Railway Clauses Consolidation Act (Scotland) 1845*), access across the level crossing was limited to the farmer, his workers and invitees – and such users were responsible for opening and closing the gates, and ensuring that it was safe to cross before proceeding. In short, they were wholly responsible for their own safety.

The driver of the lorry, one Robert Russell, had stopped and opened both gates, but eyewitnesses stated that the lorry had then stood at the crossing for about 8 minutes before moving slowly across. As it entered the crossing, the 'Flying Scotsman', the 10.00 from King's Cross to Edinburgh non-stop, approached from the east, running 11 minutes late. This train, hauled by A3 No. 2746 *Fairway*, of King's Cross Top Shed, consisted of ten eight-wheeled bogie coaches plus a sixteen-wheeled triplet Restaurant Car set and weighed 422 tons tare. Due to the convoluted rostering involving the non-stop crews, on that day it was not the Haymarket crew, but Driver H. Pennington and Fireman J. Ridley, both of Gateshead shed. Running at 60 mph, the fireman first saw the lorry when the locomotive was about 50 yards from the crossing and, immediately alerting his driver, he sounded the whistle – but the engine struck the lorry side-on without speed being reduced. The remains of the lorry were scattered up to 470 yards beyond the crossing, the driver's body being found some 112 yards from the crossing. The train was not derailed and came to stand some 640 yards beyond the point of collision. The lorry driver was the only casualty.

The Inspecting Officer, Lt Colonel A.H.I. Mount, after carefully taking statements from all concerned, in summing up came to the only conclusion possible under the circumstances: that the driver of the lorry had failed to act on the obvious message given by the railway signals and proceeded onto the crossing without being aware of the train's imminent arrival. He thus was guilty of driving without due care and attention. No blame was attached to the train crew.

COMMENT

In retrospect, this conclusion was not a little unfair and indeed, ill-considered. The Inspecting Officer assumed, it appears, that Russell would, or should, have seen the Beltonford Down starting signal cleared (lowered) for the passage of the express and that he would have understood the significance of the lowered signal. In short, Mount thus credited Russell with that 'general railway knowledge', both to the significance of the lowered signal and the direction to which it applied. That was an extraordinary assumption which was unsafe in the extreme and certainly would hold no water in today's legal minefields. Just how many people straight off the street, one wonders, would be able to confidently display that degree of 'general railway knowledge'?

One of the significant weaknesses in the operation of this type of level crossing at that time, and thus a primary causal factor, was the lack of clear and unambiguous instructions displayed on the approach sides of the crossing to assist a road user, and in particular, the unfamiliar user, as to how the crossing could be safely used and what exactly they should be alert for. The same North Belton level crossing was to see a further two accidents, with a total of a further five fatalities, before steps were taken in the early 1990s to create a new access road to the farm thus allowing the crossing to be closed off for good.

CASTLECARY: 1937

On the late afternoon of the 10th December 1937, one of the most extraordinary cases of a signal being passed at danger occurred at Castlecary station on the Edinburgh and Glasgow main line. That particular afternoon had seen severe snow storms, some of the heaviest in living memory, and darkness was falling early because of the extreme weather. At about 16.30, the 14.00 express passenger train from Dundee to Glasgow Queen Street, consisting of nine coaches and a fish van, hauled by 'Scott' Class D29 No. 9896 *Dandie Dinmont*, ran past Castlecary's Down Home signal at danger. The signalman, Sneddon by name, quite properly sent 'Train or Vehicles Running Away in Right Direction' bell signal to Dullater East signal box, where a Down goods was standing because of blocked points ahead; he fully expected that the Dundee train,

in running on, would inevitably collide with the Goods at Dullater. Sneddon did not look at the track circuit indicator in his box, and thus failed to realise that Driver McCauley of the Dundee train had been very observant, had seen the red handsignal that Sneddon had displayed as the train passed the box, and had then stopped with his train part-way beyond (18 yards) the Down Starting signal. The rear of the train was actually only 294 yards beyond his signal box and still on the platform, and would have been fully visible to the signalman had he stepped forward and looked out his window.

Sneddon, having acted correctly as the train passed, then made a quite extraordinary – and indeed most incomprehensible – decision regarding the 16.00 express from Edinburgh to Glasgow. Despite fully anticipating a collision in the forward section, he, after conferring with the signalman in rear at Greenhill Junction, quite incredibly, and quite irregularly as it turned out since he did not actually have the required 440 yard overlap, cleared back the Dundee train, and accepted the 16.00 when it was offered at 16.32 – but was of course unable to clear his Down Main line signals.

Fireman Fleming, of the standing Dundee train, entered the box at 16.35 to comply with Rule 55 and at that point clearly stated to Sneddon exactly where his train was standing. The signalman received 'Train Entering Section' bell signal at 16.36 for the Edinburgh. The station master, Scott by name, had come up to the box immediately behind Fireman Fleming and, on hearing where the Dundee was standing, both he and the signalman rushed out to lay down detonators. They were far too late, and out of the darkness and falling snow rushed the 16.00 train, running at around 70 mph. The engine was Haymarket A3 No. 2744 *Grand Parade*, with Senior Spare Driver D. Anderson at the controls, and assisted by Fireman W. Kinnear. On exploding the detonator, Anderson immediately shut off steam, applied the sanders and made an emergency brake application, but all far too late. His train ran headlong into the standing Dundee, with catastrophic consequences. The Edinburgh express continued to plough into the Dundee train for at least 100 yards before coming to a stand. The Dundee train was driven forwards for 50 yards, being reduced to matchwood in the process, and the first three coaches of the Edinburgh overshot the engine and tender. In all, thirty-five passengers were killed and 179 seriously injured. Anderson and Kinnear had a miraculous escape given that their engine was completely buried in the debris, and it was testament to the strength of the tender that the first coaches of the train overrode it, rather than crushing it.

The public inquiry was conducted by Colonel Sir Alan H.L. Mount and very much hinged on what aspect the Castlecary Down Distant signal arm had been displaying. This was the crucial point, since Driver McCauley of the Dundee train was adamant that the Distant was showing clear as he approached it. Driver Anderson, known to be an extremely reliable and vigilant engineman who, on the previous day and whilst working the same train, had slowed and queried an incorrectly displayed signal at Polmont, was equally as emphatic. Both drivers were certain that the signal arm was lying distinctly and properly in the clear position and not merely 'drooping', although both drivers were totally frank and honest by stating that neither had then observed the aspect of the Home signal.

Signalman Sneddon's evidence was contradictory and his account of what happened was considered to be untrustworthy. He, in the course of giving evidence, alleged the track circuit indicator had failed 'wrong side' in that it had not shown 'occupied' when the

Dundee came to a stand on the track circuit. But testing based on this claim was to find the equipment working as designed and thus no fault was found. He alleged that he had a clear and positive view of the Down Distant signal, 777 yards east of the box, and its backlight at all times, but under the prevailing weather conditions and the onset of darkness this was proved to be a false claim. Finally, with his allegation of indicator failure disproved, he alluded to the fact that the Dundee train must have irregularly 'set back' from the point where it came to a stop thus placing the TC indicator to 'Occupied'. This was wholly disproved. In short, he attempted to shift the blame on to anyone and everyone else! Indeed, though the finger was never pointed at him, someone had in fact crudely changed the time Fleming signed the train register from 16.35 to 16.38.

Col. Mount concluded that, given the open, honest and consistent evidence given by both drivers, and that both had been prepared to accept that the Distant was clear, that a question mark must remain as to the actual indication displayed by the signal in the severe weather conditions prevailing – the drivers were, therefore, quite properly given the benefit of the doubt. He further justified this opinion by declaring that at no time following the collision did either Sneddon or Scott once look at the Distant signal to check if it could be seen and if the backlight could be seen. Indeed, the presumption of innocence lay with both drivers since the gravest doubts existed as to whether the signal was actually within the view of the signalman before the accident. He considered that Signalman Sneddon, whilst theoretically competent in the Rules and Regulations, was a poor practical signalman who, given what had just occurred outside his box when the Dundee train had run past, had then acted in a wholly irresponsible manner by accepting the Edinburgh train and had, in Col. Mount's words, '*lost his head.*' Sneddon had then, in evidence, alleged that not one, but two, 'wrong side failures', one mechanical and one electrical, had occurred simultaneously thus leading to the accident, despite the fact the equipment alluded to had been working normally just minutes before. This allegation was, he considered, well nigh impossible and unlikely in the extreme. Both drivers were, however, criticised for running too fast in the prevailing weather conditions; the recommendations naturally called for the provision of AWS, which was a bit of a theme song with the Railway Inspectorate at the time.

Driver Anderson was, however, to be charged with manslaughter and duly appeared in the High Court of Justiciary in Edinburgh. Fellow railwaymen had stood there before him. Driver Gourlay of the Elliot Junction accident had been there, as had Signalmen Meakin and Tinsley, and Fireman Hutchinson, all players in the appalling Quintinshill tragedy. It is perhaps ironical that over the intervening years, five railwaymen, with not one iota of criminal intent in their respective minds had stood in the same dock where, over the years, Scotland's most desperate criminals had appeared.

The Lord Advocate abandoned all charges against Anderson on the second day of the trial.

COMMENT

Anderson was somewhat harshly dealt with by the company, the L&NER, who, at their internal inquiry, had more or less accepted Sneddon's account of the proceedings, apparently without question; they had then, quite unfairly, placed the full blame upon Anderson for passing a signal at danger (it must be emphasised that Anderson had passed only the one signal at danger, the Down Home signal, since other commentators such as O.S. Nock recorded that '*several signals were passed at danger*'). This extremely questionable decision (in light of the public inquiry revelations) was the reason behind Anderson having the criminal charge of manslaughter levelled against him. In the event, the day after his trial commenced at the High Court in Edinburgh, the Lord Advocate quite properly withdrew all charges and justice was done. There is little doubt that the wrong man had been arraigned. Anderson resumed his career as a driver at Haymarket and progressed into the Top link, before opting to come off the main line aged sixty, thereafter being employed as one of the pilot drivers on the Class N15 tank engine, No. 69169 (the 'big Gorgie' pilot) at Gorgie East.

However, mention must also be made of the criticism regarding the 'excessive speeds' both drivers were maintaining in the poor weather conditions existing at the time, made by Col. Mount in his report. The truth is that, if the circumstances pertaining and the alleged high speed are fully considered, it will be seen that this criticism was largely irrelevant. Consider, the Dundee train was standing, with brakes applied, only 294 yards ahead of the signal box. At the 60–70 mph the Edinburgh train was running, Anderson had only about 8½ seconds in which to react and make an emergency brake application upon exploding the detonator(s) laid just outside the box, before the impact occurred. In this short period of time, the brakes could not have begun to take any effect whatsoever. Using the BR Composite Braking Curve, at 70 mph, on level track, the Edinburgh train would have required 1,331 yards in which to be safely brought to a stand.

However, even if Anderson had been driving at a reduced speed of, say, 50 mph, then the time available for reaction would still have only been around 12 seconds; again, the brake application would still have been largely ineffective and, even at 50 mph, some 1,130 yards stopping distance were required, and thus the collision with the standing train would still have been catastrophic. The reality is that Anderson would have had to be proceeding at a ridiculously low speed of no more than 20 mph to have been able to bring his train to a stand before he struck the standing Dundee train. The excessive speed criticism was therefore somewhat of a red herring and made, most probably, as a sop to satisfy public concerns. The fact of the matter is that, given the signalman's appalling decisions, and the fact that the distant signal indication was in all probability a 'wrong side' failure due to frost and snow, both drivers were seriously misled and the collision was inevitable irrespective of speed.

STENTON CROSSING: DATE UNRECORDED

In the pre-war days of the L&NER, Driver W. (Bill) Stevenson, at the time in Senior Spare link at Haymarket, had a remarkable near miss whilst working a northbound Sunday excursion train from Newcastle to Glasgow Queen Street, with A3 No. 2500 *Windsor Lad*. Approaching Stenton occupation level crossing, between Dunbar and East Linton, and running around 80 mph, the engine gave a lurch but then steadied and continued to run on normally. However, at Prestonpans the smell of a heating axle box wafted back to the cab – but Stevenson, quite properly, decided to run on into Waverley before investigating, in order to avoid unnecessary delay to the train. The engine coupled-off in Waverley, but had to run forward to Haymarket shed quickly, to clear the station. On setting the engine on the turntable, Stevenson dropped off to investigate the heating axle and found the right-hand leading driving axlebox was extremely hot. On further investigation, he then discovered that the tyre on the left-hand driving wheel was missing entirely.

Haymarket 'Scott' No. 9339 *Ivanhoe* poses on the new 70-foot turntable having been turned after working in from Stirling with Driver W. Galloway of the latter shed in charge. The date is after 1930 and the original sand kiln is still in situ. *Bill Lynn collection*

Some urgent phone calls ensued and the missing tyre was found later, in two parts, lying in a field adjacent to the line and having brought down some of the pole route. The tyre had broken through, became detached, and had fallen cleanly away from the locomotive. Had it not done so, a serious derailment would have been the likely outcome.

FORTH BRIDGE: 1939

In October 1939, on Monday 16th to be precise, an ex-Haymarket star, 'Scott' Class D29 No. 9339 *Ivanhoe*, by this time allocated to Stirling (Shore Road) shed, was rostered to work a mid-morning passenger train from Stirling to Edinburgh via the Forth Bridge – returning with the 14.30 passenger working from Waverley over the same route. On the return journey, just as No. 9339 was working the train up the stiff climb from the River Almond Bridge towards Dalmeny station and without any prior warning, a wave of three Junkers 88 twin-engine German bombers appeared from the east and started a bombing run on two Royal Navy cruisers, HMS *Edinburgh* and HMS *Southampton*, at anchor about half a mile east of the Forth Bridge. Train crew and passengers, detained by signals at Dalmeny station on arrival, then had a ringside seat as the events of the afternoon unfolded, whilst a decision on what to do was awaited. However, Railway Officialdom, in the shape of Edinburgh Control, was in a quandary, since no official advice of enemy action had been received, nor had any air-raid warnings sounded, so there was an element of '*it's just another exercise*' thinking which coloured judgment. In the event, the driver of the 14.30 Stirling set off at 15.15 – under clear signals, but under whose authority is known not – and proceeded to take his train across the Forth Bridge, which was still under attack. Passengers were again treated to the terrifying sight of further German bombers coming in low from the

west and releasing their bombs as they flew across the bridge and train. The Forth Bridge was crossed in safety on this day which saw the first enemy air attack on the British mainland. Spitfires of two Royal Auxiliary Air Force squadrons were scrambled and fought back – and downed the first enemy planes (one credited to each squadron) in the Second World War. Defences around the bridge were thereafter strengthened, and never again did the Luftwaffe carry out low-level attacks in this vicinity.

It was not until the 19th October that *The Scotsman* newspaper reported on the fact that the RAAF had been in action above the River Forth against German bombers. Little of any real substance was contained in the article, wartime censorship being by then, no doubt, in full force, and there was ne'er a mention of the fact that a train had been on the Forth Bridge during the raid.

Incidentally, and as an interesting aside, one of the cruisers targeted that day, HMS *Edinburgh*, was herself to become the focus of some fame and attention. She suffered damage by flying splinters in the attack of that day, but after repairs at Rosyth she was to see considerably more action, including the hunt for the *Bismark*.

Later in the war, on the 29th April 1942, she left Murmansk to join Russian Convoy PQ14, loaded with gold bullion being transferred from Russia to the UK. On the 30th, during an attack on the convoy, she was struck and severely damaged by two torpedoes fired from U-boat U456. Although badly damaged, she continued to make slow headway and, on the 2nd May, actually engaged German destroyers and sank the *Schoemann*, before being torpedoed yet again. She was now beyond aid and, to protect the bullion, a sister ship, HMS *Forester*, was ordered to sink her after the crew had been taken off. The gold bullion, or at least some 95 per cent of same, was eventually recovered from the wreck in 1981.

COWLAIRS EAST JUNCTION: 1942

At approximately 16.56 on 30th January 1942, the 16.00 express passenger train from Edinburgh to Glasgow Queen Street, running about 8 minutes late and under clear signals at a speed of about 35 mph, struck, head-on, a light locomotive which was standing on the Down Main line. The driver of the 16.00 express and eight passengers were killed, the driver of the light engine and a further four passengers died later in hospital. Ten passengers received serious injury and a further forty-four complained of minor injury.

The express consisted of nine buck-eye fitted bogie coaches equipped with the continuous vacuum brake (301 tons), hauled by Class D11/2 'Director' No. 6401 *James Fitzjames* of Haymarket shed and driven by Driver Robertson with Fireman G. Broomfield of the same depot. The light engine was Class D29 'Scott' No. 9339 *Ivanhoe* (once again). The accident occurred in clear weather, about one hour before blackout, wartime daylight saving being in force.

Cowlairs East Junction signal box sat at the eastern apex of the Cowlairs triangle formed by the E&GR Main line with a facing (from Queen Street) chord line running from Cowlairs West Junction to Cowlairs North Junction and onwards towards Dumbarton. An east chord line from Cowlairs North to Cowlairs East completed the triangle. As part of the early wartime blackout conditions then in force, Cowlairs East Junction box, an old box, had all its windows painted in blue paint with only two slits, each 30 inches by 9 inches, left clear at about eye level – one in an end window at the north front corner of the box and the other in a front window in the southern front corner. As a result, the signalman, one Clements, was, in fact, working almost blind! The circumstances surrounding the accident are as follows.

A troop train arrived from Cowlairs North Junction on the Up Branch, with Class K2 2-6-0 No. 4700 *Loch Lomond* at the head. Both engine crew and locomotive were booked to be changed on the branch before the train proceeded on its journey. At this time of day there were several main line train and light engine movements taking place, and the signalman in Cowlairs East signal box was being kept very busy. In the interim, Eastfield shed had sent out two engines together to the headshunt adjacent to the Down Main line; the first into the headshunt was Class D11/1 4-4-0 No. 6378 *Bailie Macwheeble*, diagrammed to go to Singer via the Down Branch, with Class D29 4-4-0 No. 9339 *Ivanhoe*, the engine for the troop train, behind and nearest the exit signal.

Engine No. 4700 was uncoupled from the train and it was the signalman's intention to allow the engine to proceed to the Up Main to a point just clear of No. 23 Main to Main crossover and hold it there whilst the relief locomotive then reversed from the Down Main via the same No. 23 Main to Main crossover to access the Up Branch, and couple to the troop train. This he did immediately after the 16.46 Glasgow to Perth passenger train had passed clear at about 16.53, pulling off the Up Branch Home to allow No. 4700 onto the main line.

At the same time, he cleared the exit disc to permit No. 9339 to proceed from the headshunt to the Down Main, clear of No. 23 crossover road, and this the driver duly did, coming to a stand just in advance of the crossover, immediately in front of the box. At this juncture, the signalman made a fatal error. He had been offered the 16.00 ex-Edinburgh from Bishopbriggs but had correctly not accepted the bell signal because of the move taking place. Although unable to see the line in front of his box, he could see through the clear space in the end window, and from there he saw an engine (No.

6378) still standing in the headshunt. He immediately assumed, for whatever reason, that the engine for the troop train had not moved and, re-setting the road, accepted and pulled off for the Edinburgh on the Down Main.

The fireman on engine No. 4700, on the Up Main, saw the Down line signals being cleared and drew his driver's attention to the fact. The fireman then set off to run back to the signal box to warn the signalman of his error, shouting to the driver on No. 9339 as he ran, whilst his own driver moved the engine forward to the Up Starting signal in an attempt to warn the driver of the Edinburgh. He was away too late and the Edinburgh swept past at a speed of around 50 to 55 mph. The driver of No. 9339, on hearing the warning, set his engine in reverse but before it could move, it was struck by the approaching Edinburgh express. The Edinburgh was running with steam shut off and was slowing for a 10 mph speed restriction at Cowlairs West Junction – nevertheless, the speed at the point of impact was still between 30 and 35 mph. The driver of the Edinburgh was driving on the right-hand side of the 'Director', his forward view was thus restricted by the left-hand curvature and a low overbridge at this location, and he had little warning. He shouted for his fireman to jump, but the fireman instead opened the sands and held on. He survived.

In the ensuing head to head collision, both engines were seriously damaged with both smokeboxes crushed inwards, buffer beams destroyed, frames bent and both leading bogies displaced. No. 9339 was driven back some 80 yards and its tender derailed and thrown on to its side. The tender of No. 6401 was forced upwards by the underframe of the leading coach which itself was partially destroyed and the bogies were severely distorted. The second coach derailed and was thrown to the right across the tracks, the buckeye couplers having separated and been badly damaged. The underframe and bogie of this coach was forced under the underframe of the leading coach. The third and fourth coaches sustained only minor damage and the remainder of the train was completely undamaged, a testament once more to the inherent strength of L&NER coaching stock.

The casualty list was compounded by the fact that, once again, although the first vehicle was, quite properly, a brake vehicle, it had been marshalled with the passenger accommodation against the tender of No. 6401 with the brake section behind. This had been a situation which had been highlighted at the Castlecary collision, and following the recommendations of that accident, the L&NER Train Marshalling Booklet had been amended to require that a brake van be marshalled next to the locomotive wherever possible. The reason for this non-compliance was that this particular coaching set ran in set formation working a double return trip to Glasgow daily. On the 20th January, the leading brake had to be removed as defective; the replacement coach arrived at Leith Central reversed, and there was no time to turn it without delay to the train.

The Inspecting Officer, Col. A.C. Trench, concluded that the fault lay with the signalman in Cowlairs East Box (which was freely admitted by that individual), but that the blackout arrangements at the signal box were unacceptable – and that whilst light obscuration was essential at night in wartime conditions, some better arrangement, such as the provision of shutters or blinds which could be drawn back in daylight hours, should be pursued. He believed that had the signalman had clear sighting, the accident would not have happened. However, a large part of the blame lay with the fireman on locomotive No. 9339 who had failed to comply with the provisions of Rule 55(b) when his engine was detained on the Down Main line. The fireman was unclear about the different requirements of Rule 55(a) (applicable to running movements) and Rule 55(b) (specific to shunting movements), and had complied with the former clause in error. Had he gone immediately to the signal box, as required by clause (b), the signalman, who was under some considerable pressure, would have been made aware of the presence, and whereabouts, of engine No. 9339.

He also had some harsh words about non-compliance with the marshalling instructions, and whilst accepting that on the day of the coach failure there was no time to rectify the marshalling without delay to an important train, the fact that this was allowed to then continue for nine days was unacceptable.

Incidentally, the same Fireman George Broomfield was an assistant running foreman at Haymarket in 1957 when the author first started there.

FORTH BRIDGE: DATE UNRECORDED

During the Second World War, sometime in the years 1943/44, the 12.30 passenger train from Edinburgh to Perth (due Dunfermline at 13.20) became derailed on the Forth Bridge as a result of a piece of metal having fallen from a southbound freight. No one was injured but delays were considerable. This was only the second derailment ever to occur on the bridge.

The 12.30 Perth was hauled by V4 No. 3401 *Bantam Cock*, with Driver J. Swan of Haymarket at the controls.

The first derailment on the bridge occurred in 1890, the year of opening, when high winds tore a wagon sheet from a wagon carrying esparto grass, and the sheet and some bales of grass fell under the wagon's wheels. The wagon derailed but ran upright, held so by the troughs on which the rail was laid, until it reached North Queensferry and was safely brought to a stand.

GOSWICK: 1947

On Sunday, 26th October 1947, A3 No. 66 (ex 2565) *Merry Hampton* was the rostered engine for the 11.15 Edinburgh to King's Cross express passenger train. This train consisted of fifteen heavily-loaded coaches including, as coaches Nos 4, 5 and 6, a triple-articulated Kitchen/Dining Car set. The train weighed 431 tons and there were 420 passengers aboard.

The locomotive, formerly a Class A1 (latterly A10), had been rebuilt as an A3 at Doncaster and had re-entered service on the 9th December 1945, but still retaining the right-hand driving position. The driver was Tom Begbie, who had signed-on at Haymarket shed earlier in the morning. It later transpired, however, that W. Baird, who was his booked fireman, had been late in booking-on and had thus failed to read the Late Notice Case, and Begbie, who had agreed to take an unofficial passenger on the footplate – a Naval rating and brother of two firemen at Haymarket – had gone straight to the engine. Begbie had then returned to book-on but, thereafter, had also failed to observe the Late Notice regarding an alteration to Engineering Works at Goswick, which required possession of the Up Main line and thus requiring all Up trains to run via the Up Independent Goods line at Goswick. On the approach to Goswick, Begbie then failed to observe the Up Distant signal at caution. The signalman in Goswick box, thinking that the train was slowing down, pulled off the Up Independent Home signal leading to the Independent line but, as it turned out, he had imprudently cleared this signal before he had fully satisfied himself that the train was

under control and would stop. No. 66 entered the Independent line at a speed of around 60 mph and, at the inner turnout, rolled over – the train following into derailment.

The locomotive and the first eight coaches went down into a ditch running alongside a field, with the engine and tender on their side. The last six coaches remained upright and in line, with the last four not even derailed. However, the fourth coach, the leading unit of the articulated set, broke away and, taking the leading bogie with it, slid for 70 yards beyond the wreckage, coming to a rest on its side across both Up and Down Main lines. Six coaches were wrecked and another four badly damaged.

Casualties were high because of the great number of seated and standing passengers on board, and a total of twenty-seven passengers and one member of staff were killed. Fifty-nine passengers received serious injuries and another twenty-five, plus three members of staff were treated in hospital.

The public inquiry was at first chaired by Col. A.C. Trench, who unfortunately later fell ill; it was subsequently completed by Lt. Col. G.K.S. Wilson. The arrangements and sighting of the signals at Goswick were checked from a right-hand driving position on a similar class of locomotive and were found to be satisfactory, and thus, whilst the signalman was admonished for clearing the Up Independent Home signal somewhat too soon, the blame lay fairly and squarely with Driver Begbie, and to a lesser extent with Fireman Baird, for failing to read the Late Notices at Haymarket depot before leaving the shed. The presence of the Naval rating on the footplate, although irregular, played no part in the subsequent accident – although he was seriously injured and lost the opportunity to follow his two brothers to the footplate at Haymarket.

COMMENT

As has been mentioned, Haymarket drivers intensely disliked driving from the right-hand side of an engine, and following this accident the L&NER management were pressured by the trade union to replace the right-hand drive A3s at Haymarket with 'normal' left-hand drive engines. This pressure was kept up, and in 1950 the four right-hand drive A3s were replaced by four left-hand drive engines in an inter-regional transfer. Nevertheless, the former NER locomotives were all driven from the right-hand driving position and thus the arrangement and sighting of signals on the NER was done to suit this position. Goswick was a former NER signal box and the right-handed driving position was found to be irrelevant in the events leading up to this derailment, however much the Haymarket men disliked it.

PENMANSHIEL: 1949

On the evening of 23rd June 1949, the 20.00 express passenger train (the Mail) from Edinburgh to King's Cross, consisting of twelve coaches (395 tons) and hauled by A3 No. 60035 *Windsor Lad* of Haymarket shed, under the control of Driver H. Brown and Fireman E. McLeod from the same depot, was approaching Penmanshiel Tunnel whilst ascending Cockburnspath bank. The train was brought to a stand at approximately 20.40 because of the communication cord being pulled in the train, with the locomotive and eight coaches actually inside the tunnel. The tenth coach from the engine was on fire and well ablaze.

The fire had broken out suddenly, and without any prior warning, some 2½ miles beyond Cockburnspath siding and, as the train slowed, passengers broke windows and jumped to escape the blaze. Seven passengers were injured, two seriously so.

Subsequent investigation revealed that the fire had probably been started by a carelessly discarded match or cigarette, which then ignited the wooden panelling of the inner coach side. This panelling had been painted with three coats of a clear cellulose lacquer at the last overhaul and tests revealed that the lacquer ignited easily and was highly flammable, thus permitting the fire to spread quickly from the source. The coach was destroyed. The use of this lacquer was immediately prohibited.

GLASGOW QUEEN STREET TUNNEL: 1951

Here, on the 14th November 1951, Haymarket A3 No. 60100 *Spearmint* was the culprit in a collision which occurred at the foot of the incline at the entrance to Queen Street station. The engine had been brought off shed at Eastfield by Eastfield-based Driver J. Morrison and Fireman D. McKay. Morrison had made a (severe) brake test before entering the incline at Cowlairs, but on the way down he realised that the brake applications he was making were not resulting in any appreciable reduction in speed. He reversed the engine and then made an emergency brake application, but could not stop. The engine collided with the empty coaches off the incoming Leeds train which were being shunted, quite properly, across the station throat, under signal protection.

The brake failure was caused by a worn flexible vacuum hose between engine and tender, which had been worn through by rubbing. It was evident upon inspection that the rubbing of the hose had been spotted at some earlier time by an unknown fitter at Haymarket, who had then not reported the defect, but had merely plated the worn part of the hose with a metal plate to minimise the effect of the rubbing.

The public inquiry was held by Brigadier A.C. Langley, who had some fairly serious comments to make regarding the standard of mechanical inspection being carried out at Haymarket, and also to a lesser extent at Eastfield, at that time, since a similar problem had subsequently been identified on another five A3s at Haymarket.

GOSWICK: 1953

On the 28th October 1953, the 21.15 passenger train from Glasgow Queen Street to Colchester became completely derailed whilst travelling under clear signals at a speed of about 55 mph at Goswick. The train consisted of four bogie coaches, four bogie vans and a four-wheeled fish van, weighing 253 tons and hauled by Haymarket A2/1 No. 60509 *Waverley*, with Driver W. Bain and Fireman T. Hewitt, both of Haymarket Shed.

The derailment occurred after the eccentric strap in the centre valve gear became detached, the rear section striking the sleepers as it hung down. The bottom lug then caught in the stretcher-bar of the facing points at Goswick loop, bending and breaking it. The bending pulled open the left-hand switch rail and the flange of the left-hand leading driving wheel ran through the gap, the remainder of the wheels following, derailing the engine and following train. Fortunately, the train remained upright until it was brought to a stand and there were no injuries.

The public inquiry was conducted by Colonel W.P. Reed, who concluded that the accident occurred when the two nuts on the top bolt of the eccentric strap became unscrewed during the course of the journey. This had happened because a properly-sized split pin had not been fitted during the last examination at Haymarket, although he conceded that an undersized pin may well have been fitted and subsequently fallen out. No blame was attached to Driver Bain. Colonel Reed did, however, have some words to say regarding the maintenance supervision at Haymarket shed (again) in regard to the proper practice of the fitting of such nuts and split pins.

LONGNIDDRY: 1953

At about 01.18 on the 17th December 1953, the 00.41 Up special parcels train, from Edinburgh to King's Cross, ran into an obstruction on the Up line when passing through Longniddry station at a speed of around 60 mph, and became seriously derailed. The parcels train, consisted of nine bogie and nineteen four-wheeled vans, hauled by Haymarket A2 No. 60530 *Sayajirao*, was being worked by Driver

Peppercorn A2 No. 60530 *Sayajirao*, that of the unpronounceable name and long-time incumbent of Haymarket, stands dead amongst the oil barrels at the back of the new machine shop waiting fitters' attention. This was the engine which came to grief at Longniddry in 1953 after striking an obstruction between the platforms – killing the fireman and seriously injuring the driver. *Courtesy David Dunn*

D. Drummond and Fireman R. McKenzie, both of Haymarket. Fireman McKenzie was killed immediately and Driver Drummond was seriously injured.

The obstruction was a section of pre-fabricated 'decauville' 2-foot gauge track turn-out (used in the mining industry) which had become unsecured and fallen from a wagon forming part of the 21.45 freight service from Heaton to Edinburgh Niddrie West. In falling, the loose turnout struck the water column at the west end of Longniddry platform and was then thrown across onto the Up line between the platforms, at a point about 20 yards west of the Up platform running-off ramp. Drummond had no warning of the ensuing collision with the obstruction and, from the position of the controls found after the event, he had been working the engine normally. The engine was thrown over the Up platform and, having turned through 180 degrees to face Edinburgh, came to rest with wheels uppermost at the bottom of the embankment separating the platform from the North Berwick main road. The tender also turned right round but remained upright between the tracks some 40 yards beyond the engine.

The cause of the accident was improper securing of the track turn-out in the wagon, by BR staff, in the private siding of Messrs Robert Hudson Ltd at Gildersome West in the NE Region.

Driver Drummond was off work for a considerable period in consequence of the serious injuries received, but did eventually return to the footplate at Haymarket, being accommodated on the shed coal pilot.

NORTH QUEENSFERRY TUNNEL: 1955

On Sunday, 7th March 1954, the 18.55 express from Aberdeen to King's Cross, comprising thirteen bogie coaches including sleeping cars, slid to a stand in North Queensferry Tunnel and then moved backwards, with the result that the last three vehicles were derailed on the catch points just outside the tunnel. The train engine was Haymarket A4 No. 60024 *Kingfisher*, worked by Haymarket Top link men, Driver S. Storie and Passed Fireman J. Grieve. The train weighed 467 tons gross, which was an overload of just 17 tons and of little or no consequence in the circumstances leading up to the accident.

North Queensferry Tunnel is 569 yards in length and is situated on a continuous rising gradient of 1 in 70, between Inverkeithing and the Forth Bridge. The Up line through the tunnel had been relaid on that very day with new 95 lb bullhead rail and a temporary speed restriction (TSR) of 20 mph was in force.

Storie was working No. 60024 in 25% cut-off and full regulator as he started the climb, and as speed dropped he left the controls unaltered because of the TSR through the tunnel. On entering the tunnel, the engine began to slip intermittently and speed continued to fall. Storie tried to feel for the tunnel roof to ascertain whether the engine was still moving forward, the tunnel now being full of smoke. He did not realise that the engine had slipped to a stand and that the train was now moving backwards, until he felt the bang as the rear coaches derailed at the catch points and hit the cutting wall.

Brigadier C.A. Langley, who took the public inquiry, concluded that the engine had slipped to a stand on the new rail (not an uncommon occurrence) but that the driver had been seriously disadvantaged because he was unable to ascertain if the engine was still moving forward. He recommended that marker lights be provided in tunnels situated on heavy gradients. He also suggested that the catch points be repositioned at a point further away from

the mouth of the tunnel on the northern approach, but no blame was attached to the driver. As a point of interest, the assisting locomotive which came from Haymarket was driven by Driver W. Elder of Haymarket shed who later became running foreman there in the mid 1950s.

NEWCASTLETON: 1969

This incident (which has an element of farcical comedy about it) is certainly well worth recording, since it marked the great public outcry over the impending closure of the Waverley route from Edinburgh to Carlisle, and is a good example of people power.

On the night of the 5th January, diesel electric Sulzer Type 4 No. D60 was the train engine on the 21.56 Edinburgh Waverley to London St. Pancras sleeping car train. This was to be the final train over the route, but it was significantly delayed both prior to arrival, and thereafter at Newcastleton proper, because of a public demonstration orchestrated by the local Church of Scotland minister against the closure of the line. The driver was W. Fleming and the secondman G. Paterson, both of Haymarket depot.

The Area Manager, Hawick, Ossie Simpson, was first alerted to possible trouble by Traffic Inspector James (Jimmy) McBain, who was located at Newcastleton, at about 22.30. The inspector had found a set of trailing points in a crossover, which had been secured as a precaution, tampered with, and the level crossing gates at Newcastleton station chained and padlocked across the railway. Detonators were also found to have been placed on the line and there was justified suspicion of interference with the safety of the line elsewhere. On attempting to remove the chains and padlock, Traffic Inspector McBain was then confronted by an angry crowd of around forty villagers, led by the local church minister, and his Land Rover was manhandled and placed foul of the line between the crossing gates. The crowd defied all attempts to clear the line. The crowd grew by the minute and the inspector quickly recognised that a not inconsiderable contingent of police would be required if the crowd were to be controlled and removed.

The 21.56 arrived at Hawick at 23.27, and was thereafter only permitted to run forward cautiously, under Train Signalling Regulation 5 as provided for in Regulation 14(B), leaving Hawick at 00.02 and following a pilot locomotive, Clayton Type 2 No. D8606, which had been turned out by Hawick shed. This pilot locomotive was authorised to proceed cautiously and stop immediately short of the level crossing at Newcastleton. The driver of the 21.56 was instructed to follow the pilot locomotive and run as far as the Newcastleton Up Home signal only, and to keep a sharp lookout for trouble. The train arrived at the Up Home signal at 00.44, where it was detained.

The local MP Mr (later to be Sir) David Steel, who was a passenger on the train, alighted and spoke to the very large crowd now blocking the line. His attempts initially fell on deaf ears, until finally the church minister who was orchestrating the protest was forcibly removed and placed under arrest by Lothian and Borders Police. At this, the mood of the crowd grew uglier, but a second appeal by Mr Steel got the protesters to promise to disperse if the minister was released without charge, and this, very sensibly, was done.

At 01.35, D8606 was run forward to examine the line as far as Kershopefoot. On attempting to draw his train forward, Driver Fleming discovered that he was unable to create vacuum and, on examination, the vacuum bag on the last vehicle, BG E80834, was found to have been cut. The BG was isolated and the guard was

Haymarket A2 No. 60530 *Sayajirao* stands forlornly in St. Margaret's shed on 24th January 1954, showing some of the considerable damage incurred as a result of the high-speed derailment at Longniddry on the early morning of the 17th December 1953 whilst working a southbound parcels 'special' to Newcastle. The fireman was killed outright and the driver suffered serious injury which left him permanently impaired. The engine turned through 180 degrees and finished upside-down on the main road adjacent to the railway. The damage to the cab is clearly seen, with the right-hand side completely missing. The driver's position is relatively undamaged, even to the bucket seat still being *in situ*. Yeadon records No. 60530 as going for general repair to Doncaster on 15th January 1954, but the photograph says otherwise. It did, however, go into Doncaster soon after this and was returned to traffic in an amazingly short time, on 26th February 1954. *Courtesy W.S. Sellar*

BELOW: The damaged smoke deflector plate with the nameplate distorted by the derailment, along with other material recovered from the site and from the damaged locomotive, is in a wagon at St. Margaret's, waiting to go forward to Doncaster works. *Courtesy W.S. Sellar*

instructed to ride therein to Carlisle, where repairs could be effected. The pilot engine cleared Kershopefoot at 01.43 and the 21.56 finally departed from Newcastleton at 01.55, some 117 minutes late.

Damage was caused to the BG on the train and to the inspector's Land Rover, and extensive structural damage was inflicted upon the level crossing gates and locking at Newcastleton station.

The closure of the route had, quite understandably, inflamed passions in the Borders (shades of the Border Reivers) to the point where normally-peaceable townsfolk were driven to violent protest. The protest was, of course, in vain and the Waverley route was thereafter closed and the track lifted with, it must be said, indecent haste. Hawick was to become noted as being the town furthest from any railway in the whole of the UK.

DREM: 1972

Late on Saturday evening, 25th March 1972, at about 22.28, express passenger train 1E40, the 22.10 Edinburgh to King's Cross, collided with an Engineer's work train which was being set back into a siding at Drem, 17¾ miles east of Edinburgh, at a speed around 15 mph.

Train 1E40 comprised nine Mk I coaches and was hauled by EE Class 40 diesel electric locomotive No. D280. The rostered driver was Driver C.C. Rankine with an unrecorded senior secondman, accompanied by Drivers J. Hogg and G.V. Myles – all from Haymarket – who were route learning between Edinburgh and Newcastle. Hogg had already signed his route card for the entire route before the evening in question, but was completing his rostered week, and Myles, who at that time had signed for the Edinburgh to Berwick section only, was completing his route-learning over the section between Berwick and Newcastle. Rankine, therefore, had no qualms about leaving the two men in the cab, whilst he and the secondman retired to the rear cab. Myles occupied the driver's seat and drove the train out of Edinburgh.

The shunting movement at Drem, involving the Engineers work train was, quite properly, being carried out under full signal protection. Myles, however, failed to properly control the speed of the train on sighting the Drem Up Distant signal at caution and, having receiving an AWS warning which he cancelled, passed the Up Outer Home signal at danger and his train struck the side of the Engineers train. There were no injuries and little damage, but substantial consequential delay.

Major C.F. Rose, who chaired the public inquiry, concluded that Driver Myles, who was relatively inexperienced in handling Class 40 locomotives, was misled by the apparent lack of response to his initial brake application, thus making a serious error of judgment by releasing and then reapplying his brake. Driver Rankine was criticised (quite properly) for leaving the driving cab of the locomotive, since he was the responsible driver for the turn of duty and should have remained in his proper place, which was the leading cab.

CHATHILL: 1972

On the 28th May 1972, train 1E09, the 11.00 Edinburgh to King's Cross express passenger train, consisting of twelve Mk III coaches hauled by a Deltic Class 55 diesel electric locomotive (number not recorded), became derailed at Chathill whilst running at around 80 mph. The driver was C.C. Rankine (again) with Secondman G.C. Craig, both of Haymarket shed. Casualties were slight as most of the train remained upright and on the track.

The derailment was caused by the movement of the running-on end of a closure rail, which had been flame-cut after the fishplates fractured, under the wheels of the train. No blame was attached to the train or train crew.

CADDER: 1973

On the 2nd July 1973, the 16.30 express passenger (push-pull) train from Edinburgh to Glasgow Queen Street was running under clear signals at a speed of 90 mph when, on the approach to Cadder, the leading left-hand wheel of the rear locomotive derailed at the crossing of the facing connection from the Down Main line to the Down Goods line. The train ran a further 1900 yards before coming to a stand with the leading bogie of the rear locomotive completely derailed and the locomotive buffer-locked with the coach ahead. Damage was limited to the locomotive and the track. No one was injured.

The train consisted of six Mk II coaches (190 tons) powered by two Class 27/1 locomotives, each of 1250 bhp, with one locomotive at each end in push-pull formation. The rear locomotive was No.

D5400 and was one of the twelve locomotives converted for the Edinburgh/Glasgow push-pull working which commenced in 1971. The total weight of the train was 336 tons.

The driver was H. Kilpatrick of Haymarket depot who had relieved Driver Robertson of the same depot at Haymarket station at 16.34 on this outward journey.

The cause of the accident was the failure of the Gibson ring on the front left-hand wheel of the rear locomotive allowing the tyre to loosen and revolve on the wheel centre; it was believed that the Gibson ring failed either during the full-power exit from Waverley or during the brake application for the Haymarket stop. Lateral movement of the tyre then sheared the rolled-down lip, thus causing it to be held in place only by the flange during the remainder of the journey up to the point where the flange struck the nose of the points at Cadder.

Class 26 and Class 27 locomotives had a history of loose tyres and, as a result of this, BR went on to specify monobloc wheels for all future builds of high-speed traction units and rolling stock.

MORPETH: 1984

This was one of the most serious and contentious cases in recent times. On Saturday, 4th July 1984, Driver P.M. Allan – formerly of St. Margaret's shed, but a driver at Haymarket from 1972 – was rostered to work train 1E48, the 19.50 Saturdays Only sleeping car train from Aberdeen to London King's Cross, this duty requiring that he worked from Edinburgh to Newcastle and return. The train consisted of nine Mk III sleeping cars plus two bogie brakes, hauled by Class 47 diesel electric locomotive No. 47452. On the approach to Morpeth, the line speed had been raised to 100 mph, but then reducing to 80 mph at 80 miles, 16 chains. Immediately through Morpeth station, the train entered the Morpeth curve at 16 miles, 50 chains – the curve being a severe left-hand curve of 34.8 chains (700 metres) in length, where the line speed limit was 50 mph – at an excessive speed, and went into a rolling derailment to the right-hand side. The complete train ended up on its side and destroyed some private property as it continued to slide, in derailment, up the embankment. The public inquiry was held by Lt. Col. Townsend-Rose, but he was directed by the Director of Public Prosecution not to take evidence from Driver Allan since criminal charges were to be brought.

Allan appeared at Bedlington Court on the 26th October, charged on two counts. Section 17 of the *Regulation of Railways Act, 1842* and Section 34 of the *Offences Against the Person Act, 1861*. Since the latter charge could only be tried in a Crown Court, it was decided to drop the first charge and proceed with the latter.

Allan appeared at Newcastle Crown Court on the 5th June 1985 charged on three counts; the first under *The Criminal Damages Act, 1971*, and two counts under Section 34 of the *Offences Against the Person Act, 1861*. The difference in the last two charges was that the first specified '*by an unlawful act*' and the second, '*by wilful omission or neglect*'. Judge Kennedy, presiding, directed the jury that the case be judged on the third charge only.

Allan's defence was that he had suffered a bout of coughing at or around Alnemouth and that he remembered nothing thereafter. Indeed, he at one point stated that he could recall nothing of the journey after Drem.

At the trial, the case was to stand or fall on whether Allan '*had allowed himself*' to fall asleep, in which case he was guilty, or whether he had either knocked himself out or had '*blacked out'* after the coughing fit. In the event, he was quite incredibly cleared.

After the accident, Allan had had blood samples taken, since he smelled strongly of alcohol. The findings revealed that he had an alcohol reading of 84 mg per 100 ml of blood, which was well above the legal limit for road drivers. Nevertheless, and despite the fact he had admitted to an officer of the British Transport Police that he had both consumed a quantity of alcohol on his journey to work and also after he had booked on duty, this evidence was later to be ignored.

He then had lied when he claimed that he had booked on duty at Haymarket. He afterwards admitted that he had signed on by telephone to Haymarket, from the Shunters Bothy at Waverley, and thus had not been seen by anyone at the depot, although he was seen, in the passing, by the locomotive supervisor in the Waverley station as he waited for his train to arrive.

COMMENT

This accident was unusual in that there were so many violations of the BR *Rule Book* and Standing Instructions. It was, by 1984, an offence to report for duty under the influence of alcohol and a further offence to consume alcohol whilst on duty. Allan admitted to both. Then there was the reprehensible practice of allowing drivers to book-on by telephone. The argument that Allan lived on the east side of Edinburgh – and thus had to pass Waverley, where he was to take duty, to reach Haymarket – was spurious in the extreme. The reality was that there was a staff bus to take drivers booking-on at Haymarket depot to whatever place they were required to take over train working. The fact that this practice was still, in 1984, being condoned by Scottish Region management – even after a similar accident, but one with far more severe consequences, had occurred at the Eltham Well Hall curve in the Southern Region in 1972 – was disgraceful.

BR management were not exactly covered in glory in their subsequent defence, by suggesting that an illegal blood/alcohol reading was a road traffic offence and could not be applied to the railway. This was patently wrong. They then admitted that they were unwilling to adopt a system whereby an employee, believed to be under the influence of alcohol, should be breathalysed and measured against a defined legal limit, *'since it would sour relationships between the trade unions and the BRB and would, if limits were set, signify that the consumption of alcohol in small limits was acceptable, whilst believing that there should be zero tolerance.'* All in all, there was somewhat of a management cop-out.

The Morpeth accident had all the hallmarks of Eltham Well Hall, where alcohol, booking-on by telephone and over-speeding were all primary factors in an accident which resulted in a high-speed rolling derailment, and thus the outcome of the Morpeth inquiry was surprising and disgraceful – particularly since the Eltham Well Hall accident had led to a recommendation, which was accepted by the BRB, that all such irregular practices should cease. Happily, there is now a strict alcohol and drugs policy with random testing in place not only for drivers but for all safety critical staff within the UK rail industry. Today, Allan, despite his claim of mitigating factors, would just not have survived 'on the footplate'. His drinking before and on duty would have seen to that!

This case must also be looked at alongside that involving the unfortunate Driver Gourley at Elliot Junction (pages 190–92) to see how standards had changed over the years. In 1906, Allan would surely have gone to jail!

POLMONT: 1984

At approximately 17.55, on Monday 30th July, the 17.30 express passenger train (Train 1052) from Edinburgh Waverley to Glasgow Queen Street struck and killed a cow which had strayed onto the Down line, immediately to the west of Polmont Station.

The train consisted of a Mk II Driving Brake Second Open (DBSO) and five Mk III coaches, running in push-pull formation and propelled by Class 47/7 No. 47707 *Holyrood*, allocated to Haymarket Depot. It was running under clear signals at a speed of approximately 85 mph with 47707 propelling in the rear. As a consequence of the ensuing impact, the front bogie of the leading DBSO became derailed towards the cess side and the coach, now completely in derailment, then ran up a small slope. The DBSO struck a tree and came to a rest upside down with the driving cab facing back towards Edinburgh, having executed a 180-degree turn, longitudinally, when being pushed by the momentum of the remainder of the train in derailment. The second coach, a First Open (FO), was pushed forward by the coaches behind, dividing from the train and being turned end-for-end longitudinally, coming to a rest across the Up Main line at an angle of about 45 degrees, and being severely damaged by the third and fourth coaches, both SOs, as they then ran-on past, with the third SO then impacting heavily with the derailed DBSO, being severely damaged in the process. The remaining coaches and the locomotive remained upright although derailed, but all suffered damage.

Thirteen passengers were killed. A further fourteen passengers and three railway staff, including the Glasgow-based driver, R. Tennant, were removed to hospital with serious injuries. A further forty-four passengers were treated for injuries received.

The primary cause of the accident was the consequence of an act of vandalism, where a lineside fence had been torn down at the abandoned and closed West Quarter accommodation level crossing, immediately to the west of the site of the accident, thus allowing a cow to stray on to the railway line from an adjacent field. This cow, weighing no more than 750/1000 lbs, was seen to be on the lineside by the driver of the 17.15 passenger train from Glasgow Queen Street to Edinburgh as he passed the location just minutes earlier, and he then, quite properly – and as required in compliance with Section H of the (then) *Rule Book* – reported its presence to station staff when he made his station stop at Polmont. As he was in the act of reporting this, the ill-fated 17.30 ran through Polmont at speed, on its journey westwards.

The following 17.30 Glasgow Queen Street to Edinburgh passenger train had already started away from its scheduled Falkirk stop when, after leaving Falkirk Tunnel, the driver saw the derailment unfold immediately ahead. His speed was, fortunately, still low and he was able to bring his train to a stand just clear of the debris. An even more major incident was avoided by a mere couple of minutes.

The derailment, and accident, called into question the whole ethos of push-pull operation and whether this was, in fact, a safe method of train operation. An intensive study was undertaken by senior engineers from the BRB Research Establishment at Derby into the vehicle dynamics of the train, the forces this induced in the track, and the effect of propelling forces, traction and braking surges in push-pull working; it was eventually confirmed that these would not have had any untoward effect on safe train running. The safety of the DBSO, with lighter axle loadings than a locomotive, was also investigated, but as these were entirely within the design parameters for DMU/EMU coaches, this aspect was not considered a contributory factor. It was agreed, however, at the direction of the Inspecting Officer, that as a precautionary measure all the DBSOs in this push-pull fleet should be retrospectively fitted with deflector plates at the leading end. Changes were also made to Section H, 'Working of Trains' in the BR *Rule Book*, pertaining to animals on the line. Formerly, the rule specified 'animals' plural and 'on the line'.

Rules H.7.1.2 and H.7.1.3 were rewritten as follows:

7.1.2. If he (the Driver) sees any irregularity with another train, he must if possible alert the Driver of that train by sounding the horn and exhibiting a red light, or, where provided, the HAZARD WARNING indication (flashing headlights). He must also immediately inform the Signalman, stopping specially, if necessary.

7.1.3. If he (the Driver) sees any obstruction which may cause danger to other trains, he must alert the Driver of any approaching trains as shown above. He must place a track-circuit operating clip and three detonators 20 yards (or 20 metres) apart on each line affected at least 1¼ miles (or 2 km) from the obstruction. He must

immediately inform the Signalman. He must always comply with this clause whenever:

*(a)   a cow, bull or other large animal is within the boundary fence, **whether or not there is any immediate danger to trains**, or*

(b)   any other animals are on or near the line and he considers there may be a danger to trains.

Whilst animal strikes were not – and are not, even yet – uncommon in railway operation, the accident at Polmont demonstrated just how much carnage could be caused by a relatively small, single animal. Thankfully, the mitigating measures provided for in the *Rule Book*, as shown above, have ensured that there has been no repetition in the intervening years, and push-pull operation continues to be an entirely safe method of railway operation. This instruction, largely unmodified, is even today contained in the *Rule Book*, Module TW1, at Section 20.

TOP RIGHT: The date is 30th July 1984, the location is immediately west of Polmont Station on the E&GR main line. The 17.30 express passenger train from Edinburgh to Glasgow, which had been running in push-pull formation at a speed of 85 mph, lies wrecked after striking a cow which had strayed onto the line. The train, consisting of a DBSO, one Mk III FO and four Mk III SO coaches, was being propelled by diesel electric locomotive No. 47707 *Holyrood* of Haymarket shed. After the impact, the DBSO veered up the banking (on the right), struck a tree, and was pushed through 180 degrees by the rest of the train, coming to a rest upside down and turned end-for-end, with bogies ripped off and severely damaged. The following coaches pushed the FO, the second coach, up the opposite bank and also turned it end-for-end, this coach then coming to rest across the Up Main line. The third coach, an SO, virtually ran through the FO and finished in second coach position, as seen here. The DBSO, in turning round, impacted on the side of this latter coach causing serious damage. The remaining three coaches, plus locomotive, all derailed but remained upright. Fourteen passengers lost their lives, mainly all travelling in the DBSO, FO and SO (third coach). *Courtesy Scotsman Publications*

RIGHT: Another view of the Polmont accident, showing the destruction caused to the third coach (SO) as the DBSO overturned and turned end-for-end, impacting with the side of the former coach which was still moving, pushed by the remainder of the train. *Courtesy Scotsman Publications*

32 FINALE

So, what might the future hold for Haymarket? Well, railways in Scotland are entering some interesting times indeed, with the Scottish Parliament committed to expansion and further improvement of the rail network. First ScotRail is proving to be amongst the best of the many TOCs, and is committed to providing Scotland with a rail service second to none. There is ongoing talk of the need for a new, high-speed line between Edinburgh and Glasgow. Fine words, but such a project – desirable, and indeed achievable as it might be, if the will exists – would inevitably be fraught with difficulty, the least undoubtedly being the selection of a line of route across what is the busiest and most populated part of Central Scotland, and therein might well lie political suicide.

The Newbridge Junction/Bathgate/Airdrie electrification scheme is now well underway, and by early 2011 EMU trains will be providing a service of four trains in each direction, every hour, between Glasgow and Edinburgh via Bathgate. A new EMU maintenance depot is already under construction at Bathgate and thirty-three drivers' positions have been advertised (as at December 2008). With the E&GR main line electrified from Waverley as far as Newbridge Junction (8 miles, 934 yards), inevitably, full electrification of the remaining 38 miles, 1078 yards of the E&GR main line has now been authorised by the Scottish Parliament and a project team for this purpose has been set up. Electrification will require the route of the present E&GR main line to be modified, with a new chord line running from a connection from the Aberdeen (north) lines, swinging to the left around the north side of Edinburgh Airport and connecting into the existing Winchburgh Junction/Dalmeny Junction chord line. This new diversion would avoid the need for electrification (wiring) of the 7-arch and 36-arch Almond Viaducts (both listed) and the limited-clearance Winchburgh Tunnel. Indeed, there is nothing either original or inspired about this diversion proposal since, in my days as Signalling & Safety Officer, BR ScR, pre-1994, we had this very diversion surveyed and preliminary costs assumed, with draft permanent way and signalling plans prepared. This electrification could see Haymarket maintenance depot being further redesigned or expanded to service the new electric trains in whatever shape or form they might take. Perhaps!

Whilst the relaying and re-opening of the former Waverley route between Edinburgh and Galashiels (Tweedbank) was authorised in 2010, there are currently serious doubts about financial viability and whether the line should now be built. If it does go ahead, no doubt it will be the First ScotRail DMUs from Haymarket depot which will service this new route.

As a further point of interest, Haymarket Maintenance Depot may, or may not, have a new neighbour – and one which also runs on rails – with the opening of the new (but as I write, the seriously troubled Edinburgh Tram System) Airport Extension Line 1. If it does go ahead, it will actually encroach on what is currently depot ground, passing along the north side of the shed buildings and running along what is part of the main approach road to the depot.

This part of the tramway development is to be regretted, since this entrance roadway referred to, a roadway consisting of stone setts, is actually the original NBR shed entry roadway, and the last remaining NBR link with the 1894 'new' shed. Or perhaps not, since the postcode for Haymarket depot is, in fact, EH12 5NB, so perhaps the person responsible for allocating the new postcodes in the early 1970s had a sense of the ridiculous, or perhaps just a bit of railway history knowledge.

So, with this historical review now drawing to finality, and with the interesting trip I have had, not only via the many historical records, and down memory lane, but also via the modern railway, now all behind me, I like to think that the high standards set at Haymarket, oh so many years ago in the great age of steam, and the high regard in which Haymarket Motive Power Depot was then held right across the railway spectrum, are still being upheld in this brave new, highly competitive railway world.

In this year of 2011, there is at Haymarket, and on the site of the 1894 steam shed, a thoroughly modern maintenance depot, surrounded by suitably adequate, high-security measures, unthought-of and largely irrelevant in days of yore, but which befit the present-day climate. Here, maintenance, from examination through to heavy repair of the First ScotRail fleet, is carried out by highly competent and experienced engineering staff, to the highest level, and at a location where continuing high standards of Professionalism, Respect, Integrity, Safety and Security are the keystones of the Depot Mission Statement. The results are there for all to see, in the high standards of availability, train performance, punctuality and customer satisfaction currently being achieved by First ScotRail on a daily basis, and thanks, in no small part, to the efforts and dedication of the whole Haymarket team. I salute them!

Harry Knox.
Linlithgow, 2011

Haymarket Class 47/7 No. 47704, carrying the name of a former NBR Atlantic *Dunedin*, sits in the maintenance shed on 4th August 1979. This locomotive was one of the twelve to be specially fitted for push-pull working on the Edinburgh/Glasgow/Aberdeen routes, the arrangements for which can be clearly seen in this photograph. *Courtesy Gavin Morrison*

BIBLIOGRAPHY

PRIMARY SOURCES

DoT Accident Inquiry Reports (various): H.M. Stationery Office and NRM
DoT Accident Inquiry Reports (various): Railway Archives
BR/EGR/1: Minutes of Meetings of Directors E&GR, 1830–1865
BR/NBR/1: Minutes of Meetings of Directors NBR, 1865–1922
BR/EGR/1/82 Report of the Trial of William Paton (1845)

SECONDARY SOURCES

Allen, Cecil J. (1966), *The London & North Eastern Railway* (Ian Allan)
Coster, Peter (2006), *The Book of A3 Pacifics* (Irwell Press)
Coster, Peter (2006), *The Book of A4 Pacifics* (Irwell Press)
Coster, Peter (2007), *The Book of A1 and A2 Pacifics* (Irwell Press)
Coster, Peter (2008), *The Book of the V2s* (Irwell Press)
Eggington, F.B., 'High Speed Trains and their Effect on Signalling' read to IRSE, March 1938
Hamilton Ellis, C. (1955), *The North British Railway* (Ian Allan)
Hendrie, W.F. (1995), *Discovering West Lothian* (John Donald)
Highet, Campbell (1970), *Scottish Locomotive History, 1831–1923* (George Unwin & Allen)
Hoole, Ken (1977), *East Coast Main Line since 1925* (Ian Allan)
Knox, H. (2007), *Steam Days at Haymarket* (Irwell Press)
Livesey, E.H. (1939), 'Waverley to Dundee with "Mons Meg"' in *The Engineer*
MacLean, A.A. (1975), *North British Album* (Ian Allan)
Maclean, A.A. (2006), *The Edinburgh Suburban & South Side Junction Railway* (Oakwood Press)
McKillop, Norman (1958), *Enginemen Elite* (Ian Allan)
Mannion, R.J. (1996), *The Duchesses: Stanier's Masterpiece* (Allan Sutton)
Martin, Don and A.A. McLean (1990), *Edinburgh & Glasgow Railway Guidebook* (Strathkelvin District Libraries)
Meacher, Charles (1978), *LNER Footplate Memories* (Bradford Barton)
Mullay, A.J. (1989), *Non-stop! London to Scotland Steam* (Allan Sutton)
NBR Study Group (2008), *NBR Locomotive Classes and Engine Diagrams*
Nock, O.S. (1960), *Scottish Railways* (Nelson)
Nock, O.S. (1982), *The Gresley Pacifics Combined Volume* (David & Charles)
Nock, O.S. and B.K. Cooper (1987), *Historic Railway Disasters* (4th edn) (Ian Allan)
RCTS (1997), *Locomotives of the LNER*, Parts 2, 3A and 4
Rolt, L.C.T. (1955) *Red for Danger* (David & Charles)
Stephen, R.D. (1980), *Steam Supreme* (D. Bradford Barton)
Stephenson Locomotive Society (1970), *Locomotives of the NBR*
Thomas, John (1969), *The North British Railway*, Vol. 1 (David & Charles)
Thomas, John (1972), *The North British Atlantics* (David & Charles)
Thomas, John (1975), *The North British Railway*, Vol. 2 (David & Charles)
Thomas, John (1984), *A Regional History of the Railways of Great Britain, Volume 6: Scotland* (David & Charles)
Yeadon, W. (1990–), *Yeadon's Register of LNER Locomotives*, Vols 1, 2, 3, 4, 6, 9, 10, 16, 19, 26, 31, 40 and 42 Parts A and B (Book Law Publications)

Journals of the NBR Study Group (various) (NBRSG)
LNER Magazine, 1924–1947 (NRM)
The Scotsman newspaper, 1900–2000 (Scotsman Publications)
Trains Illustrated (various) (Ian Allan)

An unidentified Deltic under repair at Haymarket in the company of a Class 20 locomotive in the mid-1960s. The massive, but impressive, bulbous nose which typified the Deltics is seen to advantage in this photograph. *J. McKenzie collection*

ABOUT THE AUTHOR

Born in West Calder, Midlothian (Scotland) and educated at West Calder High School.

Joined British Railways as Junior Clerk, at Shotts (Lanarkshire), on the 15th October 1956, transferring to Haymarket MPD as an Engine Cleaner in February 1957. Acted as Cleaner/Fireman until late summer 1959. Re-entered the clerical grades at Haymarket Depot in 1959. In 1961, appointed Relief Station Master in Glasgow South District and thereafter served, amongst other roles, as a Divisional Freight Inspector, Civil Engineering Fleet Manager, Assistant Area Manager and then Area Manager at Bathgate and finally Operational Signalling & Safety Officer for the Scottish Region of BR.

Avoiding Railtrack plc at rail privatisation in 1994, joined Halcrow Transmark as an Operations & Safety Consultant. Worked in the UK and India, and relocated to Australia as Operations Projects and Safety Manager with GHD/Transmark in Sydney, working with all of the Australian Rail Authorities and also with the New Zealand Government and TranzRail.

Returned to the UK in 1999 and, as part of Halcrow Business Solutions, worked with Iarnród Éireann in Dublin as a Principal Rail Operations & Safety Consultant, but with a brief return to New Zealand in 2000. Retired from the railway industry on 31st December 2006.